⫽JEPPESEN®
Sanderson Training Products

1993-1995
PRIVATE PILOT
FAA
WRITTEN EXAM
STUDY GUIDE

- Questions, Answers, Explanations, References
- Coordinated with Jeppesen Private Pilot Manual
- Explanations Adjacent to Each Question
- Organized by Topic, Includes Full-Color Charts
- Unique Sliding Mask for Self-Testing
- Perforated and 3-Hole Punched Pages
- Airplane and Recreational Pilot Questions

© Jeppesen Sanderson, Inc., 1992, 1993, 1994
All Rights Reserved
55 Inverness Drive East, Englewood, CO 80112-5498
ISBN 0-88487-170-3

PREFACE

Thank you for purchasing this *Private Pilot Exam Study Guide*. This Study Guide will help you understand the answers to the test questions so you can take the FAA written or computer exam with confidence. It contains all FAA Recreational and Private Pilot airplane test questions. Included are the correct answers and explanations, along with study references. Explanations of why the other choices are wrong have been included where appropriate. Questions are organized by topic, with explanations conveniently located adjacent to each question. The three-hole punched, perforated pages give you great flexibility to remove and study selected sections most effectively. Full-color charts identical to those on the FAA test are included, plus our unique sliding mask for self-testing. Please note that this Exam Study Guide is intended to be a supplement to your instructor-led flight training, not a stand alone learning tool.

THE JEPPESEN SANDERSON TRAINING PHILOSOPHY

Flight training in the developing years of aviation was characterized by the separation of academics from flight training in the aircraft. For years, ground and flight training were not integrated. There were lots of books on different subjects, written by different authors, which produced a general lack of continuity in training material. The introduction of **Jeppesen Sanderson Training Products** changed all this. Our proven, professional, integrated training materials include extensive research on teaching theory and principles of how people learn best and most efficiently. Effective instruction includes determining objectives and completion standards. We employ an important principle of learning a complex skill using a step-by-step sequence known as the **building block principle**. Another important aspect of training is the principle of **meaningful repetition**, whereby each necessary concept or skill is presented several times throughout the instructional program. Jeppesen training materials incorporate this principle using different teaching tools such as textbooks, videos, exercises, exams, and this Study Guide. When these elements are combined with an instructor's class discussion and the skills learned in the simulator and airplane, you have an ideal integrated training system, with all materials coordinated.

Observation and research show that people tend to retain 10% of what they read, 20% of what they hear, 30% of what they see, and 50% of what they both hear and see together. These retention figures can be increased to as high as 90% by including active learning methods. Video and textbook materials are generally considered passive learning. Exercises, stage exams, student/instructor discussions, and skills in the simulator and airplane are considered to be active learning methods. Levels of learning include rote, understanding, application, and correlation. One of the major drawbacks with test preparation courses that concentrate only on passing the test is that they focus on rote learning, the lowest level of learning employed in a teaching situation. Students benefit from Jeppesen's professional approach through standardized instruction, a documented training record, increased learning **and** increased passing rates. Our materials are challenging and motivating, while maximizing knowledge and skill retention. Nearly 3 million pilots have learned to fly using our materials, which include:

MANUALS — Our training manuals contain the answers to many of the questions you may have as you begin your training program. They are based on the **study/review** concept of learning. This means detailed material is presented in an uncomplicated way, then important points are summarized through the use of bold type and color. The best results can be obtained when the manual is studied as an integral part of the coordinated materials. The manual is the central component for academic study and is cross-referenced to video presentations.

VIDEOS — These motivating, high-quality videos are professionally produced with actual inflight video and animated graphics. They allow you to review and reinforce essential concepts presented in the manual. The videos are available for viewing at flight and ground schools which subscribe to the Jeppesen Sanderson Training System. Call **1-800-621-JEPP** for the names of our Training System dealers in your area.

SUPPORT COMPONENTS — Supplementary items include an exercise book, stage and final exams, training syllabus, FAR/AIM manual, practical test standards, student record folder, computer, plotter, and logbook. Jeppesen Sanderson's training products are the most comprehensive pilot training materials available. They help you prepare, in conjunction with your instructor, for the FAA exam and practical test; and, more importantly, they help you become a more proficient and safer pilot.

You can purchase our products and services through your Jeppesen dealer. For product, service, or sales information call **1-800-621-JEPP, 303-799-9090, or FAX 303-784-4153**. If you have comments, questions, or need explanations about any component of our Pilot Training System, we are prepared to offer assistance at any time. If your dealer does not have a Jeppesen catalog, please request one and we will promptly send it to you. Just call the above telephone number, or write:

Marketing Manager, Training Products
Jeppesen Sanderson, Inc.
55 Inverness Drive East
Englewood, CO 80112-5498

Please direct inquiries from Europe, Africa, and the Middle East to:

Jeppesen & Co., GmbH
P.O. Box 70-05-51
Walter-Kolb-Str. 13
6000 Frankfurt/Main 70
Germany
Tel: 011-49-69-961240
Fax: 011-49-69-96124898

TABLE OF CONTENTS

PREFACE iii
INTRODUCTION ix

CHAPTER 1   Principles of Flight **1-1**
    Section A   Airplanes 1-1
    Section B   Four Forces of Flight 1-2
    Section C   Aerodynamics of Maneuvering Flight 1-4
    Section D   Stability 1-8

CHAPTER 2   The Flight Environment **2-1**
    Section A   Safety of Flight 2-1
    Section B   Airports 2-5
    Section C   Airspace 2-14
    Section D   Radio Communications 2-23
    Section E   Radar and ATC Services 2-26

CHAPTER 3   Aircraft Systems and Performance **3-1**
    Section A   Pitot-Static Instruments 3-1
    Section B   Gyroscopic Instruments 3-7
    Section C   Engine and Propeller 3-10
    Section D   Fuel and Electrical Systems 3-16
    Section E   Predicting Performance 3-17
    Section F   Weight and Balance 3-29

CHAPTER 4   Meteorology for Pilots **4-1**
    Section A   Basic Weather Theory 4-1
    Section B   Weather Patterns 4-3
    Section C   Weather Hazards 4-7

CHAPTER 5   Interpreting Weather Data **5-1**
    Section A   Printed Reports and Forecasts 5-1
    Section B   Graphic Weather Products 5-11
    Section C   Sources of Weather Information 5-18

CHAPTER 6	**Basic Navigation**	**6-1**
Section A	Aeronautical Charts	6-1
Section B	Flight Computers	6-16
Section C	Pilotage and Dead Reckoning	6-20
Section D	Sources of Flight Information	6-25

CHAPTER 7	**Radio Navigation Systems**	**7-1**
Section A	VHF Omnidirectional Range	7-1
Section B	Automatic Direction Finder	7-5
Section C	Advanced Navigation	7-10

CHAPTER 8	**Aviation Physiology**	**8-1**
Section A	Vision in Flight	8-1
Section B	Spatial Disorientation	8-3
Section C	Respiration and Altitude	8-4
Section D	Alcohol, Drugs, and Performance	8-5

CHAPTER 9	**Flight Planning and Decision Making**	**9-1**
Section A	Planning and Organizing Flights	9-1
Section B	Factors Affecting Decision Making	9-2

CHAPTER 10	**Federal Aviation Regulations**	**10-1**
Section A	FAR 1 — Definitions and Abbreviations	10-1
Section B	FAR 61 — Certification of Pilots	10-2
Section C	FAR 91 — General Operating and Flight Rules	10-13
Section D	NTSB 830 — Aircraft Accident and Incident Reporting	10-25

APPENDIX 1 Subject Matter Knowledge Codes **C-1**

APPENDIX 2 Legend Information **L-1**

APPENDIX 3 Question Cross-Reference Listing **Q-1**

INTRODUCTION

The *Private Pilot Exam Study Guide* is designed to help you prepare for the FAA written or computer test for a Recreational Pilot or Private Pilot Certificate. It covers FAA exam material that applies to airplanes, including pertinent Federal Aviation Regulations (FARs). Questions and answers pertaining to rotorcraft, gliders, balloons, and airships have been omitted.

We recommend that you use this Study Guide in conjunction with the Jeppesen Sanderson Pilot Training Course. The Study Guide is organized like the *Jeppesen Private Pilot Manual*, with nine chapters and distinctive sections within each chapter. Questions are covered in the Study Guide in the same sequence as the material is presented in the Manual. References to applicable page numbers in the Manual are included along with the answers. A separate chapter (Chapter 10) in the Study Guide is devoted to FAR questions and answers.

Within the chapters, each section contains a brief introduction and a list of questions in that section. FAA exam questions appear in the left-hand column of the Study Guide as they are printed in the FAA Written Test Book. Answers are in the right-hand column. The first line of the answer for each question is in bold type with the question number, the answer, and the page number where the question is covered in the *Jeppesen Private Pilot Manual*. There is also an abbreviation for an FAA or other authoritative source document.

Example: **3618. Answer A. JSPPM 6-14 (AIM)**

Next is a brief explanation of the correct answer, and where appropriate, an explanation of why the other answers are wrong. In some cases the incorrect answers are not explained. Examples include instances where the answers are calculated, or when the explanation of the correct answer obviously eliminates the wrong answers.

Abbreviations used in the Study Guide are as follows:

```
     AC — Advisory Circulars
    AIM — Airman's Information Manual
     AW — Aviation Weather, AC 00-6A
    AWS — Aviation Weather Services, AC 00-45C
    FAR — Federal Aviation Regulation
    FTH — Flight Training Handbook, AC 61-21A
    FTP — Flight Theory for Pilots
    IFH — Instrument Flying Handbook, AC 61-27C
  JSPPM — Jeppesen Sanderson Private Pilot Manual
    PHB — Pilot's Handbook of Aeronautical Knowledge, AC 61-23B
   PWBH — Pilot's Weight and Balance Handbook, AC 91-23A
```

Since the FAA does not provide answers with their test questions, the answers in this Study Guide are based on official reference documents and, in our judgment, are the best choice of the available answers. Some questions which were valid when the FAA Test Book was originally published may no longer be appropriate due to changes in regulations or official operating procedures. On the FAA computer exams, these questions will be corrected. For the FAA written exams, you will get credit for these questions. When taking the FAA exam, it is important to answer the questions according to the latest regulations or official operating procedures.

Two appendices from the FAA Written Test Book are included in the back of the Study Guide. These are Appendix 1, Subject Matter Knowledge Codes, which also lists reference material; and Appendix 2, which consists of a complete Directory Legend from the National Ocean Service (NOS) *Airport/Facility Directory* (A/FD). You will need to refer to this legend to answer some questions concerning A/FD information. Appendix 3 in the Study Guide consists of a numerical listing of all airplane questions. Included in this listing is a tabulation with the answer and the page number where the question appears in the Study Guide.

The figures that are referred to in many of the questions are placed throughout the Study Guide as close as practical to the applicable questions. The main exception to this placement applies to Figures 21 through 27, which are full-page, color excerpts of sectional charts. Instead of inserting these seven figures near a few chart questions in Chapter 2, they are included along with the majority of other chart questions in Chapter 6. This part of Chapter 6 also contains the full-color legend for sectional charts. Throughout the Study Guide, notations indicate figure placement when a figure is not on the same page, or facing page, as the questions. For example, the Chapter 2 questions indicate where to find Figures 21 through 27 in Chapter 6. In addition, pages in this Study Guide are three-hole punched and perforated. You can easily remove any figure you need for reference while answering a specific question.

While good study material is beneficial, it is important to realize that to become a safe, competent pilot, you need more that just the academic knowledge required to pass the test. For a comprehensive ground training program, we recommend a structured ground school with a qualified flight or ground instructor.

WHO CAN TAKE THE RECREATIONAL OR PRIVATE PILOT EXAM?
When you are ready to take the recreational or private pilot exam, you must present evidence that you have completed appropriate ground instruction or a home study course. This proof may be in the form of a graduation certificate from a pilot training course, a written statement, or a logbook entry by a certified ground or flight instructor. Although you are encouraged to obtain ground instruction, a home study course may be used. If you cannot provide one of the above documents, you may present a completed study course to an FAA aviation safety inspector for approval.

WHAT IS A RECREATIONAL PILOT?
The recreational pilot certificate has been established for several years. It is intended for those who are willing to limit their flying to a basic, single-engine aircraft with no more than 180 horsepower. Specific provisions (privileges and limitations) that apply to this certificate are listed in FAR Part 61. Recreational pilots, with additional knowledge, proficiency, and experience, may upgrade their certificates to the private or higher level.

While this Study Guide is primarily intended for Private Pilot applicants, it does contain all of the study questions for the FAA's recreational pilot test. There are 27 questions specifically for the recreational pilot test. These are questions **3038** through **3061**, as well as questions **3134**, **3135**, and **3802**.

In addition to these questions, many of the other airplane questions are applicable. However, since recreational pilot privileges do not include night flying, cross-country flights, or operations requiring the use of air-to-ground communications, questions pertaining to these subjects are not included on question selection sheets for recreational pilot applicants.

HOW TO PREPARE FOR THE EXAM

This Study Guide includes the airplane questions as they were printed in the FAA Written Test Book. By reviewing the questions and studying the material presented in the Jeppesen Sanderson Pilot Training materials, you should be well equipped to take the exam. We also suggest that you enroll in a ground school. An organized course of instruction will help you complete the course in a timely manner, and you will be able to have any questions answered. The additional instruction will be beneficial in your flight training.

You will also benefit more from your study if you test yourself as you proceed through the Study Guide. Cover the answers in the right-hand column, read each question, and choose what you consider the best answer. A sliding mask is provided for this purpose. Move the sliding mask down and read the answer and explanation for that question. You may want to mark the questions you miss for further study and review prior to taking the exam.

The sooner you take the exam after you complete your study, the better. This way, the information will be fresh in your mind, and you will be more confident when you actually take the FAA written test.

WHAT TO EXPECT ON THE EXAM

If you are taking the printed version of the exam, you will receive a question selection sheet at the start of the exam that indentifies the questions you will answer out of the Written Test Book. On the computerized version of the exam, the selection of questions is done for you and you will answer the questions that appear on the screen. You will be given a specific amount of time to complete the test, which is based on past experience with others who have taken the exam. If you are prepared, you should have plenty of time to complete the exam. Items you need to bring with you include:

    Flight computer
    Calculator (optional)
    Plotter
    Picture I.D. of yourself
    Written authorization to take the exam

When taking the FAA exam, keep the following points in mind:

1. Answer each question in accordance with the latest regulations and procedures. If the regulation or operation procedure changed after the Written Test Book was printed, you will receive credit for the affected question. These questions may be updated on the FAA computerized exams.

2. Read each question carefully before looking at the possible answers. You should clearly understand the problem before attempting to solve it.

3. After formulating an answer, determine which of the alternatives most nearly corresponds with that answer. The answer chosen should completely resolve the problem.

4. From the answers given, it may appear that there is more than one possible answer; however, there is only one answer that is correct and complete. The other answers are either incomplete or are derived from popular misconceptions.

5. Mark your answers in the space provided for each question number. Answers left unmarked will be counted as incorrect.

6. If a certain question is difficult for you, it is best to proceed to other questions. After you answer the less difficult questions, return to those which were unanswered. Be sure to identify those questions you wish to review.

7. When solving a calculator problem, select the answer nearest your solution. The problem has been checked with various types of calculators; therefore, if you have solved it correctly, your answer will be closer to the correct answer than the other choices.

TAKING THE FAA COMPUTER EXAM

One of the advantages of taking the computerized exam is you don't have to wait to get the results of the test. Generally, the results are given to you within minutes of completing the test. No computer experience is required to take the exam. Before you begin the test, an optional introductory lesson is available to familiarize you with the testing procedures. This lesson does not count toward time allocation for taking the test. Once the test is started, the screen will show you the time remaining for the completion of the test.

The method of selecting the correct answer on the computer varies with the testing center. Typically, they use the keyboard, touch screen, or a mouse. Each system allows you to mark questions that you would like to come back to for further review. The systems provide a help function as well as a person who is available to answer questions about the operation of the computer.

WHERE TO TAKE THE EXAM

Written exams are administered by some FAA Flight Standards District Offices (FSDOs), certain flight schools, and at other facilities by FAA-designated written test examiners. Testing is also administered via computer by FAA-designated testing organizations. These organizations have testing centers located throughout the U.S. You may wish to contact your nearest FSDO for information. Testing at FAA offices is done at no charge to applicants, but you can expect to pay a fee at other locations. The following is a list of computer test designees that you can call to register for the computer exam.

Aviation Business Services
795 Skyway Road
San Carlos, CA 94070
1-800-947-4228

Drake Training & Technologies
8800 Queen Avenue South
Bloomington, MN 55431
1-800-359-3278

Sylvan KEE System, Inc.
9135 Guilford Road
Columbia, MD 21046
1-800-967-1100

TRO Learning, Inc.
150 N. Martingale Road
Suite 700
Schaumburg, IL 61073
1-800-869-1100

CHAPTER 1

PRINCIPLES OF FLIGHT

SECTION A
AIRPLANES

Chapter 1 of the *Private Pilot Manual* provides a basis for your entire course of training for the private pilot certificate. Section A contains a brief overview of airplane components, aircraft classifications, and pilot certification information. Associated terms are introduced. FAA Written Test questions in Section A include:

3001, 3002, 3003, 3004.

3001. With respect to the certification of airmen, which is a category of aircraft?

A — Gyroplane, helicopter, airship, free balloon.
B — Airplane, rotorcraft, glider, lighter-than-air.
C — Single-engine land and sea, multiengine land and sea.

3001. Answer B. JSPPM 1-9 (FAR 1.1)
Airmen are certificated according to four categories of aircraft: airplane, rotorcraft, glider, and lighter-than-air. Answers (A) and (C) are wrong because they list classes of pilot certification and not categories.

3002. With respect to the certification of airmen, which is a class of aircraft?

A — Airplane, rotorcraft, glider, lighter-than-air.
B — Single-engine land and sea, multiengine land and sea.
C — Lighter-than-air, airship, hot air balloon, gas balloon.

3002. Answer B. JSPPM 1-9 (FAR 1.1)
Each category of aircraft is broken down into classes. The airplane category is divided into single-engine land and sea, and multi-engine land and sea. Answer (A) is wrong because it lists aircraft categories. Answer (C) is wrong because lighter-than-air is a category, not a class.

3003. With respect to the certification of aircraft, which is a category of aircraft?

A — Normal, utility, acrobatic.
B — Airplane, rotorcraft, glider.
C — Landplane, seaplane.

3003. Answer A. JSPPM 1-9 (FAR 1.1)
Normal, utility, and acrobatic are three of the categories under which aircraft are certified. Answer (B) lists aircraft classes, not categories. Answer (C) lists examples of airplane classes for pilot certification.

3004. With respect to the certification of aircraft, which is a class of aircraft?

A — Airplane, helicopter, glider, hot air balloon.
B — Normal, utility, acrobatic, limited.
C — Transport, restricted, provisional.

3004. Answer A. JSPPM 1-7 (FAR 1.1)
Aircraft are placed into groups having similar means of propulsion, flight, or landing. These classes include: airplane, rotorcraft, glider, and balloon. Answers (B) and (C) list aircraft categories, not classes.

SECTION B
FOUR FORCES OF FLIGHT

During flight, four basic forces act on an airplane - lift, weight, thrust, and drag. The basic aerodynamic principles concerning these forces are explained in this section. Included is a brief discussion of Bernoulli's Principle and Newton's Third Law of Motion. Frequently used aerodynamic terms are defined. Test questions in Section B include:

3201, 3202, 3203, 3204, 3205, 3219, 3220, 3311, 3317.

3201. The four forces acting on an airplane in flight are

A — lift, weight, thrust, and drag.
B — lift, weight, gravity, and thrust.
C — lift, gravity, power, and friction.

3201. Answer A. JSPPM 1-10 (FTH)
In normal (nonacrobatic) flight conditions, lift is the upward force created by airflow over and under the wings. Weight, caused by the downward pull of gravity, opposes lift. Thrust is the forward force which propels the airplane, and drag is the retarding force opposing thrust. Answer (B) does not include drag, and, while gravity causes weight, it usually is not considered one of the four forces. Answer (C) is also wrong because, while power and friction affect thrust and drag, they are not aerodynamic forces.

3202. When are the four forces that act on an airplane in equilibrium?

A — During unaccelerated flight.
B — When the aircraft is accelerating.
C — When the aircraft is at rest on the ground.

3202. Answer A. JSPPM 1-10 (FTH)
In straight-and-level, unaccelerated flight, the four forces are in equilibrium. Lift equals weight, and thrust equals drag. Answer (B) would require thrust to be greater than drag in order for the aircraft to accelerate. Answer (C) is wrong because only weight is acting on the airplane. Lift, drag, and thrust are zero (assuming no wind).

3203. (Refer to figure 1.) The acute angle A is the angle of

A — incidence.
B — attack.
C — dihedral.

3203. Answer B. JSPPM 1-14 (PHB)
The angle between the chord line and the relative wind is the angle of attack. Answer (A) cannot be correct because the angle of incidence is the angle between the wing chord line and the longitudinal axis of the airplane. Answer (C) is wrong because dihedral is the upward angle of the wings in relation to the lateral axis of the airplane.

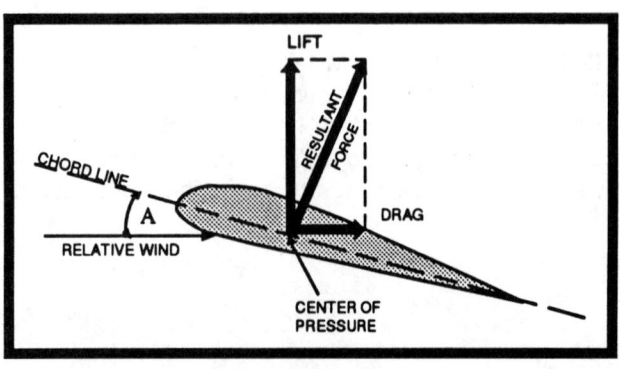

FIGURE 1.—Lift Vector.

3204. The term "angle of attack" is defined as the angle

A — between the wing chord line and the relative wind.
B — between the airplane's climb angle and the horizon.
C — formed by the longitudinal axis of the airplane and the chord line of the wing.

3204. Answer A. JSPPM 1-14 (PHB)
The angle of attack is the angle between the chord line and the relative wind. Answer (B) does not describe any aerodynamic term. Answer (C) describes the angle of incidence.

3205. What is the relationship of lift, drag, thrust, and weight when the airplane is in straight-and-level flight?

A — Lift equals weight and thrust equals drag.
B — Lift, drag, and weight equal thrust.
C — Lift and weight equal thrust and drag.

3205. Answer A. JSPPM 1-10 (FTH)
Assuming the airplane is not accelerating, thrust equals drag, and lift equals weight. Answers (B) and (C) are wrong because all four forces do not have to be equal. Thrust must be equal to drag, and lift equal to weight.

3219. One of the main functions of flaps during approach and landing is to

A — decrease the angle of descent without increasing the airspeed.
B — permit a touchdown at a higher indicated airspeed.
C — increase the angle of descent without increasing the airspeed.

3219. Answer C. JSPPM 1-19 (FTH)
Because flaps increase lift, induced drag is also increased, thus allowing a steeper angle of descent without increasing airspeed. Answer (A) is wrong because the angle of descent can be increased. Answer (B) is wrong since flaps increase lift, thereby allowing touchdown at a lower airspeed.

3220. What is one purpose of wing flaps?

A — To enable the pilot to make steeper approaches to a landing without increasing the airspeed.
B — To relieve the pilot of maintaining continuous pressure on the controls.
C — To decrease wing area to vary the lift.

3220. Answer A. JSPPM 1-10 (FTH)
Flaps increase both lift and induced drag, allowing a steeper descent without increasing airspeed. Answer (B) is wrong because flaps simply increase the camber of the wing. Trim must still be applied to relieve control pressure. Answer (C) is not correct because most flaps change the wing area very little. Some flaps will increase wing area, but none will decrease it.

3311. The angle of attack at which an airplane wing stalls will

A — increase if the CG is moved forward.
B — change with an increase in gross weight.
C — remain the same regardless of gross weight.

3311. Answer C. JSPPM 1-18 (FTP)
The critical angle of attack (angle of attack at which an airplane stalls) is determined by the lift coefficient of a particular wing configuration. An airplane will stall when the critical angle of attack is exceeded, regardless of weight or airspeed. Answers (A) and (B) are wrong because the center of gravity (CG) and weight do not affect the critical angle of attack.

3317. Angle of attack is defined as the angle between the chord line of an airfoil and the

A — direction of the relative wind.
B — pitch angle of an airfoil.
C — rotor plane of rotation.

3317. Answer A. JSPPM 1-19 (PHB)
The angle of attack is the angle between the chord line and the relative wind. Answer (B) is wrong because pitch angle describes the angle of the airplane's longitudinal axis, not the wing. Answer (C) refers to helicopters, not airplanes.

SECTION C
AERODYNAMICS OF MANEUVERING FLIGHT

Section C expands on information in the first two sections with a discussion of specific aerodynamic concepts applicable to the basic maneuvers of climbs, descents, and turns. The section also contains coverage of performance limitations and safety of flight considerations. FAA Test questions include:

3006, 3207, 3208, 3209, 3213, 3214, 3215, 3216, 3217, 3218, 3301, 3312, 3313, 3314, 3315, 3316, 3711.

3006. Which V-speed represents maneuvering speed?

A — V_A.
B — V_{LO}.
C — V_{NE}.

3006. Answer A. JSPPM 1-35 (FAR 1.1)
V_A is defined as the design maneuvering speed. Answer (B) represents maximum landing gear operating speed. Answer (C) is the never exceed speed.

3207. In what flight condition is torque effect the greatest in a single-engine airplane?

A — Low airspeed, high power, high angle of attack.
B — Low airspeed, low power, low angle of attack.
C — High airspeed, high power, high angle of attack.

3207. Answer A. JSPPM 1-37 (PHB)
Torque effect is greatest at low airspeeds, high power settings, and high angles of attack. Answer (B) is wrong because these conditions produce the least amount of torque effect. Answer (C) is also wrong because it includes high airspeed.

3208. The left turning tendency of an airplane caused by P-factor is the result of the

A — clockwise rotation of the engine and the propeller turning the airplane counter-clockwise.
B — propeller blade descending on the right, producing more thrust than the ascending blade on the left.
C — gyroscopic forces applied to the rotating propeller blades acting 90° in advance of the point the force was applied.

3208. Answer B. JSPPM 1-38 (PHB)
P-factor, or asymmetric propeller loading, normally occurs at a high angle of attack. The descending propeller blade on the right side takes a larger "bite" of the air, and produces more thrust than the ascending blade on the left. The result is a left turning tendency of the airplane. Answer (A) describes torque reaction, not P-factor. Answer (C) describes gyroscopic precession, not P-factor.

3209. When does P-factor cause the airplane to yaw to the left?

A — When at low angles of attack.
B — When at high angles of attack.
C — When at high airspeeds.

3209. Answer B. JSPPM 1-38 (PHB)
P-factor is most pronounced at high angles of attack, which cause the descending propeller blade to produce more thrust. Answer (A) is wrong because at low angles of attack, thrust produced by the ascending and descending propeller blades is almost equalized. Answer (C) is wrong because at high airspeeds, the angle of attack is lower, thus reducing the P-factor.

3213. What is the purpose of the rudder on an airplane?

A — To control yaw.
B — To control overbanking tendency.
C — To control roll.

3213. Answer A. JSPPM 1-31 (PHB)
Since the rudder moves the airplane about its vertical axis, it is used to control yaw. Answers (B) and (C) are wrong because overbanking tendency and roll are controlled by ailerons.

3214. (Refer to figure 2.) If an airplane weighs 2,300 pounds, what approximate weight would the airplane structure be required to support during a 60° banked turn while maintaining altitude?

A — 2,300 pounds.
B — 3,400 pounds.
C — 4,600 pounds.

3214. Answer C. JSPPM 1-33 (PHB)
At 60 degrees of bank, 2 G's are required to maintain level flight. This means that the airplane's wing structure must support twice the airplane's weight, or 2,300 x 2 = 4,600 pounds. Answer (A) reflects 1 G, or straight-and-level flight. Answer (B) is correct only if 1.48 G's (approximately 50° bank) are applied.

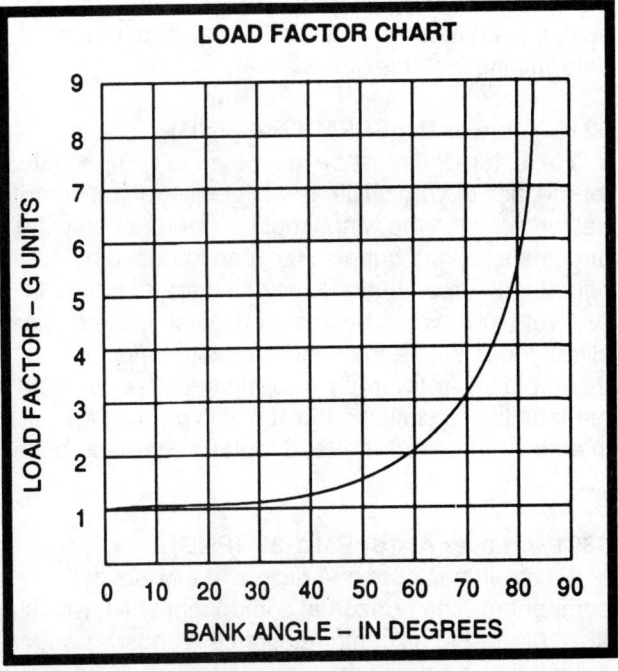

FIGURE 2.—Load Factor Chart.

3215. (Refer to figure 2.) If an airplane weighs 3,300 pounds, what approximate weight would the airplane structure be required to support during a 30° banked turn while maintaining altitude?

A — 1,200 pounds.
B — 3,100 pounds.
C — 3,960 pounds.

3215. Answer C. JSPPM 1-33 (PHB)
The load factor for 30 degrees of bank is 1.154, or about 1.2. The airplane weight (3,300) multiplied by the load factor (1.2) is 3,960 pounds which the wing structure must support. Answers (A) and (B) are both wrong because the weights are less than the airplane weight.

3216. (Refer to figure 2.) If an airplane weighs 4,500 pounds, what approximate weight would the airplane structure be required to support during a 45° banked turn while maintaining altitude?

A — 4,500 pounds.
B — 6,750 pounds.
C — 7,200 pounds.

3216. Answer B. JSPPM 1-33 (PHB)
At 45 degrees of bank the load factor is 1.414, or approximately 1.5, the wing loading would be 4,500 x 1.5, or 6,750 pounds. Answer (A) reflects only 1 G, and is therefore incorrect. Answer (C) is wrong because 1.6 G's are required to produce a load of 7,200 pounds. Therefore, (B) is the closest correct answer.

3217. The amount of excess load that can be imposed on the wing of an airplane depends upon the

A — position of the CG.
B — speed of the airplane.
C — abruptness at which the load is applied.

3217. Answer B. JSPPM 1-35 (PHB)
The amount of excess load that can be imposed on an airplane depends on its speed. If abrupt control movements or strong gusts are applied at low airspeeds, the airplane will stall before the load becomes excessive. At higher airspeeds, the increased airflow causes a greater lifting capacity. A sudden control input or gust at a high airspeed may result in an excessive load factor beyond safe limits. Answer (A) is wrong because position of the CG does not affect the load factor on the wings. Answer (C) is wrong because the amount of excess load depends on both the speed and total load. Although abruptness does affect the total load on the airplane, the determining factor is airspeed.

3218. Which basic flight maneuver increases the load factor on an airplane as compared to straight-and-level flight?

A — Climbs.
B — Turns.
C — Stalls.

3218. Answer B. JSPPM 1-32 (PHB)
In a level turn, lift must be increased to compensate for the loss of vertical lift as well as overcome centrifugal force. Since the wings must support not only the airplane's weight, but also the load imposed by centrifugal force, the load factor is greater than 1 G. Answer (A) is wrong because once established in a climb, there is no additional load factor imposed on the airplane. Answer (C) is wrong because when an airplane is in a stalled condition, it is producing insufficient lift, and the load factor decreases below 1 G.

3301. What force makes an airplane turn?

A — The horizontal component of lift.
B — The vertical component of lift.
C — Centrifugal force.

3301. Answer A. JSPPM 1-30 (PHB)
In a turn, lift has both a vertical and a horizontal component. The horizontal component of lift, which is also referred to as centripetal force, opposes centrifugal force and causes the airplane to turn. Answer (B) is wrong because the vertical component of lift opposes weight. Answer (C) is wrong because centrifugal force acts outward from the turn and opposes the horizontal component of lift.

3312. What is ground effect?

A — The result of the interference of the surface of the Earth with the airflow patterns about an airplane.
B — The result of an alteration in airflow patterns increasing induced drag about the wings of an airplane.
C — The result of the disruption of the airflow patterns about the wings of an airplane to the point where the wings will no longer support the airplane in flight.

3312. Answer A. JSPPM 1-39 (FTH)
When flying close to the ground, the airflow around an airplane is altered by interference with the surface of the earth. The resulting ground effect reduces the induced drag on the airplane. Answer (B) is wrong because the induced drag is reduced, not increased. Answer (C) is wrong because the upwash and downwash of airflow on the wing is reduced, and the airplane can fly at lower speeds.

The Principles of Flight

3313. Floating caused by the phenomenon of ground effect will be most realized during an approach to and when at

A — less than the length of the wingspan above the surface.
B — twice the length of the wingspan above the surface.
C — a higher-than-normal angle of attack.

3314. What must a pilot be aware of as a result of ground effect?

A — Wingtip vortices increase creating wake turbulence problems for arriving and departing aircraft.
B — Induced drag decreases; therefore, any excess speed at the point of flare may cause considerable floating.
C — A full stall landing will require less up elevator deflection than would a full stall when done free of ground effect.

3315. Ground effect is most likely to result in which problem?

A — Settling to the surface abruptly during landing.
B — Becoming airborne before reaching recommended takeoff speed.
C — Inability to get airborne even though airspeed is sufficient for normal takeoff needs.

3316. During an approach to a stall, an increased load factor will cause the airplane to

A — stall at a higher airspeed.
B — have a tendency to spin.
C — be more difficult to control.

3711. The most important rule to remember in the event of a power failure after becoming airborne is to

A — immediately establish the proper gliding attitude and airspeed.
B — quickly check the fuel supply for possible fuel exhaustion.
C — determine the wind direction to plan for the forced landing.

3313. Answer A. JSPPM 1-40 (FTH)
Ground effect becomes noticeable when the height of the airplane above the ground is less than the length of the wingspan. Answer (B) is wrong because it states twice the length of the wingspan. Answer (C) is wrong because ground effect is not a result of angle of attack, and at a higher angle of attack, airspeed will be lower so that floating is decreased.

3314. Answer B. JSPPM 1-39 (FTH)
Since ground effect decreases induced drag, the airplane tends to float while excess speed bleeds off. Answer (A) is wrong because the reduction in induced drag causes wingtip vortices to decrease. Answer (C) is wrong because the wings produce more lift in ground effect than out of ground effect. Therefore, more up elevator deflection would be required.

3315. Answer B. JSPPM 1-40 (FTH)
The decreased induced drag while in ground effect allows the airplane to become airborne at a lower airspeed. This may fool you into thinking the airplane is capable of flying at the lower airspeed when you climb out of ground effect. Answer (A) is wrong because ground effect tends to cause an airplane to float during landing, not settle abruptly. Answer (C) is wrong because ground effect allows an airplane to become airborne at a lower than normal airspeed.

3316. Answer A. JSPPM 1-34 (PHB)
Stall speed increases in proportion to load factor. Added G-forces cause an airplane to stall at an airspeed higher than the normal 1 G airspeed. Answer (B) is wrong because load factor normally does not affect an airplane's tendency to spin. Answer (C) is wrong because load factor does not affect controllability. Rather, this is a function of the airplane's stability.

3711. Answer A. JSPPM 1-30 (FTH)
Establishing the proper glide attitude and airspeed is critical to ensure the best possibility of reaching a suitable landing area. It also tends to reduce the possibility of a stall/spin accident. Answer (B) is an important step in attempting an engine restart, but controlling the aircraft is the first action you should take. Answer (C) is another important step, but should be taken only after establishing the proper glide speed.

SECTION D
STABILITY

The final section of Chapter 1 introduces you to important airplane design concepts such as stability, center of gravity (CG) position, and weight distribution. Stall and spin awareness is covered in the last part of this section. FAA Written Test questions include:

3210, 3211, 3212, 3287, 3288, 3309, 3310.

3210. An airplane said to be inherently stable will

A — be difficult to stall.
B — require less effort to control.
C — not spin.

3210. Answer B. JSPPM 1-42 (PHB)
An airplane that is inherently stable tends to return to its original attitude after it has been displaced, and is therefore easier to control. Answers (A) and (C) are wrong because stability does not prevent you from stalling or spinning an airplane.

3211. What determines the longitudinal stability of an airplane?

A — The location of the CG with respect to the center of lift.
B — The effectiveness of the horizontal stabilizer, rudder, and rudder trim tab.
C — The relationship of thrust and lift to weight and drag.

3211. Answer A. JSPPM 1-44 (PHB)
The longitudinal stability of an airplane is determined primarily by the location of the center of gravity (CG) in relation to the center of lift. Answer (B) is wrong because the rudder and rudder trim tab affect the directional stability. Answer (C) is wrong because this relationship affects acceleration, but not longitudinal stability.

3212. What causes an airplane (except a T-tail) to pitch nosedown when power is reduced and controls are not adjusted?

A — The CG shifts forward when thrust and drag are reduced.
B — The downwash on the elevators from the propeller slipstream is reduced and elevator effectiveness is reduced.
C — When thrust is reduced to less than weight, lift is also reduced and the wings can no longer support the weight.

3212. Answer B. JSPPM 1-45 (PHB)
At higher power settings, in airplanes other than T-tail designs, the propeller slipstream causes a greater downward force on the horizontal stabilizer. When power is reduced, this downward force on the tail is also reduced, and the nose pitches down. Answer (A) is wrong because CG is determined by how an airplane is built and loaded, and is not affected by changes in thrust and drag. Answer (C) is also wrong because most airplanes can fly with thrust less than the weight.

3287. An airplane has been loaded in such a manner that the CG is located aft of the aft CG limit. One undesirable flight characteristic a pilot might experience with this airplane would be

A — a longer takeoff run.
B — difficulty in recovering from a stalled condition.
C — stalling at higher-than-normal airspeed.

3287. Answer B. JSPPM 1-48 (FTH)
With a CG aft of the rear CG limit, the airplane becomes tail heavy and unstable in pitch because the horizontal stabilizer is less effective. This condition makes it difficult, if not impossible, to recover from a stall or spin. Answer (A) is wrong because an aft CG tends to shorten the takeoff run, and it may cause the airplane to pitch up and lift off early at a lower than normal airspeed. Answer (C) is wrong because an airplane with an aft CG requires less downward force on the tail. The airplane can fly at a lower angle of attack and will stall at a lower airspeed.

The Principles of Flight

3288. Loading an airplane to the most aft CG will cause the airplane to be

A — less stable at all speeds.
B — less stable at slow speeds, but more stable at high speeds.
C — less stable at high speeds, but more stable at low speeds.

3309. In what flight condition must an aircraft be placed in order to spin?

A — Partially stalled with one wing low
B — In a steep diving spiral
C — Stalled

3310. During a spin to the left, which wing(s) is/are stalled?

A — Both wings are stalled.
B — Neither wing is stalled.
C — Only the left wing is stalled.

3288. Answer A. JSPPM 1-48 (FTH)
In an airplane loaded to the aft CG limit, the horizontal stabilizer is less effective, causing the airplane to be less stable at all speeds. Answers (B) and (C) are wrong because an aft-loaded airplane is less stable at all speeds.

3309. Answer C. JSPPM 1-53 (FTH)
An airplane must be stalled before a spin can develop. Answer (A) is wrong because a spin occurs when both wings are in a stalled condition, with one wing more completely stalled than the other. Answer (B) is wrong because an airplane may be put into a steep diving spiral without being stalled.

3310. Answer A. JSPPM 1-53 (FTH)
In a spin, both wings are stalled. Answers (B) and (C) are wrong because both wings must be stalled for a spin to develop, although the outside wing may be less fully stalled than the inside wing.

CHAPTER 2
THE FLIGHT ENVIRONMENT

SECTION A
SAFETY OF FLIGHT

Chapter 2, Section A of the *Private Pilot Manual* contains information on visual scanning, collision avoidance, blind spots in aircraft design, right-of-way rules, and safety of flight considerations. The section also introduces some of the Federal Aviation Regulations (FARs). FAA Written Test questions that are covered in this section include:

3089, 3090, 3091, 3092, 3093, 3094, 3095, 3101, 3102, 3103, 3104, 3105, 3106, 3155, 3156, 3157, 3158, 3710, 3814, 3833, 3834, 3835, 3836.

3089. Which aircraft has the right-of-way over all other air traffic?

A — A balloon.
B — An aircraft in distress.
C — An aircraft on final approach to land.

3089. Answer B. JSPPM 2-6 (FAR 91.113)
An aircraft in distress has the right-of-way over all other aircraft. Answers (A) and (C) are wrong because an aircraft in distress has right-of-way over all other air traffic.

3090. What action is required when two aircraft of the same category converge, but not head-on?

A — The faster aircraft shall give way.
B — The aircraft on the left shall give way.
C — Each aircraft shall give way to the right.

3090. Answer B. JSPPM 2-7 (FAR 91.113)
The aircraft on the right has the right-of-way and the aircraft on the left shall give way.

3091. Which aircraft has the right-of-way over the other aircraft listed?

A — Glider.
B — Airship.
C — Aircraft refueling other aircraft.

3091. Answer A. JSPPM 2-8 (FAR 91.113)
In general, the least maneuverable aircraft normally has the right-of-way. A glider has the right-of-way over an airship, airplane, or rotorcraft. An aircraft that is towing or refueling another aircraft has the right-of-way over all other engine-driven aircraft (but not a glider).

3092. An airplane and an airship are converging. If the airship is left of the airplane's position, which aircraft has the right-of-way?

A — The airship.
B — The airplane.
C — Each pilot should alter course to the right.

3092. Answer A. JSPPM 2-6 (FAR 91.113)
See explanation for Question 3091. Since an airship is less maneuverable than an airplane, the airship has the right-of-way.

3093. Which aircraft has the right-of-way over the other aircraft listed?

A — Airship.
B — Aircraft towing other aircraft.
C — Gyroplane.

3094. What action should the pilots of a glider and an airplane take if on a head-on collision course?

A — The airplane pilot should give way to the left.
B — The glider pilot should give way to the right.
C — Both pilots should give way to the right.

3095. When two or more aircraft are approaching an airport for the purpose of landing, the right-of-way belongs to the aircraft

A — that has the other to its right.
B — that is the least maneuverable.
C — at the lower altitude, but it shall not take advantage of this rule to cut in front of or to overtake another.

3101. Except when necessary for takeoff or landing, what is the minimum safe altitude for a pilot to operate an aircraft anywhere?

A — An altitude allowing, if a power unit fails, an emergency landing without undue hazard to persons or property on the surface.
B — An altitude of 500 feet above the surface and no closer than 500 feet to any person, vessel, vehicle, or structure.
C — An altitude of 500 feet above the highest obstacle within a horizontal radius of 1,000 feet.

3102. Except when necessary for takeoff or landing, what is the minimum safe altitude required for a pilot to operate an aircraft over congested areas?

A — An altitude of 1,000 feet above any person, vessel, vehicle, or structure.
B — An altitude of 500 feet above the highest obstacle within a horizontal radius of 1,000 feet of the aircraft.
C — An altitude of 1,000 feet above the highest obstacle within a horizontal radius of 2,000 feet of the aircraft.

3093. Answer B. JSPPM 2-8 (FAR 91.113)
An aircraft towing or refueling another aircraft has the right-of-way over all other engine-driven aircraft.

3094. Answer C. JSPPM 2-8 (FAR 91.113)
When any aircraft are approaching each other head-on, both pilots should alter their course to the right. For aircraft approaching head-on, the FARs do not make a distinction between aircraft categories.

3095. Answer C. JSPPM 2-8 (FAR 91.113)
When two or more aircraft are approaching an airport for landing, the one at the lower altitude has the right-of-way, but you should not use this rule to cut in front of another aircraft.

3101. Answer A. JSPPM 2-8 (FAR 91.119)
Except for a normal takeoff and landing, you must maintain enough altitude to allow an emergency landing in the event of an engine failure without undue hazard to people or property on the surface.
Answer (B) is wrong because it combines minimum altitudes for operating over an uncongested area (500 feet above the surface), and a sparsely populated or open water area (500 feet from any person, vessel, vehicle, or structure). Answer (C) gives the wrong distances for operating over a congested area. It should be 1,000 feet above any obstacle within a horizontal radius of 2,000 feet.

3102. Answer C. JSPPM 2-9 (FAR 91.119)
See explanation for Question 3101.

3103. Except when necessary for takeoff or landing, what is the minimum safe altitude for a pilot to operate an aircraft over other than a congested area?

A — An altitude allowing, if a power unit fails, an emergency landing without undue hazard to persons or property on the surface.
B — An altitude of 500 feet AGL, except over open water or a sparsely populated area, which requires 500 feet from any person, vessel, vehicle, or structure.
C — An altitude of 500 feet above the highest obstacle within a horizontal radius of 1,000 feet.

3103. Answer B. JSPPM 2-8 (FAR 91.119)
See explanation for Question 3101.

3104. Except when necessary for takeoff or landing, an aircraft may not be operated closer than what distance from any person, vessel, vehicle, or structure?

A — 500 feet.
B — 700 feet.
C — 1,000 feet.

3104. Answer A. JSPPM 2-9 (FAR 91.119)
See explanation for Question 3101. The words person, vessel, vehicle, or structure apply for operations over a sparsely populated or open water area, and the distance is 500 feet.

3105. If an altimeter setting is not available before flight, to which altitude should the pilot adjust the altimeter?

A — The elevation of the nearest airport corrected to mean sea level.
B — The elevation of the departure area.
C — Pressure altitude corrected for nonstandard temperature.

3105. Answer B. JSPPM 2-9 (FAR 91.121)
If unable to obtain a local altimeter setting, you should set the altimeter to the field elevation prior to departure.

3106. Prior to takeoff, the altimeter should be set to which altitude or altimeter setting?

A — The current local altimeter setting, if available, or the departure airport elevation.
B — The corrected density altitude of the departure airport.
C — The corrected pressure altitude for the departure airport.

3106. Answer A. JSPPM 2-9 (FAR 91.121)
See explanation for Question 3105.

3155. Which cruising altitude is appropriate for a VFR flight on a magnetic course of 135°?

A — Even thousandths.
B — Even thousandths plus 500 feet.
C — Odd thousandths plus 500 feet.

3155. Answer C. JSPPM 2-10 (FAR 91.159)
On an easterly magnetic course (0° to 179°) above 3,000 feet AGL, VFR cruising altitudes are odd thousands plus 500 feet. Answers (A) and (B) are wrong because even thousands (plus 500 feet) are used for westbound courses above 3,000 feet AGL.

3156. Which VFR cruising altitude is acceptable for a flight on a Victor Airway with a magnetic course of 175°? The terrain is less than 1,000 feet.

A — 4,500 feet.
B — 5,000 feet.
C — 5,500 feet.

3156. Answer C. JSPPM 2-10 (FAR 91.159)
See explanation for Question 3155. Answer (C) is correct because it is the only answer with odd thousands plus 500 feet.

3157. Which VFR cruising altitude is appropriate when flying above 3,000 feet AGL on a magnetic course of 185°?

A — 4,000 feet.
B — 4,500 feet.
C — 5,000 feet.

3157. Answer B. JSPPM 2-10 (FAR 91.159)
See explanation for Question 3155. Because the course is westerly, an even thousands altitude plus 500 feet is used.

3158. Each person operating an aircraft at a VFR cruising altitude shall maintain an odd-thousand plus 500-foot altitude while on a

A — magnetic heading of 0° through 179°.
B — magnetic course of 0° through 179°.
C — true course of 0° through 179°.

3158. Answer B. JSPPM 2-10 (FAR 91.159)
VFR cruising altitudes on an easterly magnetic course (0° to 179°) are odd-thousands plus 500 feet. Answer (A) is wrong because VFR altitudes are based on course, not heading. Answer (C) is wrong because magnetic course is used, not true course.

3710. Prior to starting each maneuver, pilots should

A — check altitude, airspeed, and heading indications.
B — visually scan the entire area for collision avoidance.
C — announce their intentions on the nearest CTAF.

3710. Answer B. JSPPM 2-6 (AIM)
To ensure you can see other aircraft which may be blocked by blindspots, make clearing turns and scan the area. Answer (A) is wrong because, while it is important to maintain an instrument scan, it is critical to clear the area. Answer (C) is wrong because you should not practice maneuvers in the vicinity of an airport.

3814. What procedure is recommended when climbing or descending VFR on an airway?

A — Execute gentle banks, left and right for continuous visual scanning of the airspace.
B — Advise the nearest FSS of the altitude changes.
C — Fly away from the centerline of the airway before changing altitude.

3814. Answer A. JSPPM 2-11 (AIM)
Because of potential traffic on airways, it is important to scan. Making shallow turns allows you to compensate for blindspots. Answer (B) is wrong because FSS does not provide traffic control or advisories on airways. Answer (C) is wrong because ATC is expecting you to maintain the airway centerline.

3833. What effect does haze have on the ability to see traffic or terrain features during flight?

A — Haze causes the eyes to focus at infinity.
B — The eyes tend to overwork in haze and do not detect relative movement easily.
C — All traffic or terrain features appear to be farther away than their actual distance.

3833. Answer C. JSPPM 2-11 (AIM)
Since haze reduces visibility, objects are closer than they appear. Answers (A) and (B) are wrong because without a definite visible object, which is sometimes the case in hazy conditions, the eyes tend to relax and focus on a point in space about 3 to 5 feet away, not infinity.

3834. The most effective method of scanning for other aircraft for collision avoidance during daylight hours is to use

A — regularly spaced concentration on the 3-, 9-, and 12-o'clock positions.
B — a series of short, regularly spaced eye movements to search each 10-degree sector.
C — peripheral vision by scanning small sectors and utilizing offcenter viewing.

3834. Answer B. JSPPM 2-2 (AIM)
The eyes are able to focus clearly only on a small area, approximately 10°, so a series of short eye movements is most effective. Answer (A) is wrong because all sectors should be scanned. Answer (C) is not correct because peripheral vision and offcenter viewing are most effective at night, not during the day.

3835. Which technique should a pilot use to scan for traffic to the right and left during straight-and-level flight?

A — Systematically focus on different segments of the sky for short intervals.
B — Concentrate on relative movement detected in the peripheral vision area.
C — Continuous sweeping of the windshield from right to left.

3835. Answer A. JSPPM 2-2 (AIM)
See explanation for Question 3834.

3836. How can you determine if another aircraft is on a collision course with your aircraft?

A — The other aircraft will always appear to get larger and closer at a rapid rate.
B — The nose of each aircraft is pointed at the same point in space.
C — There will be no apparent relative motion between your aircraft and the other aircraft.

3836. Answer C. JSPPM 2-3 (AIM)
A lack of relative movement can indicate that the two aircraft are moving toward one another on a collision course. Answer (A) is not correct because there are times when the other aircraft might not appear to get larger and closer until just before a collision. Answer (B) is wrong because even though the aircraft might be headed toward the same point, different aircraft speeds, might keep them from reaching the same point at the same time.

SECTION B
AIRPORTS

This section of Chapter 2 introduces you to runway/taxiway layouts and markings, wind direction indicators, and airport lighting systems. FAA Written Test questions covered in Section B include:

3120, 3121, 3302, 3303, 3304, 3305, 3306, 3307, 3308, 3718, 3760, 3761, 3762, 3763, 3764, 3765, 3766, 3767, 3768, 3769, 3771, 3772, 3773, 3774, 3775, 3776, 3777, 3778, 3805, 3806, 3807, 3808, 3809, 3810.

3120. Each pilot of an aircraft approaching to land on a runway served by a visual approach slope indicator (VASI) shall

A — maintain a 3° glide to the runway.
B — maintain an altitude at or above the glide slope.
C — stay high until the runway can be reached in a power-off landing.

3120. Answer B. JSPPM 2-24 (FAR 91.129)
The VASI glide path provides safe obstruction clearance to the runway. Therefore, the pilot should fly at or above the glide path. Answer (A) is wrong because not all VASIs have a 3° glide path. Answer (C) is wrong because VASIs are intended to provide a glide path for a normal approach.

3121. When approaching to land on a runway served by a visual approach slope indicator (VASI), the pilot shall

A — maintain an altitude that captures the glide slope at least 2 miles downwind from the runway threshold.
B — maintain an altitude at or above the glide slope.
C — remain on the glide slope and land between the two-light bar.

3302. When taxiing with strong quartering tailwinds, which aileron positions should be used?

A — Aileron down on the downwind side.
B — Ailerons neutral.
C — Aileron down on the side from which the wind is blowing.

3303. Which aileron positions should a pilot generally use when taxiing in strong quartering headwinds?

A — Aileron up on the side from which the wind is blowing.
B — Aileron down on the side from which the wind is blowing.
C — Ailerons neutral.

3304. Which wind condition would be most critical when taxiing a nosewheel equipped high-wing airplane?

A — Quartering tailwind.
B — Direct crosswind.
C — Quartering headwind.

3305. (Refer to figure 9, area A.) How should the flight controls be held while taxiing a tricycle-gear equipped airplane into a left quartering headwind?

A — Left aileron up, elevator neutral.
B — Left aileron down, elevator neutral.
C — Left aileron up, elevator down.

3121. Answer B. JSPPM 2-24 (FAR 91.129)
See explanation for Question 3120. Answer (A) is not a requirement for using a VASI. Answer (C) is also wrong because VASIs provide a glide path to the runway. There is no requirement to land between the light bars.

3302. Answer C. JSPPM 2-21 (FTH)
With a quartering tailwind, the aileron should be down on the side from which the wind is blowing in order to prevent the wind from flowing under the wing and lifting it.

3303. Answer A. JSPPM 2-21 (FTH)
To counteract the lifting tendency of a quartering headwind, the aileron should be up on the side from which the wind is blowing.

3304. Answer A. JSPPM 2-21 (FTH)
A tricycle-gear, high-wing airplane is most susceptible to a quartering tailwind because a strong airflow beneath the wing and horizontal stabilizer can lift the airplane and tip or nose it over.

3305. Answer A. JSPPM 2-21 (FTH)
While taxiing a tricycle-gear airplane in a quartering headwind, the aileron should be up on the side from which the wind is blowing, and the elevator neutral to prevent any lifting force on the tail. In this case, the wind is from the left, so the left aileron should be up.

The Flight Environment

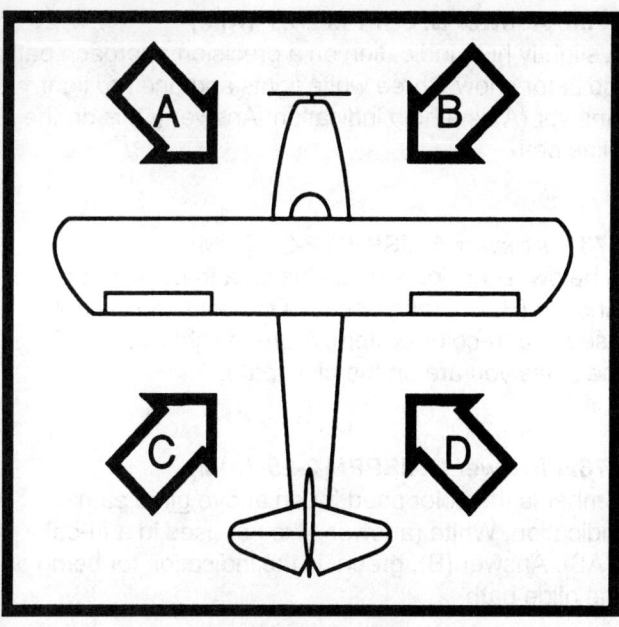

FIGURE 9.—Control Position for Taxi.

3306. (Refer to figure 9, area B.) How should the flight controls be held while taxiing a tailwheel airplane into a right quartering headwind?

A — Right aileron up, elevator up.
B — Right aileron down, elevator neutral.
C — Right aileron up, elevator down.

3307. (Refer to figure 9, area C.) How should the flight controls be held while taxiing a tailwheel airplane with a left quartering tailwind?

A — Left aileron up, elevator neutral.
B — Left aileron down, elevator neutral.
C — Left aileron down, elevator down.

3308. (Refer to figure 9, area C.) How should the flight controls be held while taxiing a tricycle-gear equipped airplane with a left quartering tailwind?

A — Left aileron up, elevator neutral.
B — Left aileron down, elevator down.
C — Left aileron up, elevator down.

3718. Airport taxiway edge lights are identified at night by

A — white directional lights.
B — blue omnidirectional lights.
C — alternate red and green lights.

3306. Answer A. JSPPM 2-21 (FTH)
In a tailwheel airplane, the aileron is held up on the upwind side, and the elevator is held up to prevent the tail from lifting. Since the tail of most tailwheel airplanes is lower than the nose while taxiing, a strong headwind blowing on a neutral or down elevator could cause the tail to rise.

3307. Answer C. JSPPM 2-21 (FTH)
For a quartering tailwind, the controls are held the same for both tailwheel and tricycle-gear airplanes. Ailerons are down on the side from which the wind is blowing. The elevator is down to prevent the wind from lifting the tail.

3308. Answer B. JSPPM 2-21 (FTH)
See explanation for Questions 3304 and 3307.

3718. Answer B. JSPPM 2-27 (FTH)
Taxiway edge lights are blue. Answer (A) is wrong because white lights are used for runway edges and centerlines. Answer (C) is wrong because alternating red and green lights are not used for taxiway lighting.

3760. A slightly high glide slope indication from a precision approach path indicator is

A — four white lights.
B — three white lights and one red light.
C — two white lights and two red lights.

3761. A below glide slope indication from a tri-color VASI is a

A — red light signal.
B — pink light signal.
C — green light signal.

3762. An above glide slope indication from a tri-color VASI is

A — a white light signal.
B — a green light signal.
C — an amber light signal.

3763. An on glide slope indication from a tri-color VASI is

A — a white light signal.
B — a green light signal.
C — an amber light signal.

3764. A below glide slope indication from a pulsating approach slope indicator is a

A — pulsating white light.
B — steady white light.
C — pulsating red light.

3765. (Refer to figure 48.) Illustration A indicates that the aircraft is

A — below the glide slope.
B — on the glide slope.
C — above the glide slope.

3766. (Refer to figure 48.) VASI lights as shown by illustration C indicate that the airplane is

A — off course to the left.
B — above the glide slope.
C — below the glide slope.

3760. Answer B. JSPPM 2-25 (AIM)
A slightly high indication on a precision approach path indicator shows three white lights and one red light. Answer (A) is a high indication. Answer (C) is on the glide path.

3761. Answer A. JSPPM 2-25 (AIM)
A below glide slope indication on a tri-color is red. Answer (B) is wrong because the color pink is not used in a tri-color system. A green light (answer C) indicates you are on the glide path.

3762. Answer C. JSPPM 2-25 (AIM)
Amber is the color used for an above glide path indication. White (answer A) is not used in a tri-color VASI. Answer (B), green, is the indication for being on the glide path.

3763. Answer B. JSPPM 2-25 (AIM)
See explanation for Question 3762.

3764. Answer C. JSPPM 2-25 (AIM)
A pulsating approach slope indicator provides a pulsating red light when below glide slope. Answer (A), pulsating white, is above glide slope. Answer (B), steady white, is on glide slope.

3765. Answer B. JSPPM 2-24 (AIM)
A red over white indication is on glide slope.

3766. Answer B. JSPPM 2-24 (AIM)
A white over white indication is above glide slope.

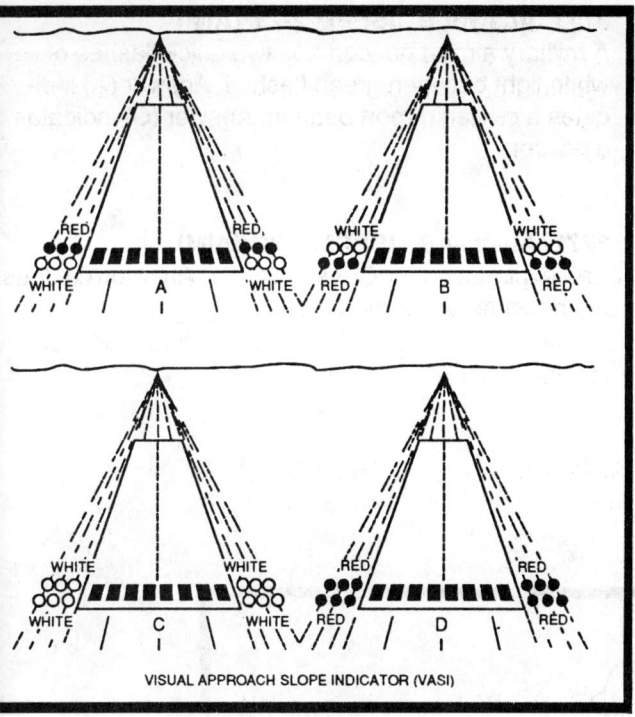

FIGURE 48.—VASI Illustrations.

3767. (Refer to figure 48.) While on final approach to a runway equipped with a standard 2-bar VASI, the lights appear as shown by illustration D. This means that the aircraft is

A — above the glide slope.
B — below the glide slope.
C — on the glide slope.

3767. Answer B. JSPPM 2-24 (AIM)
A red over red indication is below the glide slope.

3768. To set the high intensity runway lights on medium intensity, the pilot should click the microphone seven times, then click it

A — one time.
B — three times.
C — five times.

3768. Answer C. JSPPM 2-28 (AIM)
At airports with three-step pilot-controlled runway lighting system, seven clicks turns all the lights on to the maximum intensity. Five clicks turns the lights to medium. One click, (answer A) does not change the light setting. Three clicks (answer B) turns the lights to the lowest intensity.

3769. An airport's rotating beacon operated during daylight hours indicates

A — there are obstructions on the airport.
B — that weather at the airport located in Class D airspace is below basic VFR weather minimums.
C — the Air Traffic Control tower is not in operation.

3769. Answer B. JSPPM 2-23 (AIM)
When the airport beacon is on during the daytime, it usually means that the ceiling is less than 1,000 feet and/or the visibility is less than three statute miles (below basic VFR minimums). The beacon is not used to indicate obstructions (answer A), nor does it indicate that the control tower is not in operation (answer C). Remember, though, the airport beacon may not always be turned on when the weather is below VFR minimums.

3771. A military air station can be identified by a rotating beacon that emits

A — white and green alternating flashes.
B — two quick, white flashes between green flashes.
C — green, yellow, and white flashes.

3772. How can a military airport be identified at night?

A — Alternate white and green light flashes.
B — Dual peaked (two quick) white flashes between green flashes.
C — White flashing lights with steady green at the same location.

3771. Answer B. JSPPM 2-23 (AIM)
A military airport beacon has two quick flashes of white light between green flashes. Answer (A) indicates a civilian airport beacon. Answer (C) indicates a heliport.

3772. Answer B. JSPPM 2-23 (AIM)
See explanation for Question 3771. Answer (C) does not describe any airport beacon.

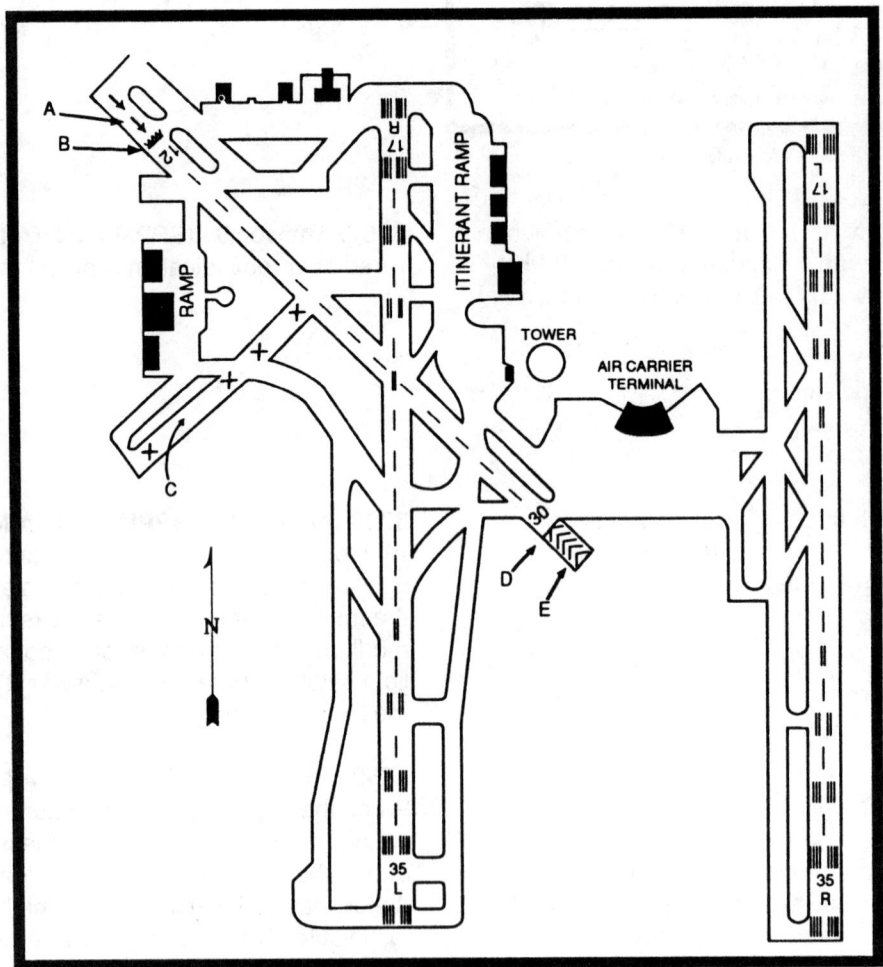

FIGURE 49.—Airport Diagram.

The Flight Environment

3773. (Refer to figure 49.) That portion of the runway identified by the letter A may be used for

A — landing.
B — taxiing and takeoff.
C — taxiing and landing.

3774. (Refer to figure 49.) According to the airport diagram, which statement is true?

A — Runway 30 is equipped at position E with emergency arresting gear to provide a means of stopping military aircraft.
B — Takeoffs may be started at position A on Runway 12, and the landing portion of this runway begins at position B.
C — The takeoff and landing portion of Runway 12 begins at position B.

3775. (Refer to figure 49.) What is the difference between area A and area E on the airport depicted?

A — "A" may be used for taxi and takeoff; "E" may be used only as an overrun.
B — "A" may be used for all operations except heavy aircraft landings; "E" may be used only as an overrun.
C — "A" may be used only for taxiing; "E" may be used for all operations except landings.

3776. (Refer to figure 49.) Area C on the airport depicted is classified as a

A — stabilized area.
B — multiple heliport.
C — closed runway.

3777. (Refer to figure 50 on page 2-12.) The arrows that appear on the end of the north/south runway indicate that the area

A — may be used only for taxiing.
B — is usable for taxiing, takeoff, and landing.
C — cannot be used for landing, but may be used for taxiing and takeoff.

3778. The numbers 9 and 27 on a runway indicate that the runway is oriented approximately

A — 009° and 027° true.
B — 090° and 270° true.
C — 090° and 270° magnetic.

3773. Answer B. JSPPM 2-17 (AIM)
At many airports, the area prior to a displaced threshold may be used for taxi and takeoff (and rollout after landing). Answers (A) and (C) are wrong because you may not land on this part of a runway.

3774. Answer B. JSPPM 2-17 (AIM)
See explanation for Question 3773. Landings may be made after the displaced threshold at position "B." Answer (A) is not correct because area "E" is a blastpad/stopway. Answer (C) is wrong because takeoffs may be started before the displaced threshold and landing rollouts may be completed in area "A."

3775. Answer A. JSPPM 2-17 (AIM)
See explanation for Question 3773. Area "E" is a blastpad/stopway, and because of its pavement strength cannot support continuous operations, but may be used as an overrun. Answer (B) in wrong because area "A" cannot be used for any landings. Answer (C) is wrong because takeoffs and landing rollouts are allowed in area "A," and area "E" is unusable.

3776. Answer C. JSPPM 2-17 (AIM)
A closed runway is marked by X's painted on its surface.

3777. Answer C. JSPPM 2-17 (AIM)
See explanation for Question 3773.

3778. Answer C. JSPPM 2-14 (AIM)
Runway numbers correspond to the magnetic, not true, direction, and are rounded to the nearest 10°, with the last zero omitted.

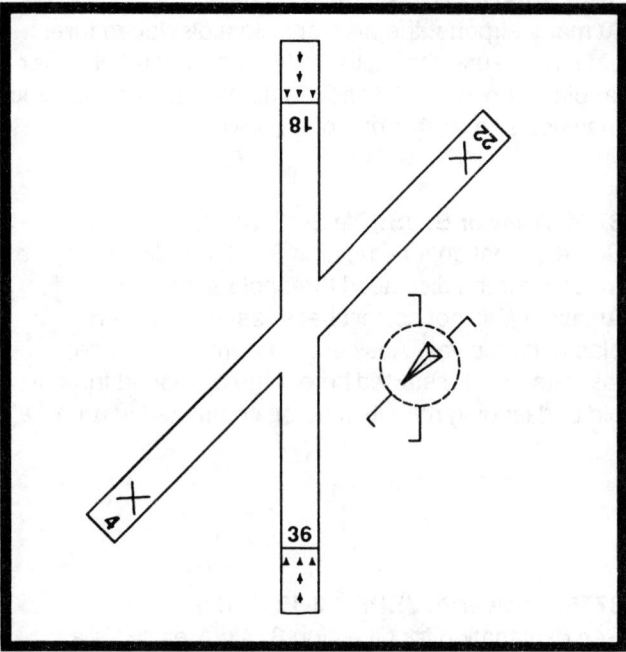

FIGURE 50.—Airport Diagram.

3805. (Refer to figure 50.) Select the proper traffic pattern and runway for landing.

A — Left-hand traffic and Runway 18.
B — Right-hand traffic and Runway 18.
C — Left-hand traffic and Runway 22.

3806. (Refer to figure 50.) If the wind is as shown by the landing direction indicator, the pilot should land on

A — Runway 18 and expect a crosswind from the right.
B — Runway 22 directly into the wind.
C — Runway 36 and expect a crosswind from the right.

3807. (Refer to figure 51.) The segmented circle indicates that the airport traffic is

A — left-hand for Runway 35 and right-hand for Runway 17.
B — left-hand for Runway 17 and right-hand for Runway 35.
C — right-hand for Runway 9 and left-hand for Runway 27.

3805. Answer B. JSPPM 2-19 (AIM)
The wind indicates a landing should be made to the south, and the segmented circle shows right-hand traffic for Runway 18. Answer (A) is wrong because the segmented circle indicates a right-hand pattern for Runway 18. Answer (C) is wrong because Runway 22 is closed.

3806. Answer A. JSPPM 2-19 (AIM)
The wind is from the southwest, so a landing on Runway 18 would provide both a headwind component and a crosswind from the right. Answer (B) is wrong because Runway 22 is closed. Answer (C) is wrong because landing on Runway 36 would be made with a tailwind and a crosswind from the left.

3807. Answer A. JSPPM 2-19 (AIM)
The segmented circle indicates left-hand traffic for Runway 35, and right-hand traffic for Runway 17. Answer (B) is opposite this. Answer (C) is wrong because left-hand traffic is used for Runway 9 and right-hand traffic for Runway 27.

The Flight Environment

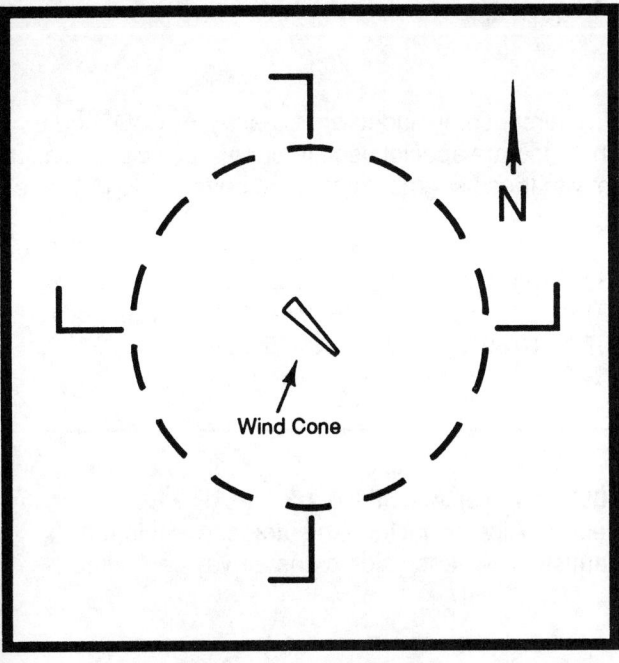

FIGURE 51.—Airport Landing Indicator.

3808. (Refer to figure 51.) The traffic patterns indicated in the segmented circle have been arranged to avoid flights over an area to the

A — south of the airport.
B — north of the airport.
C — southeast of the airport.

3809. (Refer to figure 51.) The segmented circle indicates that a landing on Runway 26 will be with a

A — right-quartering headwind.
B — left-quartering headwind.
C — right-quartering tailwind.

3810. (Refer to figure 51.) Which runway and traffic pattern should be used as indicated by the wind cone in the segmented circle?

A — Right-hand traffic on Runway 8.
B — Right-hand traffic on Runway 17.
C — Left-hand traffic on Runway 35.

3808. Answer C. JSPPM 2-19 (AIM)
Since the traffic pattern for the north-south runway is west of the field, and the pattern for the east-west runway is north of the field, there should be no flights southeast of the airport.

3809. Answer A. JSPPM 2-19 (AIM)
Since the wind cone shows wind from the northwest, a landing to the west will provide a right-quartering headwind.

3810. Answer C. JSPPM 2-19 (AIM)
With wind from the northwest, landing on Runway 35 would provide a quartering headwind. Answers (A) and (B) are wrong because you would be landing with a tailwind.

SECTION C
AIRSPACE

Section C of Chapter 2 describes various classifications for U.S. airspace. Included are Class A, B, C, D, and E controlled airspace and Class G uncontrolled airspace. Also included are special use airspace and a classification known as other airspace areas. Basic rules for flight operation with these segments are also covered. FAA Written Test questions include:

3067, 3068, 3069, 3107, 3118, 3119, 3124, 3125, 3126, 3127, 3128, 3129, 3130, 3136, 3137, 3138, 3139, 3140, 3141, 3142, 3143, 3144, 3145, 3146, 3147, 3148, 3149, 3150, 3151, 3153, 3154, 3165, 3166, 3601, 3602, 3603, 3620, 3621, 3623, 3624, 3626, 3627, 3628, 3779, 3780, 3782, 3783, 3785, 3786, 3787, 3788, 3799, 3813.

3067. The width of a Federal Airway from either side of the centerline is

A — 4 nautical miles.
B — 6 nautical miles.
C — 8 nautical miles.

3067. Answer A. JSPPM 2-34 (FAR 71.5)
Federal Airways include the airspace within four nautical miles each side of the airway centerline.

3068. Unless otherwise specified, Federal Airways include that Class E airspace extending upward from

A — 700 feet above the surface up to and including 17,999 feet MSL.
B — 1,200 feet above the surface up to and including 17,999 feet MSL.
C — the surface up to and including 18,000 feet MSL.

3068. Answer B. JSPPM 2-35 (AIM)
Federal Airways normally begin at 1,200 feet AGL and extend up to, but not including, 18,000 feet MSL. Answer (A) is not correct because 700 feet is the floor of Class E airspace associated with an airport for which an approved instrument approach procedure has been published. Answer (C) is wrong because airways do not normally begin at the surface, and do not include 18,000 feet MSL.

3069. Normal VFR operations in Class D airspace with an operating control tower require the visibility and ceiling to be at least

A — 1,000 feet and 1 mile.
B — 1,000 feet and 3 miles.
C — 2,500 feet and 3 miles.

3069. Answer B. JSPPM 2-39 (FAR 91.155)
In order to operate in Class D airspace, the VFR visibility minimum is three statute miles. In addition, the ceiling must be at least 1,000 feet. Answer (A) is incorrect because the visibility is less than that required. The 2,500 feet in answer (C) is the top of most Class D airspace areas.

3107. At what altitude shall the altimeter be set to 29.92, when climbing to cruising flight level?

A — 14,500 feet MSL.
B — 18,000 feet MSL.
C — 24,000 feet MSL.

3107. Answer B. JSPPM 2-32 (FAR 91.121)
To standardize altimeter settings in Class A airspace, all pilots are required to set their altimeters to 29.92 at and above 18,000 feet MSL.

3118. Airspace at an airport with a part-time control tower is classified as Class D airspace only

A — when the weather minimums are below basic VFR.
B — when the associated control tower is in operation.
C — when the associated Flight Service Station is in operation.

3118. Answer B. JSPPM 2-36 (AIM)
In order for airspace to be classified as Class D there must be an operating control tower. Answers (A) and (C) are incorrect because they do not address the part-time control tower.

The Flight Environment

3119. Unless otherwise authorized, two-way radio communications with Air Traffic Control are required for landings or takeoffs

A — at all tower controlled airports regardless of weather conditions.
B — at all tower controlled airports only when weather conditions are less than VFR.
C — at all tower controlled airports within Class D airspace only when weather conditions are less than VFR.

3119. Answer A. JSPPM 2-36 (FAR 91.129)
When operating at an airport where a control tower is in operation, you must be in radio contact with ATC whether or not VFR conditions exist. Therefore, answers (B) and (C) are incorrect.

3124. Two-way radio communication must be established with the Air Traffic Control facility having jurisdiction over the area prior to entering which class airspace?

A — Class C.
B — Class E.
C — Class G.

3124. Answer A. JSPPM 2-35 (FAR 91.130)
You must establish two-way communications prior to entering a Class C airspace area, and maintain it while operating within the Class C airspace. Answers (B) and (C) are wrong because two-way communications are not required in Class E or G airspace.

3125. What minimum radio equipment is required for operation within Class C airspace?

A — Two-way radio communications equipment and a 4096-code transponder.
B — Two-way radio communications equipment, a 4096-code transponder, and DME.
C — Two-way radio communications equipment, a 4096-code transponder, and an encoding altimeter.

3125. Answer C. JSPPM 2-35 (FAR 91.130, 91.215)
To operate in a Class C airspace area, you are required to have both a two-way radio and a 4096-code transponder with encoding altimeter. Answer (A) does not include the requirement for an encoding altimeter and DME is not a requirement for Class C airspace (answer B).

3126. What minimum pilot certification is required for operation within Class B airspace?

A — Recreational Pilot Certificate.
B — Private Pilot Certificate or Student Pilot Certificate with appropriate logbook endorsements.
C — Private Pilot Certificate with an instrument rating.

3126. Answer B. JSPPM 2-33 (FAR 91.131)
To operate in a Class B airspace area, a pilot must hold a private pilot certificate. However, within certain Class B airspace areas, student pilot operations may be conducted after receiving specific training and a logbook endorsement from an authorized flight instructor.

3127. What minimum pilot certification is required for operation within Class B airspace?

A — Private Pilot Certificate or Student Pilot Certificate with appropriate logbook endorsements.
B — Commercial Pilot Certificate.
C — Private Pilot Certificate with an instrument rating.

3127. Answer A. JSPPM 2-33 (FAR 91.131)
To operate in a Class B airspace area, a pilot must hold a private pilot certificate. However, within certain Class B airspace areas, student pilot operations may be conducted after receiving specific training and a logbook endorsement from an authorized flight instructor.

3128. What minimum radio equipment is required for VFR operation within Class B airspace?

A — Two-way radio communications equipment and a 4096-code transponder.
B — Two-way radio communications equipment, a 4096-code transponder, and an encoding altimeter.
C — Two-way radio communications equipment, a 4096-code transponder, an encoding altimeter, and a VOR or TACAN receiver.

3129. An operable 4096-code transponder and Mode C encoding altimeter are required in

A — Class B airspace within 30 miles of the primary airport.
B — Class D airspace.
C — Class E airspace below 10,000 feet.

3130. In which type of airspace are VFR flights prohibited?

A — Class A.
B — Class B.
C — Class C.

3136. During operations within controlled airspace at altitudes of less than 1,200 feet AGL, the minimum horizontal distance from clouds requirement for VFR flight is

A — 1,000 feet.
B — 1,500 feet.
C — 2,000 feet.

3137. What minimum visibility and clearance from clouds are required for VFR operations in Class G airspace at 700 feet AGL or below during daylight hours?

A — 1 mile visibility and clear of clouds.
B — 1 mile visibility, 500 feet below, 1,000 feet above, and 2,000 feet horizontal clearance from clouds.
C — 3 miles visibility and clear of clouds.

3138. What minimum flight visibility is required for VFR flight operations on an airway below 10,000 feet MSL?

A — 1 mile.
B — 3 miles.
C — 4 miles.

3128. Answer B. JSPPM 2-33 (FAR 91.131)
VFR operations within Class B airspace areas require a two-way radio and a 4096-code transponder with an encoding altimeter. Answer (A) does not include the requirement for an encoding altimeter, and VOR or TACAN receivers are only required for instrument flight (answer C).

3129. Answer A. JSPPM 2-33 (FAR 91.131)
A 4096-code transponder with an encoding altimeter is required for operations within a Class B airspace area. It is not required in Class D airspace or Class E airspace below 10,000 feet MSL (answers B and C).

3130. Answer A. JSPPM 2-32 (FAR 91.135)
Only IFR operations are allowed in Class A airspace. VFR flights are allowed in Class B and C airspace if authorized by ATC.

3136. Answer C. JSPPM 2-33 (FAR 91.155)
In controlled airspace below 10,000 feet, it does not matter whether you are above or below 1,200 feet AGL. The VFR cloud clearance is 2,000 feet horizontal.

3137. Answer A. JSPPM 2-40 (FAR 91.155)
For VFR flight in uncontrolled airspace below 1,200 feet during daytime, you are only required to have 1 mile visibility and remain clear of clouds. Answer (B) applies between 1,200 feet AGL and 10,000 feet MSL during daytime in uncontrolled airspace. Answer (C) applies to VFR operations in Class B airspace.

3138. Answer B. JSPPM 2-33 (FAR 91.155)
Since an airway is Class E airspace, the minimum visibility below 10,000 feet MSL is 3 statute miles.

The Flight Environment

3139. The minimum distance from clouds required for VFR operations on an airway below 10,000 feet MSL is

A — remain clear of clouds.
B — 500 feet below, 1,000 feet above, and 2,000 feet horizontally.
C — 500 feet above, 1,000 feet below, and 2,000 feet horizontally.

3140. During operations within controlled airspace at altitudes of more than 1,200 feet AGL, but less than 10,000 feet MSL, the minimum distance above clouds requirement for VFR flight is

A — 500 feet.
B — 1,000 feet.
C — 1,500 feet.

3141. VFR flight in controlled airspace above 1,200 feet AGL and below 10,000 feet MSL requires a minimum visibility and vertical cloud clearance of

A — 3 miles, and 500 feet below or 1,000 feet above the clouds in controlled airspace.
B — 5 miles, and 1,000 feet below or 1,000 feet above the clouds at all altitudes.
C — 5 miles, and 1,000 feet below or 1,000 feet above the clouds only in Class A airspace.

3142. During operations outside controlled airspace at altitudes of more than 1,200 feet AGL, but less than 10,000 feet MSL, the minimum flight visibility for VFR flight at night is

A — 1 mile.
B — 3 miles.
C — 5 miles.

3143. Outside controlled airspace, the minimum flight visibility requirement for VFR flight above 1,200 feet AGL and below 10,000 feet MSL during daylight hours is

A — 1 mile.
B — 3 miles.
C — 5 miles.

3144. During operations outside controlled airspace at altitudes of more than 1,200 feet AGL, but less than 10,000 feet MSL, the minimum distance below clouds requirement for VFR flight at night is

A — 500 feet.
B — 1,000 feet.
C — 1,500 feet.

3139. Answer B. JSPPM 2-33 (FAR 91.155)
The VFR cloud clearances for Class E airspace apply. Below 10,000 feet MSL, you must remain 500 feet below, 1,000 feet above, and 2,000 feet horizontally.

3140. Answer B. JSPPM 2-33 (FAR 91.155)
Below 10,000 feet MSL in Class C, D, and E airspace, the cloud clearances are 500 feet below, 1,000 feet above, and 2,000 feet horizontal. In Class B airspace, however, the cloud clearance is just "clear of clouds." "Clear of clouds" is not offered in answers (A) or (C). Therefore, answer (B) has to be the correct choice.

3141. Answer A. JSPPM 2-33 (FAR 91.155)
See explanation for Question 3140. The visibility and cloud clearances listed in answers (B) and (C) apply only above 1,200 feet AGL and at or above 10,000 feet MSL.

3142. Answer B. JSPPM 2-40 (FAR 91.155)
In Class G airspace at these altitudes, night VFR operations require 3 miles visibility. Answer (A) is wrong, as 1 mile is the minimum required for daytime at these altitudes. Answer (C) is wrong, since 5 miles is required above 1,200 AGL and at or above 10,000 feet MSL for both day and night.

3143. Answer A. JSPPM 2-40 (FAR 91.155)
See explanation for Question 3142. In uncontrolled airspace below 10,000 feet MSL and above 1,200 feet AGL, required daytime visibility is 1 mile.

3144. Answer A. JSPPM 2-40 (FAR 91.155)
In uncontrolled airspace below 10,000 feet MSL (both above and below 1,200 feet AGL), the VFR cloud clearance is 500 feet below. Answer (B), 1,000 feet, is the clearance above clouds at these altitudes. Answer (C), 1,500 feet, is inappropriate.

3145. The minimum flight visibility required for VFR flights above 10,000 feet MSL and more than 1,200 feet AGL in controlled airspace is

A — 1 mile.
B — 3 miles.
C — 5 miles.

3145. Answer C. JSPPM 2-33 (FAR 91.155)
At or above 10,000 feet MSL and above 1,200 feet AGL, the required visibility is 5 statute miles, whether in controlled or uncontrolled airspace.

3146. For VFR flight operations above 10,000 feet MSL and more than 1,200 feet AGL, the minimum horizontal distance from clouds required is

A — 1,000 feet.
B — 2,000 feet.
C — 1 mile.

3146. Answer C. JSPPM 2-33 (FAR 91.155)
Whether in controlled or uncontrolled airspace at these altitudes, the minimum VFR horizontal distance from clouds is 1 statute mile.

3147. During operations at altitudes of more than 1,200 feet AGL and at or above 10,000 feet MSL, the minimum distance above clouds requirement for VFR flight is

A — 500 feet.
B — 1,000 feet.
C — 1,500 feet.

3147. Answer B. JSPPM 2-33 (FAR 91.155)
For VFR flights at these altitudes, whether in controlled airspace or not, you are required to remain 1,000 feet above clouds. The only exception is for daytime operations below 1,200 feet AGL in uncontrolled airspace. In this case it is clear of clouds.

3148. No person may take off or land an aircraft under basic VFR at an airport that lies within Class D airspace unless the

A — flight visibility at that airport is at least 1 mile.
B — ground visibility at that airport is at least 1 mile.
C — ground visibility at that airport is at least 3 miles.

3148. Answer C. JSPPM 2-39 (FAR 91.155)
To take off or land under VFR in a Class D airspace area, the ceiling must be at least 1,000 feet and the ground visibility must be at least 3 statute miles. **Flight** visibility may be used if ground visibility is not available. Answers (A) and (B) are wrong since they reflect 1 statute mile visibility which only applies under special VFR.

3149. The basic VFR weather minimums for operating an aircraft within Class D airspace are

A — 500-foot ceiling and 1 mile visibility.
B — 1,000-foot ceiling and 3 miles visibility.
C — clear of clouds and 2 miles visibility.

3149. Answer B. JSPPM 2-39 (FAR 91.155)
See explanation for Question 3148. Answers (A) and (C) do not reflect normal or special VFR weather minimums.

3150. A special VFR clearance authorizes the pilot of an aircraft to operate VFR while within Class D airspace when the visibility is

A — less than 1 mile and the ceiling is less than 1,000 feet.
B — at least 1 mile and the aircraft can remain clear of clouds.
C — at least 3 miles and the aircraft can remain clear of clouds.

3150. Answer B. JSPPM 2-39 (FAR 91.157)
When authorized by ATC, special VFR allows you to operate with one statute mile visibility as long as you can remain clear of clouds.

3151. What is the minimum weather condition required for airplanes operating under special VFR in Class D airspace?

A — 1 mile flight visibility.
B — 1 mile flight visibility and 1,000-foot ceiling.
C — 3 miles flight visibility and 1,000-foot ceiling.

3153. What are the minimum requirements for airplane operations under special VFR in Class D airspace at night?

A — The airplane must be under radar surveillance at all times while in Class D airspace.
B — The airplane must be equipped for IFR with an altitude reporting transponder.
C — The pilot must be instrument rated, and the airplane must be IFR equipped.

3154. No person may operate an airplane within Class D airspace at night under special VFR unless the

A — flight can be conducted 500 feet below the clouds.
B — airplane is equipped for instrument flight.
C — flight visibility is at least 3 miles.

3165. An operable 4096-code transponder with an encoding altimeter is required in which airspace?

A — Class A, Class B (within 30 miles of the primary airport), and Class C.
B — Class D and Class E (below 10,000 feet MSL).
C — Class D and Class G (below 10,000 feet MSL).

3166. With certain exceptions, all aircraft within 30 miles of a Class B primary airport from the surface upward to 10,000 feet MSL must be equipped with

A — an operable VOR or TACAN receiver and an ADF receiver.
B — instruments and equipment required for IFR operations.
C — an operable transponder having either Mode S or 4096-code capability with Mode C automatic altitude reporting capability.

3151. Answer A. JSPPM 2-39 (FAR 91.157)
See explanation for Question 3150.

3153. Answer C. JSPPM 2-39 (FAR 91.157)
For special VFR at night, you must have a current instrument rating, and the airplane must be equipped for IFR operations. Answer (A) is wrong because radar is not a requirement for Class D airspace. Answer (B) is incorrect because a transponder is not required in Class D airspace.

3154. Answer B. JSPPM 2-39 (FAR 91.157)
See explanation for Question 3153. Answers (A) and (C) are wrong because minimums for special VFR at night are the same as for day (1 statute mile visibility and clear of clouds).

3165. Answer A. JSPPM 2-32, 33, 35 (FAR 91.215)
A transponder with an encoding transponder is required in Class A, Class B, and Class C airspace. It is not required in the areas listed in answers (B) and (C).

3166. Answer C. JSPPM 2-33 (FAR 91.215)
An appropriate transponder capable of providing altitude encoding is required to be in use when within 30 miles of a Class B primary airport. Answer (A) is incorrect because a VOR or TACAN receiver (ADF is not applicable) is only required for IFR operations within Class B airspace. Answer (B) is incorrect because IFR instruments and equipment are not required for Class B airspace operations.

3601. (Refer to figure 21 on page 6-4.) What hazards to aircraft may exist in warning areas such as Warning W-50B?

A — Unusual, often invisible, hazards such as aerial gunnery or guided missiles over international waters.
B — High volume of pilot training or unusual type of aerial activity.
C — Heavy military aircraft traffic in the approach and departure area of the North Atlantic Control Area.

3601. Answer A. JSPPM 2-41 (AIM)
Warning areas often contain hazards such as aerial gunnery or guided missiles. Answer (B) would apply to a military operations area (MOA). Answer (C) does not describe a warning area.

3602. (Refer to figure 27 on page 6-10.) What hazards to aircraft may exist in areas such as Devils Lake East MOA?

A — Unusual, often invisible, hazards to aircraft such as artillery firing.
B — High density military training activities.
C — Parachute jump operations.

3602. Answer B. JSPPM 2-41 (AIM)
A military operations area (MOA) is a block of airspace in which military training and maneuvers are conducted. Answer (A) describes activities that occur in a restricted area. Answer (C) describes a parachute jump area.

3603. (Refer to figure 22 on page 6-5.) What type military flight operations should a pilot expect along IR 644?

A — IFR training flights above 1,500 feet AGL at speeds in excess of 250 knots.
B — VFR training flights above 1,500 feet AGL at speeds less than 250 knots.
C — Instrument training flights below 1,500 feet AGL at speeds in excess of 150 knots.

3603. Answer A. JSPPM 2-43 (AIM)
"IR 644" is a military training route, on which aircraft may fly at speeds above 250 knots. "IR" designates a route used for IFR operations. Since the designation is a three digit number, the route contains one or more segments above 1,500 feet AGL. Flights along routes with four digit numbers are conducted below 1,500 feet AGL. Answer (B) is wrong because VFR flights are normally conducted on routes designated "VR."

3620. (Refer to figure 23, area 1 on page 6-6.) The visibility and cloud clearance requirements to operate VFR during daylight hours over Sandpoint Airport at less than 1,200 feet AGL are

A — 1 mile and clear of clouds.
B — 1 mile and 1,000 feet above, 500 feet below, and 2,000 feet horizontally from each cloud.
C — 3 miles and 1,000 feet above, 500 feet below, and 2,000 feet horizontally from each cloud.

3620. Answer A. JSPPM 2-40 (FAR 91.155)
Sandpoint Airport is a nontowered airport in Class G airspace. Therefore, day VFR minimums at less than 1,200 feet AGL are 1 mile and clear of clouds. Answer (B) lists the daytime minimums for flight between 1,200 feet AGL and 10,000 feet MSL in Class G airspace. Answer (C) reflects the minimums for operating below 10,000 feet MSL at night in uncontrolled airspace (Class G).

3621. (Refer to figure 27, area 2 on page 6-10.) The visibility and cloud clearance requirements to operate VFR during daylight hours over Cooperstown Airport between 1,200 feet AGL and 10,000 feet MSL are

A — 1 mile and clear of clouds.
B — 1 mile and 1,000 feet above, 500 feet below, and 2,000 feet horizontally from clouds.
C — 3 miles and 1,000 feet above, 500 feet below, and 2,000 feet horizontally from clouds.

3621. Answer B. JSPPM 2-40 (FAR 91.155)
Cooperstown Airport is a nontowered airport in Class G airspace. Therefore, day VFR minimums between 1,200 feet AGL and 10,000 feet MSL are 1 mile visibility and 1,000 feet above, 500 feet below, and 2,000 feet horizontally from clouds. Answer (A) lists the daytime minimums for flight at or below 1,200 feet AGL in Class G airspace. Answer (C) indicates the minimums for operating below 10,000 feet MSL at night in uncontrolled airspace (Class G).

The Flight Environment

3623. (Refer to figure 27, area 6 on page 6-10.) The airspace overlying and within 5 miles of Barnes County Airport is

A — Class D airspace from the surface to the floor of the overlying Class E airspace.
B — Class E airspace from the surface to 1,200 feet MSL.
C — Class G airspace from the surface to 700 feet AGL.

3623. Answer C. JSPPM 2-38 (Chart Legend)
The magenta color indicates Class E airspace. If there were magenta segmented lines around the airport, the Class E airspace would begin at the surface. Magenta shading indicates the airspace starts at 700 feet AGL. Below 700 feet the airspace is uncontrolled or Class G. Class D airspace is indicated by segmented blue lines.

3624. (Refer to figure 26, area 7 on page 6-9.) The airspace overlying McKinney Muni is uncontrolled from the surface to

A — 700 feet AGL.
B — 1,700 feet MSL.
C — 4,000 feet AGL.

3624. Answer A. JSPPM 2-38 (Chart Legend)
This location is within a magenta shaded area. Therefore, Class E airspace begins at 700 feet AGL. The 1^7 indicates the maximum elevation within the quadrangle is 1,700 feet MSL and has nothing to do with controlled airspace (answer B). The 4,000 refers to the base of the Class B airspace area overlying McKinney Municipal Airport (answer C). This base is expressed in feet above mean sea level, not AGL.

3626. (Refer to figure 24, area 3 on page 6-7.) What is the floor of the Savannah Class C airspace at the outer circle?

A — 1,200 feet AGL.
B — 1,300 feet MSL.
C — 1,700 feet MSL.

3626. Answer B. JSPPM 2-35 (AIM)
The floor of the outer circle is 1,300 feet MSL as shown by the "41" over "13" (the top or ceiling is 4,100 feet MSL). Answer (A) is not correct because while 1,200 feet AGL is usually the starting point, each Class C airspace area can be modified to fit specific locations. At Savannah, the 1,200 feet AGL has been rounded up to 1,300 feet MSL (airport elevation is 51 feet). Answer (C) is not right because the 1^7 indicates the maximum elevation within the quadrangle is 1,700 feet MSL and has nothing to do with controlled airspace.

3627. (Refer to figure 21, area 1 on page 6-4.) What minimum radio equipment is required to land and take off at Norfolk International?

A — Mode C transponder and omnireceiver.
B — Mode C transponder and two-way radio.
C — Mode C transponder, omnireceiver, and DME.

3627. Answer B. JSPPM 2-36 (FAR 91.130)
The area depicted is Class C airspace. Aircraft operating in Class C airspace must be equipped with a Mode C transponder and pilots are required to maintain two-way radio communications. Answers (A) and (C) are wrong because no navigation equipment is specified for operating in Class C airspace.

3628. (Refer to figure 26 on page 6-9.) At which airports is fixed-wing Special VFR not authorized?

A — Fort Worth Meacham and Fort Worth Spinks.
B — Dallas/Fort Worth International and Dallas Love Field.
C — Addison and Redbird.

3628. Answer B. JSPPM 2-40 (Chart Legend)
The "NO SVFR" over the airport identification name indicates that fixed-wing special VFR is not authorized. The airports listed in answers (A) and (C) permit special VFR.

3779. The vertical limit of Class C airspace above the primary airport is normally

A — 1,200 feet AGL.
B — 3,000 feet AGL.
C — 4,000 feet AGL.

3779. Answer C. JSPPM 2-35 (AIM)
The vertical limit of Class C airspace is 4,000 feet above the primary airport. This is the same for both the inner and outer circles. Answer (A) is wrong because this is the floor of the outer circle (5 n.m to 10 n.m. radius). Answer (B) is wrong because the vertical limit is 4,000 feet AGL, not 3,000 feet.

3780. The normal radius of the outer area of Class C airspace is

A — 5 nautical miles.
B — 15 nautical miles.
C — 20 nautical miles.

3782. Under what condition may an aircraft operate from a satellite airport within Class C airspace?

A — The pilot must file a flight plan prior to departure.
B — The pilot must monitor ATC until clear of the Class C airspace.
C — The pilot must contact ATC as soon as practicable after takeoff.

3783. Under what condition, if any, may pilots fly through a restricted area?

A — When flying on airways with an ATC clearance.
B — With the controlling agency's authorization.
C — Regulations do not allow this.

3785. What action should a pilot take when operating under VFR in a Military Operations Area (MOA)?

A — Obtain a clearance from the controlling agency prior to entering the MOA.
B — Operate only on the airways that transverse the MOA.
C — Exercise extreme caution when military activity is being conducted.

3786. Responsibility for collision avoidance in an alert area rests with

A — the controlling agency.
B — all pilots.
C — Air Traffic Control.

3787. The lateral dimensions of Class D airspace are based on

A — the number of airports that lie within the Class D airspace.
B — five statute miles from the geographical center of the primary airport.
C — the instrument procedures for which the controlled airspace is established.

3780. Answer C. JSPPM 2-35 (AIM)
The outer area of Class C airspace normally extends 20 nautical miles from the primary airport. Answer (A) is the dimension of the inner circle, while answer (B) is not used to define any portion of Class C airspace. The outer circle has a radius of 10 nautical miles.

3782. Answer C. JSPPM 2-35 (FAR 91.130)
A pilot must establish two-way communications with ATC as soon as practical after takeoff. Answer (A) is not a requirement for operating in Class C airspace. Answer (B) is not entirely correct, as it does not state that two-way communications must be established.

3783. Answer B. JSPPM 2-41 (FAR 91.133)
The controlling agency may grant permission to fly through a restricted area. Answer (A) is wrong because airways do not usually transit a restricted area. Answer (C) is wrong because the FARs do allow pilots to fly through restricted areas if they have authorization from the controlling agency.

3785. Answer C. JSPPM 2-41 (AIM)
Due to the possibility of military training activities, pilots operating in a MOA should use extra caution and be alert for other aircraft. Answer (A) is wrong because a clearance is not required. Answer (B) is wrong because VFR pilots are not restricted to airways in a MOA.

3786. Answer B. JSPPM 2-42 (AIM)
All pilots flying in an alert area, whether participating in activities or transitioning the area, are equally responsible for collision avoidance. Answers (A) and (C) are wrong, because even when operating under Air Traffic Control, pilots are not relieved of their responsibility for collision avoidance.

3787. Answer C. JSPPM 2-36 (AIM)
The actual lateral dimensions of Class D airspace varies with each location, but, in general, Class D airspace is based on the instrument procedures for the airports in that area. Answer (A) is wrong because, to the maximum extent practical and consistent with safety, satellite airports have been excluded from Class D airspace. Answer (B) is the dimension of the old "airport traffic area" designation, which is no longer valid.

The Flight Environment

3788. A non-tower satellite airport, within the same Class D airspace as that designated for the primary airport, requires radio communications be established and maintained with the

A — satellite airport's UNICOM.
B — associated Flight Service Station.
C — primary airport's control tower.

3788. Answer C. JSPPM 2-37 (FAR 91.129)
When approaching Class D airspace, you must contact the primary airport's control tower before entering the airspace. When departing a nontowered satellite airport, contact the controlling tower as soon as practical after takeoff. Answers (A) and (B) are wrong because the regulation specifically states you must contact the ATC facility providing air traffic services. Unicom and the Flight Service Station, in this context, do not fit the definition of an ATC facility providing these services.

3799. Which initial action should a pilot take prior to entering Class C airspace?

A — Contact approach control on the appropriate frequency.
B — Contact the tower and request permission to enter.
C — Contact the FSS for traffic advisories.

3799. Answer A. JSPPM 2-35 (AIM)
Prior to entering Class C airspace, you need to establish contact with approach control. Answer (B) is wrong because the tower sequences traffic for landing, but is not the facility to contact before entering Class C airspace. Answer (C) is not correct because flight service provides traffic advisories in an airport advisory area.

3813. What ATC facility should the pilot contact to receive a special VFR departure clearance in Class D airspace?

A — Automated Flight Service Station.
B — Air Traffic Control Tower.
C — Air Route Traffic Control Center.

3813. Answer B. JSPPM 2-39 (FAR 91.157)
The control tower is the ATC facility which issues a special VFR clearance.

SECTION D
RADIO COMMUNICATIONS

This section covers very high frequency (VHF) radio characteristics, common aviation terms, and phraseology. Coordinated Universal Time (UTC), radio procedures, and ground radio facilities are also discussed. Test questions include:

3571, 3572, 3573, 3574, 3575, 3576, 3613, 3614, 3615, 3789, 3837.

3571. (Refer to figure 28 on page 2-24.) An aircraft departs an airport in the eastern daylight time zone at 0945 EDT for a 2-hour flight to an airport located in the central daylight time zone. The landing should be at what coordinated universal time?

A — 1345Z.
B — 1445Z.
C — 1545Z.

3571. Answer C. JSPPM 2-51 (AIM)
To convert the local departure time to UTC, add 4 hours (0945 + 4:00 = 1345). Two hours later is 1545Z.

3572. (Refer to figure 28.) An aircraft departs an airport in the central standard time zone at 0930 CST for a 2-hour flight to an airport located in the mountain standard time zone. The landing should be at what time?

A— 0930 MST.
B— 1030 MST.
C— 1130 MST.

3572. Answer B. JSPPM 2-51 (AIM)
Add 2 hours to the 0930 departure time to find the arrival time of 1130 CST. Since Mountain time is one hour earlier than Central, subtract 1 hour, for a landing time of 1030 MST.

3573. (Refer to figure 28.) An aircraft departs an airport in the central standard time zone at 0845 CST for a 2-hour flight to an airport located in the mountain standard time zone. The landing should be at what coordinated universal time?

A— 1345Z.
B— 1445Z.
C— 1645Z.

3573. Answer C. JSPPM 2-51 (AIM)
Departure time (0845) plus 2 hours is 1045 CST. Convert CST to UTC by adding 6 hours, for a landing time of 1645Z.

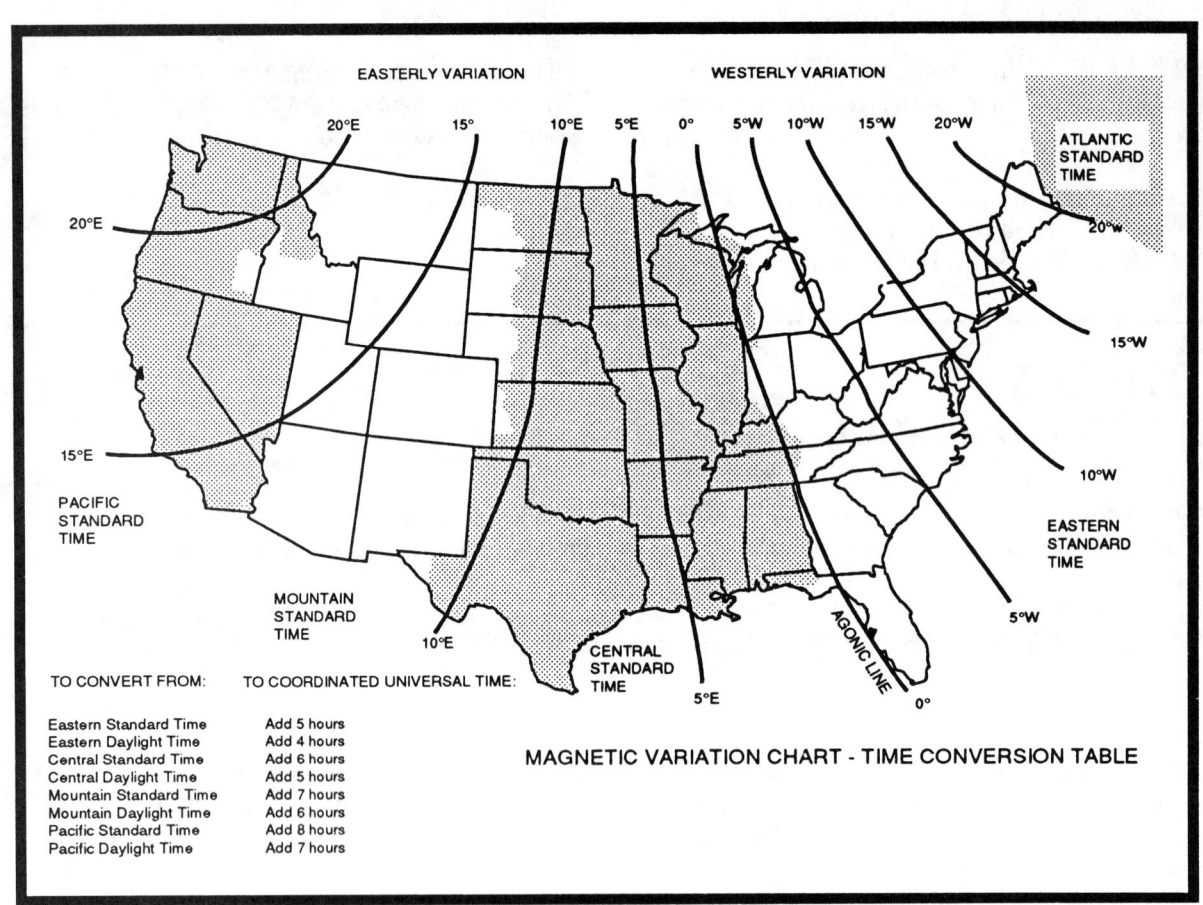

FIGURE 28.—Time Conversion Table.

3574. (Refer to figure 28.) An aircraft departs an airport in the mountain standard time zone at 1615 MST for a 2-hour 15-minute flight to an airport located in the Pacific standard time zone. The estimated time of arrival at the destination airport should be

A — 1630 PST.
B — 1730 PST.
C — 1830 PST.

3574. Answer B. JSPPM 2-51 (AIM)
Add 2:15 to 1615 MST to find the arrival time of 1830 MST. Since Pacific time is one hour earlier than MST, the arrival time is 1730 PST.

3575. (Refer to figure 28.) An aircraft departs an airport in the Pacific standard time zone at 1030 PST for a 4-hour flight to an airport located in the central standard time zone. The landing should be at what coordinated universal time?

A — 2030Z.
B — 2130Z.
C — 2230Z.

3575. Answer C. JSPPM 2-51 (AIM)
Add 4 hours to 1030 PST to find the arrival time of 1430 PST. To convert PST to UTC, add 8 hours. The landing time is 2230Z.

3576. (Refer to figure 28.) An aircraft departs an airport in the mountain standard time zone at 1515 MST for a 2-hour 30-minute flight to an airport located in the Pacific standard time zone. What is the estimated time of arrival at the destination airport?

A — 1645 PST.
B — 1745 PST.
C — 1845 PST.

3576. Answer A. JSPPM 2-51 (AIM)
Add 2:30 to 1515 MST to find the arrival time of 1745 MST. Convert MST to PST by subtracting 1 hour. The answer is 1645 PST.

3613. When flying HAWK N666CB, the proper phraseology for initial contact with McAlester AFSS is

A — "MC ALESTER RADIO, HAWK SIX SIX SIX CHARLIE BRAVO, RECEIVING ARDMORE VORTAC, OVER."
B — "MC ALESTER STATION, HAWK SIX SIX SIX CEE BEE, RECEIVING ARDMORE VORTAC, OVER."
C — "MC ALESTER FLIGHT SERVICE STATION, HAWK NOVEMBER SIX CHARLIE BRAVO, RECEIVING ARDMORE VORTAC, OVER."

3613. Answer A. JSPPM 2-57 (AIM)
The callsign for a flight service station is its name, followed by the word "radio." The aircraft's full callsign should be given, using the phonetic alphabet. Answer (B) is wrong because the phonetic alphabet is not used (i.e., "CHARLIE BRAVO" versus "CEE BEE"). Answer (C) is wrong because the correct callsign is McAlester Radio, not McAlester Flight Service Station.

3614. The correct method of stating 4,500 feet MSL to ATC is

A — "FOUR THOUSAND FIVE HUNDRED."
B — "FOUR POINT FIVE."
C — "FORTY-FIVE HUNDRED FEET MSL."

3614. Answer A. JSPPM 2-50 (AIM)
Altitudes should be stated as individual numbers with the word hundreds or thousands added as appropriate. In this case, 4,500 feet should be read as "FOUR THOUSAND FIVE HUNDRED."

3615. The correct method of stating 10,500 feet MSL to ATC is

A — "TEN THOUSAND, FIVE HUNDRED FEET."
B — "TEN POINT FIVE."
C — "ONE ZERO THOUSAND, FIVE HUNDRED."

3615. Answer C. JSPPM 2-50 (AIM)
See explanation for Question 3614. In addition, for altitudes at and above 10,000 feet MSL, each digit of the thousands is pronounced, so that 10,500 becomes "ONE ZERO THOUSAND FIVE HUNDRED."

3789. Prior to entering an Airport Advisory Area, a pilot should

A — monitor ATIS for weather and traffic advisories.
B — contact approach control for vectors to the traffic pattern.
C — contact the local FSS for airport and traffic advisories.

3789. Answer C. JSPPM 2-55 (AIM)
A local nonautomated FSS provides airport and traffic advisories for an Airport Advisory Area. Answer (A) is wrong because an ATIS may not be available, and does not give traffic advisories. Answer (B) is wrong because, whether or not you receive assistance from approach control, you should contact the local FSS for airport and traffic advisories.

3837. An ATC clearance provides

A — priority over all other traffic.
B — adequate separation from all traffic.
C — authorization to proceed under specified traffic conditions in controlled airspace.

3837. Answer C. JSPPM 2-52 (AIM)
A clearance is authorization from ATC to operate under specific conditions in controlled airspace. It does not give a pilot priority over all other traffic (answer A), as other aircraft may also have an ATC clearance. While the purpose of a clearance is to provide separation from known traffic, it does not guarantee separation from unknown or nonparticipating aircraft (answer B).

SECTION E
RADAR AND ATC SERVICES

Section E contains essential information on radar equipment, facilities, and services. Included is a discussion of transponders, radar services available for pilots operating under visual flight rules (VFR), lost communications procedures, and emergency procedures. As in previous sections, new terms are defined. The following FAA Written Test questions apply to this section:

   3111, 3112, 3113, 3114, 3115, 3116, 3191, 3759, 3791, 3792, 3793, 3794, 3795, 3796, 3797, 3798, 3800, 3801, 3802, 3803, 3804, 3811, 3812, 3819, 3820, 3821, 3822.

3111. A steady green light signal directed from the control tower to an aircraft in flight is a signal that the pilot

A — is cleared to land.
B — should give way to other aircraft and continue circling.
C — should return for landing.

3111. Answer A. JSPPM 2-72 (FAR 91.125)
A steady green light while in flight means you are cleared to land. A steady red light would be used for answer (B). A flashing green light would be used for answer (C).

3112. Which light signal from the control tower clears a pilot to taxi?

A — Flashing green.
B — Steady green.
C — Flashing white.

3113. If the control tower uses a light signal to direct a pilot to give way to other aircraft and continue circling, the light will be

A — flashing red.
B — steady red.
C — alternating red and green.

3114. A flashing white light signal from the control tower to a taxiing aircraft is an indication to

A — taxi at a faster speed.
B — taxi only on taxiways and not cross runways.
C — return to the starting point on the airport.

3115. An alternating red and green light signal directed from the control tower to an aircraft in flight is a signal to

A — hold position.
B — exercise extreme caution.
C — not land; the airport is unsafe.

3116. While on final approach for landing, an alternating green and red light followed by a flashing red light is received from the control tower. Under these circumstances, the pilot should

A — discontinue the approach, fly the same traffic pattern and approach again, and land.
B — exercise extreme caution and abandon the approach, realizing the airport is unsafe to landing.
C — abandon the approach, circle the airport to the right, and expect a flashing white light when the airport is safe for landing.

3191. No person may use an ATC transponder unless it has been tested and inspected within at least the preceding

A — 6 calendar months.
B — 12 calendar months.
C — 24 calendar months.

3112. Answer A. JSPPM 2-72 (FAR 91.125)
While on the ground, a flashing green light means cleared to taxi. A steady green light (answer B) means cleared for takeoff. A flashing white light (answer C) means return to the aircraft's starting point on the airport.

3113. Answer B. JSPPM 2-72 (FAR 91.125)
While in flight, a steady red light means give way and continue circling. A flashing red light (answer A) means that the airport is unsafe; do not land. An alternating red and green light (answer C) means to exercise extreme caution.

3114. Answer C. JSPPM 2-72 (FAR 91.125)
A flashing white light while operating on the ground means return to the starting point on the airport.

3115. Answer B. JSPPM 2-72 (FAR 91.125)
An alternating red and green signal means the same whether you are in flight or on the ground — exercise extreme caution.

3116. Answer B. JSPPM 2-72 (FAR 91.125)
An alternating red and green signal means exercise extreme caution. This is followed by a flashing red signal, which, in flight, means that the airport is unsafe.

3191. Answer C. JSPPM 2-60 (FAR 91.413)
The transponder must have been tested and inspected within the preceding 24 calendar months.

3759. To use VHF/DF facilities for assistance in locating an aircraft's position, the aircraft must have a

A — VHF transmitter and receiver.
B — 4096-code transponder.
C — VOR receiver and DME.

3759. Answer A. JSPPM 2-74 (AIM)
VHF/DF facilities use a directional antenna and a VHF radio receiver. The equipment displays the direction of the aircraft each time it transmits on its VHF radio. Answer (B) is wrong because a transponder code will show up on a radar screen, but not on a VHF/DF facility. Answer (C) is wrong because a VOR and DME will indicate an aircraft's position relative to a ground station, but is not part of the direction finder facilities on the ground.

3791. Automatic Terminal Information Service (ATIS) is the continuous broadcast of recorded information concerning

A — pilots of radar-identified aircraft whose aircraft is in dangerous proximity to terrain or to an obstruction.
B — nonessential information to reduce frequency congestion.
C — noncontrol information in selected high-activity terminal areas.

3791. Answer C. JSPPM 2-68 (AIM)
ATIS is broadcast at certain busy airports, and provides noncontrol weather and runway information.

3792. An ATC radar facility issues the following advisory to a pilot flying on a heading of 090°: "TRAFFIC 3 O'CLOCK, 2 MILES, WESTBOUND..."

Where should the pilot look for this traffic?

A — East.
B — South.
C — West.

3792. Answer B. JSPPM 2-65 (AIM)
Since the pilot is heading east, the 3 o'clock position is to the right, which is south.

3793. An ATC radar facility issues the following advisory to a pilot flying on a heading of 360°:

"TRAFFIC 10 O'CLOCK, 2 MILES, SOUTHBOUND..."

Where should the pilot look for this traffic?

A — Northwest.
B — Northeast.
C — Southwest.

3793. Answer A. JSPPM 2-65 (AIM)
Since the pilot's 12 o'clock position is north, the 10 o'clock position is northwest.

3794. An ATC radar facility issues the following advisory to a pilot during a local flight:

"TRAFFIC 2 O'CLOCK, 5 MILES, NORTHBOUND..."

Where should the pilot look for this traffic?

A — Between directly ahead and 90° to the left.
B — Between directly behind and 90° to the right.
C — Between directly ahead and 90° to the right.

3794. Answer C. JSPPM 2-65 (AIM)
Since the pilot's 12 o'clock is directly ahead, and 3 o'clock is 90° to the right, 2 o'clock is approximately 60° right.

The Flight Environment

3795. An ATC radar facility issues the following advisory to a pilot flying north in a calm wind:

"TRAFFIC 9 O'CLOCK, 2 MILES, SOUTH-BOUND..."

Where should the pilot look for this traffic?

A — South.
B — North.
C — West.

3795. Answer C. JSPPM 2-65 (AIM)
The pilot's 12 o'clock is north, so 9 o'clock is left, or west.

3796. Basic radar service in the terminal radar program is best described as

A — traffic advisories and limited vectoring to VFR aircraft.
B — mandatory radar service provided by the Automated Radar Terminal System (ARTS) program.
C — wind-shear warning at participating airports.

3796. Answer A. JSPPM 2-67 (AIM)
Basic radar service for VFR aircraft provides traffic advisories and limited vectoring on a workload-permitting basis. Basic service is not mandatory for VFR aircraft (answer B). Wind shear warning is not part of the basic radar service (answer C).

3797. From whom should a departing VFR aircraft request Stage II Terminal Radar Advisory Service during ground operations?

A — Clearance delivery.
B — Tower, just before takeoff.
C — Ground control, on initial contact.

3797. Answer C. JSPPM 2-67 (AIM)
You should notify ground control on initial contact that you are requesting radar traffic information.
Answer (A) is wrong because clearance delivery normally only provides IFR clearances. Answer (B) is wrong because ATC needs to forward the request to departure control. Requesting the service just before takeoff could delay either the departure or availability of the service. Note: The terminology for radar service is changing to Basic, TRSA, Class C, and Class B.

3798. Stage III Service in the terminal radar program provides

A — IFR separation (1,000 feet vertical and 3 miles lateral) between all aircraft.
B — warning to pilots when their aircraft are in unsafe proximity to terrain, obstructions, or other aircraft.
C — sequencing and separation for participating VFR aircraft.

3798. Answer C. JSPPM 2-67 (AIM)
Stage III service provides sequencing and separation for participating VFR aircraft. It does not always provide IFR minimum separation (answer A), because visual separation is used when conditions permit. Also, separation is not provided between all aircraft, only participating VFR aircraft and all IFR aircraft. Answer (B) is incorrect because separation is provided from other aircraft, not necessarily from obstacles and terrain. Note: The terminology for radar service is changing to Basic, TRSA, Class C, and Class B.

3800. When making routine transponder code changes, pilots should avoid inadvertent selection of which codes?

A — 0700, 1700, 7000.
B — 1200, 1500, 7000.
C — 7500, 7600, 7700.

3800. Answer C. JSPPM 2-62 (AIM)
You should avoid inadvertent selection of transponder codes which may set off false alarms at radar facilities. These codes are: 7500 for hijacking, 7600 for radio communications failure, and 7700 for emergencies.

3801. When operating under VFR below 18,000 feet MSL, unless otherwise authorized, what transponder code should be selected?

A — 1200.
B — 7600.
C — 7700.

3801. Answer A. JSPPM 2-62 (AIM)
The transponder code for VFR aircraft is 1200. Aircraft operating above 18,000 feet MSL are in Class A airspace and must have an IFR clearance. Answer (B) is wrong because 7600 is the code for radio failure. Answer (C) is wrong because 7700 is the code for emergencies.

3802. Unless otherwise authorized, if flying a transponder equipped aircraft, a recreational pilot should squawk which VFR code?

A — 1200.
B — 7600.
C — 7700.

3802. Answer A. JSPPM 2-62 (AIM)
See explanation for Question 3801.

3803. If Air Traffic Control advises that radar service is terminated when the pilot is departing Class C airspace, the transponder should be set to code

A — 0000.
B — 1200.
C — 4096.

3803. Answer B. JSPPM 2-71 (AIM)
Since you would then be operating under VFR, the transponder should be set to 1200. Answer (A) is not a designated VFR transponder code. Answer (C) is the number of discrete codes which are available on a four digit transponder with each digit starting at 0 and ending at 7.

3804. If the aircraft's radio fails, what is the recommended procedure when landing at a controlled airport?

A — Observe the traffic flow, enter the pattern, and look for a light signal from the tower.
B — Enter a crosswind leg and rock the wings.
C — Flash the landing lights and cycle the landing gear while circling the airport.

3804. Answer A. JSPPM 2-72 (AIM)
To avoid conflicts and cause the least disruption in the traffic flow, determine the landing direction, and enter the pattern. Watch the tower for a light signal and acknowledge by rocking the wings. At night, acknowledge by flashing the landing or navigation lights. Answer (B) is wrong because this does not state that you have observed the traffic flow. In addition, a crosswind entry is not normal, and rocking the wings is done to acknowledge tower light signals. Answer (C) is wrong because flashing the lights is an acknowledgement of the tower light signals. Also, cycling the gear is not a signal, and you should stay outside or above the pattern instead of circling the airport when determining traffic flow.

3811. After landing at a tower-controlled airport, when should the pilot contact ground control?

A — When advised by the tower to do so.
B — Prior to turning off the runway.
C — After reaching a taxiway that leads directly to the parking area.

3811. Answer A. JSPPM 2-72 (AIM)
The tower will normally instruct you to exit the runway and contact ground control. Answer (B) is wrong because you should exit the runway first. Answer (C) is wrong because the taxiway used to exit the runway may not lead directly to a parking area, and you must still receive a clearance from ground control to taxi.

The Flight Environment

3812. If instructed by ground control to taxi to Runway 9, the pilot may proceed

A — via taxiways and across runways to, but not onto, Runway 9.
B — to the next intersecting runway where further clearance is required.
C — via taxiways and across runways to Runway 9, where an immediate takeoff may be made.

3819. When activated, an emergency locator transmitter (ELT) transmits on

A — 118.0 and 118.8 MHz.
B — 121.5 and 243.0 MHz.
C — 123.0 and 119.0 MHz.

3820. When must the battery in an emergency locator transmitter (ELT) be replaced (or recharged if the battery is rechargeable)?

A — After one-half the battery's useful life.
B — During each annual and 100-hour inspection.
C — Every 24 calendar months.

3821. When may an emergency locator transmitter (ELT) be tested?

A — Anytime.
B — At 15 and 45 minutes past the hour.
C — During the first 5 minutes after the hour.

3822. Which procedure is recommended to ensure that the emergency locator transmitter (ELT) has not been activated?

A — Turn off the aircraft ELT after landing.
B — Ask the airport tower if they are receiving an ELT signal.
C — Monitor 121.5 before engine shutdown.

3812. Answer A. JSPPM 2-70 (AIM)
A clearance to taxi to a runway allows the pilot to proceed to that runway and cross any intersecting runways. Answer (B) is wrong because you do not have to hold at an intersecting runway and await clearance. Answer (C) is wrong because you have neither been cleared to taxi onto the runway or cleared for takeoff.

3819. Answer B. JSPPM 2-74 (AIM)
The frequencies used for ELTs are the emergency frequencies of 121.5 MHz (VHF) and 243.0 MHz (UHF).

3820. Answer A. JSPPM 2-75 (FAR 91.207)
The ELT battery must be replaced or recharged after one-half the battery's useful life.

3821. Answer C. JSPPM 2-75 (AIM)
To prevent false alerts, ELT testing should be conducted only during the first 5 minutes after any hour.

3822. Answer C. JSPPM 2-75 (AIM)
By monitoring 121.5, you will be able to hear the ELT signal if it has been activated.

CHAPTER 3

AIRCRAFT SYSTEMS AND PERFORMANCE

SECTION A
PITOT-STATIC INSTRUMENTS

This section describes the three pitot-static instruments — the airspeed indicator, altimeter, and vertical speed indicator. Included is coverage of limitations, errors, and procedures for using these key pressure differential instruments. Test questions that are covered include the following:

3247, 3248, 3249, 3250, 3251, 3252, 3253, 3254, 3255, 3256, 3257, 3258, 3259, 3260, 3261, 3262, 3263, 3264, 3265, 3266, 3267, 3268, 3269, 3270, 3271, 3272, 3273, 3274, 3386, 3388, 3390, 3391, 3392, 3393, 3394.

3247. If the pitot tube and outside static vents become clogged, which instruments would be affected?

A — The altimeter, airspeed indicator, and turn-and-slip indicator.
B — The altimeter, airspeed indicator, and vertical speed indicator.
C — The altimeter, attitude indicator, and turn-and-slip indicator.

3247. Answer B. JSPPM 3-11 (PHB)
The altimeter, the airspeed indicator, and the vertical speed indicator all use static air and would therefore be affected. Answers (A) and (C) are wrong because the turn-and-slip indicator and attitude indicator do not rely on static air.

3248. Which instrument will become inoperative if the pitot tube becomes clogged?

A — Altimeter.
B — Vertical speed.
C — Airspeed.

3248. Answer C. JSPPM 3-11 (PHB)
The airspeed indicator operates by sensing ram air (impact pressure) in the pitot tube. Answers (A) and (B) are wrong because the altimeter and VSI use pressure readings from the static air ports.

3249. Which instrument(s) will become inoperative if the static vents become clogged?

A — Airspeed only.
B — Altimeter only.
C — Airspeed, altimeter, and vertical speed.

3249. Answer C. JSPPM 3-11 (PHB)
See explanation for Question 3247.

3250. (Refer to figure 3 on page 3-2.) Altimeter 1 indicates

A — 500 feet.
B — 1,500 feet.
C — 10,500 feet.

3250. Answer C. JSPPM 3-6 (PHB)
The small 10,000' pointer is just beyond the 1, indicating that the altitude is above 10,000 feet. The wide 1,000' pointer is between 0 and 1, which indicates less than 1,000 feet. Finally, the 100' pointer is on 5. The altimeter reading is 10,500 feet.

FIGURE 3.—Altimeter

3251. (Refer to figure 3.) Altimeter 2 indicates

A — 1,500 feet.
B — 4,500 feet.
C — 14,500 feet.

3252. (Refer to figure 3.) Altimeter 3 indicates

A — 9,500 feet.
B — 10,950 feet.
C — 15,940 feet.

3253. (Refer to figure 3.) Which altimeter indicate(s) more than 10,000 feet?

A — 1, 2, and 3.
B — 1 and 2 only.
C — 1 only.

3254. Altimeter setting is the value to which the barometric pressure scale of the altimeter is set so the altimeter indicates

A — calibrated altitude at field elevation.
B — absolute altitude at field elevation.
C — true altitude at field elevation.

3255. How do variations in temperature affect the altimeter?

A — Pressure levels are raised on warm days and the indicated altitude is lower than true altitude.
B — Higher temperatures expand the pressure levels and the indicated altitude is higher than true altitude.
C — Lower temperatures lower the pressure levels and the indicated altitude is lower than true altitude.

3251. Answer C. JSPPM 3-6 (PHB)
The 10,000' pointer is above 1, the 1,000' pointer is above 4, and the 100' pointer is on 5. This indicates an altitude of 14,500 feet.

3252. Answer A. JSPPM 3-6 (PHB)
The 10,000' pointer is slightly below 1, the 1,000' pointer is above 9, and the 100' pointer is on 5. This indicates the altitude is 9,500 feet.

3253. Answer B. JSPPM 3-6 (PHB)
See explanations for Questions 3250, 3251, and 3252. Altimeter 1 indicates 10,500 feet, altimeter 2 indicates 14,500 feet, and the indication on altimeter 3 is 9,500 feet.

3254. Answer C. JSPPM 3-7 (AW)
When the current altimeter setting is set on the ground, the altimeter reads true altitude of the field, which is the actual height above mean sea level. Answer (A) is wrong because there is no such thing as calibrated altitude. Answer (B) is incorrect because absolute altitude is the actual height above the earth's surface, which would be zero at field elevation.

3255. Answer A. JSPPM 3-8 (PHB)
Because atmospheric pressure levels are raised on warm days, the aircraft will be at a higher altitude than indicated. In other words, the indicated altitude is lower than true altitude.

Aircraft Systems and Performance

3256. What is true altitude?

A — The vertical distance of the aircraft above sea level.
B — The vertical distance of the aircraft above the surface.
C — The height above the standard datum plane.

3257. What is absolute altitude?

A — The altitude read directly from the altimeter.
B — The vertical distance of the aircraft above the surface.
C — The height above the standard datum plane.

3258. What is density altitude?

A — The height above the standard datum plane.
B — The pressure altitude corrected for nonstanard temperature.
C — The altitude read directly from the altimeter.

3259. What is pressure altitude?

A — The indicated altitude corrected for position and installation error.
B — The altitude indicated when the barometric pressure scale is set to 29.92.
C — The indicated altitude corrected for nonstandard temperature and pressure.

3260. Under what condition is indicated altitude the same as true altitude?

A — If the altimeter has no mechanical error.
B — When at sea level under standard conditions.
C — When at 18,000 feet MSL with the altimeter set at 29.92.

3261. If it is necessary to set the altimeter from 29.15 to 29.85, what change occurs?

A — 70-foot increase in indicated altitude.
B — 70-foot increase in density altitude.
C — 700-foot increase in indicated altitude.

3262. The pitot system provides impact pressure for which instrument?

A — Altimeter.
B — Vertical-speed indicator.
C — Airspeed indicator.

3256. Answer A. JSPPM 3-7 (PHB)
True altitude is the actual height (vertical distance) above mean sea level. Answer (B) describes absolute altitude. Answer (C) describes pressure altitude.

3257. Answer B. JSPPM 3-8 (PHB)
Absolute altitude is the height (vertical distance) above the surface. Answer (A) describes indicated altitude. Answer (C) describes pressure altitude.

3258. Answer B. JSPPM 3-7 (PHB)
Density altitude is found by applying a correction for nonstandard temperature to the pressure altitude. Answer (A) is pressure altitude and (C) is indicated altitude.

3259. Answer B. JSPPM 3-7 (PHB)
Pressure altitude is the height above the standard datum plane when 29.92 is set in the scale. Answer(A) does not describe any type of altitude. Answer (C) describes density altitude.

3260. Answer B. JSPPM 3-8 (AW)
In this situation, both indicated and true altitude would be zero. Answers (A) and (C) are wrong because indicated altitude must be corrected for nonstandard temperature and pressure.

3261. Answer C. JSPPM 3-9 (PHB)
A one inch change of Hg in the altimeter equals 1,000 feet of altitude change in the same direction. In this case, you increased the altimeter .7 of an inch (29.85 - 29.15 = .7), therefore, the indicated altitude increased 700 feet.

3262. Answer C. JSPPM 3-4 (PHB)
The airspeed indicator senses impact pressure to provide an airspeed reading. Answers (A) and (B) are wrong because these instruments utilize only static air.

Aircraft Systems and Performance

3263. As altitude increases, the indicated airspeed at which a given airplane stalls in a particular configuration will

A — decrease as the true airspeed decreases.
B — decrease as the true airspeed increases.
C — remain the same regardless of altitude.

3263. Answer C. JSPPM 3-6 (PHB)
Since airspeed indicators are calibrated to read true airspeed only under standard sea level conditions, the indicated airspeed does not reflect lower air density at higher altitudes. As a result, the indicated airspeed of a stall remains the same. Answers (A) and (B) are not correct because indicated airspeed does not change with an increase in altitude. Answer (A) is also incorrect because true airspeed increases with altitude.

3264. What does the red line on an airspeed indicator represent?

A — Maneuvering speed.
B — Turbulence or rough-air speed.
C — Never-exceed speed.

3264. Answer C. JSPPM 3-4 (PHB)
The red line is the never-exceed speed. Answers (A) and (B) are incorrect because maneuvering, turbulent, or rough air speeds are not displayed on an airspeed indicator.

3265. (Refer to figure 4.) What is the full flap operating range for the airplane?

A — 60 to 100 MPH.
B — 60 to 208 MPH.
C — 65 to 165 MPH.

3265. Answer A. JSPPM 3-4 (PHB)
The white arc indicates the flap operating range, which, in this case, is 60 to 100. (MPH is implied from the answers.)

3266. (Refer to figure 4.) What is the caution range of the airplane?

A — 0 to 60 MPH.
B — 100 to 165 MPH.
C — 165 to 208 MPH.

3266. Answer C. JSPPM 3-4 (PHB)
The yellow arc indicates the caution range. For this aircraft, the caution range is 165 to 208. (MPH is implied from the answers.)

3267. (Refer to figure 4.) The maximum speed at which the airplane can be operated in smooth air is

A — 100 MPH.
B — 165 MPH.
C — 208 MPH.

3267. Answer C. JSPPM 3-4 (PHB)
In smooth air, an airplane can be operated in the yellow arc up to the red line, in this case, 208 MPH.

3268. (Refer to figure 4.) Which color identifies the never-exceed speed?

A — Lower limit of the yellow arc.
B — Upper limit of the white arc.
C — The red radial line.

3268. Answer C. JSPPM 3-4 (PHB)
The red line is the never-exceed speed, the yellow arc is the caution range and the white arc is the flap operating range.

3269. (Refer to figure 4.) Which color identifies the power-off stalling speed in a specified configuration?

A — Upper limit of the green arc.
B — Upper limit of the white arc.
C — Lower limit of the green arc.

3269. Answer C. JSPPM 3-5 (PHB)
The lower limit of the green arc represents the power-off stall speed in a specified configuration (usually flaps up, gear retracted). Answer (A) is the maximum structural cruising speed. Answer (B) is the maximum speed with flaps extended.

3270. (Refer to figure 4.) What is the maximum flaps-extended speed?

A — 65 MPH.
B — 100 MPH.
C — 165 MPH.

3270. Answer B. JSPPM 3-4 (PHB)
This is represented by the upper limit of the white arc, which in this case is 100 MPH.

FIGURE 4.— Airspeed Indicator.

3271. (Refer to figure 4.) Which color identifies the normal flap operating range?

A — The lower limit of the white arc to the upper limit of the green arc.
B — The green arc.
C — The white arc.

3271. Answer C. JSPPM 3-4 (PHB)
The white arc indicates the normal flap operating range.

3272. (Refer to figure 4.) Which color identifies the power-off stalling speed with wing flaps and landing gear in the landing configuration?

A — Upper limit of the green arc.
B — Upper limit of the white arc.
C — Lower limit of the white arc.

3272. Answer C. JSPPM 3-5 (PHB)
Stall speed with flaps and gear down is represented by the lower limit of the white arc. The upper limit of the green arc (Answer A) is the maximum structural cruising speed, while the upper limit of the white arc (Answer B) is the maximum flaps-extended speed.

3273. (Refer to figure 4.) What is the maximum structural cruising speed?

A — 100 MPH.
B — 165 MPH.
C — 208 MPH.

3273. Answer B. JSPPM 3-5 (PHB)
This speed is indicated by the upper limit of the green arc, which in this case is 165 MPH.

3274. What is an important airspeed limitation that is not color coded on airspeed indicators?

A — Never-exceed speed.
B — Maximum structural cruising speed.
C — Maneuvering speed.

3274. Answer C. JSPPM 3-5 (PHB)
The maneuvering speed of an airplane is not shown on the airspeed indicator. It can be found in the airplane manual or on placards. Answer (A) is not correct because this is indicated by the red radial line. Answer (B) is incorrect because this is indicated by the upper limit of the green arc.

3386. What are the standard temperature and pressure values for sea level?

A — 15°C and 29.92" Hg.
B — 59°C and 1013.2 millibars.
C — 59°F and 29.92 millibars.

3388. Under which condition will pressure altitude be equal to true altitude?

A — When the atmospheric pressure is 29.92" Hg.
B — When standard atmospheric conditions exist.
C — When indicated altitude is equal to the pressure altitude.

3390. If a flight is made from an area of low pressure into an area of high pressure without the altimeter setting being adjusted, the altimeter will indicate

A — the actual altitude above sea level.
B — higher than the actual altitude above sea level.
C — lower than the actual altitude above sea level.

3391. If a flight is made from an area of high pressure into an area of lower pressure without the altimeter setting being adjusted, the altimeter will indicate

A — lower than the actual altitude above sea level.
B — higher than the actual altitude above sea level.
C — the actual altitude above sea level.

3392. Under what condition will true altitude be lower than indicated altitude?

A — In colder than standard air temperature.
B — In warmer than standard air temperature.
C — When density altitude is higher than indicated altitude.

3393. Which condition would cause the altimeter to indicate a lower altitude than true altitude?

A — Air temperature lower than standard.
B — Atmospheric pressure lower than standard.
C — Air temperature warmer than standard.

3394. Which factor would tend to increase the density altitude at a given airport?

A — An increase in barometric pressure.
B — An increase in ambient temperature.
C — A decrease in relative humidity.

3386. Answer A. JSPPM 3-3 (PHB)
The standard atmosphere is a temperature of 15°C (59°F) and 29.92" Hg (1013.2 millibars).

3388. Answer B. JSPPM 3-8 (AW)
Pressure altitude equals true altitude when standard atmospheric conditions exist. When nonstandard conditions exist, true altitude will not equal pressure altitude. Answers (A) and (C) are wrong because they do not take into account temperatures that deviate from standard values.

3390. Answer C. JSPPM 3-9 (AW)
The aircraft will be at a higher true (actual) altitude above sea level than is indicated. In other words, the altimeter will indicate lower than the actual altitude. Answer (A) is wrong because the only time the altimeter indicates actual (true) altitude is when standard atmospheric conditions exist, and the correct altimeter setting is used. Answer (B) is not correct because the altimeter will indicate a lower, not higher, altitude than actual.

3391. Answer B. JSPPM 3-9 (AW)
Remember, "from high to low, look out below." In other words, the aircraft will be at a lower true (actual) altitude than indicated, so the altimeter indicates higher than actual.

3392. Answer A. JSPPM 3-8 (AW)
When the air is colder than standard, the aircraft's actual (true) altitude will be lower than indicated. Answer (B) is wrong because in warmer than standard conditions, true altitude will be higher than indicated. Answer (C) is wrong because there is not a direct correlation between density altitude and indicated altitude.

3393. Answer C. JSPPM 3-8 (AW)
See explanation for Question 3392. In this question, the air temperature is warmer than standard, so indicated altitude will be lower than actual (true) altitude.

3394. Answer B. JSPPM 3-7, 53 (AW)
Since density altitude is pressure altitude corrected for temperature, it increases with increased temperature. Answer (A) is wrong because an increase in barometric pressure lowers the pressure altitude. Thus, density altitude would also decrease. Answer (C) is wrong because density altitude would increase with an increase in relative humidity.

Aircraft Systems and Performance

SECTION B
GYROSCOPIC INSTRUMENTS

Section B covers the common gyroscopic instruments — the turn coordinator, heading indicator, and attitude indicator. The discussion includes the fundamental principles of rigidity in space and precession, as well as sources of power and operating procedures. Although not a gyroscopic instrument, the magnetic compass is also described in this section. The following FAA Written Test questions are covered in this section:

3275, 3276, 3277, 3278, 3279, 3280, 3281, 3282, 3283, 3284, 3286.

3275. (Refer to figure 5.) A turn coordinator provides an indication of the

A — movement of the aircraft about the yaw and roll axes.
B — angle of bank up to but not exceeding 30°.
C — attitude of the aircraft with reference to the longitudinal axis.

3275. Answer A. JSPPM 3-15 (PHB)
The turn coordinator senses movement about the vertical axis (yaw) and the longitudinal axis (roll). Answers (B) and (C) are wrong because the miniature airplane indicates rate of turn, not angle of bank, which is the attitude of the aircraft in relation to the longitudinal axis.

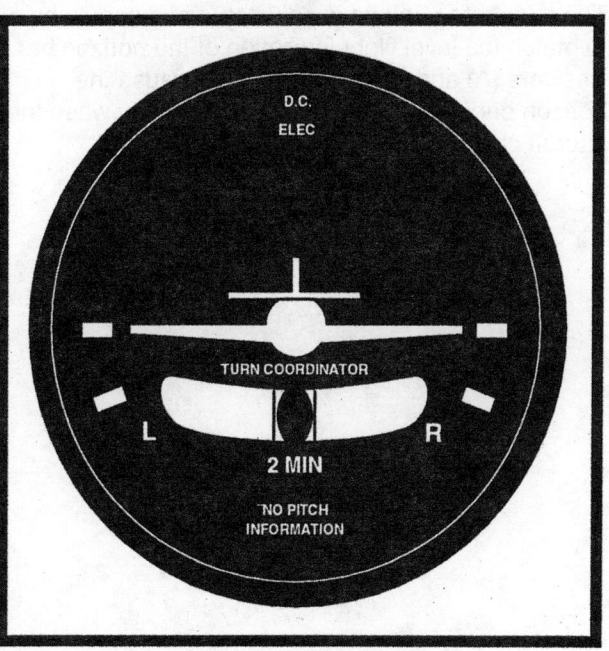

FIGURE 5.—Turn Coordinator.

3276. (Refer to figure 6 on page 3-8.) To receive accurate indications during flight from a heading indicator, the instrument must be

A — set prior to flight on a known heading.
B — calibrated on a compass rose at regular intervals.
C — periodically realigned with the magnetic compass as the gyro precesses.

3276. Answer C. JSPPM 3-18 (PHB)
To correct for precession, the pilot must realign the heading indicator with the magnetic compass at regular intervals. Answers (A) and (B) are wrong because they do not correct for precession in flight.

FIGURE 6.—Heading Indicator.

3277. (Refer to figure 7.) The proper adjustment to make on the attitude indicator during level flight is to align the

A — horizon bar to the level-flight indication.
B — horizon bar to the miniature airplane.
C — miniature airplane to the horizon bar.

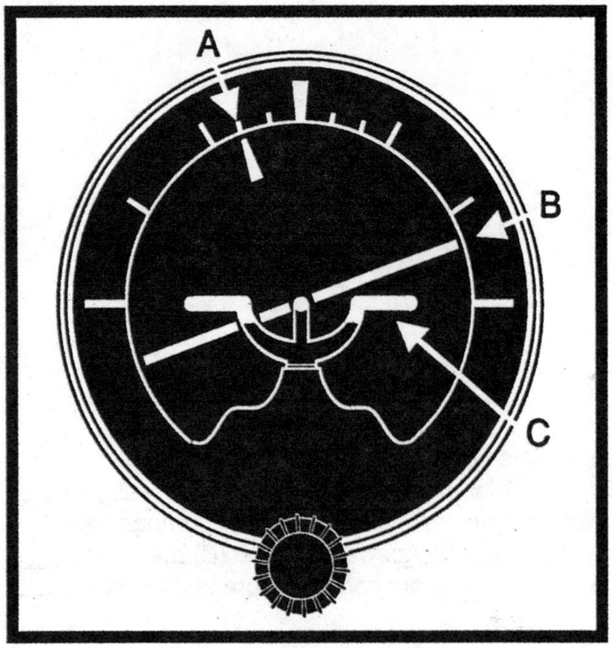

3277. Answer C. JSPPM 3-17 (PHB)
The miniature airplane is adjustable and should be set to match the level flight indication of the horizon bar. Answers (A) and (B) are incorrect because the horizon bar is not adjustable, it moves only when the aircraft changes pitch.

FIGURE 7.—Attitude Indicator.

Aircraft Systems and Performance

3278. (Refer to figure 7.) How should a pilot determine the direction of bank from an attitude indicator such as the one illustrated?

A — By the direction of deflection of the banking scale (A).
B — By the direction of deflection of the horizon bar (B).
C — By the relationship of the miniature airplane (C) to the deflected horizon bar (B).

3278. Answer C. JSPPM 3-17 (PHB)
As the airplane banks, the relationship between the miniature airplane and the horizon bar depict the direction of turn. Answer (A) is wrong because the bank scale does not deflect in the direction of bank. The combination of bank scale and pointer is used to determine bank angle only. Answer (B) is wrong because the horizon bar deflects opposite the miniature airplane; i.e., for a right turn, the horizon bar deflects to the left. (Note: Figure 7 is an example of an older style attitude indicator, not normally found in modern training airplanes.)

3279. Deviation in a magnetic compass is caused by the

A — presence of flaws in the permanent magnets of the compass.
B — difference in the location between true north and magnetic north.
C — magnetic fields within the aircraft distorting the lines of magnetic force.

3279. Answer C. JSPPM 3-19 (PHB)
Metal and electronic components in the aircraft create magnetic fields which distort the lines of magnetic force. This causes deviation errors in the compass readings. Answer (A) is wrong because deviation is not caused by flaws in the magnets. Answer (B) is incorrect because the difference between true and magnetic north is called variation, not deviation.

3280. In the Northern Hemisphere, a magnetic compass will normally indicate initially a turn toward the west if

A — a left turn is entered from a north heading.
B — a right turn is entered from a north heading.
C — an aircraft is accelerated while on a north heading.

3280. Answer B. JSPPM 3-21 (PHB)
When turning from a northerly heading, the compass initially indicates a turn in the opposite direction. When starting a right turn, toward the east, the compass begins to show a turn to the west. Answer (A) is wrong because a left turn, toward the west, would show an initial turn toward the east on the compass. Answer (C) is wrong because acceleration error does not occur when on a heading of north or south.

3281. In the Northern Hemisphere, a magnetic compass will normally indicate initially a turn toward the east if

A — an aircraft is decelerated while on a south heading.
B — an aircraft is accelerated while on a north heading.
C — a left turn is entered from a north heading.

3281. Answer C. JSPPM 3-21 (PHB)
See explanation for Question 3280. In this question, during a left turn toward the west, the magnetic compass would initially indicate a turn to the east.

3282. In the Northern Hemisphere, a magnetic compass will normally indicate a turn toward the north if

A — a right turn is entered from an east heading.
B — a left turn is entered from a west heading.
C — an aircraft is accelerated while on an east or west heading.

3282. Answer C. JSPPM 3-21 (PHB)
Acceleration error is most pronounced on east/west headings. Using the acronym ANDS (Accelerate — North, Decelerate — South), acceleration will show a turn to the north, and deceleration will show a turn to the south. Answers (A) and (B) are wrong because turning errors are not evident when beginning turns from an east or west heading.

3283. In the Northern Hemisphere, the magnetic compass will normally indicate a turn toward the south when

A — a left turn is entered from an east heading.
B — a right turn is entered from a west heading.
C — the aircraft is decelerated while on a west heading.

3283. Answer C. JSPPM 3-21 (PHB)
See explanation for Question 3282.

3284. In the Northern Hemisphere, if an aircraft is accelerated or decelerated, the magnetic compass will normally indicate

A — a turn momentarily.
B — correctly when on a north or south heading.
C — a turn toward the south.

3284. Answer B. JSPPM 3-21 (PHB)
Since acceleration and deceleration errors are most pronounced on east/west headings, accelerating or decelerating on a north or south heading will not show much of an error on the magnetic compass.

3286. During flight, when are the indications of a magnetic compass accurate?

A — Only in straight-and-level unaccelerated flight.
B — As long as the airspeed is constant.
C — During turns if the bank does not exceed 18°.

3286. Answer A. JSPPM 3-22 (PHB)
Magnetic dip causes turning and acceleration/deceleration errors. For this reason, magnetic compass indications are accurate only in straight-and-level unaccelerated flight. Answer (B) is wrong because if the airspeed is constant in a turn, the compass will still show turning errors. Answer (C) is not right because errors will occur during turns regardless of bank angle.

SECTION C
ENGINE AND PROPELLER

Section C is about the reciprocating engine, its principles of operation, and the four-stroke operating cycle. The coverage extends to include abnormal combustion, and engine systems, such as ignition, induction, oil, and cooling systems. Both fixed-pitch and constant-speed props are covered as well. FAA test questions include:

3221, 3222, 3223, 3225, 3226, 3227, 3228, 3229, 3230, 3231, 3232, 3233, 3234, 3235, 3236, 3237, 3238, 3239, 3240, 3244, 3245, 3651, 3652, 3653, 3654, 3655, 3656, 3657.

3221. Excessively high engine temperatures will

A — cause damage to heat-conducting hoses and warping of the cylinder cooling fins.
B — cause loss of power, excessive oil consumption, and possible permanent internal engine damage.
C — not appreciably affect an aircraft engine.

3221. Answer B. JSPPM 3-33 (PHB)
High temperature can cause detonation and a resulting loss of power, excessive oil consumption, and engine damage, including scoring of the cylinders and damage to pistons, rings, and valves. Answer (A) is not the best answer, since engine damage and power loss are more critical. Answer (C) is wrong because engine damage can be serious.

Aircraft Systems and Performance

3-11

3222. If the engine oil temperature and cylinder head temperature gauges have exceeded their normal operating range, the pilot may have been operating with

A — the mixture set too rich.
B — higher-than-normal oil pressure.
C — too much power and with the mixture set too lean.

3222. Answer C. JSPPM 3-34 (PHB)
With high power settings and the mixture set too lean, overheating can result. This can be indicated by a high engine oil temperature and cylinder head temperature. Answer (A) is wrong because when the mixture is too rich, temperatures are usually lower than normal. Answer (B) is wrong because high oil pressure does not normally cause high temperatures. However, low oil levels can cause high oil temperatures.

3223. One purpose of the dual ignition system on an aircraft engine is to provide for

A — improved engine performance.
B — uniform heat distribution.
C — balanced cylinder head pressure.

3223. Answer A. JSPPM 3-28 (FTH)
Dual ignition systems fire two spark plugs, which improves combustion of the fuel/air mixture and results in slightly more power. Answer (B) is incorrect because the ignition system does not affect heat distribution. Answer (C) is wrong because the ignition system does not affect cylinder head pressure.

3225. The operating principle of float-type carburetors is based on the

A — automatic metering of air at the venturi as the aircraft gains altitude.
B — difference in air pressure at the venturi throat and the air inlet.
C — increase in air velocity in the throat of a venturi causing an increase in air pressure.

3225. Answer B. JSPPM 3-29 (PHB)
The decreased pressure caused by air flowing rapidly through the venturi tube draws fuel from the float chamber. Answer (A) is wrong because air is not "metered" at the venturi. Answer (C) is not correct because the increased air velocity at the venturi throat causes a decrease in air pressure, not an increase.

3226. The basic purpose of adjusting the fuel/air mixture at altitude is to

A — decrease the amount of fuel in the mixture in order to compensate for increased air density.
B — decrease the fuel flow in order to compensate for decreased air density.
C — increase the amount of fuel in the mixture to compensate for the decrease in pressure and density of the air.

3226. Answer B. JSPPM 3-30 (FTH)
If fuel flow is not decreased with altitude, the mixture becomes too rich with fuel. Therefore, the fuel mixture must be leaned to maintain the proper fuel/air ratio. Answer (A) is wrong because air density is decreased with altitude, not increased. Answer (C) is incorrect because increasing the fuel mixture would further enrich the fuel/air mixture.

3227. During the run-up at a high-elevation airport, a pilot notes a slight engine roughness that is not affected by the magneto check but grows worse during the carburetor heat check. Under these circumstances, what would be the most logical initial action?

A — Check the results obtained with a leaner setting of the mixture.
B — Taxi back to the flight line for a maintenance check.
C — Reduce manifold pressure to control detonation.

3227. Answer A. JSPPM 3-30 (FTH)
In this case, engine roughness is probably caused by the mixture set too rich for the high altitude. When the carburetor heat is turned on, the warmer air entering the carburetor is less dense, and the mixture is further enriched. As a result, the engine roughness increases. The problem can usually be corrected by leaning the mixture. Answer (B) is wrong because the pilot should first try the runup with a leaner mixture. Answer (C) is not correct because detonation is the result of a mixture that is too lean.

3228. While cruising at 9,500 feet MSL, the fuel/air mixture is properly adjusted. What will occur if a descent to 4,500 feet MSL is made without readjusting the mixture?

A — The fuel/air mixture may become excessively lean.
B — There will be more fuel in the cylinders than is needed for normal combustion, and the excess fuel will absorb heat and cool the engine.
C — The excessively rich mixture will create higher cylinder head temperatures and may cause detonation.

3228. Answer A. JSPPM 3-30 (FTH)
With a decrease in altitude, air density increases. This means you will have to enrich the mixture as you descend, otherwise the fuel/air mixture can become excessively lean. Answers (B) and (C) are wrong because more air will enter the cylinders for the same amount of fuel, decreasing the fuel/air mixture, not increasing it.

3229. Which condition is most favorable to the development of carburetor icing?

A — Any temperature below freezing and a relative humidity of less than 50 percent.
B — Temperature between 32 and 50°F and low humidity.
C — Temperature between 20 and 70°F and high humidity.

3229. Answer C. JSPPM 3-30 (PHB)
Carburetor icing is most likely between 20° and 70°F in high humidity conditions. Answers (A) and (B) are wrong because carburetor icing is less likely with low humidity.

3230. The possibility of carburetor icing exists even when the ambient air temperature is as

A — high as 70°F and the relative humidity is high.
B — high as 95°F and there is visible moisture.
C — low as 0°F and the relative humidity is high.

3230. Answer A. JSPPM 3-30 (PHB)
(A) is the best answer because icing is more probable below 70°F with high humidity. Answer (B) is only partially correct, as icing can occur at higher temperatures, but visible moisture does not have to be present. Answer (C) is incorrect because the possibility of carburetor icing decreases below 32°F, down to 20°F. At 0°F, the humidity is generally low.

3231. If an aircraft is equipped with a fixed-pitch propeller and a float-type carburetor, the first indication of carburetor ice would most likely be

A — a drop in oil temperature and cylinder head temperature.
B — engine roughness.
C — loss of RPM.

3231. Answer C. JSPPM 3-31 (PHB)
The restricted airflow through the carburetor causes an enriched mixture and loss of RPM. Answer (A) is wrong because, while a drop in temperatures may result, they will not be the first indications of carburetor ice. Answer (B) is wrong because engine roughness may develop later, but will not be the first indication of carburetor ice.

3232. Applying carburetor heat will

A — result in more air going through the carburetor.
B — enrich the fuel/air mixture.
C — not affect the fuel/air mixture.

3232. Answer B. JSPPM 3-31 (PHB)
When the carburetor heat is turned on, the warmer air entering the carburetor is less dense, the mixture is enriched. Answer (A) is wrong because there is less air going through the carburetor. Answer (C) is not correct because the fuel/air mixture is enriched.

3233. What change occurs in the fuel/air mixture when carburetor heat is applied?

A — A decrease in RPM results from the lean mixture.
B — The fuel/air mixture becomes richer.
C — The fuel/air mixture becomes leaner.

3233. Answer B. JSPPM 3-31 (PHB)
See explanation for Question 3232. Answers (A) and (C) are wrong because the fuel/air mixture is not leaned.

Aircraft Systems and Performance

3234. Generally speaking, the use of carburetor heat tends to

A — decrease engine performance.
B — increase engine performance.
C — have no effect on engine performance.

3235. The presence of carburetor ice in an aircraft equipped with a fixed-pitch propeller can be verified by applying carburetor heat and noting

A — an increase in RPM and then a gradual decrease in RPM.
B — a decrease in RPM and then a constant RPM indication.
C — a decrease in RPM and then a gradual increase in RPM.

3236. With regard to carburetor ice, float-type carburetor systems in comparison to fuel injection systems are generally considered to be

A — more susceptible to icing.
B — equally susceptible to icing.
C — susceptible to icing only when visible moisture is present.

3237. If the grade of fuel used in an aircraft engine is lower than specified for the engine, it will most likely cause

A — a mixture of fuel and air that is not uniform in all cylinders.
B — lower cylinder head temperatures.
C — detonation.

3238. Detonation occurs in a reciprocating aircraft engine when

A — the spark plugs are fouled or shorted out or the wiring is defective.
B — hot spots in the combustion chamber ignite the fuel/air mixture in advance of normal ignition.
C — the unburned charge in the cylinders explodes instead of burning normally.

3239. If a pilot suspects that the engine (with a fixed-pitch propeller) is detonating during climb-out after takeoff, the initial corrective action to take would be to

A — lean the mixture.
B — lower the nose slightly to increase airspeed.
C — apply carburetor heat.

3234. Answer A. JSPPM 3-31 (PHB)
Since the warmer air entering the carburetor is less dense, the fuel/air mixture is enriched and power decreases. Answers (B) and (C) are wrong because performance decreases.

3235. Answer C. JSPPM 3-31 (PHB)
When carburetor heat is first applied, the mixture is enriched, and RPM decreases. Then, as the ice melts, airflow into the carburetor increases, leaning the mixture, and RPM increases. Answer (A) is wrong because it is the opposite of what happens. Answer (B) is wrong because if the RPM decreases, then remains constant, it means there was no ice in the carburetor.

3236. Answer A. JSPPM 3-32 (PHB)
Because fuel injection systems do not have a venturi throat, they are not as susceptible to icing as float-type carburetors. Answer (B) is wrong because the venturi throat makes float-type carburetors more susceptible to icing. Icing is possible when the humidity is high, regardless of whether visible moisture is present or not (answer C).

3237. Answer C. JSPPM 3-26 (PHB)
The higher the grade of fuel, the more pressure it can withstand without detonating. Conversely, lower fuel grades are more prone to detonation. Answer (A) is wrong because the mixture should be the same in all cylinders, regardless of fuel grade. Answer (B) is not correct because when detonation occurs, cylinder head temperatures increase.

3238. Answer C. JSPPM 3-26 (PHB)
Detonation occurs when the fuel/air mixture suddenly explodes in the cylinders instead of burning smoothly. Answer (A) describes conditions which would cause an engine to run rough, but not cause detonation. Answer (B) describes pre-ignition.

3239. Answer B. JSPPM 3-26 (PHB)
Detonation can occur when the engine overheats. One action to help cool the engine is to increase airspeed, thus increasing the cooling airflow around the engine. Answer (A) is incorrect because detonation can result from a mixture that is too lean. Answer (C) is wrong because carburetor heat tends to increase engine temperature, making the problem worse.

3240. The uncontrolled firing of the fuel/air charge in advance of normal spark ignition is known as

A — combustion.
B — pre-ignition.
C — detonation.

3240. Answer B. JSPPM 3-26 (PHB)
Pre-ignition occurs when the fuel/air mixture ignites too soon. Answer (A) is wrong because combustion is the normal burning of the mixture. Answer (C) is not right because detonation occurs when fuel explodes instead of burning smoothly.

3244. For internal cooling, reciprocating aircraft engines are especially dependent on

A — a properly functioning thermostat.
B — air flowing over the exhaust manifold.
C — the circulation of lubricating oil.

3244. Answer C. JSPPM 3-32 (PHB)
Engine oil lubricates moving parts, reduces friction, and removes some of the heat from the cylinders. Answer (A) is wrong because reciprocating aircraft engines are not normally equipped with a thermostat. Outside air is important for engine cooling (answer B), but the air is primarily directed to the hottest parts of the engine, especially the cylinders.

3245. An abnormally high engine oil temperature indication may be caused by

A — the oil level being too low.
B — operating with a too high viscosity oil.
C — operating with an excessively rich mixture.

3245. Answer A. JSPPM 3-34 (PHB)
If the oil level is too low, it can cause high engine oil temperatures. Answer (B) is incorrect because, while it is important to use the proper oil type and weight, it is not as likely to cause abnormally high temperatures as a low oil level would. Answer (C) is not correct because a rich mixture tends to cool the engine slightly instead of causing high temperatures.

3651. What action can a pilot take to aid in cooling an engine that is overheating during a climb?

A — Reduce rate of climb and increase airspeed.
B — Reduce climb speed and increase RPM.
C — Increase climb speed and increase RPM.

3651. Answer A. JSPPM 3-35 (PHB)
Reducing the rate of climb and increasing airspeed will increase the cooling airflow around the engine. Answers (B) and (C) are incorrect because increasing RPM increases temperature. Answer (B) is also incorrect because reducing the climb speed reduces the cooling airflow.

3652. What is one procedure to aid in cooling an engine that is overheating?

A — Enrichen the fuel mixture.
B — Increase the RPM.
C — Reduce the airspeed.

3652. Answer A. JSPPM 3-35 (PHB)
A richer fuel mixture burns at a slightly lower temperature and helps cool the engine. Answer (B) is not right because a higher RPM causes higher engine temperatures. Answer (C) is wrong because a lower airspeed reduces the cooling airflow around the engine.

3653. How is engine operation controlled on an engine equipped with a constant-speed propeller?

A — The throttle controls power output as registered on the manifold pressure gauge and the propeller control regulates engine RPM.
B — The throttle controls power output as registered on the manifold pressure gauge and the propeller control regulates a constant blade angle.
C — The throttle controls engine RPM as registered on the tachometer and the mixture control regulates the power output.

3653. Answer A. JSPPM 3-36 (PHB)
The throttle controls the power output of the engine, which is indicated on the manifold pressure gauge. The propeller control changes the pitch of the propeller blades, thus controlling engine RPM, which is indicated on the tachometer. Answer (B) is wrong because the propeller control does not maintain a constant blade angle. Rather, it varies pitch to maintain a constant speed. Answer (C) is wrong because the throttle does not directly control engine RPM, and the mixture control is not used to regulate power.

Aircraft Systems and Performance

3654. What is an advantage of a constant-speed propeller?

A — Permits the pilot to select and maintain a desired cruising speed.
B — Permits the pilot to select the blade angle for the most efficient performance.
C — Provides a smoother operation with stable RPM and eliminates vibrations.

3655. A precaution for the operation of an engine equipped with a constant-speed propeller is to

A — avoid high RPM settings with high manifold pressure.
B — avoid high manifold pressure settings with low RPM.
C — always use a rich mixture with high RPM settings.

3656. What should be the first action after starting an aircraft engine?

A — Adjust for proper RPM and check for desired indications on the engine gauges.
B — Place the magneto or ignition switch momentarily in the OFF position to check for proper grounding.
C — Test each brake and the parking brake.

3657. Should it become necessary to handprop an airplane engine, it is extremely important that a competent pilot

A — call "contact" before touching the propeller.
B — be at the controls in the cockpit.
C — be in the cockpit and call out all commands.

3654. Answer B. JSPPM 3-36 (PHB)
By selecting the proper blade angle, the pilot can convert a high percentage of engine power into thrust over a wide range of RPM and airspeed combinations. This allows the most efficient performance to be gained from the engine. Answer (A) is not correct because a constant-speed propeller is not necessary for maintaining a desired airspeed. Answer (C) is wrong because a constant-speed propeller is not necessarily smoother than a fixed-pitch propeller, nor does it operate with less vibration.

3655. Answer B. JSPPM 3-37 (PHB)
For a given RPM setting, there is a maximum allowable manifold pressure. Generally, high manifold pressures with low RPM should be avoided to prevent internal stress within the engine. Answer (A) is incorrect because higher manifold pressures are allowable with higher RPM settings, within limits. Answer (C) is incorrect because the mixture should be leaned for optimum performance.

3656. Answer A. JSPPM 3-32 (PHB)
Immediately after starting an engine, set the proper RPM and check engine gauges for proper indications. Answers (B) and (C) are wrong because these items are not the first actions to be taken. Also, answer (B) may not be included in the airplane's checklist.

3657. Answer B. JSPPM 3-38 (PHB)
When hand-propping an airplane, a competent pilot must be at the controls to prevent the airplane from moving and to set the engine controls properly. Answer (A) is not right because the person propping the engine does not have to be a pilot, nor do they have to call "contact." Answer (C) is wrong, since the pilot must be at the controls, not just in the cockpit, and the person hand-propping the engine is in charge of the starting procedure.

SECTION D
FUEL AND ELECTRICAL SYSTEMS

The two common fuel systems are the gravity-feed and the fuel pump types. Both of these are covered, along with their main components. The discussion is about typical fuel system problems, and it includes cautions about refueling and use of the proper fuel grade. The electrical systems information describes a basic 14- or 28-volt DC system, which usually is powered by an engine-driven alternator. FAA test questions covered in this section include:

3224, 3241, 3242, 3243.

3224. On aircraft equipped with fuel pumps, the practice of running a fuel tank dry before switching tanks is considered unwise because

A — the engine-driven fuel pump or electric fuel boost pump may draw air into the fuel system and cause vapor lock.
B — the engine-driven fuel pump is lubricated by fuel and operating on a dry tank may cause pump failure.
C — any foreign matter in the tank will be pumped into the fuel system.

3224. Answer A. JSPPM 3-41 (PHB)
The greatest danger in running a fuel tank dry is that air can enter the fuel system and cause vapor lock. Answers (B) and (C) can be problems, but these are secondary concerns compared to vapor lock.

3241. Which would most likely cause the cylinder head temperature and engine oil temperature gauges to exceed their normal operating ranges?

A — Using fuel that has a lower-than-specified fuel rating.
B — Using fuel that has a higher-than-specified fuel rating.
C — Operating with higher-than-normal oil pressure.

3241. Answer A. JSPPM 3-43 (PHB)
Lower grade fuels will detonate under less pressure. Using a lower fuel rating than specified can cause excessive engine temperatures. Answer (B) is incorrect because using higher grade fuel does not normally cause excessive temperatures. A high oil pressure (answer C) may be an indication of a problem, but is not as likely to cause excessive temperatures as a lower-grade fuel.

3242. What type fuel can be substituted for an aircraft if the recommended octane is not available?

A — The next higher octane aviation gas.
B — The next lower octane aviation gas.
C — Unleaded automotive gas of the same octane rating.

3242. Answer A. JSPPM 3-43 (PHB)
If the manufacturer's recommendations are followed, the next higher grade of fuel may normally be used. Answer (B) is wrong because a lower grade of fuel can cause excessive engine temperatures. Answer (C) is incorrect because automotive gas is not normally recommended.

3243. Filling the fuel tanks after the last flight of the day is considered a good operating procedure because this will

A — force any existing water to the top of the tank away from the fuel lines to the engine.
B — prevent expansion of the fuel by eliminating airspace in the tanks.
C — prevent moisture condensation by eliminating airspace in the tanks.

3243. Answer C. JSPPM 3-40 (PHB)
As the airplane cools overnight, water condenses in the tanks from vapor in the air and enters the fuel. Filling the tanks eliminates the air space and prevents condensation. Answer (A) is wrong because water is heavier than fuel and settles to the bottom of the tank. Answer (B) is wrong because fuel expands with increased temperatures. This is one reason vents are installed in fuel tanks.

Aircraft Systems and Performance 3-17

SECTION E
PREDICTING PERFORMANCE

Section E contains a wealth of information about some common performance characteristics of a training airplane. For example, performance speeds, factors affecting performance, and the pilot's operating handbook (POH) are discussed. The final part of this section includes typical examples of performance charts and tables. The following FAA test questions are covered:

3011, 3012, 3075, 3246, 3289, 3290, 3291, 3292, 3293, 3294, 3295, 3296, 3297, 3298, 3299, 3300, 3387, 3389, 3678, 3679, 3680, 3681, 3682, 3683, 3684, 3685, 3686, 3687, 3688, 3689, 3690, 3691, 3692, 3693, 3694, 3695, 3696, 3697, 3698, 3705, 3706, 3707, 3708.

3011. Which would provide the greatest gain in altitude in the shortest distance during climb after takeoff?

A — V_Y.
B — V_A.
C — V_X.

3011. Answer C. JSPPM 3-49 (FTH)
V_X is the best angle of climb. This gives you the greatest gain in altitude for horizontal distance traveled. Answer (A) is wrong because V_Y is the best rate of climb. This provides you the greatest gain in altitude over a period of time. Answer (B) is wrong because V_A is maneuvering airspeed.

3012. After takeoff, which airspeed would the pilot use to gain the most altitude in a given period of time?

A — V_Y.
B — V_X.
C — V_A.

3012. Answer A. JSPPM 3-49 (FTH)
See explanation for Question 3011.

3075. Where may an aircraft's operating limitations be found?

A — On the Airworthiness Certificate.
B — In the current, FAA-approved flight manual, approved manual material, markings, and placards, or any combination thereof.
C — In the aircraft airframe and engine logbooks.

3075. Answer B. JSPPM 3-48 (FAR 91.9)
Operating limits can be found in any of these sources. Answers (A) and (C) are incorrect because limitations are not found on the Airworthiness Certificate or in the logbooks.

3246. What effect does high density altitude, as compared to low density altitude, have on propeller efficiency and why?

A — Efficiency is increased due to less friction on the propeller blades.
B — Efficiency is reduced because the propeller exerts less force at high density altitudes than at low density altitudes.
C — Efficiency is reduced due to the increased force of the propeller in the thinner air.

3246. Answer B. JSPPM 3-52 (PHB)
Because the air is less dense, there is less airflow through the propeller, and the force and efficiency are reduced. Answers (A) and (C) are wrong because the propeller force and efficiency are reduced, not increased.

3289. If the outside air temperature (OAT) at a given altitude is warmer than standard, the density altitude is

A — equal to pressure altitude.
B — lower than pressure altitude.
C — higher than pressure altitude.

3290. Which combination of atmospheric conditions will reduce aircraft takeoff and climb performance.

A — Low temperature, low relative humidity, and low density altitude.
B — High temperature, low relative humidity, and low density altitude.
C — High temperature, high relative humidity, and high density altitude.

3291. What effect does high density altitude have on aircraft performance?

A — It increases engine performance.
B — It reduces climb performance.
C — It increases takeoff performance.

3292. (Refer to figure 8.) What is the effect of a temperature increase from 25 to 50°F on the density altitude if the pressure altitude remains at 5,000 feet?

A — 1,200-foot increase.
B — 1,400-foot increase.
C — 1,650-foot increase.

3293. (Refer to figure 8.) Determine the pressure altitude with an indicated altitude of 1,380 feet MSL with an altimeter setting of 28.22 at standard temperature.

A — 1,250 feet MSL.
B — 1,373 feet MSL.
C — 3,010 feet MSL.

3294. (Refer to figure 8.) Determine the density altitude for these conditions:
Altimeter setting 29.25
Runway temperature .... +81°F
Airport elevation .... 5,250 ft MSL

A — 4,600 feet MSL.
B — 5,877 feet MSL.
C — 8,500 feet MSL.

3289. Answer C. JSPPM 3-51 (PHB)
When the OAT is warmer than standard, the density altitude (DA) is higher than pressure altitude. Answer (A) would be correct only when the OAT is equal to standard. Answer (B) would be correct when the OAT is lower than standard.

3290. Answer C. JSPPM 3-53 (PHB)
High temperatures increase density altitude with a resulting decrease in aircraft performance. In addition, high humidity reduces engine performance.

3291. Answer B. JSPPM 3-52 (PHB)
A high density altitude decreases engine performance with a resulting reduction in climb performance.

3292. Answer C. JSPPM 3-52 (PHB)
Follow the line above 25°F up to where it intersects 5,000 feet pressure altitude, and read 3,850 feet density altitude on the left scale. Do the same with 50°F, up to 5,000 feet, and then left to read 5,500 feet. The difference is an increase of 1,650 feet.

3293. Answer C. JSPPM 3-52 (PHB)
Using the scales on the right-hand side of the chart, enter with the closest value to 28.22, which is 28.2. The pressure altitude conversion factor is +1,630. Add this to the indicated altitude of 1,380, for a pressure altitude of 3,010 feet.

3294. Answer C. JSPPM 3-52 (PHB)
First find the pressure altitude by using the pressure altitude conversion factor scale and interpolate for 29.25. The conversion factor is 626 (673 - 579 = 94 ÷ 2 = 47 + 579 = 626). This is added to 5,250 feet to find a pressure altitude of 5,876 feet. Now, find 81°F on the OAT scale at the bottom of the graph and follow its line vertically to where it intersects with the 5,876-foot pressure altitude line. From this point, follow the horizontal density altitude line to the left scale to find an approximate density altitude of 8,500 feet.

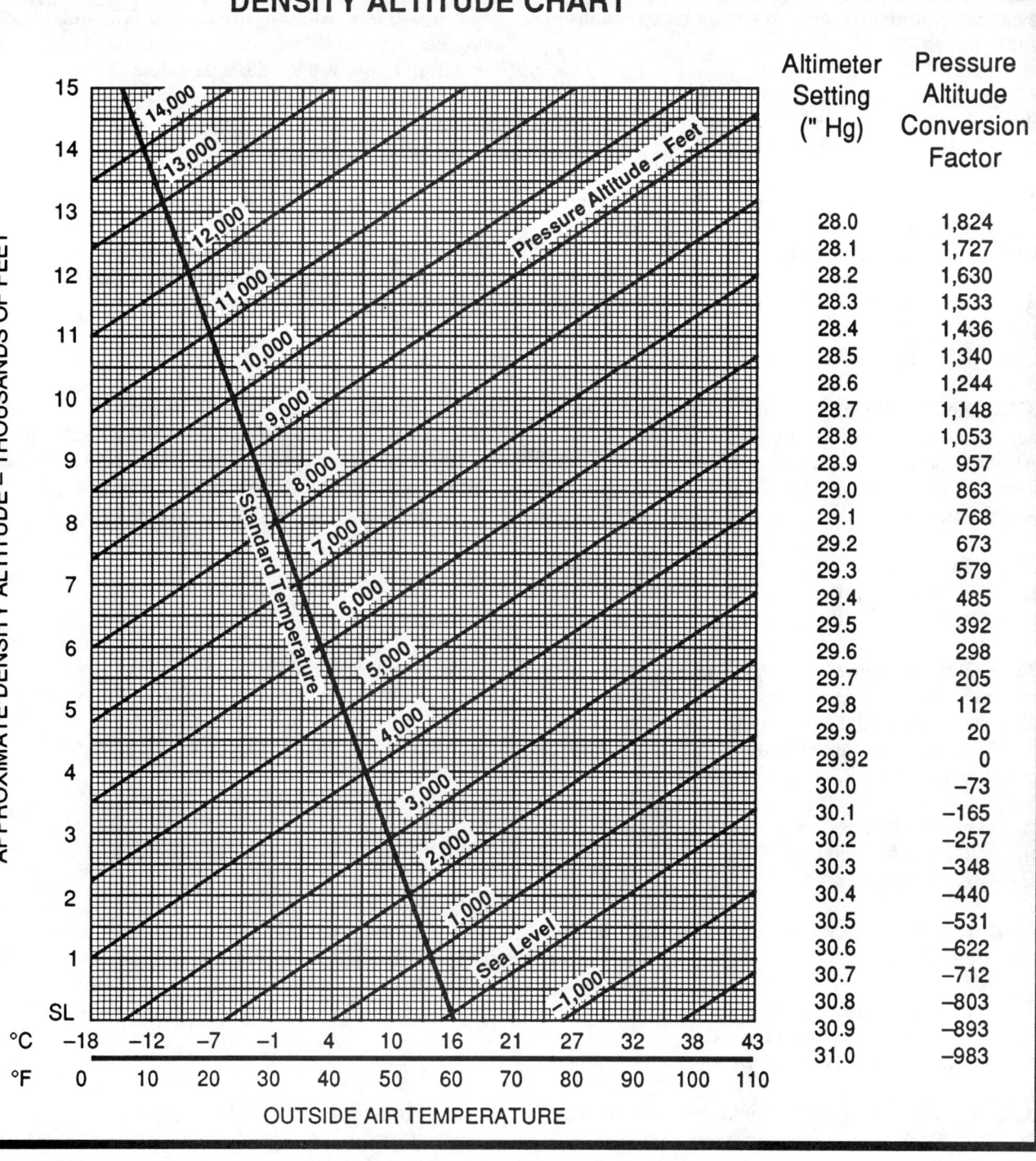

FIGURE 8.—Density Altitude Chart.

3295. (Refer to figure 8.) Determine the pressure altitude at an airport that is 3,563 feet MSL with an altimeter setting of 29.96.

— 3,527 feet MSL.
— 3,556 feet MSL.
— 3,639 feet MSL.

3295. Answer A. JSPPM 3-52 (PHB)
Find the conversion factors for 30.00 and 29.92, and interpolate to find the factor for 29.96 (-73 - 0 = -73 ÷ 2 = -36.5). Subtract 36.5 from the elevation of 3,563 feet, to find a pressure altitude of 3,526.5 feet. This is rounded to 3,527 feet.

3296. (Refer to figure 8 on page 3-19.) What is the effect of a temperature increase from 30 to 50°F on the density altitude if the pressure altitude remains at 3,000 feet MSL?

A — 900-foot increase.
B — 1,100-foot decrease.
C — 1,300-foot increase.

3297. (Refer to figure 8 on page 3-19.) Determine the pressure altitude at an airport that is 1,386 feet MSL with an altimeter setting of 29.97.

A — 1,341 feet MSL.
B — 1,451 feet MSL.
C — 1,562 feet MSL.

3298. (Refer to figure 8 on page 3-19.) Determine the density altitude for these conditions:
Altimeter setting 30.35
Runway temperature .... +25°F
Airport elevation .... 3,894 ft MSL

A — 2,000 feet MSL.
B — 2,900 feet MSL.
C — 3,500 feet MSL.

3299. (Refer to figure 8 on page 3-19.) What is the effect of a temperature decrease and a pressure altitude increase on the density altitude from 90°F and 1,250 feet pressure altitude to 60°F and 1,750 feet pressure altitude?

A — 500-foot increase.
B — 1,300-foot decrease.
C — 1,300-foot increase.

3300. What effect, if any, does high humidity have on aircraft performance?

A — It increases performance.
B — It decreases performance.
C — It has no effect on performance.

3387. If a pilot changes the altimeter setting from 30.11 to 29.96, what is the approximate change in indication?

A — Altimeter will indicate .15" Hg higher.
B — Altimeter will indicate 150 feet higher.
C — Altimeter will indicate 150 feet lower.

3296. Answer C. JSPPM 3-52 (PHB)
First you must find the density altitude (DA) for 30°F. It is 1,600 feet. At 50°F, the DA is 2,900 feet, for an increase of 1,300 feet. Keep in mind that an increase in temperature will increase density altitude.

3297. Answer A. JSPPM 3-52 (PHB)
First you must interpolate to find the conversion factor for 29.97 (-73 - 0 = -73 ÷ 8 increments = -9 x 5 increments = -45). Subtract 45 from 1,386 to find the pressure altitude of 1,341 feet.

3298. Answer A. JSPPM 3-52 (PHB)
The conversion factor for 30.35 is -394 which, when applied to 3,894, results in a pressure altitude of 3,500 feet. Enter the chart at 25°F, go up to 3,500, then left to find the density altitude of 2,000 feet.

3299. Answer B. JSPPM 3-52 (PHB)
This problem requires some interpolation. At 90°F and 1,250 feet PA, the DA is about 3,600. At 60°F and 1,750 feet PA, the DA is about 2,300. The correct answer is a decrease of 1,300 feet.

3300. Answer B. JSPPM 3-53 (PHB)
High humidity reduces engine performance by slightly increasing the density altitude of air entering the engine and retarding smooth burning of the fuel.

3387. Answer C. JSPPM 3-52 (PHB)
Each .1" change on the altimeter setting equates to about 100 feet. In this case, the change is .15 lower, or 150 feet.

Aircraft Systems and Performance

3389. Under what condition is pressure altitude and density altitude the same value?

A — At sea level, when the temperature is 0°F.
B — When the altimeter has no installation error.
C — At standard temperature.

3389. Answer C. JSPPM 3-51 (PHB)
Since density altitude is pressure altitude corrected for nonstandard temperature, DA and PA are equal only at standard temperature. Answer (A) is wrong because at sea level, standard temperature is 59°F. Answer (B) is incorrect because pressure altitude and density altitude are not dependent on an altimeter which provides indicated altitude.

3678. (Refer to figure 36.) Approximately what true airspeed should a pilot expect with 65 percent maximum continuous power at 9,500 feet with a temperature of 36°F below standard?

A — 178 MPH.
B — 181 MPH.
C — 183 MPH.

3678. Answer C. JSPPM 3-64 (PHB)
Use the left-hand portion of the table, under ISA -36°F. Interpolate between the TAS values for 8,000 feet (181 MPH) and 10,000 feet (184 MPH). The closest answer is 183 MPH.

CRUISE POWER SETTINGS
65% MAXIMUM CONTINUOUS POWER (OR FULL THROTTLE)
2800 POUNDS

PRESS ALT.	ISA −20 °C (−36 °F)							STANDARD DAY (ISA)							ISA +20 °C (+36 °F)						
	IOAT		ENGINE SPEED	MAN. PRESS	FUEL FLOW PER ENGINE		TAS		IOAT		ENGINE SPEED	MAN. PRESS	FUEL FLOW PER ENGINE		TAS		IOAT		ENGINE SPEED	MAN. PRESS	FUEL FLOW PER ENGINE		TAS
FEET	°F	°C	RPM	IN HG	PSI	GPH	KTS	MPH	°F	°C	RPM	IN HG	PSI	GPH	KTS	MPH	°F	°C	RPM	IN HG	PSI	GPH	KTS	MPH
SL	27	-3	2450	20.7	6.6	11.5	147	169	63	17	2450	21.2	6.6	11.5	150	173	99	37	2450	21.8	6.6	11.5	153	176
2000	19	-7	2450	20.4	6.6	11.5	149	171	55	13	2450	21.0	6.6	11.5	153	176	91	33	2450	21.5	6.6	11.5	156	180
4000	12	-11	2450	20.1	6.6	11.5	152	175	48	9	2450	20.7	6.6	11.5	156	180	84	29	2450	21.3	6.6	11.5	159	183
6000	5	-15	2450	19.8	6.6	11.5	155	178	41	5	2450	20.4	6.6	11.5	158	182	79	26	2450	21.0	6.6	11.5	161	185
8000	-2	-19	2450	19.5	6.6	11.5	157	181	36	2	2450	20.2	6.6	11.5	161	185	72	22	2450	20.8	6.6	11.5	164	189
10000	-8	-22	2450	19.2	6.6	11.5	160	184	28	-2	2450	19.9	6.6	11.5	163	188	64	18	2450	20.3	6.5	11.4	166	191
12000	-15	-26	2450	18.8	6.4	11.3	162	186	21	-6	2450	18.8	6.1	10.9	163	188	57	14	2450	18.8	5.9	10.6	163	188
14000	-22	-30	2450	17.4	5.8	10.5	159	183	14	-10	2450	17.4	5.6	10.1	160	184	50	10	2450	17.4	5.4	9.8	160	184
16000	-29	-34	2450	16.1	5.3	9.7	156	180	7	-14	2450	16.1	5.1	9.4	156	180	43	6	2450	16.1	4.9	9.1	155	178

NOTES:
1. Full throttle manifold pressure settings are approximate.
2. Shaded area represents operation with full throttle.

FIGURE 36.—Airplane Power Setting Table.

3679. (Refer to figure 36.) What is the expected fuel consumption for a 1,000-nautical mile flight under the following conditions?

Pressure altitude .... 8,000 ft
Temperature ....22°C
Manifold pressure .... 20.8" Hg
Wind .... Calm

A — 60.2 gallons.
B — 70.1 gallons.
C — 73.2 gallons.

3679. Answer B. JSPPM 3-64 (PHB)
The temperature of 22°C is found on the right-hand portion of the table (ISA + 20°C) at 8,000 feet. Read across to find a fuel flow of 11.5 GPH, and TAS of 164 KTS (use knots because the distance is in nautical miles). Now, find the time enroute by dividing 1,000 n.m. by 164 KTS. (Normally you would use groundspeed, but with a calm wind, TAS equals groundspeed.) The time enroute is approximately 6:06 hrs. Then multiply the time by fuel flow. The total fuel consumption is 70.1 gallons.

3680. (Refer to figure 36 on page 3-21.) What is the expected fuel consumption for a 500-nautical mile flight under the following conditions?

Pressure altitude .... 4,000 ft
Temperature .... +29°C
Manifold pressure .... 21.3" Hg
Wind .... Calm

A — 31.4 gallons.
B — 36.1 gallons.
C — 40.1 gallons.

3680. Answer B. JSPPM 3-64 (PHB)
Use the portion of the table for ISA + 20°C, and enter at 4,000 feet. Read across to find that fuel flow is 11.5 GPH and TAS is 159 KTS. For 500 n.m., the time enroute is approximately 3:08 hrs. Then, multiply fuel flow by time. The total fuel consumption is approximately 36.1 gallons.

3681. (Refer to figure 36 on page 3-21.) What fuel flow should a pilot expect at 11,000 feet on a standard day with 65 percent maximum continuous power?

A — 10.6 gallons per hour.
B — 11.2 gallons per hour.
C — 11.8 gallons per hour.

3681. Answer B. JSPPM 3-64 (PHB)
Use the center portion of the table for a standard day. You will need to interpolate to find the fuel flow for 11,000 feet which is halfway between 12,000 and 10,000 feet. The answer is 11.2 (11.5 - 10.9 = .6 ÷ 2 = .3 + 10.9 = 11.2).

3682. (Refer to figure 36 on page 3-21.) Determine the approximate manifold pressure setting with 2,450 RPM to achieve 65 percent maximum continuous power at 6,500 feet with a temperature of 36°F higher than standard.

A — 19.8" Hg.
B — 20.8" Hg.
C — 21.0" Hg.

3682. Answer C. JSPPM 3-64 (PHB)
The RPM is the same for all altitudes. Therefore, to determine what manifold pressure (MP) is required to achieve 65% maximum continuous power, enter the table under ISA + 36°F. The MP for 6,000 feet is 21.0", and for 8,000 feet it is 20.8". The interpolated MP for 6,500 feet is 20.95". The closest answer is 21.0" Hg.

3683. (Refer to figure 37.) What is the headwind component for a landing on Runway 18 if the tower reports the wind as 220° at 30 knots?

A — 19 knots.
B — 23 knots.
C — 26 knots.

3683. Answer B. JSPPM 3-55 (PHB)
First, compute the difference between the runway (180°) and the wind (220°). The result is an angle of 40 degrees. Find the intersection of the 40 degree line and the 30 knot wind velocity arc, then read across to the left side to find the headwind component of 23 knots.

3684. (Refer to figure 37.) Determine the maximum wind velocity for a 45° crosswind if the maximum crosswind component for the airplane is 25 knots.

A — 25 knots.
B — 29 knots.
C — 35 knots.

3684. Answer C. JSPPM 3-55 (PHB)
Start with the crosswind component of 25 knots at the bottom of the chart, and follow the line straight up to where it intersects the 45 degree angle line. This intersection is midway between the 30 and 40 knot wind velocity lines, or 35 knots.

3685. (Refer to figure 37.) What is the maximum wind velocity for a 30° crosswind if the maximum crosswind component for the airplane is 12 knots?

A — 16 knots.
B — 20 knots.
C — 24 knots.

3685. Answer C. JSPPM 3-55 (PHB)
Start with the crosswind component of 12 knots at the bottom of the chart, and follow the line straight up to where it intersects the 30 degree angle line. This intersection is approximately 24 knots on the wind velocity scale.

Aircraft Systems and Performance

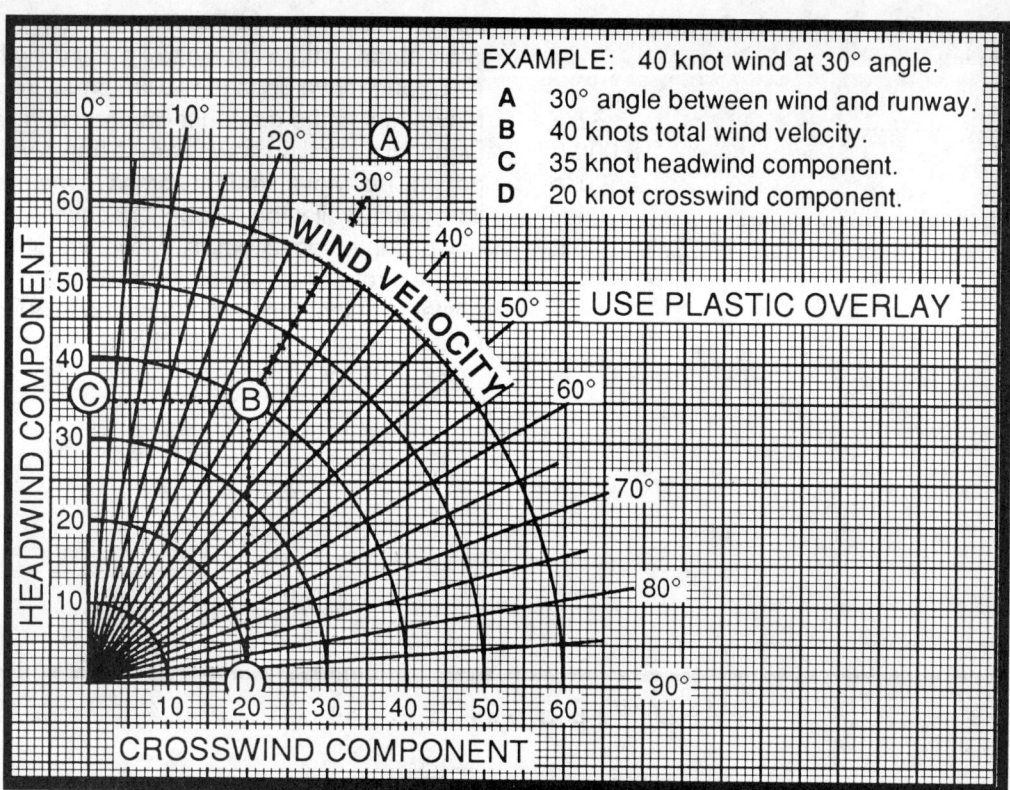

FIGURE 37.—Crosswind Component Graph.

3686. (Refer to figure 37.) With a reported wind of north at 20 knots, which runway (6, 29, or 32) is acceptable for use for an airplane with a 13-knot maximum crosswind component?

A— Runway 6.
B— Runway 29.
C— Runway 32.

3687. (Refer to figure 37.) With a reported wind of south at 20 knots, which runway (10, 14, or 24) is appropriate for an airplane with a 13-knot maximum crosswind component?

A— Runway 10.
B— Runway 14.
C— Runway 24.

3688. (Refer to figure 37.) What is the crosswind component for a landing on Runway 18 if the tower reports the wind as 220° at 30 knots?

A— 19 knots.
B— 23 knots.
C— 30 knots.

3686. Answer C. JSPPM 3-55 (PHB)
At first glance, Runway 32 is most closely aligned with north (360°). To verify, find the crosswind component for each runway. Runway 32 is 40 degrees from the wind, and since the windspeed is 20 knots, the crosswind component is slightly less than 13 knots, so Runway 32 is acceptable. Runway 6 is 60 degrees from the wind, and the crosswind component is about 17.5 knots. Runway 29 is 70 degrees from the wind, and the crosswind component is about 19 knots. Both Runways 6 and 29 exceed the 13 knot maximum crosswind component.

3687. Answer B. JSPPM 3-55 (PHB)
The same process is used as in Question 3686. Runway 14 is most closely aligned with the wind and would have the least crosswind. The crosswind angle and component for each runway is: Runway 14, 40 degrees, 12.5 knots; Runway 10, 80 degrees, 19.7 knots; Runway 24, 60 degrees, 17.5 knots. Runway 14 is the only appropriate runway because the crosswind component is less than 13 knots.

3688. Answer A. JSPPM 3-55 (PHB)
The crosswind angle is 40 degrees (220° - 180° = 40°). Find the intersection of 40 degrees and 30 knots. Then read down to find the crosswind component of about 19 knots.

3689. (Refer to figure 38.) Determine the total distance required to land.

OAT	32°F
Pressure altitude	8,000 ft
Weight	2,600 lb
Headwind component	20 kts
Obstacle	50 ft

A— 850 feet.
B— 1,400 feet.
C— 1,750 feet.

3689. Answer B. JSPPM 3-55 (PHB)
Start at the bottom left side of the chart with 32°F (0°C) and move up to the 8,000 pressure altitude line. Move right to the reference line and parallel the diagonal guide line downward to intersect the 2,600 pound line. Move straight across to the next reference line, and parallel the diagonal headwind guide line down to intersect 20 knots. Move straight across to the next reference line and parallel the diagonal obstacle height guide line upwards to 50 feet. The landing distance is read on the right side —1,400 feet.

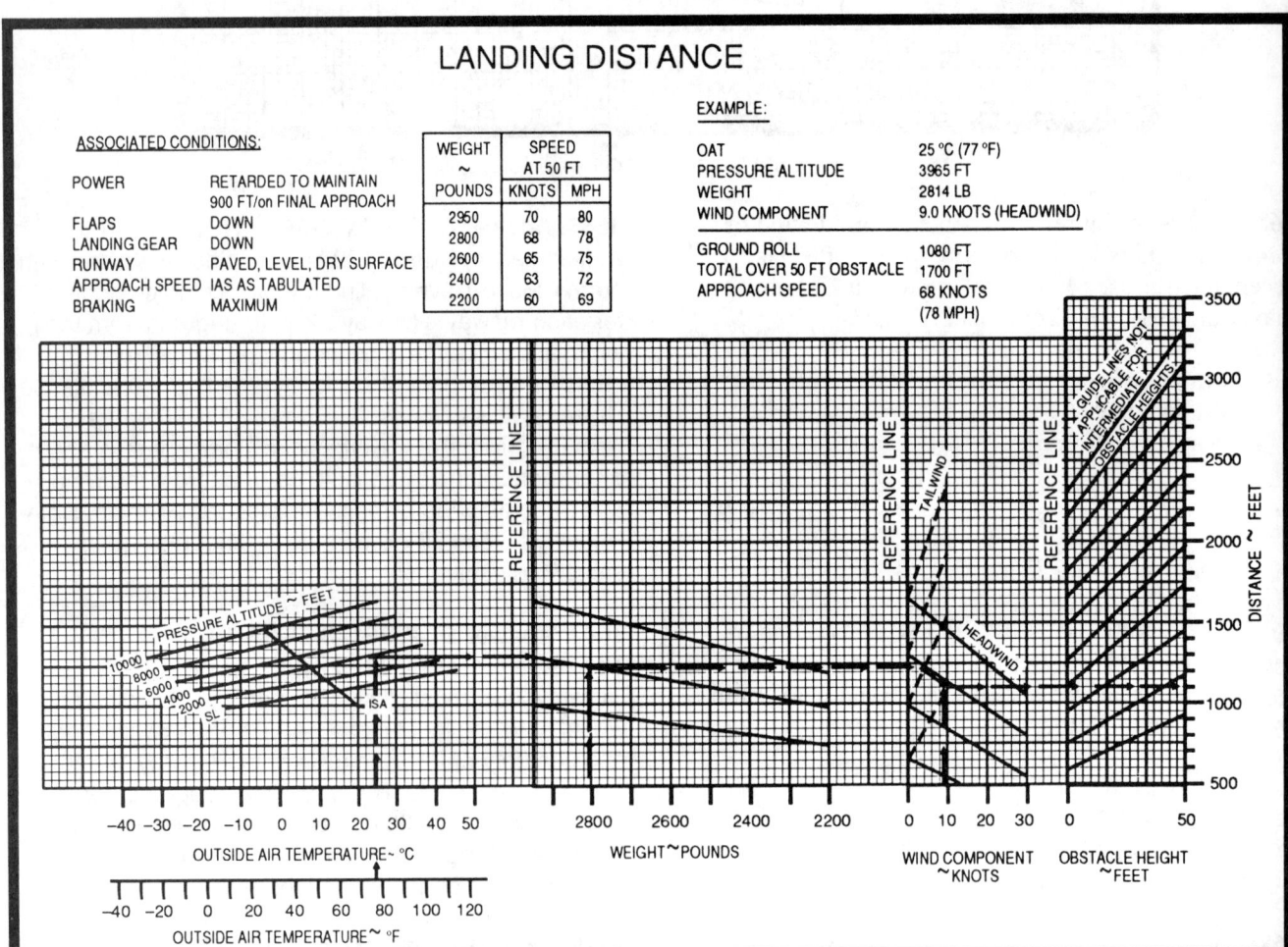

FIGURE 38.—Airplane Landing Distance Graph.

Aircraft Systems and Performance

3690. (Refer to figure 38.) Determine the total distance required to land.

OAT	Std
Pressure altitude	2,000 ft
Weight	2,300 lb
Wind component	Calm
Obstacle	None

A— 850 feet.
B— 1,250 feet.
C— 1,450 feet.

3690. Answer A. JSPPM 3-65 (PHB)
Start at the ISA (standard temperature) line and move upward to where it intersects the 2,000 foot pressure altitude line. Move right and parallel the reference lines downward to intersect 2,300 pounds. Move straight through the wind component and obstacle height sections, since the wind is calm and there is no obstacle. The landing distance is approximately 850 feet.

3691. (Refer to figure 38.) Determine the total distance required to land.

OAT	90°F
Pressure altitude	3,000 ft
Weight	2,900 lb
Headwind component	10 kts
Obstacle	50 ft

A— 1,450 feet.
B— 1,550 feet.
C— 1,725 feet.

3691. Answer C. JSPPM 3-65 (PHB)
Start with 90°F (32°C), and move upward to midway between the 2,000 and 4,000 feet pressure altitude lines. Follow the reference lines in the same manner described for the previous questions to the 2,900 pound weight, a headwind of 10 knots, and a 50 foot obstacle height. The landing distance is approximately 1,725 feet.

3692. (Refer to figure 38.) Determine the approximate ground roll distance after landing.

OAT	90°F
Pressure altitude	4,000 ft
Weight	2,800 lb
Tailwind component	10 kts

A— 1,575 feet.
B— 1,725 feet.
C— 1,950 feet.

3692. Answer C. JSPPM 3-65 (PHB)
Start with 90°F (32°C), and follow the reference lines in the same manner described for the previous questions. Be sure to move diagonally up the tailwind line. Since you are to find the ground roll, move straight through the obstacle height and read the landing distance on the right-hand scale. It is approximately 1,950 feet.

3693. (Refer to figure 39 on page 3-26.) Determine the approximate landing ground roll distance.

Pressure altitude	Sea level
Headwind	4 kts
Temperature	Std

A— 356 feet.
B— 401 feet.
C— 490 feet.

3693. Answer B. JSPPM 3-66 (PHB)
Use the table listed under sea level and 59°F, which is the standard temperature. Since you need to find the landing ground roll distance, do not include obstacle clearance. The ground roll is given as 445, but according to Note 1, you need to correct for headwind by decreasing the distance 10% for each 4 knots of headwind. In this case, subtract 10% of 445 (44.5) from 445. The closest answer is 401 feet.

LANDING DISTANCE

FLAPS LOWERED TO 40° - POWER OFF
HARD SURFACE RUNWAY - ZERO WIND

GROSS WEIGHT LB	APPROACH SPEED, IAS, MPH	AT SEA LEVEL & 59 °F		AT 2500 FT & 50 °F		AT 5000 FT & 41 °F		AT 7500 FT & 32 °F	
		GROUND ROLL	TOTAL TO CLEAR 50 FT OBS	GROUND ROLL	TOTAL TO CLEAR 50 FT OBS	GROUND ROLL	TOTAL TO CLEAR 50 FT OBS	GROUND ROLL	TOTAL TO CLEAR 50 FT OBS
1600	60	445	1075	470	1135	495	1195	520	1255

NOTES: 1. Decrease the distances shown by 10% for each 4 knots of headwind.
2. Increase the distance by 10% for each 60 °F temperature increase above standard.
3. For operation on a dry, grass runway, increase distances (both "ground roll" and "total to clear 50 ft obstacle") by 20% of the "total to clear 50 ft obstacle" figure.

FIGURE 39.—Airplane Landing Distance Table.

3694. (Refer to figure 39.) Determine the total distance required to land over a 50-foot obstacle.

Pressure altitude .... 7,500 ft
Headwind .... 8 kts
Temperature .... Std
Runway .... Dry grass

A— 1,004 feet.
B— 1,205 feet.
C— 1,506 feet.

3694. Answer B. JSPPM 3-66 (PHB)
Use the table under 7,500 feet and 32°F, which is the standard temperature. Use the value for 50 FT OBS, which is 1,255. According to Note 1 decrease the distance by 10% for each 4 knots of headwind. Since there is 8 knots of headwind, you should decrease the distance by 20% or 251 feet (1,255 x 20% = 251). The result is 1,004 feet. Since you are using a dry grass runway, you must then add 20% or 201 feet (1,004 x 20% = 201). The total landing distance is 1,205 feet. (Note that the two 20% figures do not cancel each other out. You must do the calculations in the proper order.)

3695. (Refer to figure 39.) Determine the total distance required to land over a 50-foot obstacle.

Pressure altitude .... 5,000 ft
Headwind .... 8 kts
Temperature .... 41°F
Runway .... Hard surface

A— 837 feet.
B— 956 feet.
C— 1,076 feet.

3695. Answer B. JSPPM 3-66 (PHB)
Use the table at 5,000 feet and 41°F. The distance to clear a 50 ft obstacle is 1,195. According to Note 1, decrease the distance by 20% (239') for the 8 knot headwind: (1,195 - 239 = 956 total landing distance).

3696. (Refer to figure 39.) Determine the total distance required to land over a 50-foot obstacle.

Pressure altitude .... 5,000 ft
Headwind .... Calm
Temperature .... 101°F

A— 1,076 feet.
B— 1,291 feet.
C— 1,314 feet.

3696. Answer C. JSPPM 3-66 (PHB)
Use the table at 5,000 feet and 41°F. The distance to clear a 50 ft obstacle is 1,195. Since the temperature is 60° above standard (101° - 41° = 60°), Note 2 indicates you must increase the distance by 10%. The landing distance is 1,195 + 119.5 or 1,314.5 feet. The closest answer is 1,314 feet.

Aircraft Systems and Performance

3697. (Refer to figure 39.) Determine the approximate landing ground roll distance.

Pressure altitude .... 3,750 ft
Headwind .... 12 kts
Temperature .... Std

A — 338 feet.
B — 425 feet.
C — 483 feet.

3698. (Refer to figure 39.) Determine the approximate landing ground roll distance.

Pressure altitude .... 1,250 ft
Headwind .... 8 kts
Temperature .... Std

A — 275 feet.
B — 366 feet.
C — 470 feet.

3705. (Refer to figure 41 on page 3-28.) Determine the total distance required for takeoff to clear a 50-foot obstacle.

OAT .... Std
Pressure altitude .... 4,000 ft
Takeoff weight .... 2,800 lb
Headwind component .... Calm

A — 1,500 feet.
B — 1,750 feet.
C — 2,000 feet.

3706. (Refer to figure 41 on page 3-28.) Determine the total distance required for takeoff to clear a 50-foot obstacle.

OAT .... Std
Pressure altitude .... Sea level
Takeoff weight .... 2,700 lb
Headwind component .... Calm

A — 1,000 feet.
B — 1,400 feet.
C — 1,700 feet.

3697. Answer A. JSPPM 3-66 (PHB)
This problem requires that you interpolate between the ground roll distances at 2,500 feet and 5,000 feet PA and then compensate for the headwind component. Since 3,750 feet is midway between the 5,000 and 2,500, the ground roll is 482.5 (495 - 470 = 25 ÷ 2 = 12.5 + 470 = 482.5). To correct for headwind, subtract 30% of the distance (10% for each 4 kts). 30% of 482.5 is 114.8. The landing distance is 482.5 - 144.8 or 337.7 feet. Round this figure to 338 feet to get the correct answer.

3698. Answer B. JSPPM 3-66 (PHB)
This problem requires that you interpolate between the ground roll distances at sea level and 2,500 feet PA. Since 1,250 feet is midway between the two values, the ground roll would be 457.5 (470 - 445 = 25 ÷ 2 = 12.5 + 445 = 457.5). To correct for headwind, subtract 20% of the distance (10% for each 4 kts). 20% of 457.5 is 91.5. The landing distance is 457.5 - 91.5 or 366 feet.

3705. Answer B. JSPPM 3-62 (PHB)
Since temperature is standard, start at the intersection of the ISA and 4,000 foot pressure altitude line. Move right to the reference line and follow the guide line diagonally downward to the 2,800 pound line. Since winds are calm, move straight across to the obstacle height reference line. Follow the guide line upward to the 50 foot line, which is on the right-hand border. The takeoff distance is approximately 1,700 feet.

3706. Answer B. JSPPM 3-62 (PHB)
Since temperature is standard, start at the intersection of the ISA line and sea level (S.L.). Move right to the reference line and follow the guide line diagonally downward to the 2,700 pound line. Move straight across to the obstacle height reference line, since winds are calm. Follow the guide line upward to the 50 foot line. The takeoff distance is about 1,400 feet.

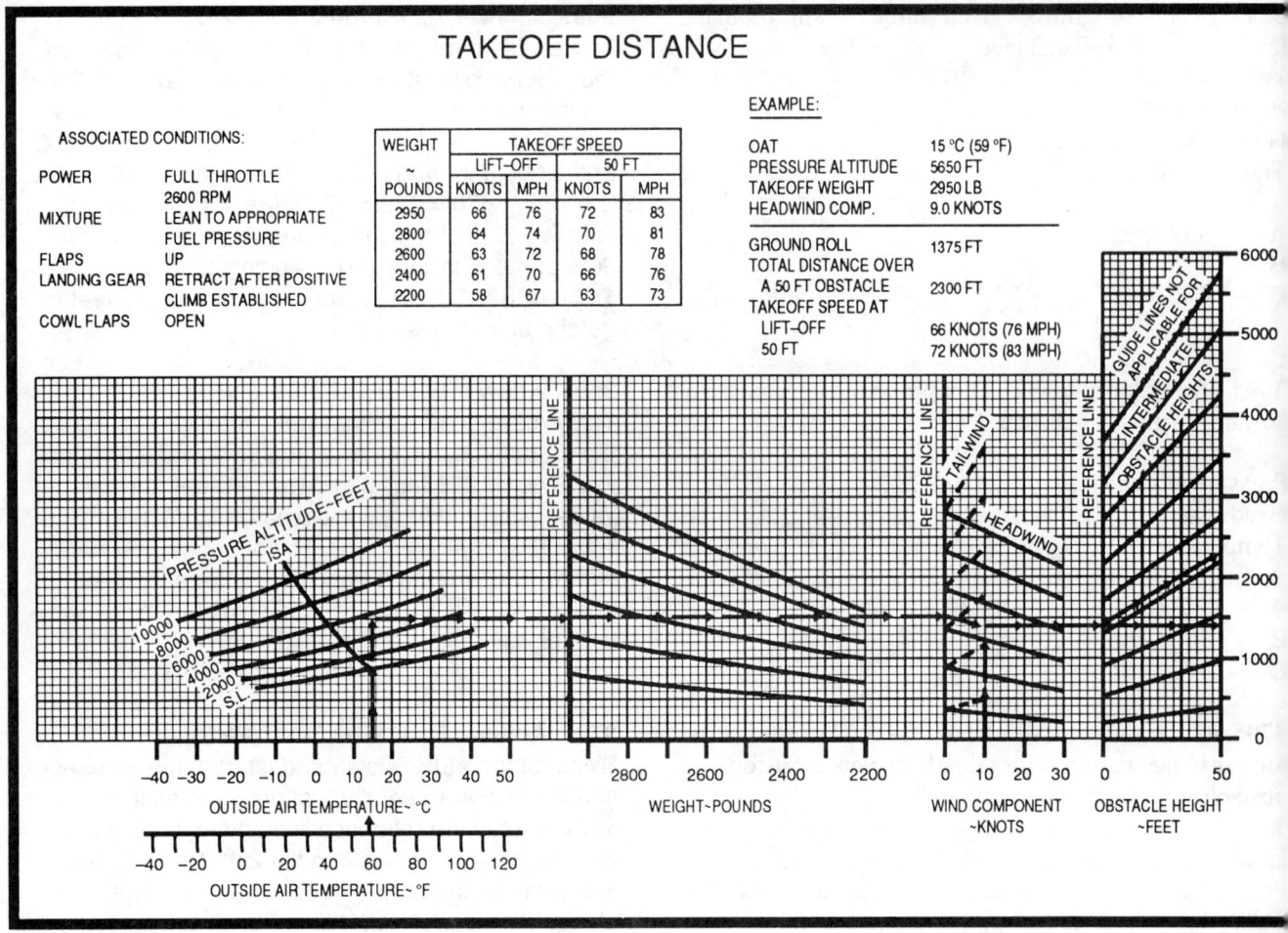

FIGURE 41.—Airplane Takeoff Distance Graph.

3707. (Refer to figure 41.) Determine the approximate ground roll distance required for takeoff.

OAT .... 100°F
Pressure altitude .... 2,000 ft
Takeoff weight .... 2,750 lb
Headwind component ....Calm

A — 1,150 feet.
B — 1,300 feet.
C — 1,800 feet.

3707. Answer A. JSPPM 3-62 (PHB)
Start at 100°F, move up to 2,000 foot pressure altitude line, then right to the reference line. Follow the guide line down to 2,750 pounds. Since winds are calm, and there is no obstacle, move straight across to the right-hand border. The ground roll is about 1,150 feet.

3708. (Refer to figure 41.) Determine the approximate ground roll distance required for takeoff.

OAT .... 90°F
Pressure altitude .... 2,000 ft
Takeoff weight .... 2,500 lb
Headwind component .... 20 kts

A — 650 feet
B — 800 feet
C — 1,000 feet

3708. Answer A. JSPPM 3-62 (PHB)
Start at 90°F, move up to 2,000 foot pressure altitude line, then right to the reference line. Follow the guide line down to 2,500 pounds. Move across to the next reference line, and follow the headwind guide line down to 20 knots. Since there is no obstacle, move straight across to the right-hand border. The ground roll is about 650 feet.

Aircraft Systems and Performance

SECTION F
WEIGHT AND BALANCE

This section expands your knowledge about an airplane's capabilities and limitations. For example, it explains how weight and balance conditions are determined. Then, you'll see why weight and weight distribution are critical factors in performance. Representative examples of weight and balance charts and tables are illustrated. Included is coverage of the weight shift formula. Test questions include the following:

3661, 3662, 3663, 3664, 3665, 3666, 3667, 3668, 3669, 3670, 3671, 3672, 3673, 3674, 3675, 3676, 3677.

3661. Which items are included in the empty weight of an aircraft?

A — Unusable fuel and undrainable oil.
B — Only the airframe, powerplant, and optional equipment.
C — Full fuel tanks and engine oil to capacity.

3661. Answer A. JSPPM 3-68 (PHB)
The empty weight of an aircraft includes unusable fuel. The term **basic empty weight** includes full engine oil. On older airplanes, the term **licensed empty weight** includes only undrainable oil. Therefore, answer (A) is the best choice. Answer (B) is wrong because empty weight also includes full operating fluids and unusable fuel. Answer (C) is wrong because empty weight does not include full fuel tanks

3662. An aircraft is loaded 110 pounds over maximum certificated gross weight. If fuel (gasoline) is drained to bring the aircraft weight within limits, how much fuel should be drained?

A — 15.7 gallons.
B — 16.2 gallons.
C — 18.4 gallons.

3662. Answer C. JSPPM 3-74 (PHB)
This problem requires converting the weight of fuel to gallons. Since the standard weight of gasoline is 6 pounds per gallon, divide 110 pounds by 6, to find an answer of 18.33, or 18.4 gallons.

3663. If an aircraft is loaded 90 pounds over maximum certificated gross weight and fuel (gasoline) is drained to bring the aircraft weight within limits, how much fuel should be drained?

A — 10 gallons.
B — 12 gallons.
C — 15 gallons.

3663. Answer C. JSPPM 3-74 (PHB)
See explanation for Question 3662. 90 pounds divided by 6 lb/gal is 15 gallons.

3664. GIVEN:

	WEIGHT (LB)	ARM (IN)	MOMENT (LB-IN)
Empty weight	1,495.0	101.4	151,593.0
Pilot and pass	380.0	64.0	—
Fuel (30 gal usable no reserve)	—	96.0	—

The CG is located how far aft of datum?

A — CG 92.44.
B — CG 94.01.
C — CG 119.8.

3664. Answer B. JSPPM 3-73 (PHB)
First, fill in the table by entering the fuel weight (30 gal x 6 lb/gal = 180 lbs). Then, multiply each weight by the arm to find the moment.

	WEIGHT (lbs)	ARM (in)	MOMENT (lb-in)
Empty weight	1,495.0	101.4	151,593.0
Pilot & pass	380.0	64.0	24,320.0
Fuel 30 gals	180.0	96.0	17,280.0
Totals	2,055.0		193,193.0

$$CG = \frac{193,193}{2,055} = 94.01$$

The CG is the total moment divided by the total weight.

3665. (Refer to figures 33 and 34 on pages 3-32 and 3-33.) Determine if the airplane weight and balance is within limits.

Front seat occupants .... 340 lb
Rear seat occupants .... 295 lb
Fuel (main wing tanks) .... 44 gal
Baggage .... 56 lb

A — 20 pounds overweight, CG aft of aft limits.
B — 20 pounds overweight, CG within limits.
C — 20 pounds overweight, CG forward of forward limits.

3665. Answer B. JSPPM 3-78 (PHB)
Again, the recommended way to do this problem is to construct a table using the information from Figures 33 and 34. Remember weight times arm equals moment. The moment can also be read from the chart. In this question the arm for the empty weight is not listed since the airplane empty weight moment is given.

	WEIGHT (lbs)	ARM (in)	MOMENT (lb-in/100)
Empty weight	2,015	—	1,554.0
Front seat	340	85	289.0
Rear seat	295	121	357.0
Fuel 44 gal	264	75	198.0
Baggage	56	140	78.4
Totals	2,970		2,476.4

The total weight is 2,970 pounds, 20 pounds over the maximum. Note, the moment in pound-inches is given with a reduction factor of 100. Thus, the total moment is actually 2,476.4 x 100, or 247,640.0. In this question, as well as in succeeding questions, some decimals have been rounded for brevity.

$$CG = \frac{2,476.4 \times 100}{2,970} = 83.4$$

This CG (83.4 inches aft of the datum) is within the limits (between 82.1 and 84.7) given in Figure 33; however, the weight is 20 pounds over the maximum figure of 2,950 lbs. listed in Figure 34. Therefore, (B) is the only correct answer.

Aircraft Systems and Performance

3666. (Refer to figures 33 and 34 on pages 3-32 and 3-33.) What is the maximum amount of baggage that can be carried when the airplane is loaded as follows?

Front seat occupants .... 387 lb
Rear seat occupants .... 293 lb
Fuel .... 35 gal

A— 45 pounds.
B— 63 pounds.
C— 220 pounds.

3666. Answer A. JSPPM 3-78 (PHB)
First, construct a table in the same manner as in Question 3665.

	WEIGHT (lbs)	ARM (in)	MOMENT (lb-in/100)
Empty weight	2,015		1,554.0
Front seat	387	85	329.0
Rear seat	293	121	354.5
Fuel 35 gal	210		158.0
Subtotal	2,905		2,395.5
Baggage	45	140	63.0
Totals	2,950		2,458.5

The known weights add up to a subtotal of 2,905. Subtract this from the maximum weight of 2,950, to find allowable baggage of 45 pounds. However, the moment limits should also be checked. Using a baggage weight of 45, the moment is 63.0. Total moments divided by total weight gives a CG of 83.3, which is within limits for the weight of 2,950 pounds.

$$CG = \frac{2{,}458.5 \times 100}{2{,}950} = 83.03$$

3667. (Refer to figures 33 and 34 on pages 3-32 and 3-33.) Calculate the weight and balance and determine if the CG and the weight of the airplane are within limits.

Front seat occupants .... 350 lb
Rear seat occupants .... 325 lb
Baggage .... 27 lb
Fuel .... 35 gal

A— CG 81.7, out of limits forward.
B— CG 83.4, within limits.
C— CG 84.1, within limits.

3667. Answer B. JSPPM 3-78 (PHB)
First, construct a weight and moment table.

	WEIGHT (lbs)	ARM (in)	MOMENT (lb-in/100)
Empty weight	2,015		1,554.0
Front seat	350	85	297.5
Rear seat	325	121	393.3
Baggage	27	140	37.8
Fuel 35 gal	210	75	158.0
Totals	2,927		2,440.6

Divide total moments by total weight to find the CG of 83.4.

$$CG = \frac{2{,}440.6 \times 100}{2{,}927} = 83.4$$

Using the Moment Limits vs. Weight from either Figure 33 or Figure 34, the CG and moment are within limits.

USEFUL LOAD WEIGHTS AND MOMENTS

OCCUPANTS

FRONT SEATS ARM 85		REAR SEATS ARM 121	
Weight	Moment/100	Weight	Moment/100
120	102	120	145
130	110	130	157
140	119	140	169
150	128	150	182
160	136	160	194
170	144	170	206
180	153	180	218
190	162	190	230
200	170	200	242

BAGGAGE OR 5TH SEAT OCCUPANT
ARM 140

Weight	Moment/100
10	14
20	28
30	42
40	56
50	70
60	84
70	98
80	112
90	126
100	140
110	154
120	168
130	182
140	196
150	210
160	224
170	238
180	252
190	266
200	280
210	294
220	308
230	322
240	336
250	350
260	364
270	378

USABLE FUEL

MAIN WING TANKS ARM 75

Gallons	Weight	Moment/100
5	30	22
10	60	45
15	90	68
20	120	90
25	150	112
30	180	135
35	210	158
40	240	180
44	264	198

AUXILIARY WING TANKS ARM 94

Gallons	Weight	Moment/100
5	30	28
10	60	56
15	90	85
19	114	107

*OIL

Quarts	Weight	Moment/100
10	19	5

*Included in basic Empty Weight

Empty Weight ~ 2015

MOM / 100 ~ 1554

MOMENT LIMITS vs WEIGHT

Moment limits are based on the following weight and center of gravity limit data (landing gear down).

WEIGHT CONDITION	FORWARD CG LIMIT	AFT CG LIMIT
2950 lb (takeoff or landing)	82.1	84.7
2525 lb	77.5	85.7
2475 lb or less	77.0	85.7

FIGURE 33.—Airplane Weight and Balance Tables.

MOMENT LIMITS vs WEIGHT (Continued)

Weight	Minimum Moment 100	Maximum Moment 100	Weight	Minimum Moment 100	Maximum Moment 100
2100	1617	1800	2600	2037	2224
2110	1625	1808	2610	2048	2232
2120	1632	1817	2620	2058	2239
2130	1640	1825	2630	2069	2247
2140	1648	1834	2640	2080	2255
2150	1656	1843	2650	2090	2263
2160	1663	1851	2660	2101	2271
2170	1671	1860	2670	2112	2279
2180	1679	1868	2680	2123	2287
2190	1686	1877	2690	2133	2295
2200	1694	1885	2700	2144	2303
2210	1702	1894	2710	2155	2311
2220	1709	1903	2720	2166	2319
2230	1717	1911	2730	2177	2326
2240	1725	1920	2740	2188	2334
2250	1733	1928	2750	2199	2342
2260	1740	1937	2760	2210	2350
2270	1748	1945	2770	2221	2358
2280	1756	1954	2780	2232	2366
2290	1763	1963	2790	2243	2374
2300	1771	1971			
2310	1779	1980	2800	2254	2381
2320	1786	1988	2810	2265	2389
2330	1794	1997	2820	2276	2397
2340	1802	2005	2830	2287	2405
2350	1810	2014	2840	2298	2413
2360	1817	2023	2850	2309	2421
2370	1825	2031	2860	2320	2428
2380	1833	2040	2870	2332	2436
2390	1840	2048	2880	2343	2444
			2890	2354	2452
2400	1848	2057	2900	2365	2460
2410	1856	2065	2910	2377	2468
2420	1863	2074	2920	2388	2475
2430	1871	2083	2930	2399	2483
2440	1879	2091	2940	2411	2491
2450	1887	2100	2950	2422	2499
2460	1894	2108			
2470	1902	2117			
2480	1911	2125			
2490	1921	2134			
2500	1932	2143			
2510	1942	2151			
2520	1953	2160			
2530	1963	2168			
2540	1974	2176			
2550	1984	2184			
2560	1995	2192			
2570	2005	2200			
2580	2016	2208			
2590	2026	2216			

FIGURE 34.—Airplane Weight and Balance Tables.

3668. (Refer to figures 33 and 34 on pages 3-32 and 3-33.) Determine if the airplane weight and balance is within limits.

Front seat occupants .... 415 lb
Rear seat occupants .... 110 lb
Fuel, main tanks .... 44 gal
Fuel, aux. tanks .... 19 gal
Baggage .... 32 lb

A — 19 pounds overweight, CG within limits.
B — 19 pounds overweight, CG out of limits forward.
C — Weight within limits, CG out of limits.

3669. (Refer to figure 35 on page 3-36.) What is the maximum amount of baggage that may be loaded aboard the airplane for the CG to remain within the moment envelope?

	WEIGHT (LB)	MOM/1000
Empty weight	1,350	51.5
Pilot and front passenger	250	—
Rear passengers	400	—
Baggage	—	—
Fuel, 30 gal	—	—
Oil, 8 qt	—	-0.2

A — 105 pounds.
B — 110 pounds.
C — 120 pounds.

3668. Answer C. JSPPM 3-78 (PHB)
First, construct a weight and moment table.

	WEIGHT (lbs)	ARM (in)	MOMENT (lb-in/100)
Empty weight	2,015		1,554.0
Front seat	415	85	352.8
Rear seat	110	121	133.1
Fuel 44 gal.	264	75	198.0
Aux 19 gal.	114	94	107.2
Baggage	32	140	44.8
Totals	2,950		2,389.9

The total weight is at the maximum limit. Divide total moments by total weight to find the CG of 81.0, which is outside the limits.

$$CG = \frac{2{,}389.9 \times 100}{2{,}950} = 81.0$$

3669. Answer A. JSPPM 3-76 (PHB)
Refer to Figure 35 to convert oil and fuel to pounds. Add up the known weights, for a total of 2,195 pounds. Subtract 2,195 pounds from 2,300 max weight to find the maximum possible baggage weight of 105 pounds. While it appears that choice A is the only correct answer, it is a good idea to check the CG limits. Use the LOADING GRAPH and find the moment for each weight.

	WEIGHT (lbs)	MOMENT (lb-in/100)
Empty wt.	1,350	51.5
Front seat	250	9.4
Rear seat	400	29.3
Fuel 30 gal	180	8.7
Oil 8 qts	15	-0.2
Subtotal	2,195	98.7
Baggage	105	10.0
Totals	2,300	108.7

Total the moments and locate the maximum weight on the CENTER OF GRAVITY MOMENT ENVELOPE graph. The intersection of the loaded weight and moment is at the upper right-hand corner of the normal category envelope, and is just barely within limits.

Aircraft Systems and Performance

3670. (Refer to figure 35 on page 3-36.) Calculate the moment of the airplane and determine which category is applicable.

	WEIGHT (LB)	MOM/1000
Empty weight	1,350	51.5
Pilot and front pass	310	—
Rear passengers	96	—
Fuel, 38 gal	—	—
Oil, 8 qt	—	-0.2

A— 79.2, utility category.
B— 80.8, utility category.
C— 81.2, normal category

3670. Answer B. JSPPM 3-76 (PHB)
Complete the table of weights and moments, using the LOADING GRAPH

	WEIGHT (lbs)	MOMENT (lb-in/100)
Empty wt	1,350	51.5
Front seat	310	11.6
Rear seat	96	7.0
Fuel 38 gal	228	11.0
Oil 8 qts	15	-0.2
Totals	1,999	80.9

The total moment is 80.9. Use the CENTER OF GRAVITY MOMENT ENVELOPE graph to find the total weight and total moment. The intersection falls within the upper right-hand corner of the utility category envelope.

3671. (Refer to figure 35 on page 3-36.) What is the maximum amount of fuel that may be aboard the airplane on takeoff if loaded as follows.

	WEIGHT (LB)	MOM/1000
Empty weight	1,350	51.5
Pilot and front passenger	340	—
Rear passengers	310	—
Baggage	45	—
Oil, 8 qt	—	—

A— 24 gallons.
B— 32 gallons.
C— 40 gallons.

3671. Answer C. JSPPM 3-76 (PHB)
Complete the table of weights and moments, using the LOADING GRAPH.

	WEIGHT (lbs)	MOMENT (lb-in/100)
Empty wt	1,350	51.5
Front seat	340	12.7
Rear seat	310	22.6
Baggage	45	4.3
Oil 8 qts	15	-0.2
Subtotal	2060	90.9
Fuel 40 gal	240	11.5
Totals	2,300	102.4

The total weight without fuel is 2,060 pounds. This is 240 pounds below the maximum of 2,300 pounds. Dividing by 6 lb/gal, the maximum fuel load is 40 gallons. It is a good idea to check the moments as well. The total moment of 102.4 is within the CG envelope, so 40 gallons is acceptable.

3672. (Refer to figure 35 on page 3-36.) Determine the moment with the following data:

	WEIGHT (LB)	MOM/1000
Empty weight	1,350	51.5
Pilot and front passenger	340	—
Fuel (std. tanks)	Capacity	—
Oil, 8 qt	—	—

A— 69.9 pound-inches.
B— 74.9 pound-inches.
C— 77.6 pound-inches.

3672. Answer B. JSPPM 3-76 (PHB)
Use the LOADING GRAPH to determine the moments. Add these to find the total moment of 74.9.

	WEIGHT (lbs)	MOMENT (lb-in/100)
Empty wt	1,350	51.5
Front seat	340	12.6
Fuel 38 gal	228	11.0
Oil 8 qts	15	-0.2
Totals	1,933	74.9

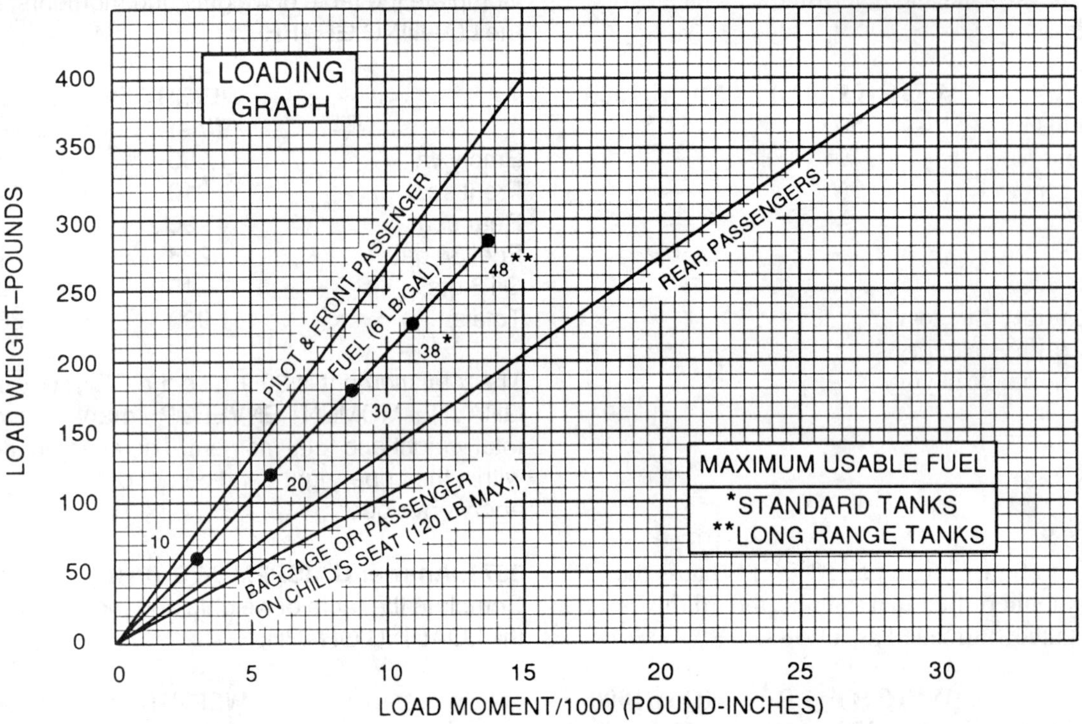

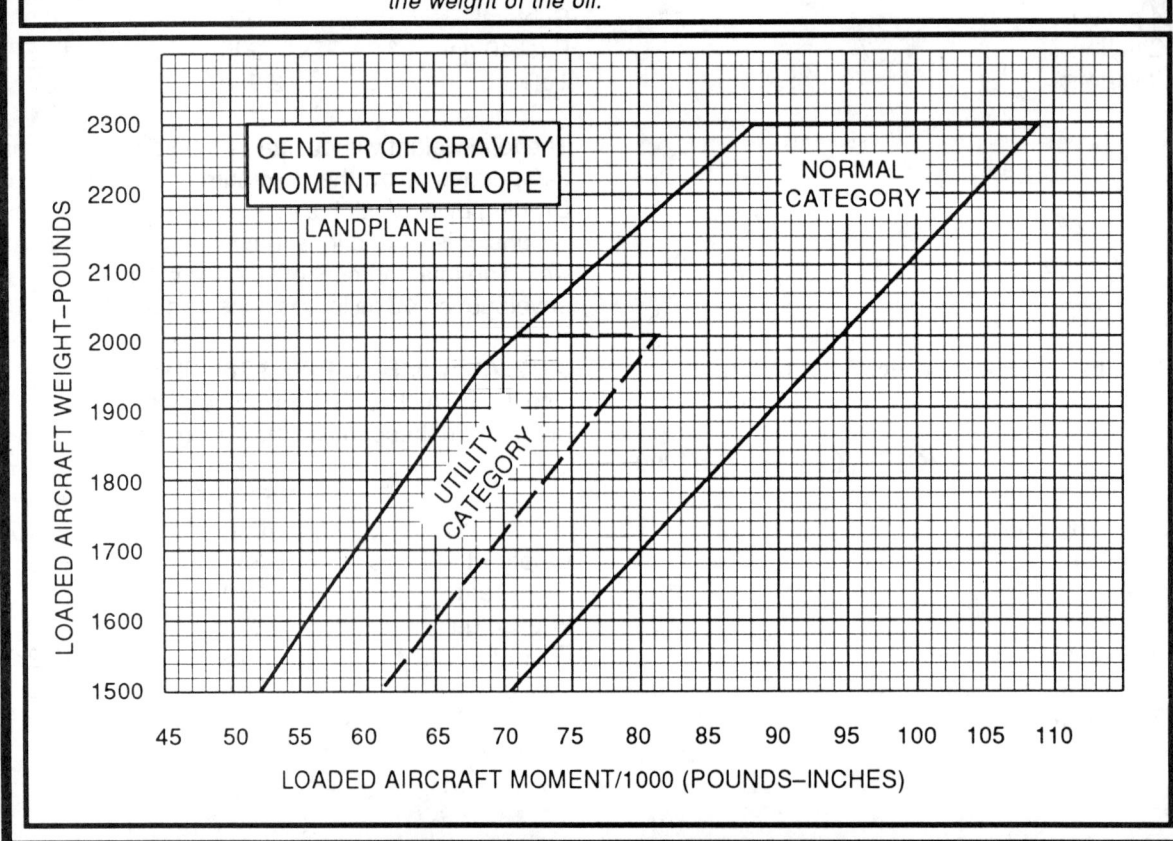

FIGURE 35.—Airplane Weight and Balance Graphs.

3673. (Refer to figure 35.) Determine the aircraft loaded moment and the aircraft category.

	WEIGHT (LB)	MOM/1000
Empty weight	1,350	51.5
Pilot and front pass	380	—
Fuel, 48 gal	288	—
Oil, 8 qt	—	—

A — 78.2, normal category.
B — 79.2, normal category.
C — 80.4, utility category.

3674. (Refer to figures 33 and 34 on pages 3-32 and 3-33.) Upon landing, the front passenger (180 pounds) departs the airplane. A rear passenger (204 pounds) moves to the front passenger position. What effect does this have on the CG if the airplane weighed 2,690 pounds and the MOM/100 was 2,260 just prior to the passenger transfer?

A — The CG moves forward approximately 3 inches.
B — The weight changes, but the CG is not affected.
C — The CG moves forward approximately 0.1 inch.

3673. Answer B. JSPPM 3-76 (PHB)
Use the LOADING GRAPH to determine the moments.

	WEIGHT (lbs)	MOMENT (lb-in/100)
Empty wt	1,350	51.5
Front seat	380	14.2
Fuel 48 gal	288	13.7
Oil 8 qts	15	-0.2
Totals	2,033	79.2

The total weight is 2,033 pounds, and the total moment is 79.2. Use the CENTER OF GRAVITY MOMENT ENVELOPE graph with the total weight and total moment. The intersection falls within the normal category, and outside the utility category.

3674. Answer A. JSPPM 3-79 (PHB)
Use the weight shift formula to determine how far the CG shifts.

$$\frac{\text{Weight Moved}}{\text{Weight of Airplane}} = \frac{\text{Distance CG Moves}}{\text{Dist. Btwn. Arms}}$$

The front passenger that departs reduces the total weight of the aircraft by 180 pounds (2,690 - 180 = 2,510.) The weight that is moved is the rear passenger (204 pounds). The arms for the front and rear passenger seats are found in Figure 33, and the difference is 121 - 85 = 36.

$$\frac{204}{2,510} = \frac{\text{Distance CG Moves}}{36}$$

$$\text{Distance CG Moves} = \frac{204 \times 36}{2,510} = 2.93$$

The change in CG is approximately 2.93, which is closest to answer (A).

3675. (Refer to figures 33 and 34 on pages 3-32 and 3-33.) Which action can adjust the airplane's weight to maximum gross weight and the CG within limits for takeoff?

Front seat occupants .... 425 lb
Rear seat occupants .... 300 lb
Fuel, main tanks .... 44 gal

A — Drain 12 gallons of fuel.
B — Drain 9 gallons of fuel.
C — Transfer 12 gallons of fuel from the main tanks to the auxiliary tanks.

3675. Answer B. JSPPM 3-79 (PHB)
Complete the weight and moment table as shown below.

	WEIGHT (lbs)	ARM (in)	MOMENT (lb-in/100)
Empty wt	2,015		1,554.0
Front seat	425	85	361.3
Rear seat	300	121	363.0
Fuel 44 gal	264	75	198.0
Total	3,004		2,476.3
Max wt	-2,950		
	54		

The total weight of 3,004 is 54 pounds over maximum weight. If we drain 54 pounds of fuel to attain the maximum weight, this is equal to 9 gallons (54 pounds ÷ 6 = 9 gallons). Now adjust the moments by entering a new fuel moment for the 35 gallons that remain, and find a total moment of 2,436.

	WEIGHT (lbs)	ARM (in)	MOMENT (lb-in/100)
Empty wt	2,015		1,554.0
Front seat	425	85	361.3
Rear seat	300	121	363.0
Fuel 35 gal	210	75	157.5
Total	2,950		2,435.8

Using the table in Figure 34, you'll find the total weight and total moment are within the limits.

3676. (Refer to figures 33 and 34 on pages 3-32 and 3-33.) What effect does a 35-gallon fuel burn (main tanks) have on the weight and balance if the airplane weighed 2,890 pounds and the MOM/100 was 2,452 at takeoff.

A — Weight is reduced by 210 pounds and the CG is aft of limits.
B — Weight is reduced by 210 pounds and the CG is unaffected.
C — Weight is reduced to 2,680 pounds and the CG moves forward.

3676. Answer A. JSPPM 3-79 (PHB)
Use the chart in Figure 33 to find the weight and moment for 35 gallons of fuel (main tanks), and subtract these values from the total weight and moment. The result is the total weight and moment after the fuel burn.

	WEIGHT (lbs)	MOMENT (lb-in/100)
Total	2,890	2,452
Fuel 35 gal	-210	-158
Adjusted	2,680	2,294

Refer to the chart in figure 34 for the weight of 2,680. The moment of 2,294 exceeds the maximum (aft) CG limit.

Aircraft Systems and Performance

3677. (Refer to figures 33 and 34 on pages 3-32 and 3-33.) With the airplane loaded as follows, what action can be taken to balance the airplane?

Front seat occupants .... 411 lb
Rear seat occupants .... 100 lb
Main wing tanks .... 44 gal

A — Fill the auxiliary wing tanks.
B — Add a 100-pound weight to the baggage compartment.
C — Transfer 10 gallons of fuel from the main tanks to the auxiliary tanks.

3677. Answer B. JSPPM 3-79 (PHB)
Construct the table as shown below, find the subtotal weight and moment, and use the Chart in Figure 34. The subtotal moment (2,222.4) at the original weight is less than the minimum (forward) limit.

	WEIGHT (lbs)	ARM (in)	MOMENT (lb-in/100)
Empty wt	2,015		1,554.0
Front seat	411	85	349.4
Rear seat	100	121	121.0
Fuel 44 gal	264	75	198.0
Subtotal	2,790		2,222.4
Baggage	100		140.0
Total	2,890		2,362.4

Since the baggage compartment is in an aft location, adding weight to this part of the airplane will shift the CG aft. Add the baggage weight and moment to the subtotals to find adjusted totals. Check the chart in Figure 34 to ensure that the moment is within limits. Answer (A) is wrong because if the auxiliary wing tanks are filled and the total weight and moment are adjusted, the moment will be less than the minimum. To check answer (C), find the original CG using the subtotals:

$$CG = \frac{\text{Total Moments}}{\text{Total Weight}} = \frac{2222.4}{2,790} = 79.7$$

Then use the weight shift formula:

$$\frac{\text{Weight Moved}}{\text{Weight of Airplane}} = \frac{\text{Distance CG Moves}}{\text{Dist. Btwn. Arms}}$$

The weight of fuel is 10 gals x 6 lb/gal = 60 lbs. The distance between arms is 94 - 75 = 19. Since the fuel is transferred from an arm of 75 to an arm of 94, the CG moves aft 0.4 inches.

$$\frac{60}{2,790} = \frac{\text{Distance CG Moves}}{19}$$

$$\text{Distance CG Moves} = \frac{60 \times 19}{2,790} = 0.4$$

The new CG is 80.1 (79.7 + 0.4). Then, find the new moment on the chart in Figure 34. The new moment is less than the minimum.

METEOROLOGY FOR PILOTS

CHAPTER 4

SECTION A
BASIC WEATHER THEORY

Section A provides a basic framework for further study of weather and its significance to flight operations. The main subject areas include the atmosphere, atmospheric circulation/pressure, temperature, and moisture (clouds, fog, precipitation, and frost). FAA test questions that are covered in this section include:

3381, 3382, 3395, 3397, 3398, 3399, 3400, 3401, 3444, 3450.

3381. Every physical process of weather is accompanied by, or is the result of, a

A — movement of air.
B — pressure differential.
C — heat exchange.

3382. What causes variations in altimeter settings between weather reporting points?

A — Unequal heating of the Earth's surface.
B — Variation of terrain elevation.
C — Coriolis force.

3395. The wind at 5,000 feet AGL is southwesterly while the surface wind is southerly. This difference in direction is primarily due to

A — stronger pressure gradient at higher altitudes.
B — friction between the wind and the surface.
C — stronger Coriolis force at the surface.

3381. Answer C. JSPPM 4-10 (AW)
Every physical process of weather such as heating, cooling, evaporation, and condensation, is caused by, or is the result of, a heat exchange. Answers (A) and (B) are wrong because air movement and pressure differential are not always involved in the physical processes of weather.

3382. Answer A. JSPPM 4-5 (AW)
Temperature changes cause variations in air pressure and density. Because the earth's surface is heated unevenly, altimeter settings will be different between weather stations. Answer (B) is wrong because altimeter settings are referenced to a standard datum, and elevation alone is not the cause of variations. Answer (C) is incorrect because Coriolis force deflects the circulation of air masses, but does not directly cause variations in altimeter settings.

3395. Answer B. JSPPM 4-7 (AW)
Above 2,000 feet AGL, wind flows along isobars. Below that altitude, friction with the earth's surface deflects the wind. Answer (A) is wrong because the pressure gradient is not always stronger at higher altitudes. Answer (C) is wrong because winds are generally calmer at lower altitudes. As a result, Coriolis force is not as effective as friction near the surface.

3397. What is meant by the term "dewpoint"?

A — The temperature at which condensation and evaporation are equal.
B — The temperature at which dew will always form.
C — The temperature to which air must be cooled to become saturated.

3398. The amount of water vapor which air can hold depends on the

A — dewpoint.
B — air temperature.
C — stability of the air.

3399. Clouds, fog, or dew will always form when

A — water vapor condenses.
B — water vapor is present.
C — relative humidity reaches 100 percent.

3400. What are the processes by which moisture is added to unsaturated air?

A — Evaporation and sublimation.
B — Heating and condensation.
C — Supersaturation and evaporation.

3401. Which conditions result in the formation of frost?

A — The temperature of the collecting surface is at or below freezing when small droplets of moisture fall on the surface.
B — The temperature of the collecting surface is at or below the dewpoint of the adjacent air and the dewpoint is below freezing.
C — The temperature of the surrounding air is at or below freezing when small drops of moisture fall on the collecting surface.

3397. Answer C. JSPPM 4-10 (AW)
When air is cooled to its dewpoint, it can hold no more moisture, and is said to be saturated. Answer (A) is incorrect because dewpoint is not a measure of condensation or evaporation. Answer (B) is wrong because the formation of dew requires the surface temperature of objects to cool below the dewpoint of the surrounding air.

3398. Answer B. JSPPM 4-10 (AW)
The amount of moisture in the air primarily depends on the temperature. For example, warm air can hold more moisture than cool air. The dewpoint (answer A) is the temperature at which the air reaches saturation (see explanation for Question 3397). Answer (C) is wrong because stability of the air does not directly affect the moisture content.

3399. Answer A. JSPPM 4-10 (AW)
Condensation occurs when water vapor changes to liquid form. Examples are when water vapor changes to clouds, fog, or dew. Answer (B) is incorrect, because the water vapor, which is present in the air, must be cooled to a temperature at or near the dewpoint before it condenses to its liquid form. Relative humidity (answer C) is a measure of how much water the air can hold. At 100% relative humidity, the air is saturated, but the water vapor may not always condense to form clouds, fog, or dew.

3400. Answer A. JSPPM 4-10 (AW)
Evaporation occurs when liquid water changes to water vapor. Sublimation is the changing of ice directly to water vapor. Both processes add moisture to the air. Answer (B) is wrong because condensation removes water vapor from the air by changing it to liquid form. Answer (C) is wrong because supersaturation can occur only in air that is already saturated after it has been cooled from a higher temperature to a temperature below the point at which saturation occurs.

3401. Answer B. JSPPM 4-12 (AW)
When the dewpoint of the surrounding air is below freezing, and the collecting surface is at or below the dewpoint, water vapor sublimates directly into ice crystals or frost instead of condensing into dew. Answer (A) describes conditions resulting in frozen dew or raindrops, which form hard, clear ice, not frost. Answer (C) is incorrect because the collecting surface must be below the dewpoint, and the dewpoint must be below freezing.

3444. If the temperature/dewpoint spread is small and decreasing, and the temperature is 62°F, what type weather is most likely to develop?

A — Freezing precipitation.
B — Thunderstorms.
C — Fog or low clouds.

3444. Answer C. JSPPM 4-12 (AW)
When the temperature/dewpoint spread decreases to zero, the likely result is the condensation of water vapor into visible moisture, such as fog or low clouds. Answer (A) is incorrect, since 62°F is well above freezing, and the water will be in liquid form, not freezing precipitation. Answer (B) is wrong because thunderstorms are associated with unstable air rather than temperature/dewpoint spread.

3450. Convective circulation patterns associated with sea breezes are caused by

A — warm, dense air moving inland from over the water.
B — water absorbing and radiating heat faster than the land.
C — cool, dense air moving inland from over the water.

3450. Answer C. JSPPM 4-9 (AW)
During the day, land surfaces become warmer than the adjacent water surfaces. This warms the air above the land causing the air to rise. The rising air is replaced by the inland flow of cooler, denser air located over the water. As the warm air flows over the water it cools and descends. This starts the cycle all over again. During the night, the process is reversed as the land cools off faster than the water. Answer (A) is wrong because cool, not warm, air moves inland. Answer (B) is incorrect because sea breezes are a result of the land, not the water, absorbing and radiating heat faster.

SECTION B
WEATHER PATTERNS

This section continues with discussions about the interaction of the forces affecting weather. Atmospheric stability, cloud types, air masses, and fronts are the major topics. Test questions in Section B are listed below:

   3383, 3384, 3385, 3402, 3403, 3404, 3405, 3406, 3407, 3408, 3409, 3410, 3412, 3413, 3414, 3415, 3416, 3421, 3422, 3423, 3424.

3383. A temperature inversion would most likely result in which weather condition?

A — Clouds with extensive vertical development above an inversion aloft.
B — Good visibility in the lower levels of the atmosphere and poor visibility above an inversion aloft.
C — An increase in temperature as altitude is increased.

3383. Answer C. JSPPM 4-16 (AW)
Normally, temperature decreases with altitude. During an inversion, cooler air is trapped beneath a warmer layer of air. Therefore, temperature increases with altitude. Answer (A) is wrong since inversions occur in stable air, and vertical development of clouds requires unstable air. Answer (B) is incorrect because weather and pollutants are trapped beneath inversions, and visibility near the surface is usually poor.

3384. The most frequent type of ground or surface-based temperature inversion is that which is produced by

A — terrestrial radiation on a clear, relatively still night.
B — warm air being lifted rapidly aloft in the vicinity of mountainous terrain.
C — the movement of colder air under warm air, or the movement of warm air over cold air.

3385. Which weather conditions should be expected beneath a low-level temperature inversion layer when the relative humidity is high?

A — Smooth air, poor visibility, fog, haze, or low clouds.
B — Light wind shear, poor visibility, haze, and light rain.
C — Turbulent air, poor visibility, fog, low stratus type clouds, and shower precipitation.

3402. The presence of ice pellets at the surface is evidence that there

A — are thunderstorms in the area.
B — has been cold frontal passage.
C — is a temperature inversion with freezing rain at a higher altitude.

3403. What measurement can be used to determine the stability of the atmosphere?

A — Atmospheric pressure.
B — Actual lapse rate.
C — Surface temperature.

3404. What would decrease the stability of an air mass?

A — Warming from below.
B — Cooling from below.
C — Decrease in water vapor.

3384. Answer A. JSPPM 4-16 (AW)
An inversion commonly forms on clear, cool nights when the ground radiates heat and cools faster than the overlying air. Answers (B) and (C) are not examples of surface-based temperature inversions. Answer (B) describes orographic lifting of air over rising terrain and answer (C) describes a cold front inversion.

3385. Answer A. JSPPM 4-16 (AW)
Low-level temperature inversions normally occur in stable, smooth air, with poor visibility due to trapped pollutants which are commonly referred to as condensation nuclei. In addition, high humidity tends to cause formation of fog and low clouds. Answers (B) and (C) are not entirely correct, because wind shear, turbulence, and showery precipitation are uncharacteristic conditions in the stable air below the inversion layer.

3402. Answer C. JSPPM 4-12 (AW)
Due to a temperature inversion, a warm layer of air is aloft and keeps the rain in liquid form. As the rain falls through colder air, it begins to freeze, finally turning into ice pellets. Ice pellets always indicate freezing rain at a higher altitude. Ice pellets can form under various conditions, and do not necessarily indicate thunderstorms (answer A). Answer (B) is wrong because ice pellets may be formed in either a warm front or a cold front.

3403. Answer B. JSPPM 4-15 (AW)
The stability of air refers to its resistance to displacement upward or downward; it is determined by the actual lapse rate. Lapse rate generally refers to the decrease in temperature with an increase in altitude. A high lapse rate tends to indicate unstable air, and a low lapse rate is an indicator of stability in the atmosphere. Answers (A) and (C) are wrong because air pressure and surface temperature do not directly affect stability.

3404. Answer A. JSPPM 4-14 (AW)
Stability is altered by a change in the lapse rate of an air mass. Warming from below or cooling from above will increase the lapse rate and make the air less stable. Cooling from below (answer B) and a decrease in water vapor (answer C) both cause the air to become more dense and tend to increase stability.

3405. What is a characteristic of stable air?

A — Stratiform clouds.
B — Unlimited visibility.
C — Cumulus clouds.

3406. Moist, stable air flowing upslope can be expected to

A — produce stratus type clouds.
B — cause showers and thunderstorms.
C — develop convective turbulence.

3407. If an unstable air mass is forced upward, what type clouds can be expected?

A — Stratus clouds with little vertical development.
B — Stratus clouds with considerable associated turbulence.
C — Clouds with considerable vertical development and associated turbulence.

3408. What feature is associated with a temperature inversion?

A — A stable layer of air.
B — An unstable layer of air.
C — Chinook winds on mountain slopes.

3409. What is the approximate base of the cumulus clouds if the surface air temperature at 1,000 feet MSL is 70°F and the dewpoint is 48°F?

A — 4,000 feet MSL.
B — 5,000 feet MSL.
C — 6,000 feet MSL.

3410. At approximately what altitude above the surface would the pilot expect the base of cumuliform clouds if the surface air temperature is 82°F and the dewpoint is 38°F?

A — 9,000 feet AGL.
B — 10,000 feet AGL.
C — 11,000 feet AGL.

3412. What are characteristics of a moist, unstable air mass?

A — Cumuliform clouds and showery precipitation.
B — Poor visibility and smooth air.
C — Stratiform clouds and showery precipitation.

3405. Answer A. JSPPM 4-17 (AW)
There is very little vertical development of clouds in stable air, and stratiform clouds and poor visibility are typical. Cumulus clouds and good visibility are indicators of unstable air.

3406. Answer A. JSPPM 4-18 (AW)
Stratus clouds are produced in stable air. When moist air flows upslope it cools to its saturation point, and clouds are formed. Showers and thunderstorms (answer B) and convective turbulence (answer C) are indicative of unstable air.

3407. Answer C. JSPPM 4-20 (AW)
Clouds with extensive vertical development are formed when unstable air is lifted. These cumulus type clouds are associated with moderate to severe turbulence. Stratus clouds (answers A and B) are a characteristic of smooth, stable air.

3408. Answer A. JSPPM 4-16 (AW)
Temperature inversions occur in stable air. Inversions cannot form in unstable air (answer B). As Chinook winds (answer C) descend, the temperature rises. This is the opposite of an inversion (cooler air under a warmer layer). In the U.S., the typical example of Chinook winds is the downslope, easterly flow from the Rocky Mountains.

3409. Answer C. JSPPM 4-16 (AW)
Cloud bases can be estimated by using a lapse rate of 4.5° F per 1,000 feet and the temperature/dewpoint spread (70 - 48 = 22). Divide 22 by 4.5 to find the approximate cloud base in thousands of feet. In this case, the cloud bases will be 4,889 (22 ÷ 4.5 x 1,000) feet above the surface, or rounded to 5,000 feet. Since the surface is 1,000 feet MSL, the cloud base should be approximately 6,000 feet MSL.

3410. Answer B. JSPPM 4-16 (AW)
See explanation for Question 3409. The temperature/dewpoint spread is 44 (82 - 38). Divide 44 by the lapse rate of 4.5°F per 1,000 feet to find cloud bases at 9,778 feet AGL, rounded to 10,000 feet AGL.

3412. Answer A. JSPPM 4-16 (AW)
Cumuliform clouds are indicative of unstable air. These clouds normally produce showery, not continuous, precipitation. Poor visibility, smooth air (answer B), and stratiform clouds (answer C) are characteristic of stable air.

3413. What are characteristics of unstable air?

A — Turbulence and good surface visibility.
B — Turbulence and poor surface visibility.
C — Nimbostratus clouds and good surface visibility.

3414. A stable air mass is most likely to have which characteristic?

A — Showery precipitation.
B — Turbulent air.
C — Smooth air.

3415. The suffix "nimbus," used in naming clouds, means

A — a cloud with extensive vertical development.
B — a rain cloud.
C — a middle cloud containing ice pellets.

3416. Clouds are divided into four families according to their

A — outward shape.
B — height range.
C — composition.

3421. The boundary between two different air masses is referred to as a

A — frontolysis.
B — frontogenesis.
C — front.

3422. One of the most easily recognized discontinuities across a front is

A — a change in temperature.
B — an increase in cloud coverage.
C — an increase in relative humidity.

3423. One weather phenomenon which will always occur when flying across a front is a change in the

A — wind direction.
B — type of precipitation.
C — stability of the air mass.

3413. Answer A. JSPPM 4-17 (AW)
The lifting motion of unstable air produces turbulence. Clouds and pollutants are not trapped as they are in stable layers of air, and good visibility is typical with unstable air. Poor surface visibility (answer B) and nimbostratus clouds (answer C) are typical of stable air masses.

3414. Answer C. JSPPM 4-17 (AW)
Stable air resists the lifting motion that is associated with turbulence, and is typically smooth. Showery precipitation (answer A) and turbulent air (answer B) are characteristics of unstable air.

3415. Answer B. JSPPM 4-18 (AW)
The word "nimbus" is the Latin word for rainstorm or cloud, and is used today to designate rain clouds, such as cumulonimbus or nimbostratus. Answer (A) describes a cumuliform cloud which commonly is called a towering cumulus. Answer (C) is wrong because nimbus means a rain cloud, not a middle cloud, or a cloud with ice pellets.

3416. Answer B. JSPPM 4-18 (AW)
Clouds are also grouped by families according to the altitudes (height range). The four families are low, middle, high, and clouds with extensive vertical development. Outward shape (answer A) and composition (answer C) are used to determine specific cloud types, such as cumulus, nimbostratus, and cirrus. These are not characteristics of the family classification.

3421. Answer C. JSPPM 4-24 (AW)
The boundary area where two air masses of different properties meet is called a front. Frontolysis (answer A) is incorrect because it means the dissipation of a weather front. Frontogenesis (answer B) means the initial formation of a front.

3422. Answer A. JSPPM 4-24 (AW)
Since a front is the boundary between air masses of differing temperatures, one of the easiest ways to recognize frontal passage is the change in temperature. Cloud coverage (answer B) may increase or decrease, depending on the type of front. A change in relative humidity (answer C) also depends on the type of front.

3423. Answer A. JSPPM 4-24 (AW)
A shift in wind direction always occurs across a front. A change in the type of precipitation (answer B) sometimes, but not always, accompanies frontal passage. The same is true of stability (answer C); it does not always change.

3424. Steady precipitation preceding a front is an indication of

A — stratiform clouds with moderate turbulence.
B — cumuliform clouds with little or no turbulence.
C — stratiform clouds with little or no turbulence.

3424. Answer C. JSPPM 4-26 (AW)
Steady precipitation, stratiform clouds, and little or no turbulence are all typical of stable air. Stratiform clouds and steady precipitation are not usually associated with moderate turbulence (answer A). Cumuliform clouds are found in unstable air and area accompanied by turbulence and showery precipitation (answer B).

SECTION C
WEATHER HAZARDS

This section covers such weather hazards as thunderstorms, turbulence, structural icing, and restrictions to visibility. This discussion addresses causes as well as the hazardous effects. FAA Written Test questions in Section C include:

3206, 3417, 3418, 3419, 3420, 3425, 3426, 3427, 3428, 3429, 3430, 3431, 3432, 3433, 3434, 3435, 3436, 3437, 3438, 3439, 3440, 3441, 3442, 3443, 3445, 3446, 3447, 3452, 3824, 3825, 3826, 3827, 3828, 3829, 3830.

3206. How will frost on the wings of an airplane affect takeoff performance?

A — Frost will disrupt the smooth flow of air over the wing, adversely affecting its lifting capability.
B — Frost will change the camber of the wing, increasing its lifting capability.
C — Frost will cause the airplane to become airborne with a higher angle of attack, decreasing the stall speed.

3206. Answer A. JSPPM 4-38 (PHB)
Frost disrupts the smooth airflow over the wing and can cause early separation of the airflow, resulting in a loss of lift. Frost does not significantly change the camber (answer B), but it can disrupt the airflow and decrease the lift. The decreased lift caused by frost can cause the stall speed to increase, not decrease (answer C).

3417. An almond or lens-shaped cloud which appears stationary, but which may contain winds of 50 knots or more, is referred to as

A — an inactive frontal cloud.
B — a funnel cloud.
C — a lenticular cloud.

3417. Answer C. JSPPM 4-35 (AW)
Lenticular clouds are the lens-shaped clouds that form at the crests of mountain waves. An inactive frontal cloud (answer A) is obviously an incorrect choice. Frontal clouds with 50-knot winds would not be stationary. A funnel cloud (answer B) is associated with a tornado, and is neither lens-shaped or stationary.

3418. Crests of standing mountain waves may be marked by stationary, lens-shaped clouds known as

A — mammatocumulus clouds.
B — standing lenticular clouds.
C — roll clouds.

3418. Answer B. JSPPM 4-35 (AW)
See explanation for Question 3417. Mammatocumulus clouds (answer A) are typically associated with thunderstorms, not mountain waves. Roll clouds (answer C) are commonly found on the leading edge of thunderstorms, not mountain waves.

3419. What clouds have the greatest turbulence?

A — Towering cumulus.
B — Cumulonimbus.
C — Nimbostratus.

3420. What cloud types would indicate convective turbulence?

A — Cirrus clouds.
B — Nimbostratus clouds.
C — Towering cumulus clouds.

3425. Possible mountain wave turbulence could be anticipated when winds of 40 knots or greater blow

A — across a mountain ridge, and the air is stable.
B — down a mountain valley, and the air is unstable.
C — parallel to a mountain peak, and the air is stable.

3426. Where does wind shear occur?

A — Only at higher altitudes.
B — Only at lower altitudes.
C — At all altitudes, in all directions.

3427. When may hazardous wind shear be expected?

A — When stable air crosses a mountain barrier where it tends to flow in layers forming lenticular clouds.
B — In areas of low-level temperature inversion, frontal zones, and clear air turbulence.
C — Following frontal passage when stratocumulus clouds form indicating mechanical mixing.

3428. A pilot can expect a wind shear zone in a temperature inversion whenever the windspeed at 2,000 to 4,000 feet above the surface is at least

A — 10 knots.
B — 15 knots.
C — 25 knots.

3419. Answer B. JSPPM 4-32 (AW)
Cumulonimbus clouds, which form thunderstorms and tornadoes, produce the most severe turbulence. Towering cumulus clouds (answer A) will have some turbulence, but not nearly as severe as a thunderstorm. Nimbostratus (answer C), a type of stratus cloud, usually has little or no turbulence.

3420. Answer C. JSPPM 4-34 (AW)
Towering cumulus clouds are formed by convective currents, caused by rising heated air. These rising air currents cause convective turbulence. Cirrus clouds (answer A) are found at high altitude and are not formed by convection. Nimbostratus clouds (answer B) usually have little or no turbulence.

3425. Answer A. JSPPM 4-35 (AW)
Mountain waves are formed when strong winds (40 knots or greater) flow across a barrier, such as a mountain ridge. When the air is stable, the flow is laminar, or layered, and creates a series of waves. Unstable air that is forced upward tends to continue rising, often creating thunderstorms. Wind flowing down a valley (answer B) will not form mountain waves. Wind blowing parallel to a mountain peak (answer C) may create some turbulence, but a single peak would not normally cause a mountain wave.

3426. Answer C. JSPPM 4-33 (AW)
Wind shear can occur at middle and high altitudes near thunderstorms or the jet stream, and near the ground in the vicinity of thunderstorms or temperature inversions. The shear can be either vertical or horizontal. Answers (A) and (B) are wrong because wind shear can occur at any altitude.

3427. Answer B. JSPPM 4-33 (AW)
Wind shear can be found above a temperature inversion when the surface air is cold and calm, and the warmer layer above it is moving at 25 knots or more. Since frontal zones are identified by a shift in the wind, wind shear can be expected. Clear air turbulence can be associated with either vertical or horizontal wind shear. Answer (A) describes a mountain wave, and wind shear may or may not be present; some turbulence is common with stratocumulus clouds (answer C), but hazardous wind shear is not typical.

3428. Answer C. JSPPM 4-33 (AW)
A temperature inversion with light surface winds may form near the surface on a clear night. You can expect a shear zone in the inversion if the winds at 2,000 to 4,000 feet are 25 knots or more. Answers (A) and (B) are incorrect because of insufficient wind speed 2,000 to 4,000 feet above the surface.

3429. One in-flight condition necessary for structural icing to form is

A — small temperature/dewpoint spread.
B — stratiform clouds.
C — visible moisture.

3429. Answer C. JSPPM 4-38 (AW)
Structural icing requires two conditions to form: (1) visible moisture, such as rain or cloud droplets, and (2) temperature of the aircraft surface must be at or below freezing. A small temperature/dewpoint spread (answer A) may be present without visible moisture. Stratiform clouds (answer B) are not the only cloud types in which icing can occur.

3430. In which environment is aircraft structural ice most likely to have the highest accumulation rate?

A — Cumulus clouds with below freezing temperatures.
B — Freezing drizzle.
C — Freezing rain.

3430. Answer C. JSPPM 4-38 (AW)
The rate of structural ice accumulation is usually the highest in freezing rain below a frontal surface. As the rain falls through air with temperatures below freezing it becomes supercooled. The supercooled drops freeze on impact with the large water droplets, and heavy rain accelerates the build up. Cumulus clouds (answer A) have varying sizes of water drops, and may not always cause a rapid buildup of ice. Freezing drizzle (answer B) has smaller droplets and icing will build up more slowly than larger drops.

3431. Why is frost considered hazardous to flight?

A — Frost changes the basic aerodynamic shape of the airfoils, thereby decreasing lift.
B — Frost slows the airflow over the airfoils, thereby increasing control effectiveness.
C — Frost spoils the smooth flow of air over the wings, thereby decreasing lifting capability.

3431. Answer C. JSPPM 4-38 (AW)
See explanation for Question 3206. Frost does not significantly change the shape of the airfoil (answer A), but will cause early separation of the airflow. The airflow over the airfoil is not slowed (answer B), and control effectiveness is not increased.

3432. How does frost affect the lifting surfaces of an airplane on takeoff?

A — Frost may prevent the airplane from becoming airborne at normal takeoff speed.
B — Frost will change the camber of the wing, increasing lift during takeoff.
C — Frost may cause the airplane to become airborne with a lower angle of attack at a lower indicated airspeed.

3432. Answer A. JSPPM 4-38 (AW)
See explanations for Questions 3206 and 3431. By disrupting the airflow over the wings, frost can prevent an airplane from becoming airborne at the normal takeoff speed. Frost does not change the camber of a wing (answer B). The disrupted airflow would prevent the airplane from becoming airborne at a lower airspeed (answer C). Ground effect, not frost, is what causes an airplane to become airborne at a lower-than-normal angle of attack and airspeed.

3433. The conditions necessary for the formation of cumulonimbus clouds are a lifting action and

A — unstable air containing an excess of condensation nuclei.
B — unstable, moist air.
C — either stable or unstable air.

3433. Answer B. JSPPM 4-30 (AW)
Three conditions are normally required for the formation of cumulonimbus clouds. These are lifting action, instability, and moisture. An excess of condensation nuclei (answer A) would aid in the formation of water droplets, but moisture must also be present. Stable air (answer C) resists any upward (or downward) displacement and, therefore, inhibits the formation of cumulonimbus clouds.

3434. What feature is normally associated with the cumulus stage of a thunderstorm?

A — Roll cloud.
B — Continuous updraft.
C — Frequent lightning.

3434. Answer B. JSPPM 4-31 (AW)
In the early, or cumulus, stage of a thunderstorm, continuous updrafts cause the cloud to build upwards. A roll cloud (answer A) forms at the leading edge of a mature thunderstorm. Frequent lightning (answer C) is seldom found in the cumulus stage, but is typical of the mature stage.

3435. Which weather phenomenon signals the beginning of the mature stage of a thunderstorm?

A — The appearance of an anvil top.
B — Precipitation beginning to fall.
C — Maximum growth rate of the clouds.

3436. What conditions are necessary for the formation of thunderstorms?

A — High humidity, lifting force, and unstable conditions.
B — High humidity, high temperature, and cumulus clouds.
C — Lifting force, moist air, and extensive cloud cover.

3437. During the life cycle of a thunderstorm, which stage is characterized predominately by downdrafts?

A — Cumulus.
B — Dissipating.
C — Mature.

3438. Thunderstorms reach their greatest intensity during the

A — mature stage.
B — downdraft stage.
C — cumulus stage.

3439. Thunderstorms which generally produce the most intense hazard to aircraft are

A — squall line thunderstorms.
B — steady-state thunderstorms.
C — warm front thunderstorms.

3440. A nonfrontal, narrow band of active thunderstorms that often develop ahead of a cold front is known as a

A — prefrontal system.
B — squall line.
C — dryline.

3435. Answer B. JSPPM 4-31 (AW)
The mature stage of a thunderstorm begins when the rain drops grow too large to be supported by the updrafts, and precipitation begins to fall. An anvil top (answer A) appears as a thunderstorm reaches the dissipating stage, not the mature stage. Maximum growth rate of the clouds (answer C) occurs during the cumulus stage, not the mature stage.

3436. Answer A. JSPPM 4-30 (AW)
See explanation for Question 3433. As moist, unstable air is lifted, it builds cumulonimbus clouds, which form thunderstorms. Unless unstable conditions are present, thunderstorms will not form, so answers (B) and (C) are incorrect.

3437. Answer B. JSPPM 4-31 (AW)
As a thunderstorm dissipates, updrafts weaken and downdrafts become predominate. Also see explanations for Questions 3434 and 3435.

3438. Answer A. JSPPM 4-31 (AW)
Thunderstorms are most violent during the mature stage, with strong updrafts and downdrafts, severe turbulence, lightning, heavy rain, hail, strong surface winds, and gust fronts. Neither the dissipating stage, with its downdrafts (answer B), or the cumulus stage (answer C) and its updrafts, are as intense as the mature stage.

3439. Answer A. JSPPM 4-32 (AW)
Squall lines often contain severe steady-state thunderstorms and present the most hazardous conditions to aircraft. Steady-state thunderstorms (answer B) by themselves are hazardous, but squall line thunderstorms are the most severe. Warm front thunderstorms (answer C) are generally not as severe as squall line thunderstorms.

3440. Answer B. JSPPM 4-32 (AW)
Squall lines are a narrow band of thunderstorms that often develop ahead of a cold front. A prefrontal system (answer A) or dry line (answer C) are not terms used to describe this narrow band of thunderstorms.

3441. If there is thunderstorm activity in the vicinity of an airport at which you plan to land, which hazardous atmospheric phenomenon might be expected on the landing approach?

A — Precipitation static.
B — Wind shear turbulence.
C — Steady rain.

3442. Upon encountering severe turbulence, which flight condition should the pilot attempt to maintain?

A — Constant altitude and airspeed.
B — Constant angle of attack.
C — Level flight attitude.

3443. What situation is most conducive to the formation of radiation fog?

A — Warm, moist air over low, flatland areas on clear, calm nights.
B — Moist, tropical air moving over cold, offshore water.
C — The movement of cold air over much warmer water.

3445. In which situation is advection fog most likely to form?

A — A warm, moist air mass on the windward side of mountains.
B — An air mass moving inland from the coast in winter.
C — A light breeze blowing colder air out to sea.

3446. What types of fog depend upon wind in order to exist?

A — Radiation fog and ice fog.
B — Steam fog and ground fog.
C — Advection fog and upslope fog.

3447. Low-level turbulence can occur and icing can become hazardous in which type of fog?

A — Rain-induced fog.
B — Upslope fog.
C — Steam fog.

3441. Answer B. JSPPM 4-33 (AW)
In the vicinity of thunderstorms, hazardous wind-shear turbulence should always be expected. Precipitation static (answer A), known as "St. Elmo's fire," is not hazardous. Steady rain (answer C) is not normally found with thunderstorms, and is not hazardous unless it is freezing.

3442. Answer C. JSPPM 4-33 (AW)
If entering severe turbulence, the best procedure is to slow to a speed not faster than maneuvering airspeed and maintain a constant level flight attitude. Variations in airspeed and altitude should be expected and tolerated. Constant altitude and airspeed (answer A) or constant angle of attack (answer B) will be practically impossible to maintain.

3443. Answer A. JSPPM 4-38 (AW)
On clear, calm nights in flat areas, radiation fog forms when moist air cools to its dewpoint. Ground fog is a form of radiation fog. Fog that forms when warm, moist air moves over a cooler surface (answer B) is called advection fog. Cold, dry air moving over warmer water (answer C) causes the formation of steam fog.

3445. Answer B. JSPPM 4-38 (AW)
See explanation for Question 3443. When warmer air moves inland, advection fog is likely to form. Warm, moist air being lifted up a mountain slope (answer A) would form upslope fog. Colder air moving over the sea (answer C) would tend to form steam fog.

3446. Answer C. JSPPM 4-38 (AW)
See explanations for Questions 3443 and 3445. Answer (C) is the only correct choice since steam fog also requires the movement of air. Both ice fog and radiation fog (answer A), also known as ground fog (answer B), form in calm air.

3447. Answer C. JSPPM 4-39 (AW)
Steam fog is formed by cold, dry air moving over warmer water. As the water particles evaporate and rise, they often freeze and fall back into the water. Icing and low-level turbulence can result. Normally, turbulence and icing are not common with rain-induced fog (answer A) or upslope fog (answer B).

3452. Which weather phenomenon is always associated with a thunderstorm?

A — Lightning.
B — Heavy rain.
C — Hail.

3824. Wingtip vortices are created only when an aircraft is

A — operating at high airspeeds.
B — heavily loaded.
C — developing lift.

3825. The greatest vortex strength occurs when the generating aircraft is

A — light, dirty, and fast.
B — heavy, dirty, and fast.
C — heavy, clean, and slow.

3826. Wingtip vortices created by large aircraft tend to

A — sink below the aircraft generating turbulence.
B — rise into the traffic pattern.
C — rise into the takeoff or landing path of a crossing runway.

3827. When taking off or landing at an airport where heavy aircraft are operating, one should be particularly alert to the hazards of wingtip vortices because this turbulence tends to

A — rise from a crossing runway into the takeoff or landing path.
B — rise into the traffic pattern area surrounding the airport.
C — sink into the flightpath of aircraft operating below the aircraft generating the turbulence.

3828. The wind condition that requires maximum caution when avoiding wake turbulence on landing is a

A — light, quartering headwind.
B — light, quartering tailwind.
C — strong headwind.

3452. Answer A. JSPPM 4-32 (AW)
Since thunder is caused by lightning, the name thunderstorm implies that lightning is always associated with a thunderstorms. Heavy rain (answer B) or hail (answer C) may not always be present, depending on the severity of the storm.

3824. Answer C. JSPPM 4-36 (PHB)
Anytime an aircraft is developing lift, air flows over the wingtip to form wingtip vortices. High speed (answer A) would tend to decrease wingtip vortices, and the heavier an aircraft (answer B), the stronger the vortices, but they are created at any weight.

3825. Answer C. JSPPM 4-36 (PHB)
Heavy aircraft, in a clean configuration, flying at low airspeeds with high angles of attack, generate the strongest vortices. A "dirty" configuration, or gear and flaps down (answers A and B), reduces the vortex strength.

3826. Answer A. JSPPM 4-36 (PHB)
Wingtip vortices tend to sink below the flight path of the aircraft which generated them. Vortices are not known to rise (answers B and C).

3827. Answer C. JSPPM 4-36 (PHB)
See explanation for Question 3826.

3828. Answer B. JSPPM 4-36 (PHB)
A light, quartering tailwind is the most hazardous because it can move the upwind vortex over the runway and forward into the landing zone. A light, quartering heading (answer A) would move the upwind vortex over the runway, but would also move it back away from the landing zone. A strong headwind (answer C) would help dissipate wake turbulence, and is not as hazardous as a light, quartering tailwind.

3829. When landing behind a large aircraft, the pilot should avoid wake turbulence by staying

A — above the large aircraft's final approach path and landing beyond the large aircraft's touchdown point.
B — below the large aircraft's final approach path and landing before the large aircraft's touchdown point.
C — above the large aircraft's final approach path and landing before the large aircraft's touchdown point.

3829. Answer A. JSPPM 4-37 (PHB)
Since wake turbulence tends to sink, a following aircraft should stay above the large aircraft's flight path and land beyond its touchdown point. Staying below the large aircraft's final approach path (answer B) or landing before its touchdown point (answers B and C) would place the aircraft in the path of the wake turbulence.

3830. When departing behind a heavy aircraft, the pilot should avoid wake turbulence by maneuvering the aircraft

A — below and downwind from the heavy aircraft.
B — above and upwind from the heavy aircraft.
C — below and upwind from the heavy aircraft.

3830. Answer B. JSPPM 4-37 (PHB)
Because wake turbulence tends to sink and drift downwind, an aircraft should stay above and upwind of the preceding aircraft. Maneuvering below and downwind (answer A) would put the aircraft into the wake turbulence. Depending on the circumstances, below and upwind (answer C) may not keep the aircraft clear.

INTERPRETING WEATHER DATA

SECTION A
PRINTED REPORTS AND FORECASTS

Section A describes the common printed reports and forecasts that pilots need to be able to use effectively. These include the surface aviation weather report (SA), pilot report (PIREP), radar weather report (RAREP), terminal forecast (FT), area forecast (FA), and the winds and temperatures aloft forecasts (FD). The following FAA test questions are covered in this section:

3462, 3463, 3464, 3465, 3466, 3467, 3472, 3473, 3474, 3475, 3476, 3478, 3479, 3480, 3481, 3482, 3483, 3484, 3485, 3486, 3487, 3488, 3489, 3490, 3491, 3492, 3493, 3500, 3501, 3502, 3503, 3504, 3505, 3506.

3462. (Refer to figure 12.) Which of the reporting stations have VFR weather?

A — All.
B — INK, BOI, and JFK.
C — INK, BOI, and LAX.

3462. Answer C. JSPPM 5-3 (AWS)
To answer this question you must know that the definition of VFR weather is a ceiling of at least 1,000 feet and a visibility of at least 3 statute miles. INK is clear with 15 miles visibility, BOI has a scattered layer at 15,000 feet with 30 miles visibility, and LAX has scattered layers at 700 feet and 25,000 feet with 6 miles visibility. Remember, a scattered layer does not constitute a ceiling. Answers (A) and (B) are wrong because neither MDW or JFK are VFR. MDW has a measured ceiling of 700 feet overcast with 1-1/2 miles visibility, and JFK has an indefinite ceiling of 500 feet with a partially obscured sky and visibility of 1/2 mile in fog.

```
INK SA 1854 CLR 15 1Ø6/ 77/63/1112G18/ØØØ
BOI SA 1854 15Ø SCT 3Ø 181/62/42/13Ø4/Ø15
LAX SA 1852 7 SCT 25Ø SCT 6FK 129/6Ø/59/25Ø4/991
MDW RS 1856 –X M7 OVC 11/2R+F 99Ø/63/61/32Ø5/98Ø/RF2  RB12
JFK RS 1853 W5 X 1/2F 18Ø/68/64/18Ø4/ØØ6/RØ4RVR22V3Ø TWR VSBY 1/4
```

FIGURE 12.—Surface Aviation Weather Report.

3463. Ceiling is defined as the height above the Earth's surface of the

A — lowest reported obscuration and the highest layer of clouds reported as overcast.
B — lowest layer of clouds or obscuring phenomena reported as broken, overcast, and not classified as thin or partial.
C — lowest layer of clouds reported as scattered, broken, or thin.

3464. (Refer to figure 12 on page 5-1.) The wind direction and velocity at JFK is from

A — 180° true at 4 knots.
B — 180° magnetic at 4 knots.
C — 040° true at 18 knots.

3465. (Refer to figure 12 on page 5-1.) What are the wind conditions at Wink, Texas (INK)?

A — Calm.
B — 110° at 12 knots, peak gusts 18 knots.
C — 111° at 2 knots, peak gusts 18 knots.

3466. (Refer to figure 12 on page 5-1.) The remarks section for MDW has RF2 and RB12 listed. These two entries mean

A — rain and fog have reduced visibility to 2 miles and rain began at 1812Z.
B — rain and fog are obscuring two-tenths of the sky and rain began at 1812Z.
C — freezing rain has reduced visibility to 2 miles and the barometer has risen .12" Hg.

3463. Answer B. JSPPM 5-4 (FAR 1.1)
A ceiling is the lowest layer of clouds or obscuration which is broken, overcast, or obscured. It cannot be classified as thin or partial. Answer (A) is wrong because, when determining a ceiling, the lowest layer of clouds is used, not the highest layer. Answer (C) is wrong because a ceiling must be broken or overcast, not scattered, and cannot be reported as thin.

3464. Answer A. JSPPM 5-3 (AWS)
The wind at JFK is shown as 1804. This means the wind is from 180 degrees at 04 knots. Winds reported on a surface aviation weather report are referenced to true north. Answer (B) is incorrect because the winds are reported as true, not magnetic. Answer (C) is incorrect because the direction is listed first, and the velocity follows.

3465. Answer B. JSPPM 5-3 (AWS)
The winds at INK are shown as 1112G18. The direction is 110 degrees, and the velocity is 12 knots, with peak gusts of 18 knots. Answer (A) is wrong because calm winds are shown as 0000. The last three zeroes in this report represent the altimeter setting (30.00). Answer (C) is wrong because only the first two digits, rounded to the nearest 10 degrees, represent the direction, while the velocity is always shown as two digits.

3466. Answer B. JSPPM 5-3 (AWS)
The obscuring phenomena are listed, followed by sky coverage in tenths. In this case, rain and fog are obscuring two-tenths of the sky. RB is the code for "rain began," and the time past the last hour is shown in minutes. Since the report was taken at 1856Z, rain began at 1812Z. Answer (A) is wrong because visibility is shown after sky condition and ceiling, followed by obstructions to vision. When visibility is included in the remarks section, it is normally done to describe variable visibility. Answer (C) is wrong because freezing rain would be shown as ZR, and RB is the code for "rain began."

Interpreting Weather Data

3467. (Refer to figure 12 on page 5-1.) What are the current conditions depicted for Chicago Midway Airport (MDW)?

A — Sky partially obscured, measured ceiling 700 overcast, visibility 1-1/2, heavy rain, fog.
B — Thin overcast, measured 700 ceiling overcast, visibility 1-1/2, heavy rain, fog.
C — Sky partially obscured, measured ceiling 700 overcast, visibility 11, occasionally 2, with rain and heavy fog.

3467. Answer A. JSPPM 5-3 (AWS)
The sky condition, -X, means partially obscured and M7 OVC means a measured ceiling of 700 feet overcast. Visibility is listed next, at 1-1/2 miles, with obstructions to vision shown as heavy rain (R+) and fog (F). Answer (B) is wrong because a thin overcast would be shown as -OVC. Answer (C) is wrong because the visibility is shown in fractions, and variations are explained in the remarks section. When precipitation is reported as light or heavy, the modifying symbol (+ or -) follows the weather symbol. Therefore, R+F shows heavy rain, not heavy fog.

3472. (Refer to figure 14.) The base and tops of the overcast layer reported by a pilot are

A — 1,800 feet MSL and 5,500 feet MSL.
B — 5,500 feet AGL and 7,200 feet MSL.
C — 7,200 feet MSL and 8,900 feet MSL.

3472. Answer C. JSPPM 5-9 (AWS)
In the PIREP, which is identified by the letters, UA, sky cover is designated by the letters, SK, followed by the base and top of each cloud layer. The overcast layer is shown as 072 OVC 089, which means the base is 7,200 feet and the tops are 8,900 feet. Altitudes are MSL unless otherwise noted. Answer (A) is wrong because it describes the broken (not overcast) layer. Answer (B) is wrong because it describes the type of turbulence, moderate (MDT), and altitudes at which it was encountered.

```
UA /OV OKC-TUL /TM 1800 /FL 120 /TP BE90 /SK 018 BKN 055 /
/072 OVC 089 /CLR ABV /TA -9/WV 0921/TB MDT 055-072 /IC LGT-MDT
CLR 072-089.
```

FIGURE 14.—Pilot Weather Reports.

3473. (Refer to figure 14.) The wind and temperature at 12,000 feet MSL as reported by a pilot are

A — 009° at 121 MPH and 90°F.
B — 090° at 21 knots and -9°F.
C — 090° at 21 knots and -9°C.

3473. Answer C. JSPPM 5-9 (AWS)
The wind direction and velocity are shown as WV 0921, which means the direction is 090 degrees magnetic and velocity is 21 knots. Temperature is designated as, TA -9, which is -9° Celsius. Answer (A) is wrong because the first two digits represent the wind direction rounded to the nearest 10 degrees. Temperature is shown in actual degrees Celsius. Answer (B) is wrong because the temperature is in Celsius, not Fahrenheit.

3474. (Refer to figure 14.) If the terrain elevation is 1,295 feet MSL, what is the height above ground level of the base of the ceiling?

A — 505 feet AGL.
B — 1,295 feet AGL.
C — 6,586 feet AGL.

3474. Answer A. JSPPM 5-9 (AWS)
The ceiling is the lowest cloud layer reported as broken, overcast, or obscured. In this case, the lowest layer is 1,800 feet broken (MSL). Subtract the ground elevation to find the AGL height (1,800 - 1,295 = 505 feet AGL). Answer (B) is wrong because this is the terrain elevation in feet MSL, not the base of the clouds. Answer (C) is obviously incorrect. According to the PIREP in Figure 14, the broken ceiling is only 1,800 feet MSL, well below the answer choice figure of 6,586 feet AGL.

3475. (Refer to figure 14 on page 5-3.) The intensity of the turbulence reported at a specific altitude is

A — moderate at 5,500 feet and at 7,200 feet.
B — moderate from 5,500 feet to 7,200 feet.
C — light to moderate from 7,200 feet to 8,900 feet.

3476. (Refer to figure 14 on page 5-3.) The intensity and type of icing reported by a pilot is

A — light to moderate.
B — light to moderate clear.
C — moderate rime.

3478. From which primary source should information be obtained regarding expected weather at the estimated time of arrival if your destination has no Terminal Forecast?

A — Low-Level Prognostic Chart.
B — Weather Depiction Chart.
C — Area Forecast.

3479. (Refer to figure 15 on page 5-5.) What ceiling is forecast for GAG between 1600Z and 0100Z?

A — 6,000 scattered, chance 10,000 broken.
B — 10,000 scattered, chance 2,500 scattered.
C — 10,000 broken, chance 5,000 broken.

3480. (Refer to figure 15 on page 5-5.) What wind conditions are expected at HBR at 1600Z?

A — Calm.
B — 150° at 15 knots.
C — 300° at 10 knots.

3475. Answer B. JSPPM 5-9 (AWS)
Turbulence is reported as TB MDT 055-072, which means moderate from 5,500 to 7,200 feet. Answer (A) is incorrect because the hyphen between two altitudes indicates turbulence between those altitudes. Answer (C) is incorrect because it describes the reported icing.

3476. Answer B. JSPPM 5-9 (AWS)
The icing is reported as IC LGT-MDT CLR 072-089. The intensity is light to moderate, and the type of icing is clear. Answer (A) is not completely correct, because the type of icing is omitted. Answer (B) is a better choice. Answer (C) is wrong because the intensity is light to moderate, and the type is clear, not rime.

3478. Answer C. JSPPM 5-11 (AWS)
The area forecast (FA) is useful to help determine expected weather at airports which do not have terminal forecasts (FTs). The low-level prognostic chart (answer A) is more useful for flight planning several hours before a flight; however, it generally does not provide enough detail for an accurate estimate of destination weather. The weather depiction chart (answer B) shows general weather conditions and is also useful for flight planning purposes, but it does not show forecast conditions.

3479. Answer C. JSPPM 5-10 (AWS)
Figure 15 is a terminal forecast (FT). The forecast cloud cover beginning at 16Z is 60SCT C100 BKN. The 6,000 foot layer is scattered and, by definition, is not a ceiling. The broken layer is designated as a ceiling by the letter "C," and is expected to be at 10,000 feet. Following the wind entry is CHC C50 BKN. This means there is a chance that the ceiling will be 5,000 feet broken. Answer (A) is wrong because 6,000 scattered is not a ceiling. Answer (B) is wrong because the 10,000-foot layer is broken, not scattered, with a chance of a 5,000-foot broken ceiling, not 2,500 feet scattered.

3480. Answer C. JSPPM 5-10 (AWS)
The time, between 1515Z and 17Z, includes the forecast for 1600Z. The wind is listed at 3010, which is 300 degrees at 10 knots. Answer (A) is wrong because the wind is listed (3010), and wind is listed anytime it is forecast to be 6 knots or greater. Answer (B) is wrong because it is time of the FT — (1515). Wind is listed after the sky condition, not at the beginning of the report.

Interpreting Weather Data

```
OK FT 011447

GAG FT 011515 100 SCT 250 SCT 2610. 16Z 60 SCT C100 BKN 3315G22 CHC C50 BKN
   5TRW. 01Z 250 SCT 3515G25. 09Z VFR WIND..

HBR FT 011515 C120 BKN 250 BKN 3010. 17Z 100 SCT C250 BKN 3215G25 CHC C30 BKN
   3TRW. 00Z 250 SCT 3515G25. 092 VFR WIND..

MLC FT 011515 C20 BKN 1815 BKN OCNL SCT. 20Z C30 BKN 1815G22 CHC C20 BKN
   1TRW. 03Z C30 BKN 2015 CHC C7 X 1/2TRW+G40. 09Z MVFR CIG TRW..

OKC FT 011515 C12 BKN 140 BKN 1815G28 LWR BKN V SCT. 18Z C30 BKN 250 BKN
   2315G25 LWR BKN OCNL SCT CHC C7 X 1/2TRW+G40. 21Z CFP 100 SCT C250 BKN
   3315G25 CHC C30 BKN 5TRW-. 02Z 100 SCT 250 SCT 3515G25. 09Z VFR WIND..

PNC FT 011515 C100 BKN 250 BKN 1810. 16Z CFP 20 SCT C100 BKN 3115 SCT V BKN. 00Z
   250 SCT 3515G25. 09Z VFR WIND..

TUL FT 011515 C20 BKN 1915G22. 19Z C30 BKN 1815G25 CHC 3TRW. 23Z CFP C100 BKN
   250 BKN 3215G25 CHC C30 BKN 5TRW. 09Z VFR WIND..
```

FIGURE 15.—Terminal Forecast.

3481. (Refer to figure 15.) What is the outlook for weather conditions at MLC?

A — Ceilings 2,000 to 3,000 feet with southerly winds.
B — Ceiling 700 feet, sky obscured, visibility 1/2 mile in thundershowers.
C — Ceilings 1,000 to 3,000 feet with thunderstorms and rain showers.

3482. (Refer to figure 15.) The wind condition in the Terminal Forecast 6-hour categorical outlook for PNC is for

A — velocities of 25 knots or stronger.
B — a wind shift from south to northwest.
C — the wind to change from a gusty condition to calm.

3483. (Refer to figure 15.) When is the wind forecast to shift at TUL?

A — 1500Z.
B — By 2300Z.
C — Between 2300Z and 0900Z the next day.

3481. Answer C. JSPPM 5-9 (AWS)
The outlook, which is the last entry of the FT, reads MVFR CIG TRW. Marginal VFR (MVFR) is defined as a ceiling between 1,000 and 3,000 feet inclusive, and TRW means thunderstorms and rain showers. Answers (A) and (B) are wrong because they are taken from the main body of the FT, not the six-hour categorical outlook.

3482. Answer A. JSPPM 5-11 (AWS)
As with Question 3481, the outlook is the last entry, VFR WIND. This means VFR conditions are expected, with winds of 25 knots or greater. Answer (B) is wrong because a wind shift is shown throughout the body of the FT, but not in the outlook. Answer (C) is wrong because winds are not shown as calm anywhere in the forecast.

3483. Answer B. JSPPM 5-11 (AWS)
First, check the forecast wind direction for each time period listed. At 1515Z, the wind is forecast to be from 190 degrees, and at 19Z it is from 180 degrees. Then, at 23Z it will be from 320 degrees. Therefore, a significant wind shift is forecast to occur by 23Z. Answer (A) is wrong because the FT is valid beginning at 1515Z. Answer (C) is wrong because no shift in wind direction is shown between 23Z and 09Z.

3484. (Refer to figure 15 on page 5-5.) According to the Terminal Forecast for OKC, the cold front should pass through

A — between 1800Z and 2100Z.
B — by 2100Z.
C — after 2100Z.

3484. Answer B. JSPPM 5-10 (AWS)
The forecast at 18Z is for low clouds and winds from the southwest. The period (.) prior to 21Z indicates that changes are expected. By 21Z, a cold front is expected to pass, accompanied by a wind shift to the northwest. It would seem that both answers (A) and (B) could be correct. However, a literal reading of the FT would be, by 21Z, cold front passage; therefore, (B) is the better answer. Answer (C) is wrong, because each time period lists the changes expected to occur by that time, not after that time.

3485. (Refer to figure 15 on page 5-5.) What type conditions are forecast for OKC from 1800Z to 2100Z?

A — MVFR and VFR.
B — MVFR, VFR, and IFR.
C — VFR and IFR.

3485. Answer B. JSPPM 5-10 (AWS)
The definition of IFR is a ceiling 500 to less than 1,000 feet and/or visibility 1 to less than 3 miles. The "C7" in the report indicates IFR. MVFR is defined as a ceiling 1,000 feet to 3,000 feet and/or visibility 3 to 5 miles inclusive. The "C30" indicates MVFR conditions. VFR is defined as a ceiling greater than 3,000 feet and visibility greater than 5 miles. The "C250" indicates VFR conditions. Therefore, the only correct answer is (B).

3486. (Refer to figure 15 on page 5-5.) What is the outlook for the weather condition at TUL?

A — VFR with winds 25 knots or more with the direction not forecast.
B — Chance of ceilings 3,000 feet broken, visibility 5 miles in thunderstorms and rain showers.
C — VFR with winds 320° at 15 knots with gusts to 25 knots.

3486. Answer A. JSPPM 5-10 (AWS)
The outlook, the last entry in the FT, is for VFR WIND. This means the weather is forecast to be VFR, and when wind is listed, it means that winds are expected to be 25 knots or greater. Wind direction is not listed. Answer (B) is wrong because this is included in the remarks section for 23Z. Answer (C) is wrong because this describes the prevailing forecast conditions by 23Z.

3487. To best determine general forecast weather conditions over several states, the pilot should refer to

A — Area Forecasts.
B — Weather Depiction Charts.
C — Satellite Maps.

3487. Answer A. JSPPM 5-11 (AWS)
An area forecast (FA) covers the expected general weather conditions over several states. The FA also provides information on general weather conditions at airports that are not covered by other weather reports or forecasts. Answer (B) is wrong because a weather depiction chart is a "snapshot" of observed weather at the valid time of the report; it is not a forecast. Answer (C) is wrong because satellite maps are made of existing weather conditions, and are not a forecast of expected weather.

Interpreting Weather Data

3488. (Refer to figure 16 on page 5-8.) What is the forecast ceiling and visibility for Tennessee from 2300Z through 0500Z?

A — 500 feet to less than 1,000 feet, and 1 mile to less than 3 miles.
B — 1,000 to 3,000 feet, and 3 to 5 miles.
C — 3,000 feet or greater, and 5 miles or greater.

3489. To determine the freezing level and areas of probable icing aloft, the pilot should refer to the

A — Radar Summary Chart.
B — Weather Depiction Chart.
C — Area Forecast.

3490. The section of the Area Forecast entitled "SIG CLDS AND WX" contains a summary of

A — cloudiness and weather significant to flight operations broken down by states or other geographical areas.
B — forecast sky cover, cloud tops, visibility, and obstructions to vision along specific routes.
C — weather advisories still in effect at the time of issue.

3491. (Refer to figure 16 on page 5-8.) What hazards are forecast in the Area Forecast for TN, AL, and the coastal waters?

A — Thunderstorms with severe or greater turbulence, severe icing, and low-level wind shear.
B — Moderate rime icing above the freezing level to 10,000 feet.
C — Moderate turbulence from 25,000 to 38,000 feet due to the jetstream.

3488. Answer C. JSPPM 5-12 (AWS)
(NOTE: The Area Forecast format was changed in 1991, but Figure 16 and associated questions use the old format.) The last section shown, DFWC SGFNT CLOUD AND WX, lists a valid time for the outlook (OTLK) of 042300-050500. This time is from 2300Z on the 4th day of the month to 0500Z on the 5th. Under Tennessee (TN), the outlook (OTLK) is for VFR. The definition in AC 00-45 for VFR is no ceiling, or a ceiling greater than 3,000 feet and visibility greater than 5 miles. Although answer (C) includes 3,000 feet and 5 miles, and is not entirely correct, it is the closest answer. Answer (A) is not correct because it fits the definition for IFR. Answer (B) is incorrect because this would be marginal VFR (MVFR).

3489. Answer C. JSPPM 5-12 (AWS)
The old Area Forecast format, as shown in Figure 16, has an icing section, which describes areas of icing and freezing levels. (NOTE: The new FA format only makes reference to icing conditions in the Hazards/Flight Precautions section by listing affected states. Freezing levels and areas of icing are now found only in the applicable AIRMET or SIGMET.) Answer (A) is wrong because a radar summary chart depicts areas of precipitation, particularly thunderstorms. Areas of icing and freezing levels are not shown. Answer (B) is wrong because a weather depiction chart shows areas if IFR and MVFR weather, but no areas of icing or freezing levels.

3490. Answer A. JSPPM 5-14 (AWS)
The SIG CLDS AND WX section describes cloud cover and weather which are significant to flight operations. Affected areas are listed by states or other geographical areas, such as coastal waters, or outlined by VORs. Answer (B) is incorrect because each section of an Area Forecast covers specific areas, not routes. Answer (C) is incorrect because weather advisories are not mentioned in the SIG CLDS AND WX section, but are referenced in the HAZARDS/FLT PRCTNS section (old format only).

3491. Answer C. JSPPM 5-12 (AWS)
The HAZARDS section lists turbulence for TN, AL, and coastal waters. For more detail, refer to the TURBULENCE section (DFWT). In this area, occasional moderate turbulence is forecast from 25,000 to 38,000 feet due to the jetstream. Answer (A) is wrong because this statement is taken from the standard note in the HAZARDS section. Thunderstorms are not included in the area forecast. Answer (B) is wrong because these icing conditions are forecast only for TN, not AL or the coastal waters.

```
DFWH FA 041040
HAZARDS VALID UNTIL 042300
OK TX AR LA TN MS AL AND CSTL WTRS
FLT PRCTNS...TURBC...TN AL AND CSTL WTRS
         ...ICG...TN
         ...IFR...TX
TSTMS IMPLY PSBL SVR OR GTR TURBC SVR ICG AND LLWS
NON MSL HGTS NOTED BY AGL OR CIG
THIS FA ISSUANCE INCORPORATES THE FOLLOWING AIRMETS STILL IN
EFFECT...NONE.

DFWS FA 041040
SYNOPSIS VALID UNTIL 050500
AT 11Z RDG OF HI PRES ERN TX NWWD TO CNTRL CO WITH HI CNTR
OVR ERN TX. BY 05Z HI CNTR MOVS TO CNTRL LA.

DFWI FA 041040
ICING AND FRZLVL VALID UNTIL 042300
TN
FROM SLK TO HAT TO MEM TO ORD TO SLK
OCNL MDT RIME ICGIC ABV FRZLVL TO 100. CONDS ENDING BY 17Z.
FRZLVL 80 CHA SGF LINE SLPG TO 120 S OF A IAH MAF LINE.

DFWT FA 041040
TURBC VALID UNTIL 042300
TN AL AND CSTL WTRS
FROM SLK TO FLO TO 90S MOB TO MEI TO BUF TO SLK
OCNL MDT TURBC 250-380 DUE TO JTSTR. CONDS MOVG SLOLY EWD
AND CONTG BYD 23Z.

DFWC FA 041040
SGFNT CLOUD AND WX VALID UNTIL 042300...OTLK 042300-050500
IFR...TX
FROM SAT TO PSX TO BRO TO MOB TO SAT
VSBY BLO 3F TIL 15Z.
OK AR TX LA MS AL AND CSTL WTRS
80 SCT TO CLR EXCP VSBY BLO 3F TIL 15Z OVR PTNS S CNTRL TX.
OTLK...VFR.
TN
CIGS 30-50 BKN 100 VSBYS OCNLY 3-5F BCMG AGL 40-50 SCT TO
CLR BY 19Z. OTLK...VFR.
```

FIGURE 16.—Area Forecast.

3492. (Refer to figure 16.) What type obstructions to vision, if any, are forecast for the entire area from 2300Z until 0500Z the next day?

A — None of any significance, VFR is forecast.
B — Visibility 3 to 5 miles in fog.
C — Visibility below 3 miles in fog over southcentral Texas.

3492. Answer A. JSPPM 5-13 (AWS)
Obstructions to vision are included in the SGFNT CLOUD AND WX section. The period from 2300Z to 0500Z is the time for the outlook (OTLK). The outlook for the entire area is for VFR. Answer (B) is wrong because visibility of 3 to 5 miles in fog is listed only for TN, and this will clear up by 19Z. Answer (C) is wrong because the low visibility is forecast only until 15Z. The outlook for all of Texas is VFR.

Interpreting Weather Data

3493. (Refer to figure 16.) What sky condition and type obstructions to vision are forecast for all the area except TN from 1040Z until 2300Z?

A — Ceilings 3,000 to 5,000 feet broken, visibility 3 to 5 miles in fog.
B — 8,000 feet scattered to clear expect visibility below 3 miles in fog until 1500Z over southcentral Texas.
C — Generally ceilings 3,000 to 8,000 feet to clear with visibility sometimes below 3 miles in fog.

3500. (Refer to figure 17.) What wind is forecast for STL at 6,000 feet?

A — 210° magnetic at 13 knots.
B — 230° true at 25 knots.
C — 232° true at 5 knots.

3493. Answer B. JSPPM 5-13 (AWS)
This forecast is included in the SGFNT CLOUD AND WX section from the valid time of 1040Z up until the outlook time of 2300Z. Apart from the separate forecasts for TX and TN, the rest of the area is forecast to have 8,000 feet scattered to clear, except visibility below 3 miles in fog until 15Z over portions of southcentral Texas. Answer (A) is incorrect because this is the forecast for TN. Answer (C) is incorrect because this combines the forecast for TN with the rest of the area, and the area with visibility below 3 miles is limited to parts of TX only.

3500. Answer B. JSPPM 5-15 (AWS)
The wind information is given as 2325+07. The first two digits represent the wind direction in relation to true north, 230 degrees. The next two digits are the speed, which in this case is 25 knots. Answer (A) is wrong because the direction is true, not magnetic, and the direction and speed in this answer are listed under 3,000 feet, not 6,000 feet. Answer (C) is wrong because only the first two digits represent the wind direction rounded to the nearest 10 degrees, and the speed is always shown with two digits.

```
FD WBC 151745
BASED ON 151200Z DATA
VALID 1600Z FOR USE 1800-0300Z.  TEMPS NEG ABV 24000
```

FT	3000	6000	9000	12000	18000	24000	30000	34000	39000
ALS			2420	2635-08	2535-18	2444-30	245945	246755	246862
AMA		2714	2725+00	2625-04	2531-15	2542-27	265842	256352	256762
DEN			2321-04	2532-08	2434-19	2441-31	235347	236056	236262
HLC		1707-01	2113-03	2219-07	2330-17	2435-30	244145	244854	245561
MKC	0507	2006+03	2215-01	2322-06	2338-17	2348-29	236143	237252	238160
STL	2113	2325+07	2332+02	2339-04	2356-16	2373-27	239440	730649	731960

FIGURE 17.—Winds and Temperatures Aloft Forecast.

3501. (Refer to figure 17.) What wind is forecast for STL at 18,000 feet?

A — 230° true at 56 knots.
B — 235° true at 06 knots.
C — 235° magnetic at 06, peak gusts to 16 knots.

3501. Answer A. JSPPM 5-15 (AWS)
The wind information is given as 2356-16. The first two digits represent the wind direction in relation to true north, 230°. The next two digits are the speed, which in this case is 56 knots. The temperature is -16°C. Answer (B) is wrong because only the first two digits are used for the wind direction. Answer (C) is wrong because the wind direction is true, not magnetic, and wind gusts are not listed in the winds aloft forecast.

3502. (Refer to figure 17 on page 5-9.) Determine the wind and temperature aloft forecast for DEN at 30,000 feet.

A — 023° magnetic at 53 knots, temperature 47°C.
B — 230° true at 53 knots, temperature -47°C.
C — 235° true at 34 knots, temperature -7°C.

3502. Answer B. JSPPM 5-15 (AWS)
The wind and temperature information is listed as 235347. The wind direction and speed is 230 degrees at 53 knots. Notice the heading for the forecast states that temperatures are negative above 24,000 feet. In this case, the number 47 represents -47°C. Answer (A) is wrong because the direction is true, not magnetic. The wind direction is rounded to the nearest 10 degrees, and the temperature is negative, not positive. Answer (C) is wrong because only the first two digits represent the wind direction rounded to the nearest 10 degrees, the speed is the next two digits, and the temperature is the last two digits.

3503. (Refer to figure 17 on page 5-9.) Determine the wind and temperature aloft forecast for 3,000 feet at MKC.

A — 050° true at 7 knots, temperature missing.
B — 360° magnetic at 5 knots, temperature -7°C.
C — 360° true at 50 knots, temperature +7°C.

3503. Answer A. JSPPM 5-15 (AWS)
The wind information is given as 0507, which is 050 degrees true at 7 knots. No temperatures are given at the 3,000 feet level. Answers (B) and (C) are incorrect because the first two digits represent the wind direction (true, not magnetic), the next two digits are the speed, and temperature is not given.

3504. (Refer to figure 17 on page 5-9.) What wind is forecast for STL at 34,000 feet?

A — 007° magnetic at 30 knots.
B — 073° true at 6 knots.
C — 230° true at 106 knots.

3504. Answer C. JSPPM 5-15 (AWS)
The wind information is shown as 730649. Winds of 100 to 199 knots have 50 added to the direction. To decode, subtract 50 from 73 to find the direction of 23, or 230 degrees. The wind speed of 06 is added to 100, for a speed of 106 knots. Answers (A) and (B) are not right because the first two digits represent wind direction rounded to the nearest 10 degrees. The next two digits represent the speed, and are added to 100, for a wind speed of 106 knots.

3505. What values are used for Winds Aloft Forecasts?

A — Magnetic direction and knots.
B — Magnetic direction and miles per hour.
C — True direction and knots.

3505. Answer C. JSPPM 5-14 (AWS)
The best rule of thumb is to remember that all forecast winds are given in true direction, and speed is always in knots.

3506. When the term "light and variable" is used in reference to a Winds Aloft Forecast, the coded group and windspeed is

A — 0000 and less than 7 knots.
B — 9900 and less than 5 knots.
C — 9999 and less than 10 knots.

3506. Answer B. JSPPM 5-15 (AWS)
The direction is shown as 99, which means the direction is variable. When the second two digits are listed as 00, the speed is less than 5 knots.

SECTION B
GRAPHIC WEATHER PRODUCTS

In Section B, the main graphic weather reports that are covered are the surface analysis, weather depiction, radar summary, and low-level significant prognostic charts. Each has an intended information purpose, as well as specific features and certain limitations. FAA Written Test questions in this section include:

3507, 3508, 3509, 3510, 3511, 3512, 3513, 3514, 3515, 3516, 3517, 3518, 3519, 3520, 3521, 3522, 3523, 3524.

3507. (Refer to figure 18 on page 5-12.) What is the status of the front that extends from New Mexico to Indiana?

A — Stationary.
B — Occluded.
C — Retreating.

3507. Answer A. JSPPM 5-17 (AWS)
This front is depicted with rounded warm front symbols on one side and triangular cold front symbols on the other side. This symbology indicates a stationary front. An occluded front (answer B) has both warm and cold front symbols on the same side. No symbols are used to depict a retreating front (answer C).

3508. (Refer to figure 18 on page 5-12.) The IFR weather in eastern Texas is due to

A — intermittent rain.
B — fog.
C — dust devils.

3508. Answer B. JSPPM 5-19 (AWS)
The shaded area in eastern Texas is an area of IFR weather. The symbol with two horizontal lines (=) indicates fog. Intermittent rain (answer A) would be shown with a single solid dot next to a station model, and none is shown in this area. The corkscrew symbol, which is used to depict dust devils (answer C), is not included in Figure 18.

3509. (Refer to figure 18 on page 5-12.) Of what value is the Weather Depiction Chart to the pilot?

A — For determining general weather conditions on which to base flight planning.
B — For a forecast of cloud coverage, visibilities, and frontal activity.
C — For determining frontal trends and air mass characteristics.

3509. Answer A. JSPPM 5-18 (AWS)
The weather depiction chart shows a "birds eye" view of general weather conditions over a wide area, and is useful for flight planning purposes by showing areas of adverse weather. It depicts actual weather conditions, and is not a forecast (answer B). Although it does show locations of fronts, it does not indicate trends or high and low pressure areas (answer C).

3510. (Refer to figure 18 on page 5-12.) The marginal weather in southeast New Mexico is due to

A — reported thunderstorms.
B — 600-foot overcast ceilings.
C — low visibility.

3510. Answer C. JSPPM 5-20 (AWS)
The outlined area enclosed by contoured lines without shading in southeastern New Mexico indicates marginal VFR weather. The station model shows 6,000 feet overcast, visibility 4 miles, with rain showers and a thunderstorm. Three to five miles visibility is the marginal condition. Answer (A) is incorrect because a thunderstorm by itself does not specifically indicate marginal weather. There are no areas with 600-foot ceilings (answer B) in New Mexico, since this would be shown as a shaded area.

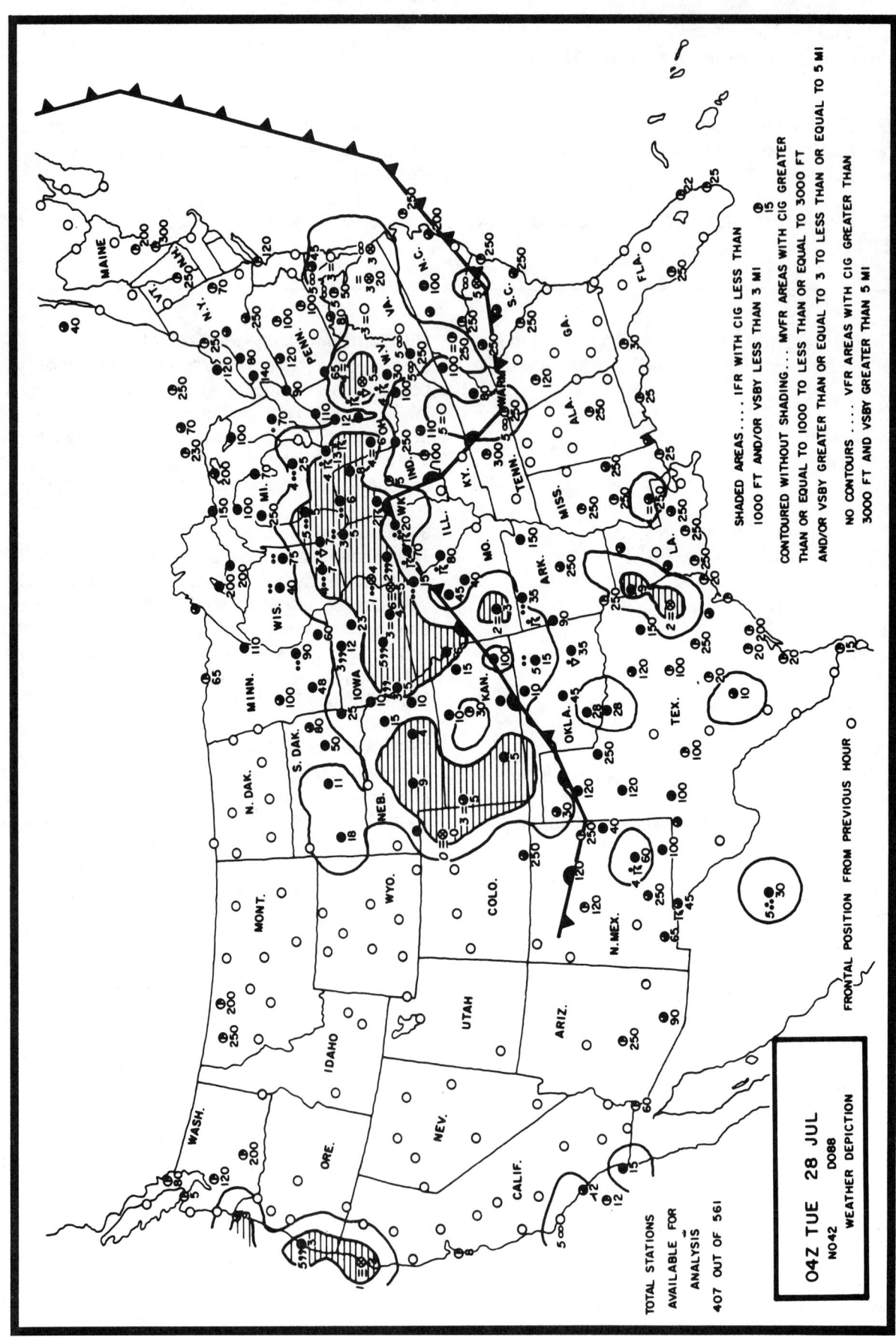

FIGURE 18.—Weather Depiction Chart.

Interpreting Weather Data

3511. (Refer to figure 18 on page 5-12.) What weather phenomenon is causing IFR conditions along the coast of Oregon and California?

A — Squall line activity.
B — Low ceilings.
C — Heavy rain showers.

3511. Answer B. JSPPM 5-19 (AWS)
Under each station model, the number indicates the ceiling in hundreds of feet AGL, and the number to the left is the visibility. The two station models in this area show ceilings of 300 feet in Oregon and 200 feet in northern California. A squall line (answer A) would be indicated by a series of thunderstorm symbols. Neither are shown here. No heavy rain shower symbols (answer C) are shown in this area.

3512. (Refer to figure 18 on page 5-12.) According to the Weather Depiction Chart, the weather for a flight from central Arkansas to southeast Alabama is

A — broken clouds at 2,500 feet.
B — visibility from 3 to 5 miles.
C — broken to scattered clouds at 25,000 feet.

3512. Answer C. JSPPM 5-19 (AWS)
Along this route, the station models show broken and scattered clouds, with clear skies in southeast Alabama. The number 250 is the cloud layer in hundreds of feet, which is 25,000 feet. Broken clouds of 2,500 feet (answer A) would be depicted as 25, not 250. Areas with visibility of 3 to 5 miles (answer B) would be included in a contoured area, but this route has no areas enclosed by contours.

3513. Radar weather reports are of special interest to pilots because they indicate

A — large areas of low ceilings and fog.
B — location of precipitation along with type, intensity, and trend.
C — location of broken to overcast clouds.

3513. Answer B. JSPPM 5-21 (AWS)
Radar weather reports show areas of precipitation; type, such as rain showers; intensity, such as light or heavy; and trend of intensity, such as increasing or decreasing. Printed radar reports show only precipitation, not areas of low ceiling or fog (answer A) or locations of clouds (answer C).

3514. What information is provided by the Radar Summary Chart that is not shown on other weather charts?

A — Lines and cells of hazardous thunderstorms.
B — Ceilings and precipitation between reporting stations.
C — Types of clouds between reporting stations.

3514. Answer A. JSPPM 5-22 (AWS)
Individual thunderstorm cells as well as lines of thunderstorms are depicted on radar summary charts. Since the radar returns are reflected off precipitation, not clouds, they do not show ceilings (answer B) or types of clouds (answer C).

3515. (Refer to figure 19, area A on page 5-14.) What is the direction and speed of movement of the radar return?

A — 020° at 20 knots.
B — East at 15 knots.
C — Northeast at 22 knots.

3515. Answer B. JSPPM 5-22 (AWS)
The movement pennant points in the direction of movement, which in this case is to the east. Each barb on the pennant indicates 10 knots, and half barbs are 5 knots, so the speed of movement here is 15 knots. The number 220 should not be confused with direction and speed (answers A and C). It indicates the top of the precipitation echo in hundreds of feet MSL (22,000 feet).

3516. (Refer to figure 19, area C on page 5-14.) What type of weather is occurring in the radar return?

A — Continuous rain.
B — Heavy rain showers.
C — Rain showers increasing in intensity.

3516. Answer C. JSPPM 5-22 (AWS)
The symbol in area C is RW+. The RW means rain shower, and the + symbol means the intensity is increasing or a new echo. Rain (answer A) would be shown as R only, which implies continuous rain rather than showers. The + symbol does not indicate heavy rain showers (answer B). The intensity of the precipitation is shown by the contour levels. In this area there is a single contour, which means the precipitation is light to moderate.

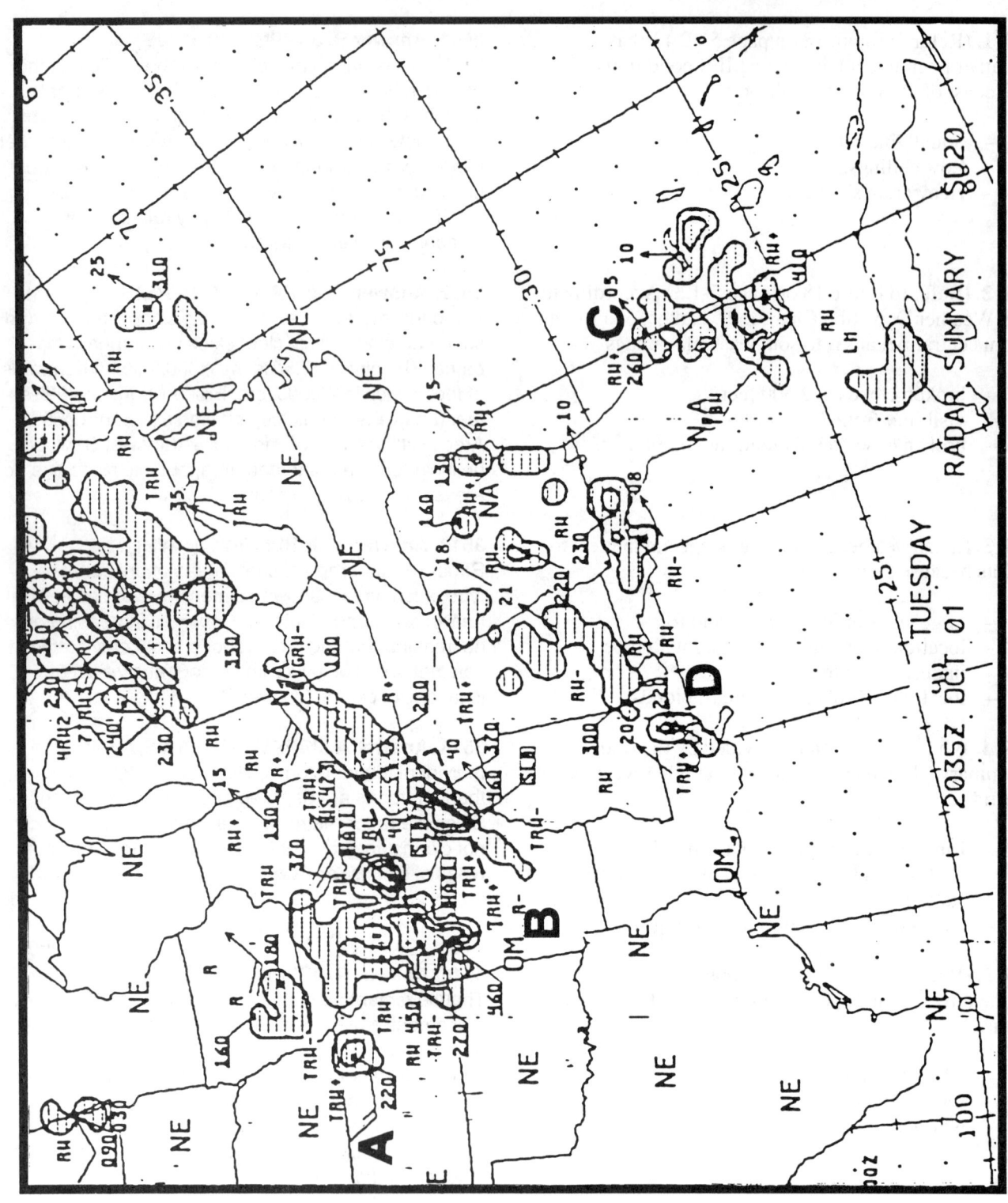

FIGURE 19.—Radar Summary Chart.

3517. (Refer to figure 19, area D.) What is the direction and speed of movement of the radar return?

A— Southeast at 30 knots.
B— Northeast at 20 knots.
C— West at 30 knots.

3517. Answer B. JSPPM 5-22 (AWS)
The arrow points in the direction of movement, which is northeast. The number 20 represents the speed in knots. The number 300 should not be confused with direction and speed (answers A and C). This is the top of the precipitation return.

3518. (Refer to figure 19, area D.) The top of the precipitation is

A — 2,000 feet.
B — 20,000 feet.
C — 30,000 feet.

3518. Answer C. JSPPM 5-22 (AWS)
The top of the precipitation is shown in hundreds of feet MSL. This question requires some interpretation, since it is not clear which highest precipitation top is referenced. The two numbers in this area are 300 (30,000 feet) and 220 (22,000 feet). Therefore, 30,000 feet is the only correct answer.

3519. (Refer to figure 19, area B.) What does the dashed line enclose?

A — Areas of heavy rain.
B — Severe weather watch area.
C — Areas of hail 1/4 inch in diameter.

3519. Answer B. JSPPM 5-23 (AWS)
The dashed line encloses a severe weather watch area. These areas are designated for tornadoes or severe thunderstorms. Other hazardous weather phenomenon may also be included in the weather watch area. Heavy rain (answer A) would be indicated as R+ and hail (answer C) is shown with the word "Hail" enclosed in a small box.

3520. (Refer to figure 20 on page 5-16.) How are Significant Weather Prognostic Charts best used by a pilot?

A — For overall planning at all altitudes.
B — For determining areas to avoid (freezing levels and turbulence).
C — For analyzing current frontal activity and cloud coverage.

3520. Answer B. JSPPM 5-24 (AWS)
In addition to outlining areas of instrument flight rule (IFR) and marginal visual flight rule (MVFR) weather, these charts include freezing levels and areas of turbulence. Since the significant weather panels are valid from the surface up to 24,000 feet, they are intended for planning flights below this altitude, not all altitudes (answer A). These charts do not depict current frontal activity (answer C) because they are forecasts, not observations. The lower two panels are 12- and 24-hour surface progs and the upper two panels are 12- and 24-hour progs for the surface up to 400 millibars, or approximately 24,000 feet.

3521. (Refer to figure 20 on page 5-16.) Interpret the weather symbol depicted in southern California on the 12-hour Significant Weather Prognostic Chart.

A — Moderate turbulence, surface to 18,000 feet.
B — Thunderstorm tops at 18,000 feet.
C — Base of clear air turbulence, 18,000 feet.

3521. Answer A. JSPPM 5-25 (AWS)
On the upper left panel, this symbol indicates moderate turbulence. The figure 180 means the turbulence is from the surface up to 18,000 feet. No thunderstorm symbol is shown in this area (answer B). Figures shown above a line represent the top of the turbulence, and figures below a line show the base of the turbulence (answer C).

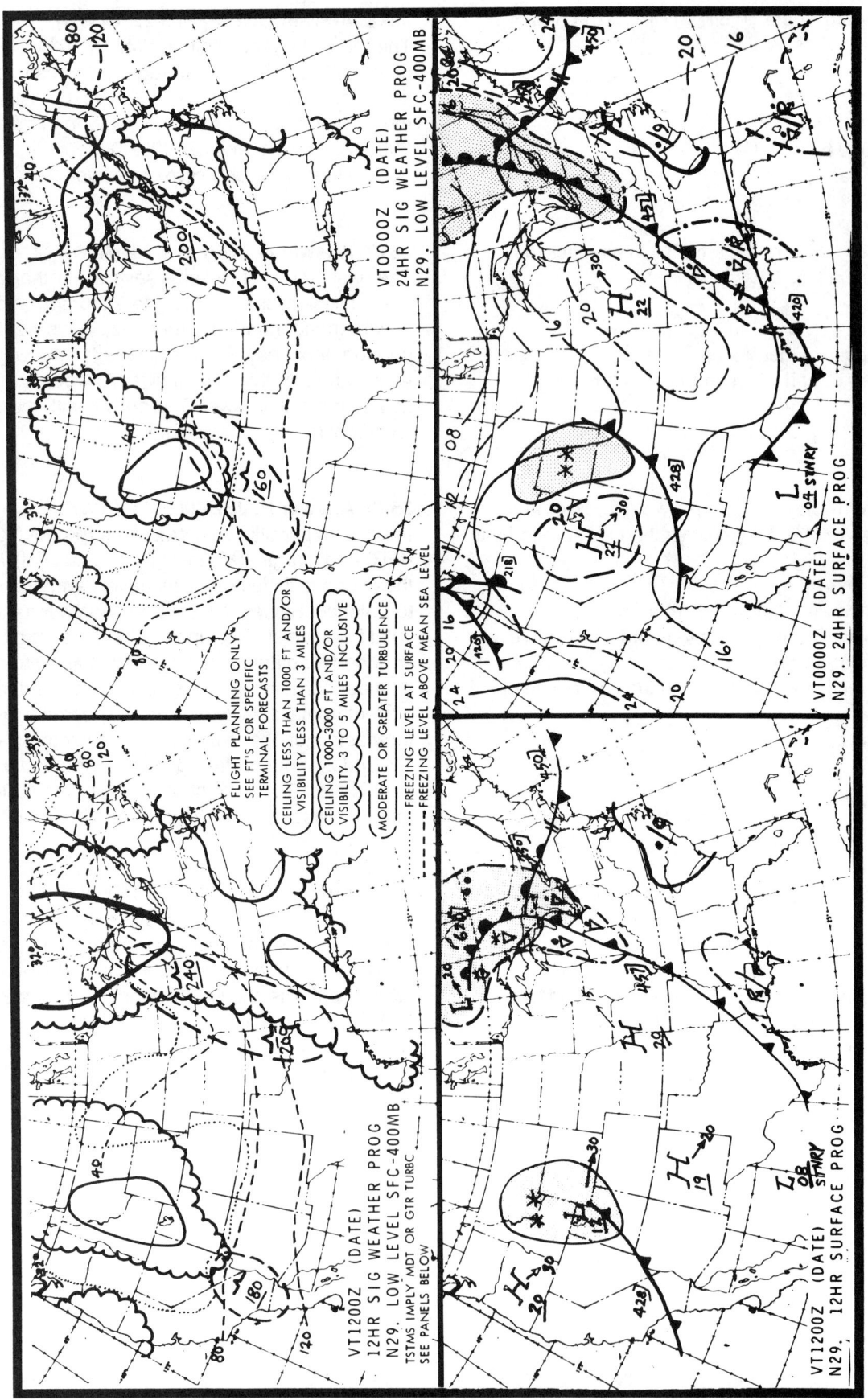

FIGURE 20.—Significant Weather Prognostic Chart.

Interpreting Weather Data

3522. (Refer to figure 20.) What weather is forecast for the Gulf Coast area just ahead of the cold front during the first 12 hours?

A — Ceiling 1,000 to 3,000 feet and/or visibility 3 to 5 miles with intermittent thundershowers and rain showers.
B — IFR with moderate or greater turbulence over the coastal areas.
C — Rain and thunderstorms moving northeastward ahead of the front.

3522. Answer A. JSPPM 5-26 (AWS)
On the lower left panel, the outlined area along the Gulf Coast shows showery precipitation ahead of the cold front. The symbols indicate thunderstorms and rain showers. Since the area is not shaded, coverage is less than half the area, so intermittent showers could be implied. The upper left panel shows most of the coastline enclosed by scalloped lines, indicating ceilings between 1,000 and 3,000 feet and/or visibility of 3 to 5 miles inclusive. The only IFR weather in this region (answer B) is shown by the oval-shaped solid line covering parts of Louisiana and Mississippi. IFR conditions are not expected along the coast, nor is any turbulence indicated. Although movement of the air mass is indicated by the frontal position, no specific movement of the rain and thunderstorms (answer C) is depicted. Movement of thunderstorms is shown on the radar summary chart.

3523. (Refer to figure 20.) The low pressure associated with the cold front in the western states is forecast to move

A — east at 30 knots.
B — northeast at 12 knots.
C — southeast at 30 knots.

3523. Answer A. JSPPM 5-24 (AWS)
The low pressure area on the lower left panel is shown with an arrow pointing in the direction of movement (east) and the speed in knots is shown as 30. The underlined two-digit number 12 beneath the low pressure symbol represent the sea level pressure in millibars, not movement of the low (answer B). In this case, the pressure is 1012.0 millibars. Note, this indication of millibar pressure differs from the three-digit reference included in a surface aviation weather report. The high pressure system in Oregon is moving southeast at 30 knots (answer C), not the low pressure system.

3524. (Refer to figure 20.) At what altitude is the freezing level over northeastern Oklahoma on the 24-hour Significant Weather Prognostic Chart?

A — 4,000 feet.
B — 8,000 feet.
C — 10,000 feet.

3524. Answer B. JSPPM 5-24 (AWS)
The upper right panel shows a dashed line representing the freezing level which crosses northeastern Oklahoma. On each side of the chart, this line connects with the number 80, which indicates MSL height of the freezing level in hundreds of feet. The 4,000-foot freezing level (answer A) crosses North Dakota and the Great Lakes region. Since 10,000 feet (answer C) is not shown, it could be interpolated between the 8,000-and 12,000-foot levels. The 10,000-foot freezing level would cross southern, not northeastern, Oklahoma.

SECTION C
SOURCES OF WEATHER INFORMATION

Section C contains a discussion of the primary sources for pilots. These include three types of briefings and a variety of supplement sources. Many of the latter are automated outlets such as the pilot's automatic telephone weather answering service (PATWAS). In addition, in-flight sources of weather information are included. This section covers the following FAA Written Test questions:

3453, 3454, 3455, 3456, 3457, 3458, 3459, 3460, 3461, 3494, 3495, 3496, 3497, 3498, 3499, 3526, 3527, 3528, 3616, 3617, 3823.

3453. Individual forecasts for specific routes of flight can be obtained from which weather source?

A — Transcribed Weather Broadcasts (TWEB's).
B — Terminal Forecasts.
C — Area Forecasts.

3453. Answer A. JSPPM 5-30 (AWS)
The information in a transcribed weather broadcast (TWEB) varies, but generally it contains route-oriented data. Terminal and area forecasts (answers B and C) contain terminal forecasts and forecasts for large geographical areas respectively, not route-oriented information.

3454. Transcribed Weather Broadcasts (TWEB's) may be monitored by tuning the appropriate radio receiver to certain

A — airport advisory frequencies.
B — VOR and NDB frequencies.
C — ATIS frequencies.

3454. Answer B. JSPPM 5-30 (AWS)
TWEB's are broadcast over certain VOR and NDB frequencies. Airport advisory frequencies (answer A) are used by an FSS at uncontrolled airports to provide general airport information to pilots. Automatic terminal information service (ATIS) frequencies (answer C) are used to broadcast recorded airport information.

3455. When telephoning a weather briefing facility for preflight weather information, pilots should state

A — the aircraft identification or the pilot's name.
B — true airspeed.
C — fuel on board.

3455. Answer A. JSPPM 5-27 (AWS)
Pilots should give their name or the aircraft number, as well as other specific information, to the weather briefer. True airspeed (answer B) or fuel on board (answer C) are not required. These are items that are included on a flight plan.

3456. To get a complete weather briefing for the planned flight, the pilot should request

A — a general briefing.
B — an abbreviated briefing.
C — a standard briefing.

3456. Answer C. JSPPM 5-27 (AIM)
A standard briefing is the most compete type of weather briefing. Since the three types of briefings are standard, abbreviated, and outlook, the term "general briefing" (answer A) is not used. An abbreviated briefing (answer B) may be obtained when the pilot has used other sources of weather data for a preliminary briefing, and needs to update that information.

3457. Which type weather briefing should a pilot request, when departing within the hour, if no preliminary weather information has been received?

A — Outlook briefing.
B — Abbreviated briefing.
C — Standard briefing.

3457. Answer C. JSPPM 5-27 (AIM)
See explanation for Question 3456. An outlook briefing (answer A) is used for long-range planning, six or more hours ahead of time. Answer (B), the abbreviated briefing, is intended primarily for updating previous briefing information.

Interpreting Weather Data

3458. Which type of weather briefing should a pilot request to supplement mass disseminated data?

A — An outlook briefing.
B — A supplemental briefing.
C — An abbreviated briefing.

3459. To update a previous weather briefing, a pilot should request

A — an abbreviated briefing.
B — a standard briefing.
C — an outlook briefing.

3460. A weather briefing that is provided when the information requested is 6 or more hours in advance of the proposed departure time is

A — an outlook briefing.
B — a forecast briefing.
C — a prognostic briefing.

3461. When requesting weather information for the following morning, a pilot should request

A — an outlook briefing.
B — a standard briefing.
C — an abbreviated briefing.

3494. To obtain a continuous transcribed weather briefing, including winds aloft and route forecasts for a cross-country flight, a pilot should monitor a

A — Transcribed Weather Broadcast (TWEB) on an ADF radio receiver.
B — VHF radio receiver tuned to an Automatic Terminal Information Service (ATIS) frequency.
C — regularly scheduled weather broadcast on a VOR frequency.

3495. What is indicated when a current CONVECTIVE SIGMET forecasts thunderstorms?

A — Moderate thunderstorms covering 30 percent of the area.
B — Moderate or severe turbulence.
C — Thunderstorms obscured by massive cloud layers.

3458. Answer C. JSPPM 5-29 (AIM)
See explanation for Questions 3456 and 3457. The term "supplemental briefing" (answer B) is not used.

3459. Answer A. JSPPM 5-29 (AIM)
See explanation for Questions 3456 and 3457.

3460. Answer A. JSPPM 5-29 (AIM)
See explanation for Question 3457. The terms "forecast briefing" (answer B) and "prognostic briefing" (answer C) are not official names for weather briefings provided by an FSS on the National Weather Service.

3461. Answer A. JSPPM 5-29 (AIM)
Assuming this would be 6 or more hours away, the pilot would request an outlook briefing (see explanation for Questions 3456 and 3457).

3494. Answer A. JSPPM 5-30 (AIM)
The answers to this question can be somewhat misleading, since a TWEB can be broadcast over either an NDB (ADF) or a VOR. However, some VORs broadcast only local information and do not include route forecasts. In general, most TWEBs include route information, so answer (A) appears to be the most correct choice.

3495. Answer C. JSPPM 5-33 (AIM)
None of these answers is entirely correct, but by process of elimination, answer (C) is the best choice. One of the criteria for issuing a Convective SIGMET is embedded thunderstorms. A Convective SIGMET is issued when level 4 thunderstorms (very strong, not moderate) cover 40 percent (not 30 percent) of an area (answer A). Severe or greater turbulence is implied, not moderate or severe (answer B).

3496. What information is contained in a CONVECTIVE SIGMET?

A — Tornadoes, embedded thunderstorms, and hail 3/4 inch or greater in diameter.
B — Severe icing, severe turbulence, or widespread dust storms lowering visibility to less than 3 miles.
C — Surface winds greater than 40 knots or thunderstorms equal to or greater than video integrator processor (VIP) level 4.

3497. SIGMET's are issued as a warning of weather conditions hazardous to which aircraft?

A — Small aircraft only.
B — Large aircraft only.
C — All aircraft.

3498. Which in-flight advisory would contain information on severe icing?

A — Convective SIGMET.
B — SIGMET.
C — AIRMET.

3499. AIRMET's are issued as a warning of weather conditions particularly hazardous to which aircraft?

A — Small single-engine aircraft.
B — Large multiengine aircraft.
C — All aircraft.

3526. When telephoning a weather briefing facility for preflight weather information, pilots should

A — identify themselves as pilots.
B — tell the number of hours they have flown within the preceding 90 days.
C — state the number of occupants on board and the color of the aircraft.

3496. Answer A. JSPPM 5-33 (AIM)
Convective SIGMETs are issued for any of the following phenomena: tornadoes, lines of thunderstorms, embedded thunderstorms, areas of level 4 thunderstorms covering 40 percent of the area, and hail of 3/4 inch or greater in diameter. Severe icing and severe turbulence (answer B) are implied but not specified in the advisory. Convective SIGMETs are not issued for surface winds over 40 knots (answer C); however, if the surface winds are 50 knots, or greater, a Convective SIGMET may be issued.

3497. Answer C. JSPPM 5-33 (AWS)
SIGMETs are issued for weather potentially hazardous to all aircraft. An AIRMET advises of weather which is of operational interest to all aircraft, but may be hazardous to aircraft with limited capabilities, such as light single-engine airplanes.

3498. Answer B. JSPPM 5-33 (AWS)
A SIGMET contains more severe conditions than an AIRMET. A SIGMET covers severe icing, while an AIRMET covers moderate icing (answer C). Severe icing is implied, but not covered, in Convective SIGMETs (answer A).

3499. Answer A. JSPPM 5-32 (AWS)
See explanation for Question 3497.

3526. Answer A. JSPPM 5-27 (AWS)
You should identify yourself as a pilot and include concise facts about your flight, as follows:
1. Type of flight VFR or IFR
2. Aircraft identification or pilot's name
3. Aircraft type
4. Departure point
5. Route of flight
6. Destination
7. Altitude
8. Estimated time of departure
9. Estimated time enroute or estimated time of arrival

Briefers do not need to know how many hours the pilot has flown recently (answer B). They also do not need to know the number of occupants or color of the aircraft (answer C); this information will be on the flight plan.

3527. When telephoning a weather facility for preflight weather information, pilots should state

A — the full name and address of the pilot in command.
B — the intended route, destination, and type of aircraft.
C — the radio frequencies to be used.

3528. When telephoning a weather briefing facility for preflight weather information, pilots should state

A — the full name and address of the formation commander.
B — that they possess a current pilot certificate.
C — whether they intend to fly VFR only.

3616. How should contact be established with an En Route Flight Advisory Service (EFAS) station, and what service would be expected?

A — Call EFAS on 122.2 for routine weather, current reports on hazardous weather, and altimeter settings.
B — Call flight assistance on 122.5 for advisory service pertaining to severe weather.
C — Call Flight Watch on 122.0 for information regarding actual weather and thunderstorm activity along proposed route.

3617. What service should a pilot normally expect from an En Route Flight Advisory Service (EFAS) station?

A — Actual weather information and thunderstorm activity along the route.
B — Preferential routing and radar vectoring to circumnavigate severe weather.
C — Severe weather information, changes to flight plans, and receipt of routine position reports.

3823. Below FL180, en route weather advisories should be obtained from an FSS on

A — 122.0 MHz.
B — 122.1 MHz.
C — 123.6 MHz.

3527. Answer B. JSPPM 5-27 (AWS)
The briefer is able to tailor the briefing and supply pertinent information if the route, destination, and aircraft type are known. Providing aircraft type gives the briefer a general idea of its capabilities (altitude, de-icing equipment, power, etc.). The pilot's full name and address (answer A) are not necessary, as this information will be on the flight plan. The briefer does not need to know the radio frequencies (answer C).

3528. Answer C. JSPPM 5-27 (AWS)
It is important that the briefer knows whether a pilot intends to fly VFR or IFR, so that the information can help the pilot make a go/no-go decision. The pilot's full name and address (answer A) are not necessary for the briefer (whether a formation or single airplane). Since a pilot should not be flying without a current pilot certificate (answer B), there is no need to state the obvious.

3616. Answer C. JSPPM 5-31 (AWS)
Below FL180, EFAS is contacted on 122.0. Actual weather and thunderstorm activity along the pilot's route is provided. The frequency is not 122.2 (answer A) or 122.5 (answer B).

3617. Answer A. JSPPM 5-31 (AWS)
See explanation for Question 3616. EFAS provides weather information only, not routing or radar vectoring (answer B). It is not intended for updates to flight plans, or position reports (answer C).

3823. Answer A. JSPPM 5-31 (AIM)
See explanation for Question 3616.

CHAPTER 6

BASIC NAVIGATION

SECTION A
AERONAUTICAL CHARTS

Chapter 6 of the Private Pilot Manual introduces the basic navigational skills required for cross-country flying. Section A explains VFR aeronautical charts and how to interpret symbols, such as terrain, landmarks, airspace, airport data, and navigation aids. The following FAA Written Test questions are covered in Section A:

3117, 3530, 3535, 3536, 3543, 3567, 3599, 3600, 3604, 3605, 3606, 3607, 3608, 3609, 3610, 3611, 3612, 3618, 3622, 3625, 3629, 3630, 3631, 3632, 3633, 3634, 3635, 3636, 3637, 3638, 3639, 3640, 3641, 3642, 3643, 3831.

3117. A blue segmented circle on a Sectional Chart depicts which class airspace?

A — Class B.
B — Class C.
C — Class D.

3117. Answer C. JSPPM 6-16 (Chart Legend)
Class D airspace is designated on sectional charts by a blue segmented circle. Class B airspace is indicated by a solid blue line. Class C airspace is designated by a solid magenta line. Therefore, answers (A) and (B) are incorrect.

3530. (Refer to figure 21, area 3 on page 6-4.) Determine the approximate latitude and longitude of Currituck County Airport.

A — 36°24'N — 76°01'W.
B — 36°48'N — 76°01'W.
C — 47°26'N — 75°58'W.

3530. Answer A. JSPPM 6-7 (PHB)
This airport is located to the northeast of the number "3." Starting at the bottom of the chart at the 36° latitude, count upwards along the longitudinal line until you are opposite the airport. Each tick mark represents one minute of latitude, so the airport is located at 36°24'N. It also lies slightly more than one tick mark west of the 76° longitude line. In the United States (Western Hemisphere), longitude increases as you go west. Therefore, the airport is located at 36°24'N and 76°01'W.

3535. (Refer to figure 22, area 2 on page 6-5.) Which airport is located at approximately 47°39'30"N latitude and 100°53'00"W longitude?

A — Linrud.
B — Crooked Lake.
C — Johnson.

3535. Answer B. JSPPM 6-7 (PHB)
Note that the 48° latitude line crosses the top third of the chart. The latitude line along the bottom third is 30' less, or 47°30'N. Count up 9 1/2 tick marks (minutes) for 47°39'30"N. Since the airport's longitude is less than 101°W, move to the right of the 101° line seven tick marks to arrive at 100°53'00"W. This intersection is at Crooked Lake Airport.

3536. (Refer to figure 22, area 3 on page 6-5.) Which airport is located at approximately 47°21'N latitude and 101°01'W longitude?

A — Underwood.
B — Evenson.
C — Washburn.

3536. Answer C. JSPPM 6-7 (PHB)
See explanation for Question 3535. In this question, the latitude must be counted down from the 47°30' line, to arrive at 47°21'N. One minute to the west of the 101° longitude line (101°01'W) is the Washburn Airport.

3543. (Refer to figure 23, area 3 on page 6-6.) Determine the approximate latitude and longitude of Shoshone County Airport.

A — 47°02'N — 116°11'W.
B — 47°32'N — 116°11'W.
C — 47°32'N — 116°41'W.

3567. (Refer to figure 27, area 2 on page 6-10.) What is the approximate latitude and longitude of Cooperstown Airport?

A — 47°25'N — 98°06'W.
B — 47°25'N — 99°54'W.
C — 47°55'N — 98°06'W.

3599. (Refer to figure 26, area 4 on page 6-9.) The floor of Class B airspace overlying Hicks Airport (T67) north-northwest of Fort Worth Meacham Field is

A — at the surface.
B — 3,200 feet MSL.
C — 4,000 feet MSL.

3600. (Refer to figure 26, area 2 on page 6-9.) The floor of Class B airspace at Addison Airport is

A — at the surface.
B — 3,000 feet MSL.
C — 3,100 feet MSL.

3604. (Refer to figure 21, area 3 on page 6-4.) What is the recommended communications procedure for a landing at Currituck County Airport?

A — Transmit intentions on 122.9 MHz when 10 miles out and give position reports in the traffic pattern.
B — Contact Elizabeth City FSS for airport advisory service.
C — Contact New Bern FSS for area traffic information.

3605. (Refer to figure 22, area 2 on 6-5.) The CTAF/MULTICOM frequency for Garrison Municipal is

A — 122.8 MHz.
B — 122.9 MHz.
C — 123.0 MHz.

3543. Answer B. JSPPM 6-7 (PHB)
The airport is located just over two minutes (tick marks) north of the 47°30'N latitude line, which puts it at 47°32'N. It also lies 11 tick marks west of the 116° longitude line. Since longitude increases as you go west in the Western Hemisphere, you need to add 11 minutes to 116°. This puts the airport at 47°32'N 116°11'W.

3567. Answer A. JSPPM 6-7 (PHB)
The airport is located about 25 minutes (tick marks) north of the 47° latitude line, which puts it at 47°25'N. It is about 6 minutes (tick marks) west of the 98° longitude line, which makes the location 98°06'W.

3599. Answer C. JSPPM 6-14 (Chart Legend)
The altitudes of this portion of the Class B airspace are indicated by "100" over "40." This means the Class B airspace extends from a floor of 4,000 feet MSL up to 10,000 feet MSL. Answer (A) is wrong because the Class B airspace does not begin at the surface in this area. Answer (B) is incorrect because 3,200 feet MSL is the ceiling of the Class D airspace associated with Fort Worth Meacham.

3600. Answer B. JSPPM 6-14 (Chart Legend)
The altitudes of this portion of the Class B airspace are indicated by "100" over "30." This means the Class B airspace extends from a floor of 3,000 feet MSL up to 10,000 feet MSL.

3604. Answer A. JSPPM 6-11 (AIM)
The CTAF symbol is next to the frequency of 122.9. The normal procedure is to transmit intentions when 10 miles out and give position reports in the pattern. An FSS (answers B and C) provides airport advisory service only when located at airports without a tower. The flight service stations at Elizabeth City and New Bern do not provide airport advisory service for Currituck County.

3605. Answer B. JSPPM 6-11 (AIM)
The frequency next to the CTAF symbol at Garrison Municipal is the multicom frequency of 122.9. The frequencies 122.8 (answer A) and 123.0 (answer C) are standard UNICOM frequencies, but there is no indication they are used at Garrison Municipal.

LEGEND 1.—Sectional Aeronautical Chart.

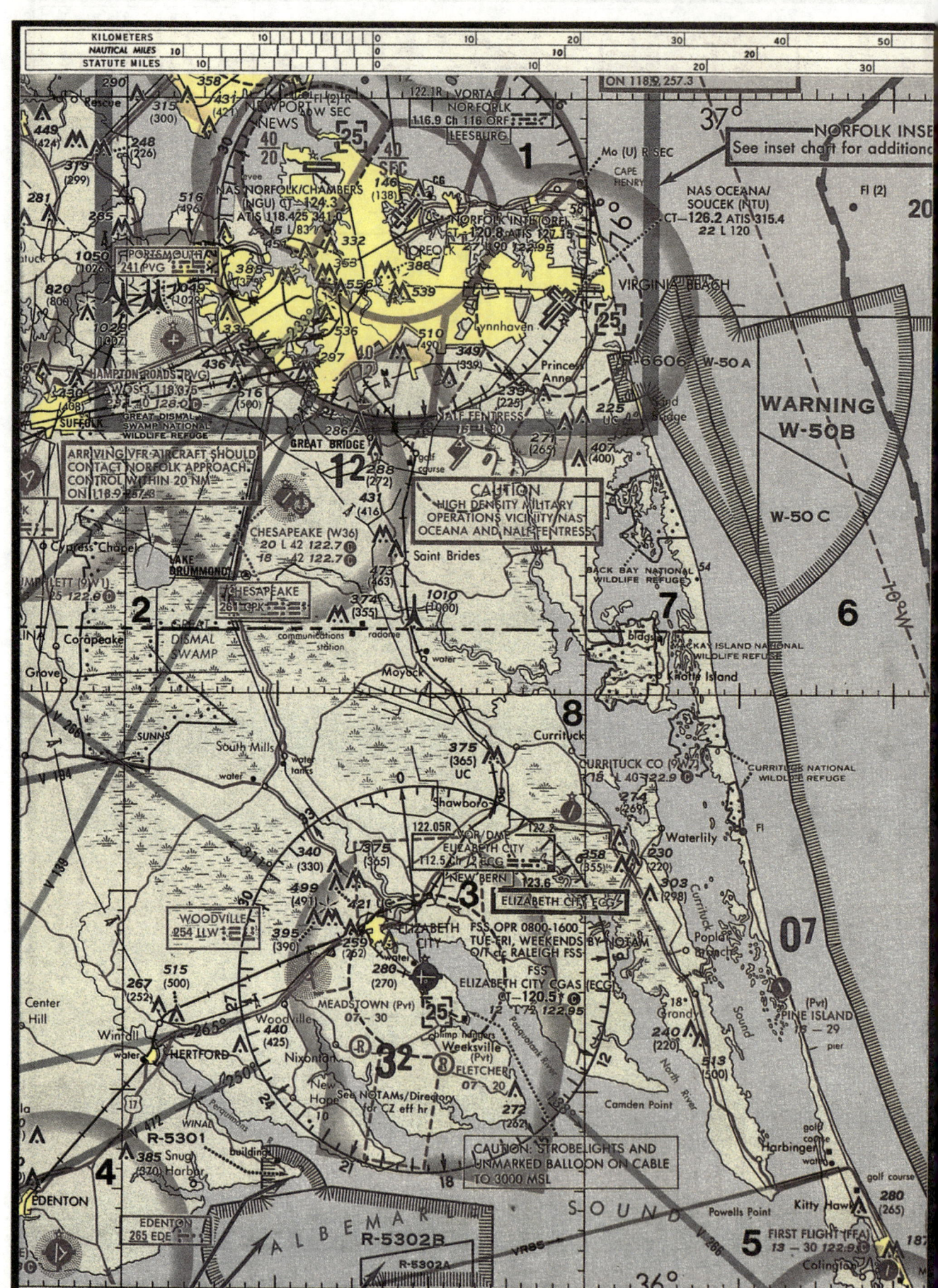

FIGURE 21.—Sectional Chart Excerpt.

FIGURE 22.—Sectional Chart Excerpt.

FIGURE 23.—Sectional Chart Excerpt.

Basic Navigation

FIGURE 24.—Sectional Chart Excerpt.

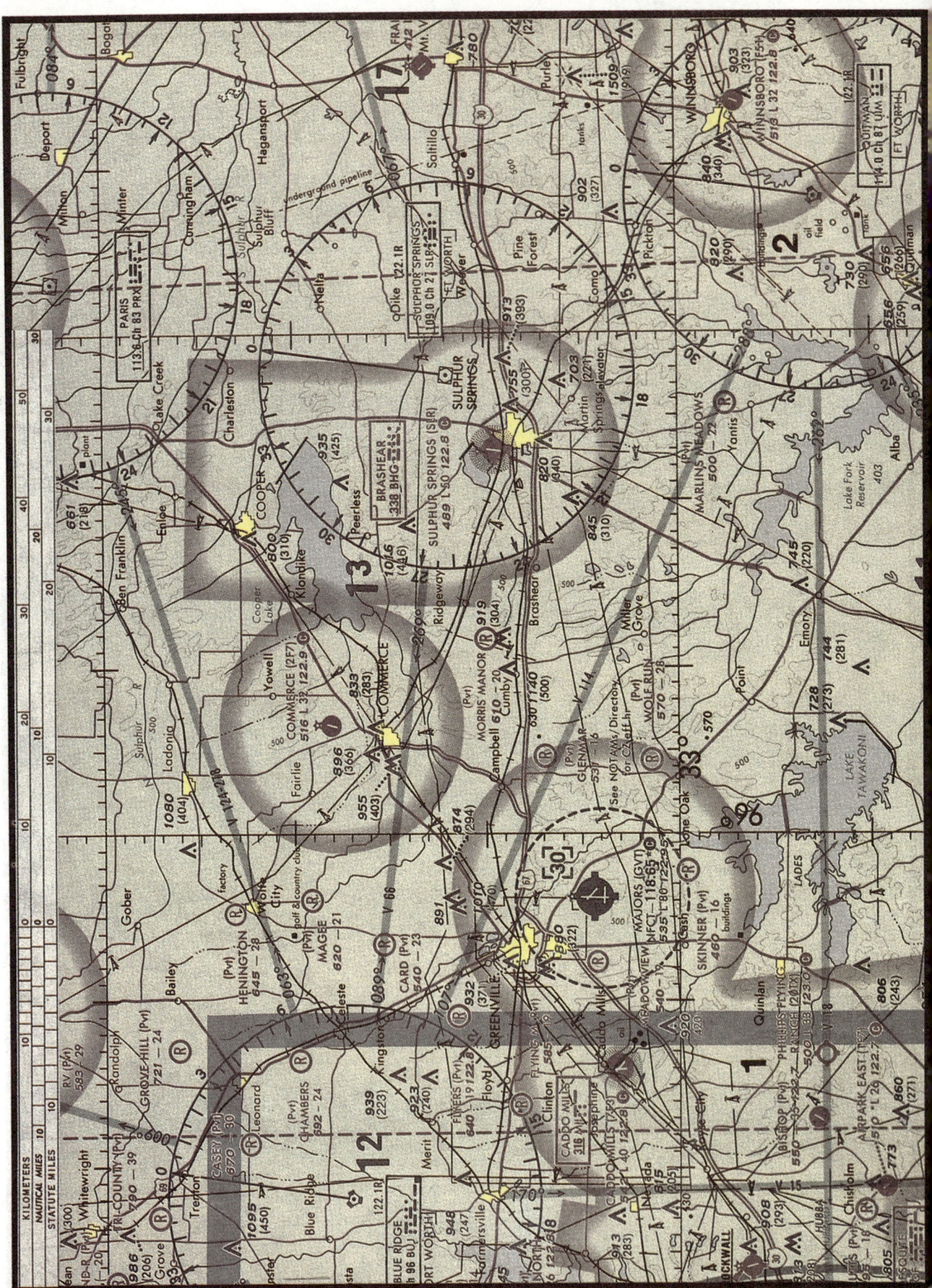

FIGURE 25.—Sectional Chart Excerpt.

FIGURE 26.—Sectional Chart Excerpt.

FIGURE 27.—Sectional Chart Excerpt.

Basic Navigation

```
COEUR D'ALENE
   COEUR D'ALENE AIR TERMINAL   (COE)   9 NW   UTC-8(-7DT)   N47°46.46' W116°49.17'           GREAT FALLS
      2318   B   S4   FUEL 80, 100, JET A   OX 1, 2                                              H-1B, L-9A
      RWY 05-23: H7400X140 (ASPH-GRVD)   S-57, D-95, DT-165   HIRL   0.7%up NE                   IAP
      RWY 05: MALSR.         RWY 23: REIL. VASI(V4L)—GA 3.0° TCH 39'.
      RWY 01-19: H5400X70 (ASPH)   S-50, D-83, DT-150   LIRL
      RWY 01: Rgt tfc.      RWY 19: Thld dsplcd 410'.
      AIRPORT REMARKS: Attended Mon-Fri 1500-0100Z‡. Rwy 23 REIL's out of service indefinitely. Rwy 05-23 potential
         standing water and/or ice on center 3000' of rwy. Arpt conditions avbl on UNICOM. Rwy 19 is designated calm
         wind rwy. ACTIVATE LIRL Rwy 01-19, HIRL Rwy 05-23 and MALSR Rwy 05—CTAF.
      WEATHER DATA SOURCES: AWOS-3 135.075 (208) 772-8215.
      COMMUNICATIONS: CTAF 119.1   UNICOM 122.8
         SPOKANE FSS (SFF) TF 1-800-527-3960. NOTAM FILE COE.
         RCO 122.1R 108.8T (SPOKANE FSS)
       ® SPOKANE APP/DEP CON 132.1
         TOWER 119.1 (1700-2300Z‡ Sat-Sun ocassional Mon-Fri).   GND CON 121.8
      RADIO AIDS TO NAVIGATION: NOTAM FILE COE.
         (T) VOR/DME 108.8   COE   Chan 25   N47°46.42' W116°49.24'   at fld. 2290/19E.
            DME portion unusable 280°-350° byd 15 NM blo 11000' 220°-240° byd 15 NM.
         LEENY NDB (LOM) 347   CO   N47°44.57' W116°57.66'   053° 6.0 NM to fld.
         ILS 110.7   I-COE   Rwy 05   LOM LEENY NDB.
```

FIGURE 32.—Airport/Facility Directory Excerpt.

3606. (Refer to figure 23, area 2 on page 6-6; and figure 32.) If Coeur D'Alene Tower is not in operation, which frequency should be used as a Common Traffic Advisory Frequency (CTAF) to self-announce position and intentions?

A— 119.1 MHz.
B— 122.1/108.8 MHz.
C— 122.8 MHz.

3606. Answer A. JSPPM 6-11 (AIM)
The control tower frequency, designated "CT -119.1" is next to a CTAF symbol. This means that the same frequency is used for CTAF when the tower is closed. The frequencies 122.1 and 108.8 (answer B) that are depicted on and in the VOR/DME box, are used to communicate with Spokane FSS. 122.8 (answer C) is the UNICOM frequency.

3607. (Refer to figure 23, area 2 on page 6-6; and figure 32.) If Coeur D'Alene Tower is not in operation, which frequency should be used as a Common Traffic Advisory Frequency (CTAF) to monitor airport traffic?

A— 119.1 MHz.
B— 122.1/108.8 MHz.
C— 122.8 MHz.

3607. Answer A. JSPPM 6-11 (AIM)
The control tower frequency, designated "CT -119.1" is next to a CTAF symbol. This means that the same frequency is used for CTAF when the tower is closed. You should use the CTAF to monitor traffic.

3608. (Refer to figure 23, area 2 on page 6-6; and figure 32.) What is the correct UNICOM frequency to be used at Coeur D'Alene to request fuel?

A— 119.1 MHz.
B— 122.1/108.8 MHz.
C— 122.8 MHz.

3608. Answer C. JSPPM 6-11 (AIM)
To request fuel, transportation, or other airport information of a general nature use the UNICOM frequency, not CTAF. The UNICOM frequency for Coeur D'Alene is 122.8.

3609. (Refer to figure 26, area 3 on page 6-9.) If Redbird Tower is not in operation, which frequency should be used as a Common Traffic Advisory Frequency (CTAF) to monitor airport traffic?

A— 120.3 MHz.
B— 122.95 MHz.
C— 126.35 MHz.

3609. Answer A. JSPPM 6-11 (AIM)
Since the tower frequency, designated "CT - 120.3" is next to the CTAF symbol, the CTAF frequency is the tower frequency. UNICOM is 122.95 (answer B), and ATIS is 126.35 (answer C).

3610. (Refer to figure 27, area 2 on page 6-10.) What is the recommended communication procedure when inbound to land at Cooperstown Airport?

A — Broadcast intentions when 10 miles out on the CTAF/MULTICOM frequency, 122.9 MHz.
B — Contact UNICOM when 10 miles out on 122.8 MHz.
C — Circle the airport in a left turn prior to entering traffic.

3611. (Refer to figure 27, area 4 on page 6-10.) The CTAF/UNICOM frequency at Jamestown Airport is

A — 122.0 MHz.
B — 123.0 MHz.
C — 123.6 MHz.

3612. (Refer to figure 27, area 6 on page 6-10.) What is the CTAF/UNICOM frequency at Barnes County Airport?

A — 122.0 MHz.
B — 122.8 MHz.
C — 123.6 MHz.

3618. (Refer to figure 27, area 3 on page 6-10.) When flying over Arrowwood National Wildlife Refuge, a pilot should fly no lower than

A — 2,000 feet AGL.
B — 2,500 feet AGL.
C — 3,000 feet AGL.

3622. (Refer to figure 27, area 3 on page 6-10.) Identify the airspace over Dalamar Farms Airport that exists from the surface to 14,500 feet MSL.

A — Class G airspace — surface to 14,500 feet MSL.
B — Class G airspace — surface to 3,500 feet MSL; Class E airspace — 3,500 feet MSL to 14,500 feet MSL.
C — Class G airspace — surface to 3,500 feet MSL; Class E airspace — 3,500 feet MSL to 10,000 feet MSL; Class G airspace — 10,000 feet MSL to 14,500 feet MSL.

3625. (Refer to figure 26, area 4 on page 6-9.) The airspace directly overlying Fort Worth Meacham is

A — Class B airspace to 10,000 feet MSL.
B — Class C airspace to 5,000 feet MSL.
C — Class D airspace to 3,200 feet MSL.

3610. Answer A. JSPPM 6-11 (AIM)
The CTAF/MULTICOM frequency, 122.9, is depicted next to the CTAF symbol. Pilots should broadcast intentions on this frequency when 10 miles from the field. When a separate CTAF is listed, the UNICOM frequency (answer B) is used only for fuel and other requests, not traffic pattern calls. Answer (C) is wrong because when radios are available, you should make the standard calls prior to entering the traffic pattern.

3611. Answer B. JSPPM 6-11 (AIM)
The CTAF symbol is next to the frequency 123.0. Answer (A) is wrong because 122.0 is the standard Enroute Fight Advisory Service (Flight Watch) frequency. Answer (C) is incorrect because 123.6 is an FSS frequency.

3612. Answer B. JSPPM 6-11 (AIM)
The CTAF symbol is next to the UNICOM frequency 122.8. 122.0 is the frequency for Flight Watch, and 123.6 is an FSS frequency used for airport advisory service.

3618. Answer A. JSPPM 6-14 (AIM)
Pilots are requested to maintain a minimum of 2,000 feet above National Wildlife Refuges.

3622. Answer A. JSPPM 6-15 (Chart Legend)
Even though this airfield is located within an MOA, it is still in uncontrolled or Class G airspace. Class G airspace extends up to the base of the overlying controlled airspace, which for this area is 14,500 feet MSL. The 3,500 and 10,000 feet MSL references in answers (B) and (C) apply to the area of V55 which does not exist when the Devils Lake East MOA is active.

3625. Answer C. JSPPM 6-14 (Chart Legend)
The blue segmented circle indicates Fort Worth Meacham is located in Class D airspace. The [32] indicates the ceiling of the Class D airspace is 3,200 feet MSL. Above the Class D airspace is a section of Class E airspace extending from 3,200 feet to 4,000 feet. Class B airspace starts at 4,000 feet MSL (not the surface) and extends to 10,000 feet MSL (answer A). There is no Class C airspace in this area of the chart (answer B).

Basic Navigation

3629. (Refer to figure 23, area 3 on page 6-6.) The vertical limits of that portion of Class E airspace designated as a Federal Airway over Magee Airport are

A — 1,200 feet AGL to 10,000 feet MSL.
B — 7,500 feet MSL to 12,500 feet MSL.
C — 7,500 feet MSL to 17,999 feet MSL.

3630. (Refer to figure 22 on page 6-5.) On what frequency can a pilot receive a Transcribed Weather Broadcast (TWEB) in the vicinity of area 1?

A — 117.1 MHz.
B — 118.0 MHz.
C — 122.0 MHz.

3631. (Refer to figure 21, area 5 on page 6-4.) The CAUTION box denotes what hazard to aircraft?

A — Guy wires extending from radio or TV towers.
B — Tall bridge over the inlet to the body of water.
C — Cable extending from radar-outfitted blimps.

3632. (Refer to figure 21, area 2 on page 6-4.) The flag symbol at Lake Drummond represents

A — a compulsory reporting point for Norfolk Class C airspace.
B — a compulsory reporting point for Hampton Roads Airport.
C — a visual checkpoint used to identify position for initial callup to Norfolk Approach Control.

3633. (Refer to figure 21, area 2 on page 6-4.) The elevation of the Chesapeake Municipal Airport is

A — 20 feet.
B — 36 feet.
C — 360 feet.

3634. (Refer to figure 22 on page 6-5.) The terrain elevation of the light tan area between Minot (area 1) and Audubon Lake (area 2) varies from

A — sea level to 2,000 feet MSL.
B — 2,000 feet to 2,500 feet MSL.
C — 2,000 feet to 2,700 feet MSL.

3629. Answer C. JSPPM 6-15 (Chart Legend)
The airway is outlined by a blue tint band. Usually the floor of an airway is 1,200 feet AGL, but, in this case, the floor is depicted by the dark blue notation "7500 MSL." As a Federal Airway, it extends up to, but not including, the base of Class A airspace, or 17,999 feet. If there was no altitude figure shown, the floor would be 1,200 feet AGL (answer A). The upper limit is neither 10,000 feet nor 12,500 feet MSL (answers A and B).

3630. Answer A. JSPPM 6-13 (Chart Legend)
The small square in the corner of the Minot VORTAC indicates that weather information (TWEB or HIWAS) is available over the VOR frequency, which is 117.1 (answer A). However, the underline under the frequency indicates there is **NO VOICE** transmissions available. The TACAN channel is 118, but does not broadcast a TWEB. The frequency 118.0 MHz (answer B) is not listed. 122.0 (answer C) is the standard EFAS frequency, not a TWEB.

3631. Answer C. JSPPM 6-18 (Chart Legend)
The CAUTION box does not exactly match any of the answers. However, it does state "strobelights and unmarked balloon on cable." Therefore, the closest answer is (C). There is no CAUTION for guy wires (answer A) or a tall bridge (answer B).

3632. Answer C. JSPPM 6-13 (Chart Legend)
The flag represents a visual checkpoint used to identify your position for approach control. Since the flag is 22 nautical miles southwest of Norfolk International Airport, it can be assumed that the checkpoint is used when contacting Norfolk Approach. The flag does not indicate a compulsory reporting point (answers A and B).

3633. Answer A. JSPPM 6-10 (Chart Legend)
The elevation is the first number listed beneath the airport name. In this case, it is 20 feet. The location identifier, W36, should not be confused with the elevation, so neither 36 feet (answer B) nor 360 feet (answer C) is correct.

3634. Answer B. JSPPM 6-4 (Chart Legend)
The colored scale shows that the tan area represents terrain above 2,000 feet MSL. In addition, the legend states that the contour interval is 500 feet. Between Minot and Audubon Lake, there are no contour lines in the tan area, which indicates there is no terrain above 2,500 feet. A check of the airports in this area shows their elevations are all less than 2,500 feet. In addition, tower heights in MSL minus their AGL heights all yield base elevations less than 2,500 feet.

3635. (Refer to figure 22 on page 6-5.) Which public use airports depicted are indicated as having fuel and a rotating beacon?

A — Minot and Mercer County Regional Airport.
B — Minot and Garrison.
C — Mercer County Regional Airport and Garrison.

3636. (Refer to figure 24 on page 6-7.) The flag symbols at Statesboro Airport, Claxton-Evans County Airport, and Ridgeland Airport are

A — outer boundaries of Savannah Class C airspace.
B — airports with special traffic patterns.
C — visual checkpoints to identify position for initial callup prior to entering Savannah Class C airspace.

3637. (Refer to figure 24, area 3 on page 6-7.) What is the height of the lighted obstacle approximately 7 nautical miles southwest of Savannah International?

A — 1,500 feet AGL.
B — 1,532 feet AGL.
C — 1,549 feet AGL.

3638. (Refer to figure 24, area 3 on page 6-7.) The top of the lighted stack approximately 12 nautical miles from the Savannah VORTAC on the 350° radial is

A — 305 feet AGL.
B — 400 feet AGL.
C — 430 feet AGL.

3639. (Refer to figure 25, area 1 on page 6-8.) What minimum altitude is necessary to vertically clear the obstacle on the northeast side of Airpark East Airport by 500 feet?

A — 1,010 feet MSL.
B — 1,273 feet MSL.
C — 1,283 feet MSL.

3640. (Refer to figure 25, area 2 on page 6-8.) What minimum altitude is necessary to vertically clear the obstacle on the southeast side of Winnsboro Airport by 500 feet?

A — 823 feet MSL.
B — 1,013 feet MSL.
C — 1,403 feet MSL.

3635. Answer A. JSPPM 6-9 (Chart Legend)
Tick marks around the airport symbol indicate fuel available, and a star on the top of the symbol represents a rotating beacon. Minot and Mercer County Regional are the only airports on the chart depicted in this manner. Garrison (answers B and C) has neither symbol.

3636. Answer C. JSPPM 6-13 (Chart Legend)
The flag symbols represent visual checkpoints used to identify your position for approach control. These checkpoints are used when contacting Savannah Approach Control. Answer (A) is not correct because the outer circle of a Class C airspace area (10 n.m. radius) is depicted by a heavy magenta line, and the outer area (20 n.m. radius) is not depicted. Special traffic patterns (answer B) are depicted on sectional charts with crosshatching accompanied by a note, "F.A.R. 93," not a flag.

3637. Answer B. JSPPM 6-17 (Chart Legend)
About 6 nautical miles southwest of the center of Savannah International airport is a lighted obstacle with its elevation marked as 1,549 (1,532). The first number is height in MSL, and the number in parentheses is height AGL. 1,500 (answer A) is the MSL height of a nearby tower, while 1,549 (answer C) is MSL height of the obstacle in question.

3638. Answer B. JSPPM 6-17 (Chart Legend)
The callout "430 (400)" near the lighted stack indicates the obstacle height is 430 feet MSL (not AGL), and 400 feet AGL.

3639. Answer B. JSPPM 6-17 (Chart Legend)
To clear the obstacle by 500 feet, you need to add 500 to the obstacle height of 773 feet MSL. The answer is 1,273 feet MSL. The airport elevation (510) plus 500 feet is 1,010 feet MSL (answer A). Answer (C), 1,283 feet MSL, can be derived by adding the airport elevation to the obstacle height.

3640. Answer C. JSPPM 6-17 (Chart Legend)
In this question, you need to add 500 feet to the obstacle height of 903 feet MSL. The answer is 1,403 feet MSL. Answer (A) can be found by adding 500 feet to 323 feet, which is the AGL height. However, this would place the aircraft below the top of the 903-foot obstacle. Answer (B) can be found by adding 500 feet to the airport elevation of 513 feet.

3641. (Refer to figure 26, area 2 on page 6-9.) The control tower frequency for Addison Airport is

A— 122.95 MHz.
B— 126.0 MHz.
C— 133.4 MHz.

3641. Answer B. JSPPM 6-10 (Chart Legend)
The tower frequency at Addison Airport is 126.0 as indicated by the letters "CT." Answer (A) is wrong because 122.95 is the UNICOM frequency. 133.4 (answer C) is the ATIS frequency.

3642. (Refer to figure 26, area 8 on page 6-9.) What minimum altitude is required to fly over the Cedar Hill TV towers in the congested area south of NAS Dallas?

A— 2,533 feet MSL.
B— 2,849 feet MSL.
C— 3,349 feet MSL.

3642. Answer C. JSPPM 6-17 (FAR 91.119)
Since we are told that this is a congested area, 1,000 feet should be added to the highest obstacle. These towers are shown with a height of 2,349 feet MSL, so the minimum altitude would be 3,349 feet MSL.

3643. (Refer to figure 26, area 6 on page 6-9.) The navigation facility at Dallas Love Field is a

A— VOR.
B— VORTAC.
C— VOR/DME.

3643. Answer NCA. JSPPM 6-12 (Chart Legend)
There is no longer a symbol at Dallas Love Field. Previous editions showed a VOR symbol enclosed by a square box. This is the symbol for a VOR/DME. A VOR without DME (answer A) would not be enclosed by a box. A VORTAC (answer B) symbol is triangular shaped, such as the one at Dallas-Fort Worth.

3831. Pilots flying over a national wildlife refuge are requested to fly no lower than

A— 1,000 feet AGL.
B— 2,000 feet AGL.
C— 3,000 feet AGL.

3831. Answer B. JSPPM 6-14 (AIM)
Pilots should fly no lower than 2,000 feet AGL over a national wildlife area.

SECTION B
FLIGHT COMPUTERS

Flight computers, whether mechanical or electronic, are essential for flight planning. The basic principles are explained in this section. In addition, detailed procedures are included for solving typical navigation problems during flight planning and while in flight. Types of problems discussed include time-speed-distance, fuel consumption, density altitude, standard temperature, airspeed calculations, wind corrections, and conversions. Test questions included in Section B are:

3529, 3534, 3540, 3541, 3542, 3548, 3549, 3554, 3562, 3563.

3529. (Refer to figure 21, on page 6-4.) En route to First Flight Airport (area 5), your flight passes over Hampton Roads Airport (area 2) at 1456 and then over Chesapeake Municipal at 1501. At what time should your flight arrive at First Flight?

A — 1516.
B — 1521.
C — 1526.

3529. Answer C. JSPPM 6-25 (PHB)
This question requires you to calculate groundspeed and then estimated time of arrival.
1. Determine the actual groundspeed (GS) of the aircraft.
    a. Measure the distance between Hampton Roads Airport and Chesapeake Municipal using your plotter (10 n.m.).
    b. Determine the elapsed time (15:01 -14:56 = 5 min.).
    c. Determine the GS (10 n.m. in 5 min. = 2 n.m./min. x 60 min. = 120 n.m. per hour groundspeed).
2. Determine the estimated time of arrival (ETA) at First Flight Airport.
    a. Measure the distance between Chesapeake Municipal and First Flight Airport (50 n.m.).
    b. Determine the time enroute between the two points (50 n.m. at 2 n.m./min. = 25 minutes).
    c. If the aircraft was over Chesapeake Municipal at 15:01, the ETA at First Flight Airport is 15:26 (15:01 + 25 min. = 15:26).

3534. (Refer to figure 22 on page 6-5.) What is the estimated time en route from Mercer County Regional Airport (area 3) to Minot International (area 1)? The wind is from 330° at 25 knots and the true airspeed is 100 knots.
Add 3-1/2 minutes for departure and climb-out.

A — 44 minutes.
B — 48 minutes.
C — 52 minutes.

3534. Answer B. JSPPM 6-37 (PHB)
This question requires you to calculate groundspeed and then complete a time-speed-distance problem.
1. Measure the distance between Mercer County Regional Airport and Minot International (59 n.m.).
2. Determine the True Course (TC) (012°).
3. Determine the groundspeed using your flight computer.
    a. Enter the wind direction and speed (330° True at 25 kts.).
    b. Enter the TC (012°).
    c. Enter the True Air Speed (TAS) (100 kts.).
    d. GS = 80 kts.
4. Determine the time enroute using your flight computer (59 n.m. at 80 n.m./hr. = 44 min.15 sec.).
5. Add departure and climb-out time (3 min. 30 sec. + 44 min. 15 sec. = 47 min. 45 sec.). This is rounded to 48 minutes.

Basic Navigation

6-17

3540. (Refer to figure 23 on page 6-6.) What is the estimated time en route from Sandpoint Airport (area 1) to St. Maries Airport (area 4)? The wind is from 215° at 25 knots and the true airspeed is 125 knots.

A — 27 minutes.
B — 30 minutes.
C — 34 minutes.

3540. Answer C. JSPPM 6-37 (PHB)
This question requires you to calculate groundspeed and then complete a time-speed-distance problem.
1. Measure the distance from Sandpoint Airport to St. Maries Airport (58 n.m.).
2. Determine the TC (180°).
3. Determine groundspeed using your flight computer.
   a. Enter the wind direction and speed (215°True at 25 kts.)
   b. Enter the TC (180°).
   c. Enter the True Airspeed (125 kts.).
   d. GS = 104 kts.
4. Determine the time enroute using your flight computer (58 n.m. at 104 n.m./hr. = 33 min 30 sec.). This is rounded to 34 minutes.

3541. (Refer to figure 23 on page 6-6.) Determine the estimated time en route for a flight from Priest River Airport (area 1) to Shoshone County Airport (area 3). The wind is from 030 at 12 knots and the true airspeed is 95 knots. Add 2 minutes for climb-out.

A — 23 minutes.
B — 27 minutes.
C — 31 minutes.

3541. Answer C. JSPPM 6-37 (PHB)
This question requires you to calculate groundspeed and then complete a time-speed-distance problem.
1. Measure the distance from Priest River Airport to Shoshone County Airport (48 n.m.).
2. Determine the True Course (143°).
3. Determine groundspeed using your flight computer.
   a. Enter the wind direction and speed (030° at 12 kts.).
   b. Enter the True Course (143°).
   c. Enter the True Airspeed (95 kts.).
   d. GS = 99 kts.
4. Determine the time enroute using your flight computer (48 n.m. at 99 n.m./hr. = 29 min.).
5. Add 2 min. for departure and climb-out (2 min. + 29 min. = 31 min.).

3542. (Refer to figure 23 on page 6-6.) What is the estimated time en route for a flight from St. Maries Airport (area 4) to Priest River airport (area 1)? The wind is from 300° at 14 knots and the true airspeed is 90 knots. Add 3 minutes for climb-out.

A — 38 minutes.
B — 43 minutes.
C — 48 minutes.

3542. Answer B. JSPPM 6-37 (PHB)
This question requires you to calculate groundspeed and then complete a time-speed-distance problem.
1. Measure the distance from St. Maries Airport to Priest River Airport (53 n.m.).
2. Determine the True Course (345°).
3. Determine groundspeed using your flight computer.
   a. Enter the wind direction and speed (300° at 14 kts.).
   b. Enter the True Course (345°).
   c. Enter the TAS (90 kts.).
   d. GS = 80 kts.
4. Determine the time enroute using your flight computer (53 n.m. at 80 n.m./hr. = 39 min. 45 sec.).
5. Add 3 min. for departure and climb-out (3 min. + 39 min. 45 sec. = 42 min. 45 sec.). This is rounded to 43 minutes.

3548. (Refer to figure 24 on page 6-7.) What is the estimated time en route for a flight from Allendale County Airport (area 1) to Claxton-Evans County Airport (area 2)? The wind is from 090° at 16 knots and the true airspeed is 90 knots. Add 2 minutes for climb-out.

A — 33 minutes.
B — 37 minutes.
C — 41 minutes.

3548. Answer B. JSPPM 6-37 (PHB)
This question requires you to calculate groundspeed and then complete a time-speed-distance problem.
1. Measure the distance from Allendale County to Claxton-Evans County Airport (57 n.m.).
2. Determine the True Course (212°).
3. Determine the groundspeed using your flight computer.
   a. Enter the wind direction and speed (090° at 16 kts.).
   b. Enter the True Course (212°).
   c. Enter the TAS (90 kts.).
   d. GS = 97 kts.
4. Determine the time enroute using your flight computer (57 n.m. at 97 n.m./hr. = 35 min. 15 sec.).
5. Add 2 min. for departure and climb-out (2 min. + 35 min. 15 sec. = 37 min. 15 sec.). This is rounded to 37 minutes.

3549. (Refer to figure 24 on page 6-7.) What is the estimated time en route for a flight from Claxton-Evans County Airport (area 2) to Hampton Varnville Airport (area 1)? The wind is from 290° at 18 knots and the true airspeed is 85 knots. Add 2 minutes for climb-out.

A — 35 minutes.
B — 39 minutes.
C — 44 minutes.

3549. Answer B. JSPPM 6-37 (PHB)
This question requires you to calculate groundspeed and then complete a Time-Speed-Distance problem.
1. Measure the distance from Claxton-Evans County Airport to Hampton Varnville Airport (57 n.m.).
2. Determine the True Course (045°).
3. Determine the groundspeed using your flight computer.
   a. Enter the wind direction and speed (290° at 18 kts.).
   b. Enter the True Course (045°).
   c. Enter the TAS (85 kts.).
   d. GS = 91 kts.
4. Determine the time enroute using your flight computer (57 n.m. at 91 n.m./hr. = 37 min. 30 sec.).
5. Add 2 minutes for departure and climb-out (2 min. + 37 min. 30 sec. = 39 min. 30 sec.). The closest answer is 39 minutes.

Basic Navigation

6-19

3554. (Refer to figure 24 on page 6-7.) While en route on Victor 185, a flight crosses the 248° radial of Allendale VOR at 0951 and then crosses the 216° radial of Allendale VOR at 1000. What is the estimated time of arrival at Savannah VORTAC?

A — 1023.
B — 1028.
C — 1036.

3554. Answer C. JSPPM 6-37 (PHB)
This question requires you to calculate groundspeed and then estimated time of arrival.
1. Determine the actual groundspeed of the aircraft.
   a. Measure the distance along Victor 185 where it crosses the 248° radial and the 216° radial of Allendale VOR (10 n.m.).
   b. Determine the elapsed time. (10:00 - 09:51 = 9 min.).
   c. Determine the groundspeed (10 n.m. in 9 min. = 67 kts.).
2. Determine the Estimated Time of Arrival (ETA) over the Savannah VORTAC.
   a. Measure the distance along Victor 185 from the 216° radial of Allendale VORTAC to the Savannah VORTAC (40 n.m.).
   b. Determine time enroute (GS is 67 kts.) (40 n.m. at 67 n.m./hr. = 36 min. 30 sec.).
   c. Determine estimated time of arrival (10:00 + 36 min. 30 sec. = 10:36).

3562. (Refer to figure 26 on page 6-9.) What is the estimated time en route for a flight from Denton Muni (area 1) to Addison (area 2)? The wind is from 200° at 20 knots, the true airspeed is 110 knots, and the magnetic variation is 7° east.

A — 13 minutes.
B — 16 minutes.
C — 19 minutes.

3562. Answer A. JSPPM 6-37 (PHB)
This question requires you to calculate groundspeed, then complete a time-speed-distance problem.
1. Measure the distance from Denton Muni to Addison Airport (23 n.m.).
2. Determine True Course (128°).
3. Determine the groundspeed using your flight computer.
   a. Enter the wind direction and speed (200° at 20 kts.).
   b. Enter the True Course (128°).
   c. Enter the TAS (110 kts.).
   d. GS = 102 kts.
4. Determine time enroute (23 n.m. at 102 n.m./hr = 13 min. 30 sec.). The closest answer is 13 minutes.

3563. (Refer to figure 26 on page 6-9.) Estimate the time enroute from Addison (area 2) to Redbird (area 3). The wind is from 300° at 15 knots, the true airspeed is 120 knots, and the magnetic variation is 7° east.

A — 8 minutes.
B — 11 minutes.
C — 14 minutes.

3563. Answer A. JSPPM 6-37 (PHB)
This question requires you to calculate groundspeed, then complete a time-speed-distance problem.
1. Measure the distance from Addison Airport to Redbird Airport (17 n.m.).
2. Determine the True Course (186°).
3. Determine the groundspeed using your flight computer.
   a. Enter the wind direction and speed (300° at 15 kts.).
   b. Enter the TC (186°).
   c. Enter the TAS (120 kts.).
   d. GS = 125 kts.
4. Determine time enroute (17 n.m. at 125 n.m./hr. = 8 min. 8 sec.). The closest answer is 8 minutes.

SECTION C
PILOTAGE AND DEAD RECKONING

This section introduces you to VFR navigation using pilotage, or navigating by reference to checkpoints. Also explained is dead reckoning, which allows you to predict the movement of your airplane along an intended route. The use of a navigation log and how to fill out a flight plan are also covered. FAA Written Test questions in this section include:

3531, 3538, 3545, 3546, 3547, 3550, 3551, 3556, 3565, 3568, 3815, 3816, 3817, 3818.

3531. (Refer to figure 21 on page 6-4.) Determine the magnetic course from First Flight Airport (area 5) to Hampton Roads Airport (area 2).

A — 312°.
B — 321°.
C — 330°.

3531. Answer C. JSPPM 6-46 (PHB)
This question requires you to find the magnetic course by determining true course, then correcting it for magnetic variation.
1. Use your plotter to determine True Course (321°).
2. Locate the nearest isogonic line to the course (9°W).
3. Convert TC to MC by correcting for variation. (Since this is a west variation, you must add it to the true course.)
TC ± Variation = MC (321° + 9° = 330°)

3538. (Refer to figure 22 on page 6-5.) Determine the magnetic heading for a flight from Mercer County Regional Airport (area 3) to Minot International (Area 1). The wind is from 330° at 25 knots, the true airspeed is 100 knots, and the magnetic variation is 11° east.

A — 002°.
B — 012°.
C — 351°.

3538. Answer C. JSPPM 6-46 (PHB)
This question requires you to find magnetic heading. This is done by first determining true heading by correcting true course for winds. Then, correct true heading for magnetic variation.
1. Use your plotter to determine true course (012°).
2. Use your flight computer to determine true heading.
   a. Enter wind direction and speed (330° at 25 kts.).
   b. Enter the true course (012°).
   c. Enter the TAS (100 kts.).
   d. TH = 002°
3. Convert TH to MH by correcting for magnetic variation (11°E). (Since this is an east variation, you must subtract it from the true heading.)
TH ± Variation = MH (002° - 11° = 351°)

Basic Navigation

3545. (Refer to figure 23 on page 6-6.) Determine the magnetic heading for a flight from Sandpoint Airport (area 1) to St. Maries Airport (area 4). The wind is from 215° at 25 knots and the true airspeed is 125 knots.

A — 161°.
B — 167°.
C — 181°.

3545. Answer B. JSPPM 6-46 (PHB)
This question requires you to find magnetic heading. This is done by first determining true heading by correcting true course for winds. Then, correct true heading for magnetic variation.
1. Use your plotter to determine true course (181°).
2. Use your flight computer to determine true heading.
   a. Enter the wind direction and speed (215° at 25 kts.).
   b. Enter the true course (181°).
   c. Enter the TAS (125 kts.).
   d. TH = 187°
3. Convert TH to MH by correcting for magnetic variation (19°E). Since this is an east variation, you must subtract it from the true heading.)
TH ± Variation = MH (187° - 19° = 168°)
The closest answer is 167°.

3546. (Refer to figure 23 on page 6-6.) What is the magnetic heading for a flight from Priest River Airport (area 1) to Shoshone County Airport (area 3)? The wind is from 030° at 12 knots and the true airspeed is 95 knots.

A — 116°.
B — 123°.
C — 130°.

3546. Answer A. JSPPM 6-46 (PHB)
This question requires you to find magnetic heading. This is done by first determining true heading by correcting true course for winds. Then, correct true heading for magnetic variation.
1. Use your plotter to determine true course (143°).
2. Use your flight computer to determine true heading.
   a. Enter the wind direction and speed (030° at 12 kts.).
   b. Enter the true course (143°).
   c. Enter the TAS (95 kts.).
   d. TH = 136°
3. Convert TH to MH by correcting for magnetic variation (19°E). (Since this is an east variation, you must subtract it from the true heading.)
TH ± Variation = MH (136° - 19° = 117°)
The closest answer is 116°.

3547. (Refer to figure 23 on page 6-6.) Determine the magnetic heading for a flight from St. Maries Airport (area 4) to Priest River Airport (area 1). The wind is from 300° at 14 knots and the true airspeed is 90 knots.

A — 319°.
B — 325°.
C — 331°.

3547. Answer A. JSPPM 6-46 (PHB)
This question requires you to find magnetic heading. This is done by first determining true heading by correcting true course for winds. Then, correct true heading for magnetic variation.
1. Use your plotter to determine true course (345°).
2. Use your flight computer to determine true heading.
   a. Enter the wind direction and speed (300° at 14 kts.).
   b. Enter the true course (345°).
   c. Enter the TAS (90 kts.).
   d. TH = 339°
3. Convert TH to MH by correcting for magnetic variation (19°E). (Since this is an east variation, you must subtract it from the true heading.)
TH ± Variation = MH (339° - 19° = 320°)
The closest answer is 319°.

3550. (Refer to figure 24 on page 6-7.) Determine the compass heading for a flight from Allendale County Airport (area 1) to Claxton-Evans County Airport (area 2). The wind is from 090° at 16 knots and the true airspeed is 90 knots.

A — 200°.
B — 205°.
C — 211°.

3550. Answer C. JSPPM 6-46 (PHB)
This question requires you to find compass heading. This is done by first determining true heading by correcting true course for winds. Then, correct true heading for magnetic variation, and finally correct magnetic heading for compass error.
1. Use your plotter to determine true course (212°).
2. Use your flight computer to determine true heading.
   a. Enter the wind direction and speed (090° at 16 kts.).
   b. Enter the true course (212°).
   c. Enter the TAS (90 kts.).
   d. TH = 203°
3. Convert TH to MH by correcting for magnetic variation (4°W). (Since this is a west variation, you must add it to the true heading.)
   TH ± Variation = MH (203° + 4° = 207°)
4. Use the compass correction card at the top of Figure 24 to determine compass error. For a heading of approximately 210°, add 4° (207° + 4° = 211°).

3551. (Refer to figure 24 on page 6-7.) Determine the compass heading for a flight from Claxton-Evans County Airport (area 2) to Hampton Varnville Airport (area 1). The wind is from 290° at 18 knots and the true airspeed is 85 knots.

A — 034°.
B — 038°.
C — 042°.

3551. Answer A. JSPPM 6-46 (PHB)
This question requires you to find compass heading. This is done by first determining true heading by correcting true course for winds. Then, correct true heading for magnetic variation, and finally correct magnetic heading for compass error.
1. Use your plotter to determine true course (045°).
2. Use your flight computer to determine true heading.
   a. Enter the wind direction and speed (290° at 18 kts.).
   b. Enter the true course (045°).
   c. Enter the TAS (85 kts.).
   d. TH = 034°
3. Convert TH to MH by correcting for magnetic variation (4°W). (Since this is a west variation, you must add it to the true heading.)
   TH ± Variation = MH (034° + 4° = 038°)
4. Use the compass correction card at the top of Figure 24 to determine compass error. For a heading of approximately 030°, subtract 3°. (038° - 3° = 035°)
The closest answer is 034°.

Basic Navigation

3556. (Refer to figure 25 on page 6-8.) Determine the magnetic course from Airpark East Airport (area 1) to Winnsboro Airport (area 2). Magnetic variation is 6°30'E.

A — 075°.
B — 082°.
C — 091°.

3556. Answer A. JSPPM 6-46 (PHB)
This question requires you find the magnetic course by determining true course, then correcting it for magnetic variation.
1. Use your plotter to determine True Course (082°).
2. Locate the nearest isogonic line to the course (6°30'E). (Add West, Subtract East variation)
3. Convert TC to MC by correcting for variation. (Since this is an east variation, you must subtract it from true course.)
   TC ± Variation = MC (082° - 6°30' = 075° 30')
   The closest answer is 075°.

3565. (Refer to figure 26 on page 6-9.) Determine the magnetic heading for a flight from Fort Worth Meacham (area 4) to Denton Muni (area 1). The wind is from 330° at 25 knots, the true airspeed is 110 knots, and the magnetic variation is 7° east.

A — 003°.
B — 017°.
C — 023°.

3565. Answer A. JSPPM 6-46 (PHB)
This question requires you to find magnetic heading. This is done by first determining true heading by correcting true course for winds. Then, correct true heading for magnetic variation.
1. Use your plotter to determine true course (021°).
2. Use your flight computer to determine true heading.
   a. Enter the wind direction and speed (330° at 25 kts.).
   b. Enter the true course (021°).
   c. Enter the TAS (110 kts.).
   d. TH = 011°
3. Convert TH to MH by correcting for magnetic variation (7°E). (Since this is an east variation, you must subtract it from the true heading.)
   TH ± Variation = MH (011° - 7° = 004°)
   The closest answer is 003°.

3568. (Refer to figure 27 on page 6-10.) Determine the magnetic course from Breckheimer (Pvt) Airport (area 1) to Jamestown Airport (area 4).

A — 013°.
B — 021°.
C — 181°.

3568. Answer C. JSPPM 6-46 (PHB)
This question requires you find the magnetic course by determining true course, then correcting it for magnetic variation.
1. Use your plotter to determine True Course (189°).
2. Locate the nearest isogonic line to the course (8°E).
3. Convert TC to MC by correcting for variation. (Since this is an east variation, you must subtract it from true course.)
   TC ± Variation = MC (189° - 8° = 181°).

3815. (Refer to figure 52.) If more than one cruising altitude is intended, which should be entered in block 7 of the flight plan?

A — Initial cruising altitude.
B — Highest cruising altitude.
C — Lowest cruising altitude.

3815. Answer A. JSPPM 6-50 (PHB)
The initial cruising altitude should be entered on the flight plan. Any subsequent altitude changes should be requested from the enroute controller. If the highest or lowest cruising altitude (answers B and C) is entered, air traffic control will assume that this altitude is the initial cruising altitude.

3816. (Refer to figure 52.) What information should be entered in block 9 for a VFR day flight?

A — The name of the airport of first intended landing.
B — The name of destination airport if no stopover for more than 1 hour is anticipated.
C — The name of the airport where the aircraft is based.

3816. Answer B. JSPPM 6-50 (PHB)
FAR 91.153 states that the flight plan shall include the point of first intended landing. However, the AIM says to enter the destination airport. It also recommends that for a stopover of more than 1 hour, a separate flight plan should be filed. Therefore, answer (B) is a correct statement, and we believe it is the best answer. Answer (A) would not be entirely correct for a flight which includes a stopover of less than 1 hour. The aircraft's home base (answer C) is entered in block 14, not block 9.

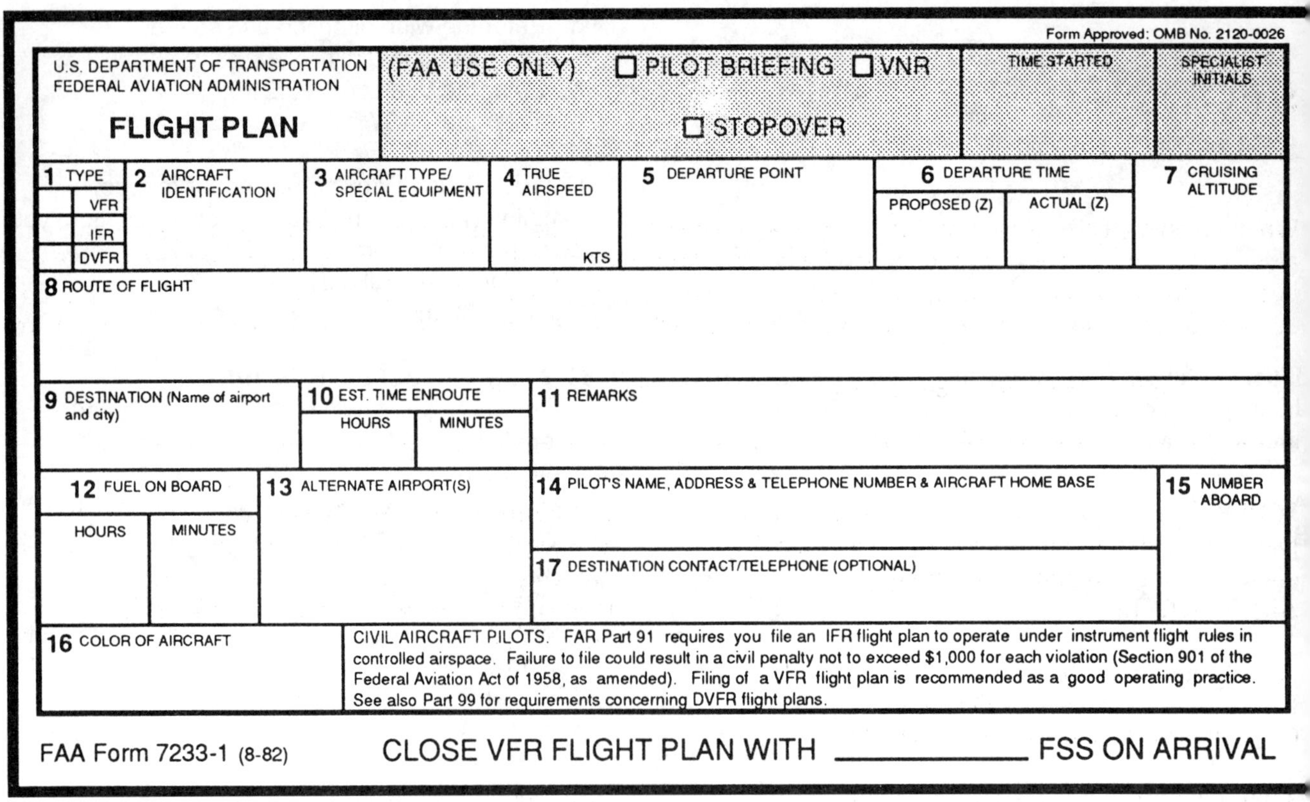

Form Approved: OMB No. 2120-0026

U.S. DEPARTMENT OF TRANSPORTATION
FEDERAL AVIATION ADMINISTRATION

FLIGHT PLAN

(FAA USE ONLY) ☐ PILOT BRIEFING ☐ VNR ☐ STOPOVER | TIME STARTED | SPECIALIST INITIALS

1 TYPE: VFR / IFR / DVFR
2 AIRCRAFT IDENTIFICATION
3 AIRCRAFT TYPE/ SPECIAL EQUIPMENT
4 TRUE AIRSPEED KTS
5 DEPARTURE POINT
6 DEPARTURE TIME: PROPOSED (Z) / ACTUAL (Z)
7 CRUISING ALTITUDE
8 ROUTE OF FLIGHT
9 DESTINATION (Name of airport and city)
10 EST. TIME ENROUTE: HOURS / MINUTES
11 REMARKS
12 FUEL ON BOARD: HOURS / MINUTES
13 ALTERNATE AIRPORT(S)
14 PILOT'S NAME, ADDRESS & TELEPHONE NUMBER & AIRCRAFT HOME BASE
15 NUMBER ABOARD
17 DESTINATION CONTACT/TELEPHONE (OPTIONAL)
16 COLOR OF AIRCRAFT

CIVIL AIRCRAFT PILOTS. FAR Part 91 requires you file an IFR flight plan to operate under instrument flight rules in controlled airspace. Failure to file could result in a civil penalty not to exceed $1,000 for each violation (Section 901 of the Federal Aviation Act of 1958, as amended). Filing of a VFR flight plan is recommended as a good operating practice. See also Part 99 for requirements concerning DVFR flight plans.

FAA Form 7233-1 (8-82) CLOSE VFR FLIGHT PLAN WITH ________ FSS ON ARRIVAL

FIGURE 52.— Flight Plan Form.

Basic Navigation 6-25

3817. (Refer to figure 52.) What information should be entered in block 12 for a VFR day flight?

A — The estimated time en route plus 30 minutes.
B — The estimated time en route plus 45 minutes.
C — The amount of usable fuel on board expressed in time.

3817. Answer C. JSPPM 6-50 (PHB)
The fuel on board is the total amount of fuel in hours and minutes (usable fuel is assumed). The estimated time en route (answers A and B) is entered in block 10, not block 12. The reserve fuel (30 minutes VFR, 45 minutes IFR) is not entered on the flight plan; however, the fuel on board should always be at least 30 or 45 minutes greater than the time en route.

3818. How should a VFR flight plan be closed at the completion of the flight at a controlled airport?

A — The tower will automatically close the flight plan when the aircraft turns off the runway.
B — The pilot must close the flight plan with the nearest FSS or other FAA facility upon landing.
C — The tower will relay the instructions to the nearest FSS when the aircraft contacts the tower for landing.

3818. Answer B. JSPPM 6-51 (PHB)
To close a VFR flight plan, you must notify an FSS or other FAA facility. The control tower (answers A and C) does not automatically close VFR flight plans.

SECTION D
SOURCES OF FLIGHT INFORMATION

When planning a cross-country flight, you need to know how to find current information on airports, navigational aids, and other procedural or regulatory details affecting safety of flight. This kind of information is found in several publications which are discussed in this section. They include the Airport/Facility Directory, the Airman's Information Manual, Notices to Airmen, advisory circulars, and the J-AID. The applicable FAA questions in Section D are:

3619, 3709, 3838, 3839, 3840, 3841, 3842, 3843, 3854, 3855, 3856.

3619. (Refer to figure 23, area 2 and legend 1 on pages 6-6 and 6-3.) For information about the parachute jumping and glider operations at Silverwood Airport, refer to

A— notes on the border of the chart.
B— the Airport/Facility Directory.
C— the Notices to Airmen (NOTAM) publication.

3619. Answer B. JSPPM 6-57 (Chart Legend)
The Airport/Facility Directory lists information on parachute jumping areas. This information is not found on the border of the chart (answer A) or in the NOTAM publication (answer C).

3709. FAA advisory circulars (some free, other at cost) are available to all pilots and are obtained by

A — distribution from the nearest FAA district office.
B — ordering those desired from the Government Printing Office.
C — subscribing to the Federal Register.

3709. Answer B. JSPPM 6-60 (PHB)
Advisory circulars may be ordered directly from the Government Printing Office. FAA district offices (answer A) do not stock advisory circulars for sale to the public. The Federal Register (answer C) contains notices of proposed rulemaking and final rules, but does not contain advisory circulars.

172 **NEBRASKA**

LINCOLN MUNI (LNK) 4 NW UTC–6(–5DT) N40°51 05' W96°45 55' OMAHA
  1214 B S4 FUEL 100LL, JET A TPA—2214(1000) ARFF Index C H-1E, 3F, 4F, L-11B
  RWY 17R-35L: H12901X200 (ASPH-CONC-GRVD) S-100 D-200, DT-400 HIRL IAP
    RWY 17R: MALSR. VASI(V4L)—GA 3.0° TCH 55'. Rgt tfc Arresting device
    RWY 35L: MALSR. VASI(V4L)—GA 3.0° TCH 55'. Arresting device.
  RWY 14-32: H8620X150 (ASPH-CONC-GRVD) S-80, D-170. DT-280 MIRL
    RWY 14: REIL. VASI(4VL)—GA 3.0° TCH 48'. RWY 32: VASI(4VL)—GA 3.0° TCH 53' Thld dsplcd 431' Pole
  RWY 17L-35R: H5500X100 (ASPH-CONC-AFSC) S-49 D-60 HIRL 0.8% up N
    RWY 17L: VASI(V4L)—GA 3.0° TCH 33'. RWY 35R: VASI(V4L)—GA 3.0° TCH 35'. Pole. Rgt tfc
  AIRPORT REMARKS: Attended continuously. Arresting barrier located 2200' in from thld 17R and 1500' in from thld 35L. Arresting barrier in place departure end Rwy 17R-35L during military operations and approach end during emergencies. Airport manager advise 43000 lbs GWT single wheel Rwy 17L-35R. For MALSR Rwy 17R and 35L ctc twr.; When twr clsd MALSR Rwy 17R and 35L preset on med ints. and REIL Rwy 14 left on when wind favor. NOTE: See SPECIAL NOTICE-Simultaneous Operations on Intersecting Runways.
  WEATHER DATA SOURCES: ASOS (402) 474-9214. LLWAS
  COMMUNICATIONS: CTAF 118.5 ATIS 118.05 UNICOM 122 95
    COLUMBUS FSS (OLU) TF 1-800-WX-BRIEF. NOTAM FILE LNK
    RCO 122.65 (COLUMBUS FSS)
  ® APP/DEP CON 124.0 (170°-349°) 124.8 (350°-169°) (1200-0600Z‡)
  ® MINNEAPOLIS CENTER APP/DEP CON 128.75 (0600-1200Z‡)
    TOWER 118.5 125.7 (1200-0600Z‡) GND CON 121.9 CLNC DEL 120 7
    ARSA ctc APP CON
  RADIO AIDS TO NAVIGATION: NOTAM FILE LNK. VHF/DF ctc COLUMBUS FSS
    (H) VORTACW 116.1 LNK Chan 108 N40°55.43' W96°44.52 181° 4.5 NM to fld. 1370/9E
    POTTS NDB (MHW/LOM) 385 LN N40°44.83' W96°45.75' 355° 6.2 NM to fld. Unmonitored when twr clsd
    ILS 111.1 I-OCZ Rwy 17R. MM and OM unmonitored.
    ILS 109.9 I-LNK Rwy 35L LOM POTTS NDB. MM unmonitored. LOM unmonitored when twr clsd.
  COMM/NAVAID REMARKS: Emerg frequency 121.5 not available at tower.

LOUP CITY MUNI (NE03) 1 NW UTC–6(–5DT) N41°17.42' W98°59.44' OMAHA
  2070 B FUEL 100LL L-11B
  RWY 15-33: H3200X50 (ASPH) S-8 LIRL
    RWY 33: Trees.
  RWY 04-22: 2100X100 (TURF)
    RWY 04: Tree. RWY 22: Road.
  AIRPORT REMARKS: Unattended. For svc call 308-745-0328.
  COMMUNICATIONS: CTAF 122.9
    COLUMBUS FSS (OLU) TF 1-800-WX-BRIEF. NOTAM FILE OLU.
  RADIO AIDS TO NAVIGATION: NOTAM FILE OLU.
    WOLBACH (H) VORTAC 114.8 OBH Chan 95 N41°22.54' W98°21.22' 250° 29.3 NM to fld. 2010/10E

MARTIN FLD (See SO SIOUX CITY)

McCOOK MUNI (MCK) 2 E UTC–6(–5DT) N40°12.38' W100°35.51' OMAHA
  2579 B S4 FUEL 100LL, JET A ARFF Index Ltd. H-2D, L-11A
  RWY 12-30: H5998X100 (CONC) S-30, D-38 MIRL 0.6% up NW IAP
    RWY 12: MALS. VASI(V4L)—GA 3.0° TCH 33'. Tree. RWY 30: REIL. VASI(V4L)—GA 3.0° TCH 42'.
  RWY 03-21: H3999X75 (CONC) S-30, D-38 MIRL
    RWY 03: VASI(V2L)—GA 3.0° TCH 26'. Rgt tfc. RWY 21: VASI(V2L)—GA 3.0° TCH 26'.
  RWY 17-35: 1350X200 (TURF)
  AIRPORT REMARKS: Attended daylight hours. Parachute Jumping. Deer on and in vicinity of arpt. Arpt closed to air carrier operations with more than 30 passengers except 24 hour PPR, call arpt manager 308-345-2022. Avoid McCook State (abandoned) arpt 7 miles NW on the MCK VOR/DME 313° radial at 8.3 DME. ACTIVATE VASI Rwys 12 and 30 and MALS Rwy 12—CTAF. Control Zone effective 1100-0500Z‡, except holidays.
  COMMUNICATIONS: CTAF/UNICOM 122.8
    COLUMBUS FSS (OLU) TF 1-800-WX-BRIEF. NOTAM FILE MCK.
    RCO 122.6 (COLUMBUS FSS)
  ® DENVER CENTER APP/DEP CON 132.7
  RADIO AIDS TO NAVIGATION: NOTAM FILE MCK.
    (L) VORW/DME 116.5 MCK Chan 112 N40°12.23' W100°35.66' at fld. 2550/11E.

MILLARD (See OMAHA)

MILLER FLD (See VALENTINE)

FIGURE 53.—Airport/Facility Directory Excerpt.

Basic Navigation

3838. (Refer to figure 53.) When approaching Lincoln Municipal from the west at noon for the purpose of landing, initial communications should be with

A — Lincoln Approach Control on 124.0 MHz.
B — Minneapolis Center on 128.75 MHz.
C — Lincoln Tower on 118.5 MHz.

3838. Answer A. JSPPM 6-55 (A/FD)
The communications section of the Airport/Facility Directory indicates that the airport is in Class C airspace (formerly ARSA), and that you should contact approach control. When west of the airport (170° - 349°), the frequency to use is 124.0. To confirm that Lincoln Approach Control is operational at noon, check the hours of operation. These are listed as 1200 — 0600Z, which is 0600 — 2400 local standard time. Minneapolis Center (answer B) would be contacted between 0600 and 1200 Z, which is midnight to 6 A.M. local standard time. Contact should be made with approach control, where available, prior to contacting the tower (answer C).

3839. (Refer to figure 53.) Which type radar service is provided to VFR aircraft at Lincoln Municipal?

A — Sequencing to the primary Class C airport and standard separation.
B — Sequencing to the primary Class C airport and conflict resolution so that radar targets do not touch, or 1,000 feet vertical separation.
C — Sequencing to the primary Class C airport, traffic advisories, conflict resolution, and safety alerts.

3839. Answer C. JSPPM 6-55 (AIM)
The VFR services provided within a Class C airspace area (formerly ARSA) include: sequencing all arriving aircraft to the primary Class C airport; providing traffic advisories and conflict resolutions between IFR and VFR aircraft so that radar targets do not touch, or 500 feet vertical separation, and between VFR aircraft, traffic advisories and safety alerts.

3840. (Refer to figure 53.) What is the recommended communications procedure for landing at Lincoln Municipal during the hours when the tower is not in operation?

A — Monitor airport traffic and announce your position and intentions on 118.5 MHz.
B — Contact UNICOM on 122.95 MHz for traffic advisories.
C — Monitor ATIS for airport conditions, then announce your position on 122.95 MHz.

3840. Answer A. JSPPM 6-55 (A/FD)
The CTAF frequency is listed as 118.5, and is used when the tower is not in operation. Standard procedures are to monitor airport traffic and announce your position on CTAF. UNICOM (answers B and C) is not used for airport advisories when a CTAF is listed. It is a good idea to listen to ATIS, but it might not be updated after the tower closes.

3841. (Refer to figure 53.) Where is Loup City Municipal located with relation to the city?

A — Northeast approximately 3 miles.
B — Northwest approximately 1 mile.
C — East approximately 10 miles.

3841. Answer B. JSPPM 6-55 (A/FD)
The first line of the A/FD includes the distance and direction from the associated city. The entry 1 NW indicates that the airport is 1 mile northwest of the city. The entry (NE03) is the location identifier, not a direction and distance (answer A). The last line of the A/FD entry contains the entry 2010/10E, which is the site elevation of the VORTAC, followed by the magnetic variation, not direction and distance (answer C).

3842. (Refer to figure 53 on page 6-26.) Traffic patterns in effect at Lincoln Municipal are

A — to the right on Runway 17L and Runway 35L; to the left on Runway 17R and Runway 35R.
B — to the left on Runway 17L and Runway 35L; to the right on Runway 17R and Runway 35R.
C — to the right on Runways 14 — 32.

3843. The letters VHF/DF appearing in the Airport/Facility Directory for a certain airport indicate that

A — this airport is designated as an airport of entry.
B — the Flight Service Station has equipment with which to determine your direction from the station.
C — this airport has a direct-line phone to the Flight Service Station.

3854. FAA advisory circulars containing subject matter specifically related to Airmen are issued under which subject number?

A — 60.
B — 70.
C — 90.

3855. FAA advisory circulars containing subject matter specifically related to Airspace are issued under which subject number?

A — 60.
B — 70.
C — 90.

3856. FAA advisory circulars containing subject matter specifically related to Air Traffic Control and General Operations are issued under which subject number?

A — 60.
B — 70.
C — 90.

3842. Answer B. JSPPM 6-55 (A/FD)
Remarks following the runway data for each runway include nonstandard traffic patterns. Left-hand patterns are used if not otherwise stated. Right-hand traffic is noted for Runway 17R and Runway 35R. Left traffic is used for Runways 17L, 35L, 14, and 32.

3843. Answer B. JSPPM 6-55 (A/FD)
Some Flight Service Stations have direction finding equipment. This capability is noted in the A/FD listing for the FSS airport under Radio Aids to Navigation. An airport of entry (answer A) is designated by the letters AOE. Flight service phone numbers (answer C) are listed in the A/FD, usually with an 800 number.

3854. Answer A. JSPPM 6-60 (AC 00-2)
Advisory circulars relating to Airmen are issued under subject number 60. Airspace is covered under number 70 (answer B), and 90 covers Air Traffic Control and General Operating Rules (answer C).

3855. Answer B. JSPPM 6-60 (AC 00-2)
See explanation for Question 3854.

3856. Answer C. JSPPM 6-60 (AC 00-2)
See explanation for Question 3854.

CHAPTER 7
RADIO NAVIGATION SYSTEMS

SECTION A
VHF OMNIDIRECTIONAL RANGE

This chapter of the *Private Pilot Manual* explains the radio navigation aids which are especially important in your cross-country flying. This first section discusses the components of the VOR system, including distance measuring equipment (DME), and how to use this equipment in the airplane. The following FAA Written Test questions are covered in this section:

3532, 3533, 3539, 3552, 3553, 3559, 3560, 3561, 3566, 3570, 3577, 3578, 3579, 3598.

3532. (Refer to figure 21 on page 6-4.) What is your approximate position on low altitude airway Victor 1, southwest of Norfolk (area 1), if the VOR receiver indicates you are on the 340° radial of Elizabeth City VOR (area 3)?

A — 15 nautical miles from Norfolk VORTAC.
B — 18 nautical miles from Norfolk VORTAC.
C — 23 nautical miles from Norfolk VORTAC.

3532. Answer B. JSPPM 7-10 (PHB)
Using the compass rose of the Elizabeth City VOR, draw a line along the 340° radial until it intersects Victor 1. Measure the distance from this point to the Norfolk VORTAC. The distance is 18 nautical miles. 15 n.m. from Norfolk (answer A) is the intersection of Victor 1 and the 345° radial. 23 n.m. from Norfolk VORTAC (answer C) is the intersection of Victor 1 and the 330° radial. Don't be misled by the number 340 which appears near the 33 on the compass rose. This is the elevation of an obstacle.

3533. (Refer to figure 21, area 3; and figure 29 on pages 6-4 and 7-2.) The VOR is tuned to Elizabeth City VOR, and the aircraft is positioned over Shawboro. Which VOR indication is correct?

A — 5.
B — 6.
C — 8.

3533. Answer C. JSPPM 7-5 (PHB)
Shawboro is along the 030° radial of the Elizabeth City VOR. With 210° selected on the VOR indicator, the CDI needle should be centered with a "TO" indication. This is what is shown on VOR indicator #8. VOR indicator #5 (answer A) needs a "FROM" indication to be correct. VOR indicator #6 (answer B) shows the aircraft left of Shawboro.

3539. (Refer to figure 22 on page 6-5.) What course should be selected on the omnibearing selector (OBS) to make a direct flight from Mercer County Regional Airport (area 3) to the Minot VORTAC (area 1) with a TO indication?

A — 001°.
B — 012°.
C — 181°.

3539. Answer A. JSPPM 7-8 (PHB)
The magnetic course can be determined by plotting a line from Mercer County Regional Airport to the Minot VORTAC. The line intersects the minot VORTAC compass rose at 181°. The reciprocal of 181° is 001°. This is what you would set in the OBS. 012° (answer B) is the true course to the Minot VORTAC. 181° (answer C) is the reciprocal of the desired OBS course.

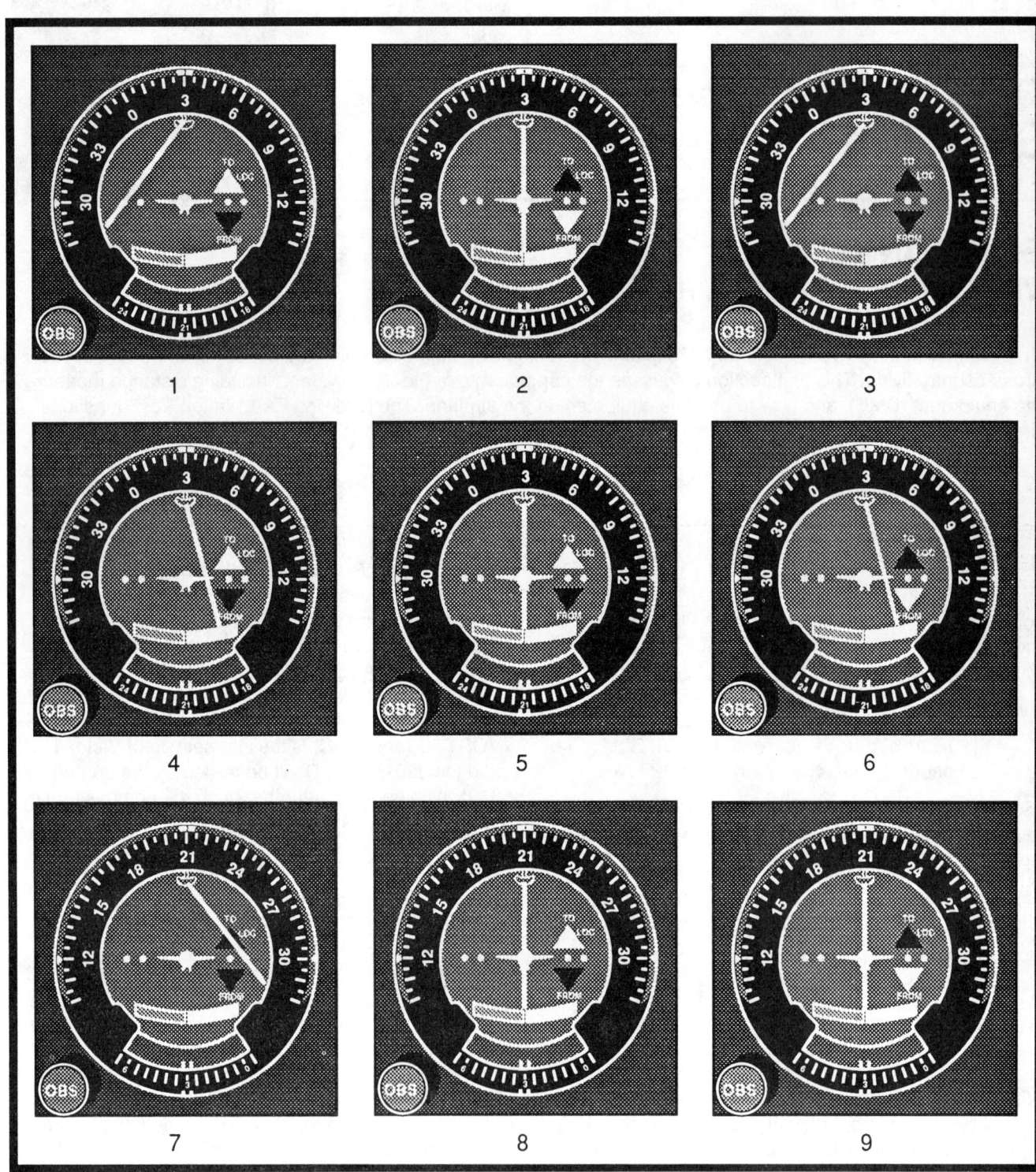

FIGURE 29.—VOR.

3552. (Refer to figure 24 on page 6-7.) What is the approximate position of the aircraft if the VOR receivers indicate the 310° radial of Savannah VORTAC (area 3) and the 190° radial of Allendale VOR (area 1)?

A — Town of Guyton.
B — Town of Springfield.
C — 3 miles east of Marlow.

3553. (Refer to figure 24 on page 6-7.) On what radial should the VOR receiver (OBS) be set to navigate direct from the Hampton Varnville Airport (area 1) to Savannah VORTAC (area 3)?

A — 005°.
B — 185°.
C — 200°.

3559. (Refer to figure 25 on page 6-8.) What is the approximate position of the aircraft if the VOR receivers indicate the 250° radial of Sulphur Springs VORTAC (area 2) and the 130° radial of Blue Ridge VORTAC (area 1)?

A — Caddo Mills Airport.
B — Meadowview Airport.
C — 3 miles southeast of Caddo Mills Airport.

3560. (Refer to figure 25 on page 6-8.) On what radial should the VOR receiver (OBS) be set in order to navigate direct from Majors Airport (area 1) to Quitman VORTAC (area 2)?

A — 101°.
B — 108°.
C — 281°.

3552. Answer A. JSPPM 7-10 (PHB)
The intersection of these two radials places the aircraft over the town of Guyton. The town of Springfield (answer B) is northeast of Guyton, at the intersection of the 185° radial of Allendale VOR and the 323° radial of Savannah VOR. Three miles east of Marlow (answer C) is derived from the intersection of the 185° radial of Allendale VOR and the 300° radial of Savannah VOR.

3553. Answer B. JSPPM 7-8 (PHB)
If you draw a line between Hampton Varnville Airport and Savannah VORTAC, it crosses the Savannah compass rose at 005°. To navigate inbound with a "TO" indication, would require the reciprocal of 005°, or 185°, to be set in the OBS. If 005° were set in the OBS (answer A) the TO-FROM indicator would display "FROM." A 200° inbound course (answer C) would not be a direct route from Hampton Varnville to Savannah VORTAC.

3559. Answer B. JSPPM 7-10 (PHB)
The intersection of these two radials puts the aircraft near the Meadowview Airport. The Caddo Mills Airport (answer A) lies along the 250° radial from Sulphur Springs VORTAC and the 150° radial from Blue Ridge VORTAC. If the aircraft were about 3 miles southeast of Caddo Mills Airport (answer C), the cross radials would be the 245° radial from Sulphur Springs VORTAC and the 150° radial from Blue Ridge VORTAC.

3560. Answer A. JSPPM 7-8 (PHB)
A direct course from Majors Airport to Quitman VORTAC crosses the compass rose at 283°. The inbound course to be set in the OBS is the reciprocal of 283°, or 103°. The closest answer is 101° (answer A). The inbound course to Quitman VORTAC on Victor 114 is 108° (answer B), but this is not a direct route from Majors Airport. 281° (answer C) is the approximate outbound course from the Quitman VORTAC.

3561. (Refer to figure 25, area 1; and figure 29 on pages 6-8 and 7-2.) The VOR is tuned to Blue Ridge VORTAC, and the aircraft is positioned over the town of Lone Oak, southeast of Majors Airport. Which VOR indication is correct?

A — 1.
B — 4.
C — 7.

3566. (Refer to figure 26, area 5 on page 6-9.) The VOR is tuned to the Dallas/Fort Worth VORTAC. The omnibearing selector (OBS) is set on the 253° radial, with a TO indication, and a right course deviation indicator (CDI) deflection. What is the aircraft's position from the VORTAC?

A — East-northeast.
B — North-northeast.
C — West-southwest.

3570. (Refer to figure 27, areas 4 and 3; and figure 29 on pages 6-10 and 7-2.) The VOR is tuned to Jamestown VOR, and the aircraft is positioned over the town of Wimbledon. Which VOR indication is correct?

A — 1.
B — 4.
C — 6.

3577. (Refer to figure 29, illustration 1 on page 7-2.) The VOR receiver has the indications shown. What is the aircraft's position relative to the station?

A — North.
B — East.
C — South.

3578. (Refer to figure 29, illustration 3 on page 7-2.) The VOR receiver has the indications shown. What is the aircraft's position relative to the station?

A — East
B — Southeast.
C — West.

3561. Answer C. JSPPM 7-5 (PHB)
Using your plotter, you can determine that Lone Oak lies near the 120° radial of the Blue Ridge VORTAC. Because all of the VOR indicators in figure 29 have either 030° or 210° set in the OBS, you must determine the position of the aircraft in relation to these settings and the VOR station. Since the 120° radial is 90° from the 030°/210° settings, the TO-FROM indicator will be blank. With the OBS set to 210°, the CDI will be deflected to the right, which is the display on VOR indicator #7 (answer C). VOR indicator #1 (answer A) shows a 030° setting with a left deflection, but it has a "TO" indication. Answer (B) is wrong because VOR indicator #4 shows a 030° setting with a right deflection.

3566. Answer A. JSPPM 7-8 (PHB)
A course of 253° will take the aircraft to the station. This means the aircraft is currently on the east side of the station near the 073° radial. A CDI deflection to the right places the aircraft to the left of the 073° radial. East-northeast (answer A) is the best answer given. If the aircraft was north-northeast of the station (answer B), the CDI needle would be deflected to the left. If it was west-southwest of the station (answer C), the TO-FROM indicator would show "FROM."

3570. Answer C. JSPPM 7-5 (PHB)
The aircraft is on the 023° radial of the Jamestown VOR. This puts it to the left of the outbound course of 030°. Since it's an outbound course, the VOR indicator will have a "FROM" indication. This is the display on VOR indicator #6. Answers (A) and (B) both show a 030° course with a "TO" indication. This would put the aircraft on the other side of the station.

3577. Answer C. JSPPM 7-5 (PHB)
With the 030° course selected, a "TO" indication, and a left CDI deflection, the aircraft is right of course, between the 120° and 210° radials. Therefore, south is the correct answer. North and east (answers A and B) are outside the defined quadrant.

3578. Answer B. JSPPM 7-5 (PHB)
Since the TO-FROM indicator is blank, the aircraft is either over the station or on either the 120° or 300° radial. These radials are 90° from the 030° setting. The left CDI deflection puts the aircraft right of the selected radial. Therefore, the correct answer is southeast of the station. If the aircraft was east of the station (answer A), the TO-FROM indicator would show "FROM." If the aircraft was west of the station (answer C), a "TO" indication would be displayed.

Radio Navigation Systems

3579. (Refer to figure 29, illustration 8 on page 7-2.) The VOR receiver has the indications shown. What radial is the aircraft crossing?

A — 030°.
B — 210°.
C — 300°.

3579. Answer A. JSPPM 7-5 (PHB)
The selected course of 210° would take the aircraft to the station, as indicated by a "TO" in the TO-FROM window. This places the aircraft northeast of the station on the reciprocal radial of 210°, which is the 030° radial. If the aircraft was on the 210° radial (answer B) with 210° in the OBS, a "FROM" indication would be displayed. If the aircraft was crossing the 300° radial (answer C), the TO-FROM indicator would be blank, because 300° is 90° from 210°.

3598. When the course deviation indicator (CDI) needle is centered during an omnireceiver check using a VOR test signal (VOT), the omnibearing selector (OBS) and the TO/FROM indicator should read

A — 180° FROM, only if the pilot is due north of the VOT.
B — 0° TO or 180° FROM, regardless of the pilot's position from the VOT.
C — 0° FROM or 180° TO, regardless of the pilot's position from the VOT.

3598. Answer C. JSPPM 7-12 (AIM)
No matter where the aircraft is located in relation to the VOT, the VOR should always read 180° with a "TO" indication or 0° with a "FROM" indication.

SECTION B
AUTOMATIC DIRECTION FINDER

Another radio navigation system is the automatic direction finder (ADF). In Section B, ADF components, navigation procedures, limitations, and cautions are discussed. The associated ground facilities, called nondirectional radio beacons (NDBs), are also included. FAA test questions include:

3580, 3581, 3582, 3583, 3584, 3585, 3586, 3587, 3588, 3589, 3590, 3591, 3592, 3593, 3594, 3595, 3596, 3597.

3580. (Refer to figure 30, illustration 1 on page 7-6.) Determine the magnetic bearing TO the station.

A — 030°.
B — 180°.
C — 210°.

3580. Answer C. JSPPM 7-19 (PHB)
(Note: With a movable-card indicator, the magnetic heading of the aircraft is set under the top index. The bearing pointer indicates the magnetic bearing TO the station, and the tail of the needle indicates the magnetic bearing FROM the station.) In this illustration, the needle is pointing to 210°, which is the magnetic bearing TO the station. The tail of the needle is on 030° (answer A). This is the magnetic bearing FROM the station. 180° (answer B) is not a logical answer.

3581. (Refer to figure 30, illustration 2 on page 7-6.) What magnetic bearing should the pilot use to fly TO the station?

A — 010°.
B — 145°.
C — 190°.

3581. Answer C. JSPPM 7-19 (PHB)
(Refer to the note for Question 3580 for more details.) The pointer is on the 190° magnetic bearing TO the station. The tail is on the 010° (answer A), which is the magnetic bearing FROM the station. A bearing of 145° TO the station (answer B) is not a logical answer.

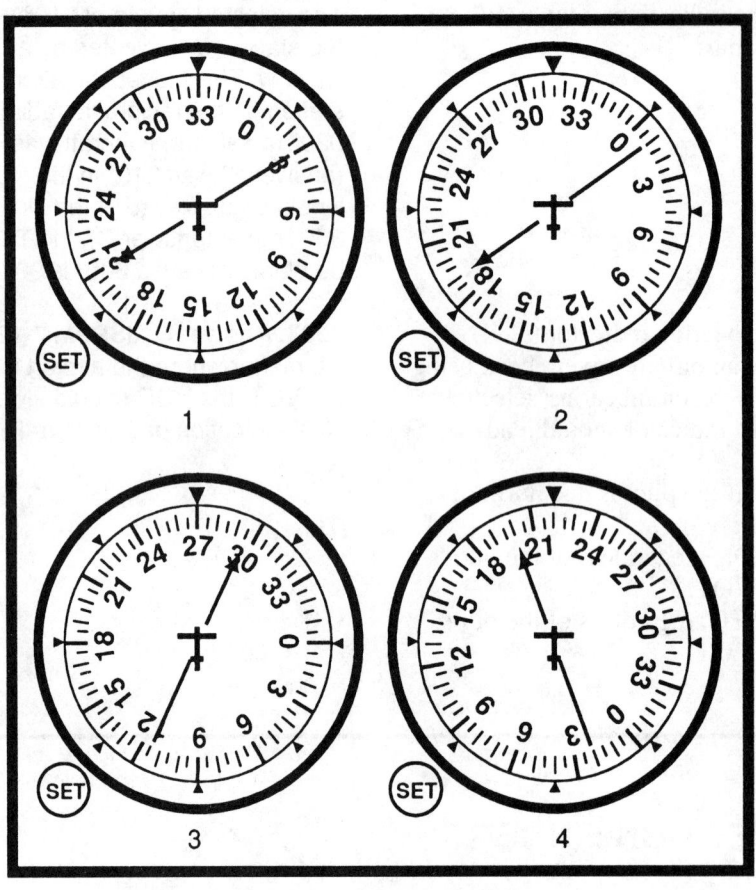

FIGURE 30.–ADF (Movable Card).

3582. (Refer to figure 30, illustration 2.) Determine the approximate heading to intercept the 180° bearing TO the station.

A — 040°.
B — 160°.
C — 220°.

3582. Answer C. JSPPM 7-19 (PHB)
The tail of the needle is on the 010° magnetic bearing FROM the station. This indicates the aircraft is northeast of the station. To intercept the 180° bearing which would put the aircraft north of the station, you need to turn toward the southwest. A heading of 220° will provide an intercept of 40°. A heading of 040° (answer A) will not intercept the 180° bearing. Instead it will take the aircraft away from the station to the northeast. A heading of 160° (answer B) will take the aircraft southeast of the station, and the 180° bearing will not be intercepted.

3583. (Refer to figure 30, illustration 3.) What is the magnetic bearing FROM the station?

A — 025°.
B — 115°.
C — 295°.

3583. Answer B. JSPPM 7-19 (PHB)
(Refer to the note for Question 3580 for more details.) The tail of the pointer is on the 115° magnetic bearing FROM the station. Answer (A), 025°, is not a logical answer. 295° (answer C) is the magnetic bearing TO the station.

3584. (Refer to figure 30.) Which ADF indication represents the aircraft tracking TO the station with a right crosswind?

A — 1.
B — 2.
C — 4.

3585. (Refer to figure 30, illustration 1.) What outbound bearing is the aircraft crossing?

A — 030°.
B — 150°.
C — 180°.

3586. (Refer to figure 30, illustration 1.) What is the relative bearing TO the station?

A — 030°.
B — 210°.
C — 240°.

3587. (Refer to figure 30, illustration 2.) What is the relative bearing TO the station?

A — 190°.
B — 235°.
C — 315°.

3588. (Refer to figure 30, illustration 4.) What is the relative bearing TO the station?

A — 020°.
B — 060°.
C — 340°.

3589. (Refer to figure 31, illustration 1 on page 7-8.) The relative bearing TO the station is

A — 045°.
B — 180°.
C — 315°.

3584. Answer C. JSPPM 7-19 (PHB)
To track to the station in a no-wind condition, the head of the bearing pointer would be under the heading index. With a cross-wind from the right, the heading would be adjusted a few degrees to the right. Answer (C) is the only correct indication. The ADF indicators for answers (A) and (B) show the aircraft tracking FROM the station.

3585. Answer A. JSPPM 7-19 (PHB)
The tail of the needle indicates the magnetic bearing FROM the station, or the outbound bearing. In this case, it is 030°. 150° (answer B) is the reciprocal of the magnetic heading, not the magnetic bearing. Answer (C), 180°, is not a logical choice.

3586. Answer C. JSPPM 7-19 (PHB)
(Note: The relative bearing is the number of degrees between the aircraft's magnetic heading and the magnetic bearing to the station, measured clockwise from the aircraft's heading. The ADF formula is magnetic heading (MH) plus relative bearing (RB) equals magnetic bearing (MB).)

To solve for **relative bearing** use the formula
MB - MH = RB (if the number is negative, add 360°.)
In this problem MB = 210° and MH = 33°
210° - 330° = -120 + 360° = 240°.

3587. Answer B. JSPPM 7-19 (PHB)
(Refer to the note for Question 3586 for more details.)

To solve for **relative bearing** use the formula
MB - MH = RB (if the number is negative, add 360°.)
In this problem MB = 190° and MH = 315°
190° - 315° = -125 + 360° = 235°.

3588. Answer C. JSPPM 7-19 (PHB)
(Refer to the note for Question 3586 for more details.)

To solve for **relative bearing** use the formula
MB - MH = RB (if the number is negative, add 360°.)
In this problem MB = 200° and MH = 220°
200° - 220° = -20 + 360° = 340°.

3589. Answer C. JSPPM 7-19 (PHB)
(Note: With a fixed-card indicator, the relative bearing is read directly from the bearing pointer.) In this example, the needle is pointing to 315°. Answer (A), 045°, is the difference between the relative bearing TO the station and 360°. Answer (B), 180°, is not a logical choice.

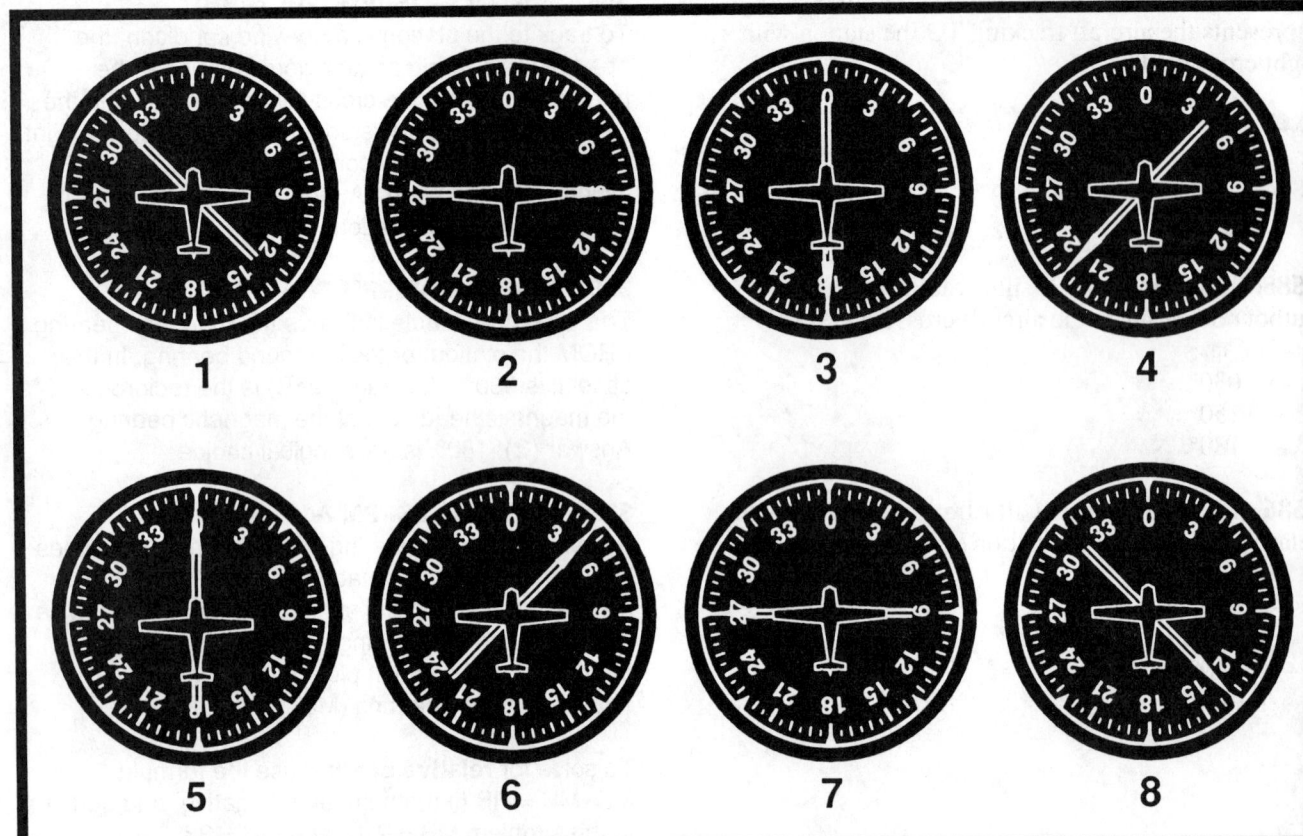

FIGURE 31.—ADF (Fixed Card).

3590. (Refer to figure 31, illustration 2.) The relative bearing TO the station is

A — 090°.
B — 180°.
C — 270°.

3591. (Refer to figure 31, illustration 3.) The relative bearing TO the station is

A — 090°.
B — 180°.
C — 270°.

3592. (Refer to figure 31, illustration 4.) On a magnetic heading of 320°, the magnetic bearing TO the station is

A — 005°.
B — 185°.
C — 225°.

3590. Answer A. JSPPM 7-19 (PHB)
The relative bearing TO the station is read directly under the bearing pointer, which is on 090°. Answer(B), 180°, is not a logical answer. Answer (C), 270°, is next to the tail of the needle, and is the relative bearing FROM the station.

3591. Answer B. JSPPM 7-19 (PHB)
The relative bearing TO the station is read directly under the pointer, which, in this case, is 180°. Answers (A) and (C), are not logical answers.

3592. Answer B. JSPPM 7-19 (PHB)
(Note: The relative bearing is the number of degrees between the aircraft's magnetic heading and the magnetic bearing to the station, measured clockwise from the aircraft's heading. The ADF formula is magnetic heading (MH) plus relative bearing (RB) equals magnetic bearing (MB).)

To solve for **magnetic bearing** use the formula MH + RB = MB. (If the number is higher than 360° subtract 360°.)
In this problem MH = 320° and RB = 225°
320° + 225° = 545° - 360° = 185°.

3593. (Refer to figure 31, illustration 5.) On a magnetic heading of 035°, the magnetic bearing TO the station is

A — 035°.
B — 180°.
C — 215°.

3594. (Refer to figure 31, illustration 6.) On a magnetic heading of 120°, the magnetic bearing TO the station is

A — 045°.
B — 165°.
C — 270°.

3595. (Refer to figure 31, illustration 6.) If the magnetic bearing TO the station is 240°, the magnetic heading is

A — 045°.
B — 105°.
C — 195°.

3596. (Refer to figure 31, illustration 7.) If the magnetic bearing TO the station is 030°, the magnetic heading is

A — 060°.
B — 120°.
C — 270°.

3597. (Refer to figure 31, illustration 8.) If the magnetic bearing TO the station is 135°, the magnetic heading is

A — 135°.
B — 270°.
C — 360°.

3593. Answer A. JSPPM 7-19 (PHB)
(Refer to the note for Question 3592 for more details.)

To solve for **magnetic bearing** use the formula
MH + RB = MB. (If the number is higher than 360° subtract 360°.)
In this problem MH = 035° and RB = 000°
035° + 000° = 035°.

3594. Answer B. JSPPM 7-19 (PHB)
(Refer to the note for Question 3592 for more details.)

To solve for **magnetic bearing** use the formula
MH + RB = MB. (If the number is higher than 360° subtract 360°.)
In this problem MH = 120° and RB = 045°
120° + 045° = 165°.

3595. Answer C. JSPPM 7-19 (PHB)
(Note: The relative bearing is the number of degrees between the aircraft's magnetic heading and the magnetic bearing to the station, measured clockwise from the aircraft's heading. The ADF formula is magnetic heading (MH) plus relative bearing (RB) equals magnetic bearing (MB).)

To solve for **magnetic heading** use the formula
MB - RB = MH. (If the number is negative, add 360°.)
In this problem MB = 240° and RB = 045°
240° - 045° = 195°.

3596. Answer B. JSPPM 7-19 (PHB)
(Refer to the note for Question 3595 for more details.)

To solve for **magnetic heading** use the formula
MB - RB = MH. (If the number is negative, add 360°.)
In this problem MB = 030° and RB = 270°
030° - 270° = -240° + 360° = 120°.

3597. Answer C. JSPPM 7-19 (PHB)
(Refer to the note for Question 3595 for more details.)

To solve for **magnetic heading** use the formula
MB - RB = MH. (If the number is negative, add 360°.)
In this problem MB = 135° and RB = 135°
135° - 135° = 000° or 360°.

SECTION C
ADVANCED NAVIGATION

This section of Chapter 7 provides an overview of area navigation (RNAV), long range navigation (LORAN), and advanced avionic instruments. No FAA Written Test questions are specifically covered in Section C.

CHAPTER 8

AVIATION PHYSIOLOGY

SECTION A
VISION IN FLIGHT

Since you, as the pilot in command of an airplane, determine how a flight is conducted, it is important to understand how your mind and body work. Chapter 8 of the *Private Pilot Manual* will help you learn the limitations of your body within the flight environment, and how you can best deal with them. Section A discusses the key role of vision and how it relates to flying during the day, as well as at night. You should be aware of blindspots and visual illusions and how to compensate for them. The FAA questions covered in this section are:

3712, 3713, 3714, 3715, 3716, 3717, 3719, 3849.

3712. What is the most effective way to use the eyes during night flight?

A — Look only at far away, dim lights.
B — Scan slowly to permit offcenter viewing.
C — Concentrate directly on each object for a few seconds.

3712. Answer B. JSPPM 8-5 (FTH)
The rods in the retina are used for night vision. Because they are not located directly behind the pupil, you must use offcenter viewing. Also, in dim light, you might need to move your eyes more slowly to prevent blurring of images than during the day. Answer (A) is impractical since the eyes tend to focus on lights and could miss items of importance. Answer (C) is wrong because if the eye concentrates directly on an object for even a few seconds, the image on the retina begins to fade.

3713. The best method to use when looking for other traffic at night is to

A — look to the side of the object and scan slowly.
B — scan the visual field very rapidly.
C — look to the side of the object and scan rapidly.

3713. Answer A. JSPPM 8-5 (FTH)
The most effective method of night scanning is to use offcenter vision, which means looking to the side of an object, and to scan slowly to prevent blurring. Rapid scanning (answer B) does not allow the image to focus clearly. Answer (C) is also wrong because scanning should be done slowly, not rapidly.

3714. The most effective method of scanning for other aircraft for collision avoidance during nighttime hours is to use

A — regularly spaced concentration on the 3-, 9-, and 12-o'clock positions.
B — a series of short, regularly spaced eye movements to search each 30-degree sector.
C — peripheral vision by scanning small sectors and utilizing offcenter viewing.

3714. Answer C. JSPPM 8-5 (FTH)
As with the previous questions, scanning should be done slowly, in small sectors, using offcenter (peripheral) vision. Answer (A) is wrong because scanning should not be concentrated in a few specific areas. Both day and night scanning should be done in sectors of 10 degrees, not 30 degrees (answer B).

3715. During a night flight, you observe a steady red light and a flashing red light ahead and at the same altitude. What is the general direction of movement of the other aircraft?

A — The other aircraft is crossing to the left.
B — The other aircraft is crossing to the right.
C — The other aircraft is approaching head-on.

3716. During a night flight, you observe a steady white light and a flashing red light ahead and at the same altitude. What is the general direction of movement of the other aircraft?

A — The other aircraft is flying away from you.
B — The other aircraft is crossing to the left.
C — The other aircraft is crossing to the right.

3717. During a night flight, you observe steady red and green lights ahead and at the same altitude. What is the general direction of movement of the other aircraft?

A — The other aircraft is crossing to the left.
B — The other aircraft is flying away from you.
C — The other aircraft is approaching head-on.

3719. VFR approaches to land at night should be accomplished

A — at a higher speed.
B — with a steeper descent.
C — the same as during daytime.

3849. What preparation should a pilot make to adapt the eyes for night flying?

A — Wear sunglasses after sunset until ready for flight.
B — Avoid red lights at least 30 minutes before the flight.
C — Avoid bright white lights at least 30 minutes before the flight.

3715. Answer A. JSPPM 8-6 (FTH)
The steady red light is a position light on the left wing and the flashing red light is an anticollision beacon. If you are looking at the left wingtip, the other aircraft would be crossing to the left. If the other aircraft was crossing to the right (answer B), you would see a green light on the wingtip, not a red light. If the other aircraft was approaching head-on (answer C), you would see both red and green wingtip position lights.

3716. Answer A. JSPPM 8-6 (FTH)
The white position light is on the tail and the flashing red light is the anticollision light. Therefore, you would be looking at the rear of the aircraft, which indicates it is flying away from you. If the aircraft was crossing to the left or to the right (answers B and C), you would be able to see either the steady red or green wingtip position light.

3717. Answer C. JSPPM 8-6 (FTH)
In this case, you are seeing both wingtip lights. If there was no white tail light in between them, you would most likely be looking head-on at the aircraft. If the aircraft was crossing to the left (answer A), you would not be able to see the green light on the right wingtip. If the aircraft was flying away from you (answer B), you should be able to see a white tail light. Although the question does not mention which side each light is on, you could tell that an aircraft is approaching head-on if the red light is to your right and the green light is to your left.

3719. Answer C. JSPPM 8-7 (FTH)
You should try to make night VFR approaches the same as day approaches. Using a higher airspeed (answer A) could result in floating, while using a steeper descent (answer B) could make it difficult to judge altitude when it comes time to flare the airplane for landing.

3849. Answer C. JSPPM 8-4 (AIM)
The rods in the human eye can take up to 30 minutes to fully adapt to the dark. Bright lights must be avoided for this amount of time. While sunglasses (answer A) can reduce light intensity, they are not as effective as simply avoiding bright lights for 30 minutes. Avoiding red lights (answer B) is not correct, since red cockpit lighting preserves night vision.

SECTION B
SPATIAL DISORIENTATION

When you enter the three-dimensional realm of flight, your body is subjected to motion and forces which often send confusing signals to your brain. This section provides you with an understanding of how these sensations in your body are created and how you can cope with them. The three senses which provide you with an awareness of your position are visual, vestibular, and kinesthetic. A discussion of spatial disorientation and illusions, and how to minimize their effects is also presented. Test questions in this section are:

    3850, 3851, 3852, 3853.

3850. The danger of spatial disorientation during flight in poor visual conditions may be reduced by

A — shifting the eyes quickly between the exterior visual field and the instrument panel.
B — having faith in the instruments rather than taking a chance on the sensory organs.
C — leaning the body in the opposite direction of the motion of the aircraft.

3851. A state of temporary confusion resulting from misleading information being sent to the brain by various sensory organs is defined as

A — spatial disorientation.
B — hyperventilation.
C — hypoxia.

3852. Pilots are more subject to spatial disorientation if

A — they ignore the sensations of muscles and inner ear.
B — body signals are used to interpret flight attitude.
C — eyes are moved often in the process of cross-checking the flight instruments.

3853. If a pilot experiences spatial disorientation during flight in a restricted visibility condition, the best way to overcome the effect is to

A — rely upon the aircraft instrument indications.
B — concentrate on yaw, pitch, and roll sensations.
C — consciously slow the breathing rate until symptoms clear and then resume normal breathing rate.

3850. Answer B. JSPPM 8-12 (AIM)
To avoid spatial disorientation, a pilot must rely on the instruments in the cockpit and not the feelings from the sensory organs. Answer (A) is wrong because when visual conditions are poor, scanning outside is not very effective. Shifting the eyes quickly will only add to spatial disorientation. Answer (C) is not a good option, as it would tend to increase spatial disorientation.

3851. Answer A. JSPPM 8-12 (AC 67-2)
Spatial disorientation occurs when the brain receives conflicting messages from the sensory organs. Answer (B), hyperventilation, is a breathing rate that is too rapid or too deep. Answer (C), hypoxia, is a state of oxygen deficiency in the blood.

3852. Answer B. JSPPM 8-12 (AC 67-2)
Spatial disorientation is more likely to occur when a pilot believes the signals from the body's sensory organs. Answer (A) is wrong because pilots are more subject to spatial disorientation if they rely on the body's sensations. Answer (C), moving the eyes often, is wrong because the key is to focus on the instruments, rely on them, and avoid rapid head movements.

3853. Answer A. JSPPM 8-12 (AIM)
Since the brain receives confusing messages from the body's senses, the pilot must rely on the aircraft's instruments. Concentrating on pitch, roll, and yaw sensations (answer B) will cause or increase spatial disorientation. Slowing the breathing rate (answer C) will reduce hyperventilation, but by itself will not overcome the effects of spatial disorientation.

SECTION C
RESPIRATION AND ALTITUDE

As you fly above the earth, you can experience the effects of reduced atmospheric pressure. A lack of oxygen can have drastic effects on the pilot of an airplane. This section explains the respiration process, how your body uses oxygen, how to recognize hypoxia, how hyperventilation affects your body, and the effects of changing atmospheric pressure. FAA questions covered in Section C are:

3832, 3844, 3845, 3846, 3847, 3848.

3832. Large accumulations of carbon monoxide in the human body result in

A — tightness across the forehead.
B — loss of muscular power.
C — an increased sense of well-being.

3832. Answer B. JSPPM 8-19 (AC 20-32)
The key word in this question is "large" accumulations. This condition can produce a loss of muscle power. Answers (A) and (C) describe symptoms of hypoxia.

3844. Which statement best defines hypoxia?

A — A state of oxygen deficiency in the body.
B — An abnormal increase in the volume of air breathed.
C — A condition of gas bubble formation around the joints or muscles.

3844. Answer A. JSPPM 8-17 (AIM)
Hypoxia occurs when the body tissues do not receive enough oxygen. Answer (B) would occur during hyperventilation, when the breathing rate is to fast and too deep. Answer (C) describes decompression sickness, or the "bends," which can occur during and after scuba diving.

3845. Rapid or extra deep breathing while using oxygen can cause a condition known as

A — hyperventilation.
B — aerosinusitis.
C — aerotitis.

3845. Answer A. JSPPM 8-20 (AIM)
Hyperventilation occurs when the breathing rate is too rapid or too deep. It can occur with or without the use of supplemental oxygen. Answer (B), aerosinusitis, is an inflammation of the sinuses. Answer (C), aerotitis, is an inflammation of the middle ear. Both are caused by changes in air pressure.

3846. Which would most likely result in hyperventilation?

A — Emotional tension, anxiety, or fear.
B — The excessive consumption of alcohol.
C — An extremely slow rate of breathing and insufficient oxygen.

3846. Answer A. JSPPM 8-20 (AIM)
Emotional tension, anxiety, and fear can cause the rapid, deep breathing associated with hyperventilation. Excessive consumption of alcohol (answer B), does not cause hyperventilation. Answer (C) is wrong because a slow breathing rate is used to recover from hyperventilation. Also, hyperventilation is caused by insufficient carbon dioxide, not oxygen, in the body.

3847. A pilot should be able to overcome the symptoms or avoid future occurrences of hyperventilation by

A — closely monitoring the flight instruments to control the airplane.
B — slowing the breathing rate, breathing into a bag, or talking aloud.
C — increasing the breathing rate in order to increase lung ventilation.

3847. Answer B. JSPPM 8-21 (AIM)
Slowing the breathing rate is one of the best ways to stop hyperventilation. Also, breathing into a bag and talking out loud are helpful. Answer (A) will not help control the breathing rate. Increasing the breathing rate (answer C), is a cause of hyperventilation, not a cure.

3848. Susceptibility to carbon monoxide poisoning increases as

A — altitude increases.
B — altitude decreases.
C — air pressure increases.

3848. Answer A. JSPPM 8-19 (AC 20-32)
Since carbon monoxide poisoning is a form of hypoxia, its effects are increased with altitude, where there is less oxygen available. As altitude decreases (answer B), oxygen increases, and the effects of CO poisoning are decreased instead of increased. As altitude decreases, air pressure increases (answer C), and the effect is the same as in Answer (B).

SECTION D
ALCOHOL, DRUGS, AND PERFORMANCE

Section D is included in the *Private Pilot Manual* to describe how alcohol and seemingly harmless medication (drugs) can cause serious side effects for a pilot. No FAA questions are specifically covered in this section.

CHAPTER 9

FLIGHT PLANNING AND DECISION MAKING

SECTION A
PLANNING AND ORGANIZING FLIGHTS

A well-planned cross-country flight requires you to bring together the various skills and information you have learned and apply them to your operation. Chapter 9 of the *Private Pilot Manual* is a summation of the flight planning process you should use when preparing for a cross-country flight. Section A discusses the planning process, route selection, weather considerations, completing a navigation log, and cockpit management. FAA Written Test questions in this section are:

3187, 3658, 3659, 3660.

3187. How long does the Airworthiness Certificate of an aircraft remain valid?

A — As long as the aircraft has a current Registration Certificate.
B — Indefinitely, unless the aircraft suffers major damage.
C — As long as the aircraft is maintained and operated as required by Federal Aviation Regulations.

3187. Answer C. JSPPM 9-9 (PHB)
The Airworthiness Certificate remains valid only as long as the aircraft is maintained and operated in accordance with the FARs. Answer (A) is incorrect because the Airworthiness Certificate is dependent on the maintenance and operation of the aircraft, not the registration. Obviously, answer (B) is wrong because the Airworthiness Certificate is valid only as long as the aircraft is properly maintained and operated. Minor damage could make an Airworthiness Certificate invalid.

3658. In regard to preflighting an aircraft, what is the minimum expected of a pilot prior to every flight?

A — Drain fuel from each quick drain.
B — Perform a walk-around inspection of the aircraft.
C — Check the required documents aboard the aircraft.

3658. Answer B. JSPPM 9-8 (PHB)
The pilot should always perform a walk-around inspection of the aircraft prior to every flight. An inspection of fuel from the quick drains (answer A) may not be required for every flight. Some manufacturers recommend the fuel be checked prior to the first flight of the day and after each refueling. A check for the required documents (answer C) should be made prior to the first flight of the day and whenever another pilot has operated the aircraft, but the check should not be necessary on succeeding flights.

3659. Why is the use of a written checklist recommended for preflight inspection and engine start?

A — To ensure that all necessary items are checked in a logical sequence.
B — For memorizing the procedures in an orderly sequence.
C — To instill confidence in the passengers.

3659. Answer A. JSPPM 9-8 (PHB)
A written checklist is useful to ensure that the preflight is done in a logical sequence and that all necessary items are checked. Memorizing the procedures (answer B) is not recommended since items can be forgotten. While using a checklist may give some passengers a measure of confidence (answer C), that is not the reason to use one. The objective is to ensure that all required items are checked.

3660. What special check should be made on an aircraft during preflight after it has been stored an extended period of time?

A — ELT batteries and operation.
B — Condensation in the fuel tanks.
C — Damage or obstructions caused by animals, birds, or insects.

3660. Answer C. JSPPM 9-9 (PHB)
Aircraft that have been stored for a long time are often used for nesting by birds, animals, and insects. This can cause obstructions in air intakes and vents, engine compartments, wings, and fuselage, in addition to damaging the components. The ELT (answer A) must be tested and maintained according to the manufacturer's instructions, and the batteries replaced or recharged after one-half their useful life. The batteries should be checked for expiration, but the ELT may not require an operational check, depending on how long the aircraft has been in storage. Condensation in the fuel tanks (answer B) should be checked prior to the first flight of the day and after each refueling. This is not a special check for aircraft which have been stored.

SECTION B
FACTORS AFFECTING DECISION MAKING

Although FAA question material is not included in this section, a lot of important pilot information is covered. Subjects such as situational awareness, hazardous attitudes, risk assessment, and stress management are discussed.

FEDERAL AVIATION REGULATIONS

CHAPTER 10

SECTION A
PART 1 — DEFINITIONS AND ABBREVIATIONS

A good understanding of Parts 1, 61, 91, and NTSB 830 of the Federal Aviation Regulations (FARs) is crucial for operating an airplane safely in the National Airspace System. While some information from the FARs is incorporated into the *Private Pilot Manual*, you should study a current publication of the FARs to make sure you learn all appropriate "rules of the air." An FAR book, published by Jeppesen Sanderson, is available along with other private pilot training materials. The FAR book includes a "Recommended Study List" and a series of exercises with answers to help you in your study. This section covers the FAA Written Test questions dealing with the definitions and abbreviations from Part 1. These questions include:

3005, 3007, 3008, 3009, 3010, 3014, 3015.

3005. The definition of nighttime is

A — sunset to sunrise.
B — 1 hour after sunset to 1 hour before sunrise.
C — the time between the end of evening civil twilight and the beginning of morning civil twilight.

3005. Answer C. (FAR 1.1)
Night is the time between the end of evening civil twilight and the beginning of morning civil twilight. Answer (A) describes the time during which aircraft lights must be used according to FAR 91.209. Answer (B) reflects the night experience currency requirements found in FAR 61.57.

3007. Which V-speed represents maximum flap extended speed?

A — V_{FE}.
B — V_{LOF}.
C — V_{FC}.

3007. Answer A. (FAR 1.2)
V_{FE} is defined as maximum flap extended speed. Answer (B) represents lift-off speed. Answer (C) is used to describe maximum speed for stability characteristics.

3008. Which V-speed represents maximum landing gear extended speed?

A — V_{LE}.
B — V_{LO}.
C — V_{FE}.

3008. Answer A. (FAR 1.2)
V_{LE} is defined as maximum landing gear extended speed. Answer (B) is maximum landing gear operating speed. Answer (C) represents maximum flap extended speed.

3009. V_{NO} is defined as the

A — normal operating range.
B — never-exceed speed.
C — maximum structural cruising speed.

3009. Answer C. (FAR 1.2)
V_{NO} is defined as maximum structural cruising speed. Answer (A) is not defined by any V-speed. Answer (B), never-exceed speed, is represented by V_{NE}.

3010. V_{S0} is defined as the

A — stalling speed or minimum steady flight speed in the landing configuration.
B — stalling speed or minimum steady flight speed in a specified configuration.
C — stalling speed or minimum takeoff safety speed.

3010. Answer A. (FAR 1.2)
V_{S0} is stalling speed or minimum steady flight speed in a landing configuration. Answer (B) is represented by V_{S1}. Answer (C) has two V-speeds. Stalling speed is V_S and minimum takeoff safety speed is $V_{2\,min}$.

3014. Which operation would be described as preventive maintenance?

A — Servicing landing gear wheel bearings.
B — Alteration of main seat support brackets.
C — Engine adjustments to allow automotive gas to be used.

3014. Answer A. (FAR 1.1, FAR 43 — APPENDIX A)
Preventive maintenance involves simple or minor preservation operations. Servicing landing gear is an example of preventive maintenance listed in FAR Part 43, Appendix A. Answers (B) and (C) are alterations, and are not listed in Appendix A.

3015. Which operation would be described as preventive maintenance?

A — Repair of landing gear brace struts.
B — Replenishing hydraulic fluid.
C — Repair of portions of skin sheets by making additional seams.

3015. Answer B. (FAR 1.1, FAR 43 — APPENDIX A)
Replenishing hydraulic fluid is listed as preventive maintenance in FAR Part 43, Appendix A. Answers (A) and (C) are not listed in Appendix A and they are considered as repair work.

SECTION B
PART 61 — CERTIFICATION: PILOTS AND FLIGHT INSTRUCTORS

As a pilot applicant, you need to know the Part 61 requirements for obtaining certificates and ratings, as well as the associated privileges and limitations. This section covers the following FAA Written Test questions from Part 61:

3016, 3017, 3018, 3019, 3020, 3021, 3022, 3023, 3024, 3025, 3026, 3027, 3028, 3029, 3030, 3031, 3032, 3033, 3034, 3035, 3036, 3037, 3038, 3039, 3040, 3041, 3042, 3043, 3044, 3045, 3046, 3047, 3048, 3049, 3050, 3051, 3052, 3053, 3054, 3055, 3056, 3057, 3058, 3059, 3060, 3061, 3064, 3065, 3066.

3016. What document(s) must be in your personal possession while operating as pilot in command of an aircraft.

A — Certificates showing accomplishment of a checkout in the aircraft and a current biennial flight review.
B — A pilot certificate with an endorsement showing accomplishment of an annual flight review and a pilot logbook showing recency of experience.
C — An appropriate pilot certificate and an appropriate current medical certificate.

3016. Answer C. (FAR 61.3)
Both the medical certificate and pilot certificate are required to be in your personal possession while you are acting as pilot in command. Answers (A) and (B) are incorrect because there are no regulations requiring pilots to have in their personal possession "proof" of currency.

3017. When must a current pilot certificate be in the pilot's personal possession.

A — When acting as a crew chief during launch and recovery.
B — Only when passengers are carried.
C — Anytime when acting as pilot in command or as a required crewmember.

3018. Private pilots acting as pilot in command, or in any other capacity as a required pilot flight crewmember, must have in their personal possession while aboard the aircraft a current

A — logbook endorsement to show that a flight review has been satisfactorily accomplished.
B — medical certificate and an appropriate pilot certificate.
C — endorsement on the pilot certificate to show that a flight review has been satisfactorily accomplished.

3019. Each person who holds a pilot certificate or a medical certificate shall present it for inspection upon the request of the Administrator, the National Transportation Safety Board, or any

A — authorized representative of the Department of Transportation.
B — person in a position of authority.
C — federal, state, or local law enforcement officer.

3020. A Third-Class Medical Certificate is issued on August 10, this year. To exercise the privileges of a Private Pilot Certificate, the medical certificate will be valid until midnight on

A — August 10, 2 years later.
B — August 31, 2 years later.
C — August 31, 3 years later.

3021. A Third-Class Medical Certificate is issued on May 3, this year. To exercise the privileges of a Private Pilot Certificate, the medical certificate will be valid until midnight on

A — May 3, 1 year later.
B — May 31, 1 year later.
C — May 31, 2 years later.

3017. Answer C. (FAR 61.3)
You must have a current pilot certificate in your personal possession whenever you are pilot in command or acting as a required pilot flight crewmember. Answer (A) is incorrect because a crew chief is not a required pilot flight crewmember. Answer (B) is wrong because it makes no difference whether you are carrying passengers or not.

3018. Answer B. (FAR 61.3)
You must have both the medical certificate and pilot certificate in your personal possession. Answers (A) and (C) are incorrect because you are not required to have proof of flight reviews in your personal possession.

3019. Answer C. (FAR 61.3)
By regulation you, as the pilot, are required to present your pilot certificate upon request of the administrator, an authorized representative of the National Transportation Safety Board (NTSB) or any Federal, State, or local law enforcement officer. Answers (A) and (B) are incorrect because a representative of the Department of Transportation or a person in a position of authority could mean someone other than an administrator, NTSB representative, or law enforcement officer.

3020. Answer B. (FAR 61.23)
A third-class medical is good until the end of the 24th calendar month after the date of issue (calendar month is defined as to the end of the month). Answer (A) is wrong because a third-class medical expires at the end of the month. Answer (C) is wrong because a third-class medical certificate is good for two years, not three.

3021. Answer C. (FAR 61.23)
A third-class medical is good until the end of the 24th calendar month after the date of issue. Answer (A) is wrong because a third-class medical expires at the end of the month and is good for two years. Answer (B) is wrong because a third-class medical certificate is good for two years, not one.

3022. For private pilot operations, a Second-Class Medical Certificate issued on July 15, this year, will expire at midnight on

A — July 15, 2 years later.
B — July 31, 1 year later.
C — July 31, 2 years later.

3022. Answer C. (FAR 61.23)
To exercise the privileges of a commercial pilot, a second-class medical is good until the end of the 12th calendar month after the date of issue. For private pilot operations, a second-class medical is good until the end of the 24th calendar month after the date of issue. Answer (A) is wrong because a medical certificate expires at the end of the month. Answer (B) is incorrect because a second-class medical certificate expires at the end of one year for a commercial pilot, not a private pilot.

3023. For private pilot operations, a First-Class Medical Certificate issued on October 21, this year, will expire at midnight on

A — October 21, 2 years later.
B — October 31, next year.
C — October 31, 2 years later.

3023. Answer C. (FAR 61.23)
To exercise the privileges of an ATP, a first-class medical is good until the end of the 6th calendar month after the date of issue. Between the beginning of the 7 month and the end of the 12th month, the first-class medical carries 2nd class privileges. From the beginning of the 13th month to the end of the 24th calendar month, a first-class medical is good only for operations requiring a 3rd class medical. Answer (A) is wrong because a medical certificate expires at the end of the month. Answer (B) is incorrect because a first-class medical expires at the end of six months for an ATP, one year for a commercial pilot, and two years for a private pilot.

3024. The pilot in command is required to hold a type rating in which aircraft?

A — Aircraft operating under an authorization issued by the Administrator.
B — Aircraft having a gross weight of more than 12,500 pounds.
C — Aircraft involved in ferry flights, training flights, or test flights.

3024. Answer B. (FAR 1.1, 61.5, 61.31)
FAR 61.5 and 61.31 indicates that a type rating is required for large aircraft. FAR 1.1 defines large aircraft as having a gross weight greater than 12,500 pounds. Answers (A) and (C) are incorrect because a type rating is not required for either kind of operation.

3025. What is the definition of a high-performance airplane?

A — An airplane with 180 horsepower, or retractable landing gear, flaps, and a fixed-pitch propeller.
B — An airplane with more than 200 horsepower, or retractable landing gear, flaps, and a controllable propeller.
C — An airplane with a normal cruise speed in excess of 200 knots, flaps, and a controllable propeller.

3025. Answer B. (FAR 61.31)
A high performance airplane is defined as an airplane having more than 200 horsepower, or one that has retractable landing gear, a controllable propeller, and flaps. Answer (A) is incorrect because the airplane does not have a controllable propeller. Answer (C) is incorrect because it does not indicate that the airplane has more than 200 horsepower or retractable gear.

Federal Aviation Regulations

3026. Before a person holding a Private Pilot Certificate may act as pilot in command of a high-performance airplane, that person must have

A — passed a flight test in that airplane from an FAA inspector.
B — an endorsement in that person's logbook that he/she is competent to act as pilot in command.
C — received flight instruction from an authorized flight instructor who then endorses that person's logbook.

3026. Answer C. (FAR 61.31)
In order to act as pilot in command of a high-performance airplane, you must have received flight instruction in a high-performance airplane and had your logbook endorsed indicating you received the instruction. Answer (A) is wrong because a flight test is not required for a high performance endorsement. Answer (B) is wrong because flight instruction in a high-performance airplane is not indicated.

3027. In order to act as pilot in command of a high-performance airplane, a pilot must have

A — made three solo takeoffs and landings in a high-performance airplane.
B — received flight instruction in an airplane that has more than 200 horsepower, or retractable landing gear, flaps, and a controllable propeller.
C — passed a flight test in a high-performance airplane.

3027. Answer B. (FAR 61.31)
A person holding a private or commercial pilot certificate may not act as pilot in command of an airplane that has more than 200 horsepower, or that has retractable landing gear, flaps, and controllable propeller, unless the pilot has received flight instruction from an authorized flight instructor who has certified in the pilot's logbook that he or she is competent to pilot a high performance airplane. Keep in mind that an airplane with less than 200 horsepower can qualify as a high performance airplane if that airplane has retractable landing gear, a controllable propeller, and flaps. Answers (A) and (C) are incorrect because there are no solo or flight test requirements for high performance airplanes.

3028. To act as pilot in command of an aircraft carrying passengers, a pilot must show by logbook endorsement the satisfactory completion of a flight review or completion of a pilot proficiency check within the preceding

A — 6 calendar months.
B — 12 calendar months.
C — 24 calendar months.

3028. Answer C. (FAR 61.56)
To act as pilot in command of any aircraft, whether you are carrying passengers or not, you must have, within the preceding 24 calendar months, complied with the flight review requirements. Answers (A) and (B) are the wrong time frames for flight review requirements.

3029. If recency of experience requirements for night flight are not met and official sunset is 1830, the latest time passengers may be carried is

A — 1829.
B — 1859.
C — 1929.

3029. Answer C. (FAR 61.57)
No person may act as pilot in command of an aircraft carrying passengers during the period beginning 1 hour after sunset and ending 1 hour before sunrise, unless that person meets night experience requirements. Answers (A) and (B) are wrong because the times are less than one hour after sunset.

3030. To act as pilot in command of an aircraft carrying passengers, the pilot must have made at least three takeoffs and three landings in an aircraft of the same category, class, and if a type rating is required, of the same type, within the preceding

A — 90 days.
B — 12 calendar months.
C — 24 calendar months.

3030. Answer A. (FAR 61.57)
To meet recent flight experience requirements for carrying passengers, the pilot in command must have, within the preceding 90 days, made three takeoffs and landings (to a full stop for night currency requirements). Answers (B) and (C) are incorrect because they exceed the 90 day time period.

3031. To act as pilot in command of an aircraft carrying passengers, the pilot must have made three takeoffs and three landings within the preceding 90 days in an aircraft of the same

A — make and model.
B — category and class, but not type.
C — category, class, and type, if a type rating is required.

3032. The takeoffs and landings required to meet the recency of experience requirements for carrying passengers in a tailwheel airplane

A — may be touch and go or full stop.
B — must be touch and go.
C — must be to a full stop.

3033. The three takeoffs and landings that are required to act as pilot in command at night must be done during the time period from

A — sunset to sunrise.
B — 1 hour after sunset to 1 hour before sunrise.
C — the end of evening civil twilight to the beginning of morning civil twilight.

3034. To meet the recency of experience requirements to act as pilot in command carrying passengers at night, a pilot must have made at least three takeoffs and three landings to a full stop within the preceding 90 days in

A — the same category and class of aircraft to be used.
B — the same type of aircraft to be used.
C — any aircraft.

3035. If a certificated pilot changes permanent mailing address and fails to notify the FAA Airmen Certification Branch of the new address, the pilot is entitled to exercise the privileges of the pilot certificate for a period of only

A — 30 days after the date of the move.
B — 60 days after the date of the move.
C — 90 days after the date of the move.

3031. Answer C. (FAR 61.57)
To meet the recency of experience requirements for carrying passengers, FAR 61.57(c) states that you must have made three takeoffs and landings within the preceding 90 days in an aircraft of the same category and class, and if a type rating is required, of the same type. Answer (A) is wrong because make and model is more restrictive than category and class. Answer (B) is incorrect because currency requirements must be met for each aircraft requiring a type rating.

3032. Answer C. (FAR 61.57)
FAR 61.57(c) states that to meet the recency of experience requirement in a tailwheel airplane, the landings must have been made to a full stop. Answers (A) and (B) are incorrect because a touch and go is not an option for meeting currency requirements in a tailwheel airplane.

3033. Answer B. (FAR 61.57)
To act as pilot in command of an aircraft carrying passengers between one-hour after sunset and one-hour before sunrise, the pilot must have, within the preceding 90 days, made three takeoffs and landings to a full stop. Answer (A) is not applicable because this is the time period when aircraft lights must be used. Answer (C) is wrong because this is the definition of night, not the time period in the recent flight experience regulation.

3034. Answer A. (FAR 61.57)
No person may act as pilot in command of an aircraft carrying passengers at night unless that person has made three takeoffs and three landings to a full stop within the preceding 90 days. The takeoffs and landings must be at night and in the same category and class of aircraft that is to be used for the carriage of passengers.

3035. Answer A. (FAR 61.60)
As a pilot, you may not exercise the privileges of your certificate after 30 days from the date of your permanent mailing address change unless you notify the FAA's Airman Certificate Branch in writing of the new address. Answers (B) and (C) are incorrect because the time specified exceeds the 30 day limitation.

3036. A certificated private pilot may not act as pilot in command of an aircraft towing a glider unless there is entered in the pilot's logbook a minimum of

A — 100 hours of pilot flight time in any aircraft.
B — 100 hours of pilot flight time in powered aircraft.
C — 200 hours of pilot flight time in powered aircraft.

3036. Answer B. (FAR 61.69)
If you plan to act as the pilot in command of an aircraft towing a glider with only a private pilot certificate, you must have logged at least 100 hours of pilot flight time in powered aircraft. Answer (A) is wrong because the 100 hours must be in powered aircraft. Answer (C) is incorrect because the 200 hours total pilot flight time is only required if the pilot does not have at least 100 hours in powered aircraft.

3037. To act as pilot in command of an aircraft towing a glider, a person is required to have made within the preceding 12 months

A — at least three flights as observer in a glider being towed by an aircraft.
B — at least three flights in a powered glider.
C — at least three actual or simulated glider tows while accompanied by a qualified pilot.

3037. Answer C. (FAR 61.69)
The pilot in command of an aircraft towing a glider must have, within the preceding 12 months, made at least three actual or simulated glider tows while accompanied by a qualified pilot, or made at least three flights as PIC of a glider towed by an aircraft. Answer (A) is wrong because the requirement is for three flights as PIC in a glider, not as an observer. Answer (B) is incorrect because the requirement applies to a glider, not a powered glider.

3038. A recreational pilot acting as pilot in command must have in his/her personal possession while aboard the aircraft

A — a current logbook endorsement to show that a flight review has been satisfactorily accomplished.
B — the current and appropriate pilot and medical certificates.
C — the pilot logbook to show recent experience requirements to serve as pilot in command have been met.

3038. Answer B. (FAR 61.3)
A current and appropriate medical certificate and pilot certificate are both required to be in the pilot's personal possession. Answers (A) and (C) are incorrect because there are no regulatory requirements for pilots to have proof of currency in their personal possession.

3039. A Third-Class Medical Certificate was issued on August 10, this year. To exercise the privileges of a Recreational Pilot Certificate, the medical certificate will expire on

A — August 10, 2 years later.
B — August 31, 2 years later.
C — August 31, 3 years later.

3039. Answer B. (FAR 61.23)
A third-class medical, which is appropriate to exercise the privileges of a recreational pilot, expires at the end of the 24th calendar month after the date of issue. Answer (A) is wrong because a medical certificate expires at the end of the month. Answer (C) is obviously incorrect because it indicates three years instead of two years.

3040. If a recreational pilot had a flight review on August 8, this year, when is the next flight review required?

A — August 8, 2 years later.
B — August 31, next year.
C — August 31, 2 years later.

3040. Answer C. (FAR 61.56)
To act as pilot in command of an aircraft, a recreational pilot must have, within the preceding 24 calendar months, complied with the biennial flight review (BFR) requirement. Answers (A) and (B) are wrong because the listed dates are less than the 24 calendar months stipulated for the BFR requirement.

3041. Each recreational pilot is required to have

A — a biennial flight review.
B — an annual flight review.
C — a semiannual flight review.

3042. If a recreational pilot had a flight review on August 8, this year, when is the next flight review required?

A — August 8, next year.
B — August 31, next year.
C — August 31, 2 years later.

3043. How many passengers is a recreational pilot allowed to carry on board?

A — One.
B — Two.
C — Three.

3044. According to regulations pertaining to privileges and limitations, a recreational pilot may

A — be paid for the operating expenses of a flight.
B — share the operating expenses of a flight with a passenger.
C — not be paid in any manner for the operating expenses of a flight.

3045. In regard to privileges and limitations, a recreational pilot may

A — fly for compensation or hire.
B — share the operating expenses of the flight with the passenger.
C — not be paid in any manner for the operating expenses of a flight.

3046. What is the maximum distance recreational pilots may fly from the airport/heliport at which they received instruction?

A — 25 nautical miles.
B — 50 nautical miles.
C — 100 nautical miles.

3041. Answer A. (FAR 61.56)
In order for any pilot to act as pilot in command of an aircraft, that person must have, within the preceding 24 calendar months, complied with the biennial flight review (BFR) requirements. Answer (B) is incorrect because an annual flight review is not required. Answer (C) is incorrect because the BFR is biennial, or once every two years, instead of semiannual, which means twice a year.

3042. Answer C. (FAR 61.56)
To act as pilot in command of an aircraft, a recreational pilot must have, within the preceding 24 calendar months (calendar month is defined as to the end of the month), complied with the biennial flight review (BFR) requirement. Answer (A) is wrong because the listed date is considerably less than 24 calendar months. Answer (B) is incorrect because there is no requirement for an annual (12 calendar months) flight review.

3043. Answer A. (FAR 61.101)
According to the limitations specified in FAR 61.101(a)(1), a recreational pilot may not carry more than one passenger. Answers (B) and (C) are incorrect because they both exceed the passenger limit for recreational pilots.

3044. Answer B. (FAR 61.101)
The regulations clearly indicate that a recreational pilot may share the operating expenses of a flight with a passenger. Answer (A) is incorrect because it indicates that the recreational pilot will be paid for all operating expenses and will not share in the cost. Answer (C) is incorrect because it indicates that a recreational pilot cannot share operating expenses of a flight in any manner.

3045. Answer B. (FAR 61.101)
According to FAR 61.101(a)(2), a recreational pilot may share the operating expenses of the flight with the passenger. Answer (A) is incorrect because a recreational pilot cannot fly for hire under any circumstances. Answer (C) is incorrect because it indicates that a recreational pilot cannot share the operating expenses of the flight.

3046. Answer B. (FAR 61.101)
A recreational pilot may act as pilot in command only when the flight is within 50 nautical miles of an airport at which the pilot has received instruction. Answer (A) is incorrect because it is less than the maximum distance of 50 nautical miles. Answer (C) is incorrect because it is more than the maximum distance.

3047. A recreational pilot may act as pilot in command of an aircraft that is certificated for a maximum of how many occupants?

A — Two.
B — Three.
C — Four.

3048. A recreational pilot may act as pilot in command of an aircraft with a maximum engine horsepower of

A — 160.
B — 180.
C — 200.

3049. What exception, if any, permits a recreational pilot to act as pilot in command of an aircraft carrying a passenger for hire?

A — If the passenger pays no more than the operating expenses.
B — If a donation is made to a charitable organization for the flight.
C — There is no exception.

3050. May a recreational pilot act as pilot in command of an aircraft in furtherance of a business?

A — Yes, if the flight is only incidental to that business.
B — Yes, providing the aircraft does not carry a person or property for compensation or hire.
C — No, it is not allowed.

3051. With respect to daylight hours, what is the earliest time a recreational pilot may take off?

A — One hour before sunrise.
B — At sunrise.
C — At the beginning of morning civil twilight.

3052. If sunset is 2021 and the end of evening civil twilight is 2043, when must a recreational pilot terminate the flight?

A — 2021.
B — 2043.
C — 2121.

3047. Answer C. (FAR 61.101)
This regulation states that a recreational pilot may not act as pilot in command of an aircraft that is certificated for more than four occupants. Answers (A) and (B) are wrong because they are less than the maximum occupancy limit for recreational pilots.

3048. Answer B. (FAR 61.101)
A recreational pilot may not act as pilot in command of an aircraft that is certificated with more than 180 horsepower. Answer (A) is incorrect because it is less than the maximum horsepower limit for recreational pilots. Answer (C) is wrong because it exceeds the 180 maximum horsepower limit for recreational pilots.

3049. Answer C. (FAR 61.101)
A recreational pilot may only share operating expenses with a passenger, there are no exceptions. Answer (A) is wrong because it implies that the passenger is permitted to pay all of the operating expenses. Answer (B) is incorrect because recreational pilots are specifically prohibited from being a participant in a passenger-carrying airlift sponsored by a charitable organization.

3050. Answer C. (FAR 61.101)
The regulation specifically states that a recreational pilot is prohibited from flying in furtherance of a business. Answer (A) is incorrect because, even if the flight is incidental to business, it is still considered in the furtherance of business. Answer (B) is incorrect because, even if the flight is not conducted for compensation or hire, the intended purpose is still considered for the furtherance of business.

3051. Answer B. (FAR 61.101)
A recreational pilot may not act as pilot in command of an aircraft between sunset and sunrise. Therefore the earliest takeoff time is sunrise. Answer (A) refers to night as defined for currency purposes under FAR 61.57. Answer (C) is also incorrect. It is part of the definition of night under FAR 1.1.

3052. Answer A. (FAR 61.101)
As indicated in the previous answer, a recreational pilot may not act as pilot in command of an aircraft between sunset and sunrise. Answers (B) and (C) are incorrect because both of these times are after 2021.

3053. When may a recreational pilot operate to or from an airport that lies within Class C airspace?

A — Anytime the control tower is in operation.
B — When the ceiling is at least 1,000 feet and the surface visibility is at least 3 miles.
C — For the purpose of obtaining an additional certificate or rating while under the supervision of an authorized flight instructor.

3053. Answer C. (FAR 61.101)
A recreational pilot may operate in airspace, such as Class C airspace, that requires communication with air traffic control only when such operations are conducted for the purpose of obtaining additional certificates or ratings. These operations must be under the supervision of an authorized flight instructor. Answer (A) is incorrect because it does not state that the operation is for the purpose of obtaining an additional certificate or rating. Answer (B) is incorrect because it implies that as long as visibility minimums are maintained, a recreational pilot may enter Class C airspace.

3054. Under what conditions may a recreational pilot operate at an airport that lies within Class D airspace and that has a part-time control tower in operation?

A — When the tower is in operation, the ceiling is at least 2,500 feet and the visibility is at least 3 miles.
B — When the tower is in operation, the ceiling is at least 3,000 feet and the visibility is more than 1 mile.
C — When the tower is closed, the ceiling is at least 1,000 feet, and the visibility is at least 3 miles.

3054. Answer C. (FAR 61.101, 91.155)
A recreational pilot may not operate in airspace in which communications are required with ATC. An example is within Class D airspace. However, Class D airspace is only valid when the tower is operational. When the tower is closed, this airspace becomes Class E. If the ceiling is at least 1,000 feet AGL, and the visibility is at least three miles, a recreational pilot may legally operate at an airport in Class E airspace under visual flight rules (VFR). Answers (A) and (B) are wrong because the tower is operational, which makes the airspace Class D.

3055. When may a recreational pilot fly above 10,000 feet MSL?

A — When 2,000 feet AGL or below.
B — When 2,500 feet AGL or below.
C — When outside of controlled airspace.

3055. Answer A. (FAR 61.101)
A recreational pilot cannot fly above an altitude of 10,000 feet MSL, unless the aircraft is within 2,000 feet of the ground. Answer (B) is wrong because a recreational pilot may fly above 10,000 feet when at 2,000 feet AGL, or less, not 2,500 feet above the surface. Answer (C) is incorrect because whether the airspace is controlled or uncontrolled, a recreational pilot is not authorized to fly above 10,000 feet MSL unless the aircraft is within 2,000 feet AGL.

3056. During daytime, what is the minimum flight or surface visibility required for recreational pilots in Class G airspace below 10,000 feet MSL?

A — 1 mile.
B — 3 miles.
C — 5 miles.

3056. Answer B. (FAR 61.101)
A recreational pilot may not act as pilot in command of an aircraft when the flight or surface visibility is less than three statute miles. Answer (A) is wrong; the minimum daytime visibility requirement is three statute miles, not one. Answer (C) is incorrect because the minimum daytime flight or surface visibility for a recreational pilot in either controlled or uncontrolled airspace is three, not five, statute miles.

3057. During daytime, what is the minimum flight visibility required for recreational pilots in controlled airspace below 10,000 feet MSL?

A — 1 mile.
B — 3 miles.
C — 5 miles.

3057. Answer B. (FAR 61.101)
This question and the answer choices are almost identical to the previous question (3056). A recreational pilot may not act as pilot in command of an aircraft when the flight or surface visibility is less than three statute miles. Answer (A) is less than the recreational pilot's minimum and therefore is incorrect. Answer (C) is incorrect because it corresponds to either the visibility minimum above 10,000 MSL, or the night visibility minimum that applies to a student pilot.

3058. Under what conditions, if any, may a recreational pilot demonstrate an aircraft in flight to a prospective buyer?

A — The buyer pays all the operating expenses.
B — The flight is not outside the United States.
C — None.

3058. Answer C. (FAR 61.101)
FAR 61.101(b)(12) specifically prohibits recreational pilots from demonstrating an aircraft in flight to prospective buyers. Answers (A) and (B) are obviously incorrect because there are no conditions under which a recreational pilot can demonstrate an aircraft, in flight, to a prospective buyer.

3059. When, if ever, may a recreational pilot act as pilot in command in an aircraft towing a banner?

A — If the pilot has logged 100 hours of flight time in powered aircraft.
B — If the pilot has an endorsement in his/her pilot logbook from an authorized flight instructor.
C — It is not allowed.

3059. Answer C. (FAR 61.101)
FAR 61.101(b)(14) specifically prohibits recreational pilots from towing any object. Answers (A) and (B) are eliminated with selection of answer (C).

3060. When must a recreational pilot have a pilot-in-command flight check?

A — Every 400 hours.
B — Every 180 days.
C — If the pilot has less than 400 total flight hours and has not flown as pilot in command in an aircraft within the preceding 180 days.

3060. Answer C. (FAR 61.101)
A recreational pilot who has logged fewer than 400 flight hours and who has not logged pilot-in-command time in an aircraft within the preceding 180 days may not act as pilot in command of an aircraft until the pilot receives flight instruction from an authorized flight instructor who certifies in the pilot's logbook that the recreational pilot is competent to act as pilot in command. Answers (A) and (B) are incomplete and incorrect.

3061. A recreational pilot may fly as sole occupant of an aircraft at night while under the supervision of a flight instructor provided the flight or surface visibility is at least

A — 3 miles.
B — 4 miles.
C — 5 miles.

3061. Answer C. (FAR 61.101)
For the purpose of obtaining additional certificates or ratings, while under the supervision of an authorized flight instructor, a recreational pilot may fly as sole occupant of an aircraft between sunset and sunrise, provided the flight or surface visibility is at least five statute miles. Answers (A) and (B) are less than the required minimum.

3064. In regard to general privileges and limitations, a private pilot may

A — act as pilot in command of an aircraft carrying a passenger for compensation if the flight is in connection with a business or employment.
B — share the operating expenses of a flight with a passenger.
C — not be paid in any manner for the operating expenses of a flight.

3065. According to regulations pertaining to general privileges and limitations, a private pilot may

A — be paid for the operating expenses of a flight if at least three takeoffs and three landings were made by the pilot within the preceding 90 days.
B — share the operating expenses of a flight with the passengers.
C — not be paid in any manner for the operating expenses of a flight.

3066. What exception, if any, permits a private pilot to act as pilot in command of an aircraft carrying passengers who pay for the flight?

A — If the passengers pay all the operating expenses.
B — If a donation is made to a charitable organization for the flight.
C — There is no exception.

3064. Answer B. (FAR 61.118)
A private pilot may share the operating expenses of the flight with the passenger. Answer (A) is incorrect because a private pilot cannot fly for hire under any circumstances. Answer (C) is incorrect because it indicates that a private pilot cannot share in the operating expenses of a flight.

3065. Answer B. (FAR 61.118)
According to FAR 61.118(b), a private pilot may share the operating expenses of the flight with the passenger. Answer (A) is incorrect because it indicates that the private pilot will be paid for all operating expenses and will not share in the cost. Answer (C) is incorrect because it indicates that a private pilot cannot share the operating expenses of the flight.

3066. Answer B. (FAR 61.118)
Paragraph 61.118(d) of the FARs indicates a private pilot may act as pilot in command of an aircraft used in a passenger-carrying airlift sponsored by a charitable organization, and for which the passengers make a donation to the organization. Answer (A) is incorrect because it indicates that the private pilot will be paid for all operating expenses and will not share in the cost. Answer (C) is incorrect because it applies to recreational pilots.

SECTION C
PART 91 — GENERAL OPERATING AND FLIGHT RULES

Generally, automobile drivers understand and obey the traffic rules that help them avoid accidents, as well as traffic court. Likewise, you, as a pilot, must know and follow the "rules of the air" in order to operate an airplane safely and legally. The rules covered in this section should be an important part of your aeronautical knowledge. The test questions covered are:

3013, 3070, 3071, 3072, 3073, 3074, 3076, 3077, 3078, 3079, 3080, 3081, 3082, 3083, 3084, 3085, 3086, 3087, 3088, 3096, 3097, 3098, 3099, 3100, 3108, 3109, 3110, 3123, 3131, 3132, 3134, 3135, 3159, 3160, 3161, 3162, 3163, 3164, 3167, 3168, 3169, 3170, 3171, 3172, 3173, 3178, 3179, 3180, 3181, 3182, 3183, 3184, 3185, 3186, 3188, 3189, 3190, 3192, 3193, 3781.

3013. Preventive maintenance has been performed on an aircraft. What paperwork is required?

A — A full, detailed description of the work done must be entered in the airframe logbook.
B — The date the work was completed, and the name of the person who did the work must be entered in the airframe and engine logbook.
C — The signature, certificate number, and kind of certificate held by the person approving the work and a description of the work must be entered in the aircraft maintenance records.

3070. The final authority as to the operation of an aircraft is the

A — Federal Aviation Administration.
B — pilot in command.
C — aircraft manufacturer.

3071. The person directly responsible for the pre-launch briefing of passengers for a flight is the

A — safety officer.
B — pilot in command.
C — ground crewmember.

3072. If an in-flight emergency requires immediate action, the pilot in command may

A — deviate from the FAR's to the extent required to meet the emergency, but must submit a written report to the Administrator within 24 hours.
B — deviate from the FAR's to the extent required to meet that emergency.
C — not deviate from the FAR's unless prior to the deviation approval is granted by the Administrator.

3013. Answer C. (FAR 91.417, FAR Part 43.9)
FAR 91.417 states that records of preventive maintenance must include a description of the work performed, the date of completion, and the signature and certificate number of the person approving the aircraft for return to service. In addition, FAR 43.9 also indicates that the kind of certificate held by the person approving the work must be included in the record. Answers (A) and (B) are incorrect because if there are separate logbooks for the engine, propeller, and airframe normally only that kind of work would be recorded in the appropriate logbook.

3070. Answer B. (FAR 91.3)
As clearly indicated in the regulation, the pilot in command of an aircraft is directly responsible for, and is the final authority as to, the operation of that aircraft. Therefore (B) is the only correct answer.

3071. Answer B. (FAR 91.3)
The pilot in command of an aircraft is directly responsible for operation of that aircraft. Therefore, the pilot in command is responsible for pre-launch passenger briefing on safety belts according to FAR 91.107, as well as other pertinent information. Answers (A) and (C) normally do not apply to private pilot operations.

3072. Answer B. (FAR 91.3)
In an in-flight emergency requiring immediate action, the pilot in command may deviate from any rule to the extent required to meet that emergency. Answer (A) is incorrect because a written report is not required unless it is requested from the FAA. Answer (C) is incorrect because it is not practicable (if not impossible) to get prior permission to deviate from a FAR in an actual emergency situation.

3073. When must a pilot who deviates from a regulation during an emergency send a written report of that deviation to the Administrator?

A — Within 7 days.
B — Within 10 days.
C — Upon request.

3074. Who is responsible for determining if an aircraft is in condition for safe flight?

A — A certificated aircraft mechanic.
B — The pilot in command.
C — The owner or operator.

3076. Under what conditions may objects be dropped from an aircraft?

A — Only in an emergency.
B — If precautions are taken to avoid injury or damage to persons or property on the surface.
C — If prior permission is received from the Federal Aviation Administration.

3077. A person may not act as a crewmember of a civil aircraft if alcoholic beverages have been consumed by that person within the preceding

A — 8 hours.
B — 12 hours.
C — 24 hours.

3078. Under what condition, if any, may a pilot allow a person who is obviously under the influence of drugs to be carried aboard an aircraft?

A — In an emergency or if the person is a medical patient under proper care.
B — Only if the person does not have access to the cockpit or pilot's compartment.
C — Under no condition.

3079. No person may attempt to act as a crewmember of a civil aircraft with

A — .008 percent by weight or more alcohol in the blood.
B — .004 percent by weight or more alcohol in the blood.
C — .04 percent by weight or more alcohol in the blood.

3073. Answer C. (FAR 91.3)
The regulations clearly indicate that a written report is not required, unless a report is requested from the FAA. Answers (A) and (B) are incorrect because they indicate that a written report must automatically be submitted upon deviation of the FARs during an emergency.

3074. Answer B. (FAR 91.7)
The pilot in command of a civil aircraft is responsible, and has final authority, for determining whether that aircraft is in condition for safe flight. Answers (A) and (C) indicate that the pilot in command does not make the final determination.

3076. Answer B. (FAR 91.15)
Objects can be dropped from an aircraft in flight, if reasonable precautions are taken to avoid injury or damage to persons or property. Answer (A) is incorrect because it indicates that objects are always prohibited from being dropped. Answer (C) is incorrect because there is no requirement for FAA notification.

3077. Answer A. (FAR 91.17)
A common saying used in aviation for this regulation is "eight hours from bottle to throttle." In other words, no person may act or attempt to act as a crewmember of a civil aircraft within eight hours after the consumption of any alcoholic beverage.

3078. Answer A. (FAR 91.17)
Except in an emergency, no pilot of a civil aircraft may allow a person who appears to be intoxicated or who demonstrates by manner or physical indications that the individual is under the influence of drugs (except a patient under proper care) to be carried in that aircraft. Answer (B) is incorrect because there are no provisions for limiting passenger access to the cockpit. Answer (C) is incorrect because a person under medical care can be under the influence of drugs.

3079. Answer C. (FAR 91.17)
No person may act or attempt to act as a crewmember of a civil aircraft while having .04 percent by weight or more alcohol in the blood. Answers (A) and (B) are incorrect because the alcohol blood contents are far below the limit set by the regulations.

3080. Which preflight action is specifically required of the pilot prior to each flight?

A — Check the aircraft logbooks for appropriate entries.
B — Become familiar with all available information concerning the flight.
C — Review wake turbulence avoidance procedures.

3081. Preflight action, as required for all flights away from the vicinity of an airport, shall include

A — the designation of an alternate airport.
B — a study of arrival procedures at airports/ heliports of intended use.
C — an alternate course of action if the flight cannot be completed as planned.

3082. In addition to other preflight actions for a VFR flight away from the vicinity of the departure airport, regulations specifically require the pilot in command to

A — review traffic control light signal procedures.
B — check the accuracy of the navigation equipment and the emergency locator transmitter (ELT).
C — determine runway lengths at airports of intended use and the aircraft's takeoff and landing distance data.

3083. Flight crewmembers are required to keep their safety belts and shoulder harnesses fastened during

A — takeoffs and landings.
B — all flight conditions.
C — flight in turbulent air.

3080. Answer B. (FAR 91.103)
Each pilot in command shall, before beginning a flight, become familiar with all available information concerning that flight. Answer (A) is incorrect because it addresses only the aircraft preflight inspection. Answer (C) is wrong because not all of the available information concerning the flight is utilized.

3081. Answer C. (FAR 91.103)
The preflight action for flights away from the vicinity of an airport include checking weather reports and forecasts, fuel requirements, alternatives available if the flight cannot be completed as planned, and any known traffic delays. Answer (A) is incorrect because alternate airports are only a requirement for instrument flight rules. Answer (B) is not a specific requirement under FAR 91.103 and is incorrect because the pilot is not using all of the available information concerning the flight.

3082. Answer C. (FAR 91.103)
For any flight, a pilot must determine runway lengths at airports of use and the airplane's takeoff and landing distance data. Answers (A) and (B) are not specific to FAR 91.103.

3083. Answer A. (FAR 91.105)
According to the regulation, safety belts are required during takeoff and landing and while enroute. In addition, shoulder harnesses are required during takeoff and landing, unless the seat of the crewmembers' stations are not equipped with shoulder harnesses, or the crewmembers are not able to perform their duties with the shoulder harness fastened. Answers (B) and (C) are incorrect because shoulder harnesses are only required during takeoff and landing.

3084. Which best describes the flight conditions under which flight crewmembers are specifically required to keep their safety belts and shoulder harnesses fastened?

A — Safety belts during takeoff and landing; shoulder harnesses during takeoff and landing.
B — Safety belts during takeoff and landing; shoulder harnesses during takeoff and landing and while en route.
C — Safety belts during takeoff and landing and while en route; shoulder harnesses during takeoff and landing.

3085. With respect to passengers, what obligation, if any, does a pilot in command have concerning the use of safety belts?

A — The pilot in command must instruct the passengers to keep safety belts fastened for the entire flight.
B — The pilot in command must brief the passengers on the use of safety belts and notify them to fasten their safety belts during taxi, takeoff, and landing.
C — The pilot in command has no obligation in regard to passengers' use of safety belts.

3086. With certain exceptions, safety belts are required to be secured about passengers during

A — taxi, takeoffs, and landings.
B — all flight conditions.
C — flight in turbulent air.

3087. Safety belts are required to be properly secured about which persons in an aircraft and when?

A — Pilots only, during takeoffs and landings.
B — Passengers, during taxi, takeoffs, and landings only.
C — Each person on board the aircraft during the entire flight.

3088. No person may operate an aircraft in formation flight

A — over a densely populated area.
B — in Class D airspace under special VFR.
C — except by prior arrangement with the pilot in command of each aircraft.

3084. Answer C. (FAR 91.105)
During takeoff and landing, and while enroute, each required flight crewmember shall keep the safety belt fastened while at the crewmember station. In addition, each required flight crewmember shall, during takeoff and landing, keep the shoulder harness fastened while at the crewmember station. Answer (A) is wrong because safety belts are required while enroute. Answer (B) is incorrect because shoulder harnesses are not required while en route.

3085. Answer B. (FAR 91.107)
The pilot in command must ensure that each person on board is briefed on how to fasten and unfasten the safety belt and shoulder harness, as well as ensure all persons on board are notified to fasten their safety belt (and shoulder harness, if installed) during taxi, takeoff, or landing. Answer (A) is incorrect because safety restraints are only required for passengers during taxi, takeoff, and landings. Answer (C) is incorrect because FAR 91.107 specifically puts the responsibility and obligation on the pilot in command.

3086. Answer A. (FAR 91.107)
Passengers are only required to have safety belts (and shoulder harnesses, if installed) fastened during taxi, takeoff, and landing. Answers (B) and (C) are incorrect because safety restraints are not required at all times, nor are they required during turbulent air conditions.

3087. Answer B. (FAR 91.107)
Passengers are required to have safety belts (and shoulder harnesses, if installed) fastened during taxi, takeoff, and landing. Answer (A) is incorrect because pilots must wear restraints while enroute and while at their stations. Answer (C) is incorrect because safety restraints are not required at all times for passengers or crewmembers when they are not at their station.

3088. Answer C. (FAR 91.111)
No person may operate an aircraft in formation flight except by arrangement with the pilot in command of each aircraft in the formation. Answers (A) and (B) are incorrect because there are no special restrictions concerning formation flight over densely populated areas or in Class D airspace.

3096. A seaplane and a motorboat are crossing courses. If the motorboat is to the left of the seaplane, which has the right-of-way?

A — The motorboat.
B — The seaplane.
C — Both should alter course to the right.

3096. Answer B. (FAR 91.115)
When an aircraft, or an aircraft and a vessel, are on crossing courses, the aircraft or vessel to the other's right has the right-of-way. Answer (A) is incorrect because the aircraft is to the right of the motorboat and has the right-of-way. Answer (C) is wrong because it applies only to vehicles approaching head on.

3097. Unless otherwise authorized, what is the maximum indicated airspeed at which a person may operate an aircraft below 10,000 feet MSL?

A — 200 knots.
B — 250 knots.
C — 288 knots.

3097. Answer B. (FAR 91.117)
Unless otherwise authorized by the Administrator, no person may operate an aircraft below 10,000 feet MSL at an indicated airspeed of more than 250 knots. Answer (A) is incorrect because this airspeed limitation applies when operating below 2,500 feet above the surface when within four nautical miles of the primary airport of a Class C or D airspace area. It is also the airspeed limitation for operating within the airspace underlying a Class B airspace area, or in a VFR corridor designated through such a Class B airspace area. Answer (C) is incorrect because the correct answer is 288 mph not 288 knots.

3098. Unless otherwise authorized, the maximum indicated airspeed at which aircraft may be flown when at or below 2,500 feet AGL and within four nautical miles of the primary airport of Class B airspace is

A — 200 knots.
B — 230 knots.
C — 250 knots.

3098. Answer C. (FAR 91.117)
FAR 91.117 indicates that the maximum speed within Class B airspace is 250 knots. Answer (A) is wrong because this is the maximum speed you can travel when at or below 2,500 feet above the surface when within 4 n.m. of the primary airport of Class C or D airspace. Answer (B) is wrong because this is the maximum speed in these areas in miles per hour, not knots.

3099. When flying in the airspace underlying Class B airspace, the maximum speed authorized is

A — 200 knots.
B — 230 knots.
C — 250 knots.

3099. Answer A. (FAR 91.117)
No person may operate an aircraft in the airspace underlying a Class B airspace area, or in a VFR corridor designated through a Class B airspace area, at an indicated airspeed of more than 200 knots. Answer (B) is wrong because the correct answer is 230 mph not 230 knots. Answer (C) is incorrect because this speed applies to either the speed restriction below 10,000 feet MSL, or the speed restriction for operations within a Class B airspace area.

3100. When flying in a VFR corridor designated through Class B airspace, the maximum speed authorized is

A — 180 knots.
B — 200 knots.
C — 250 knots.

3100. Answer B. (FAR 91.117)
No person may operate an aircraft in a VFR corridor designated through a Class B airspace area, or in the airspace underlying a Class B airspace area, at an indicated airspeed of more than 200 knots. Answer (A) is wrong because 180 knots does not apply to any airspeed restriction. Answer (C) is incorrect because this speed applies to either the speed restriction below 10,000 feet MSL, or the speed restriction for operations within a Class B airspace area.

3108. When an ATC clearance has been obtained, no pilot in command may deviate from that clearance, unless that pilot obtains an amended clearance. The one exception to this regulation is

A — when the clearance states "at pilot's discretion."
B — an emergency.
C — if the clearance contains a restriction.

3109. When would a pilot be required to submit a detailed report of an emergency which caused the pilot to deviate from an ATC clearance?

A — When requested by ATC.
B — Immediately.
C — Within 7 days.

3110. What action, if any, is appropriate if the pilot deviates from an ATC instruction during an emergency and is given priority?

A — Take no special action since you are pilot in command.
B — File a detailed report within 48 hours to the chief of the appropriate ATC facility, if requested.
C — File a report to the FAA Administrator, as soon as possible.

3123. Which is the correct traffic pattern departure procedure to use at a noncontrolled airport?

A — Depart in any direction consistent with safety, after crossing the airport boundary.
B — Make all turns to the left.
C — Comply with any FAA traffic pattern established for the airport.

3131. What is the specific fuel requirement for flight under VFR during daylight hours in an airplane?

A — Enough to complete the flight at normal cruising speed with adverse wind conditions.
B — Enough to fly to the first point of intended landing and to fly after that for 30 minutes at normal cruising speed.
C — Enough to fly to the first point of intended landing and to fly after that for 45 minutes at normal cruising speed.

3108. Answer B. (FAR 91.123)
According the FAR 91.23(a), when an ATC clearance has been obtained, no pilot in command may deviate from that clearance, except in an emergency, unless an amended clearance is obtained. Answer (A) is incorrect because "at pilot's discretion" means that the pilot must still comply with the clearance. Answer (C) is incorrect because a clearance restriction has no bearing on complying with ATC instructions.

3109. Answer A. (FAR 91.3, 91.123)
According to FAR 91.123(d), a pilot in command who deviates from a clearance and then is given priority by ATC because of that emergency, shall submit a detailed report of that emergency within 48 hours to the manager of that ATC facility, if requested by ATC. Answer (B) is incorrect because you are allowed 48 hours to submit the report. Answer (C) is a specification found for reporting an overdue aircraft under NTSB 830.15(a).

3110. Answer B. (FAR 91.123)
A pilot in command who is given priority by ATC because of an emergency, shall submit a detailed report of that emergency within 48 hours to the manager of that ATC facility, if requested by ATC. Answer (A) is incorrect because of the above reason. Answer (C) is incorrect because according to FAR 91.3, you must file a report with an FAA administrator (not ATC) when an FAR was violated, as a result of an emergency, and a report is requested from the administrator.

3123. Answer C. (FAR 91.127)
Each person operating an aircraft to or from an airport without an operating control tower shall, in the case of an aircraft departing the airport, comply with any traffic patterns established for that airport in Part 93. Answers (A) and (B) are incorrect because they will not always comply with established traffic patterns.

3131. Answer B. (FAR 91.151)
For day VFR flight in an airplane, there must be enough fuel (considering wind and forecast weather conditions) to fly to the first point of intended landing, and, assuming normal cruising speed, 30 minutes thereafter. Answer (A) is incorrect because the fuel required is based on forecasted weather, not adverse winds. Answer (C) is incorrect because it is based on night VFR.

3132. What is the specific fuel requirement for flight under VFR at night in an airplane?

A — Enough to complete the flight at normal cruising speed with adverse wind conditions.
B — Enough to fly to the first point of intended landing and to fly after that for 30 minutes at normal cruising speed.
C — Enough to fly to the first point of intended landing and to fly after that for 45 minutes at normal cruising speed.

3134. What minimum visibility and clearance from clouds are required for a recreational pilot in Class G airspace at 1,200 feet AGL or below during daylight hours?

A — 1 mile visibility and clear of clouds.
B — 3 miles visibility and clear of clouds.
C — 3 miles visibility, 500 feet below the clouds.

3135. Outside controlled airspace, the minimum flight visibility requirement for a recreational pilot flying VFR above 1,200 feet AGL and below 10,000 feet MSL during daylight hours is

A — 1 mile.
B — 3 miles.
C — 5 miles.

3159. In addition to a valid Airworthiness Certificate, what documents or records must be aboard an aircraft during flight?

A — Aircraft engine and airframe logbooks, and owner's manual.
B — Radio operator's permit, and repair and alteration forms.
C — Operating limitations and Registration Certificate.

3160. When must batteries in an emergency locator transmitter (ELT) be replaced or recharged, if rechargeable?

A — After any inadvertent activation of the ELT.
B — When the ELT has been in use for more than 1 cumulative hour.
C — When the ELT can no longer be heard over the airplane's communication radio receiver.

3132. Answer C. (FAR 91.151)
For night VFR flight in an airplane, there must be enough fuel (considering wind and forecast weather conditions) to fly to the first point of intended landing, and assuming normal cruising speed, 45 minutes thereafter. Answer (A) is incorrect because the fuel required is based on forecasted weather, not adverse winds. Answer (B) is incorrect because it is based on day VFR.

3134. Answer B. (FAR 61.101, 91.155)
VFR minimums for uncontrolled airspace at 1,200 feet AGL, or below, is one mile visibility and clear of clouds. However, recreational pilots must have at least three miles visibility. Answer (A) is incorrect because it only applies to private, commercial, and ATP pilots. Answer (C) is incorrect because the aircraft only has to remain clear of clouds when within 1,200 feet AGL, or below, in uncontrolled airspace.

3135. Answer B. (FAR 61.101, 91.155)
For recreational pilots, the visibility minimum below 10,000 feet MSL, is three miles. Answer (A) is wrong because it is the visibility minimum for uncontrolled airspace at or below 1,200 feet AGL and is not applicable to recreational pilots. Answer (C) is incorrect because it is the visibility minimum for airspace above 1,200 feet AGL and above 10,000 feet MSL.

3159. Answer C. (FAR 91.203, 91.9)
An acronym commonly used by pilots for remembering the required certificates and documents is ARROW. The ARROW acronym means AIRWORTHINESS certificate; aircraft REGISTRATION; RADIO station permit; OPERATING limitations; and WEIGHT and balance. Answer (A) is incorrect because engine and airframe logbooks are not required to be in the aircraft. Answer (B) is incorrect because repair and alteration forms are not required to be in the aircraft.

3160. Answer B. (FAR 91.207)
Batteries used in the emergency locator transmitters must be replaced (or recharged, if the battery is rechargeable) when the transmitter has been in use for more than one cumulative hour. Answer (A) is incorrect because the ELT can be reset after an inadvertent activation well before one cumulative hour has occurred. Answer (C) is incorrect because it is well past the one cumulative hour specification.

3161. When are non-rechargeable batteries of an emergency locator transmitter (ELT) required to be replaced?

A — Every 24 months.
B — When 50 percent of their useful life expires.
C — At the time of each 100-hour or annual inspection.

3162. Except in Alaska, during what time period should lighted position lights be displayed on an aircraft?

A — End of evening civil twilight to the beginning of morning civil twilight.
B — 1 hour after sunset to 1 hour before sunrise.
C — Sunset to sunrise.

3163. When operating an aircraft at cabin pressure altitudes above 12,500 feet MSL up to and including 14,000 feet MSL, supplemental oxygen shall be used during

A — the entire flight time at those altitudes.
B — that flight time in excess of 10 minutes at those altitudes.
C — that flight time in excess of 30 minutes at those altitudes.

3164. Unless each occupant is provided with supplemental oxygen, no person may operate a civil aircraft of U.S. registry above a maximum cabin pressure altitude of

A — 12,500 feet MSL.
B — 14,000 feet MSL.
C — 15,000 feet MSL.

3167. No person may operate an aircraft in acrobatic flight when

A — flight visibility is less than 5 miles.
B — over any congested area of a city, town, or settlement.
C — less than 2,500 feet AGL.

3168. In which controlled airspace is acrobatic flight prohibited?

A — Class D airspace, Class E airspace designated for Federal Airways.
B — All Class E airspace above 1,500 feet AGL.
C — All Class G airspace.

3161. Answer B. (FAR 91.207)
Non-rechargeable batteries used in the ELT must be replaced when 50 percent of their useful life, as established by the manufacturer, has expired. Answer (A) is incorrect because the useful half life of the ELT battery is not fixed, and it may vary from manufacturer to manufacturer. Answer (C) is wrong because a 100-hour or annual inspection could occur well before or well after the time an ELT battery needs to be replaced or recharged.

3162. Answer C. (FAR 91.209)
No person may, during the period from sunset to sunrise, operate an aircraft unless it has lighted position lights. Answer (A) is wrong because it reflects the FAR 1.1 definition for night, which is used for logging time. Answer (B) is incorrect because it is the terminology used to define currency requirements for carrying passengers.

3163. Answer C. (FAR 91.211)
Between cabin pressure altitudes of 12,500 feet MSL and 14,000 feet MSL, the required minimum flight crew is required to use supplemental oxygen for any duration of the flight past 30 minutes. Answers (A) and (B) greatly exceed the oxygen requirements.

3164. Answer C. (FAR 91.211)
At cabin pressure altitudes above 15,000 feet MSL, each occupant of the aircraft must be provided with supplemental oxygen. Answers (A) and (B) are incorrect because at those altitudes, only required crewmembers must use oxygen for any portion of the flight past 30 minutes.

3167. Answer B. (FAR 91.303)
No person may operate an aircraft in acrobatic flight over any congested area of a city, town, or settlement. Answer (A) is incorrect because the minimum visibility for acrobatic flight is three miles. Answer (C) is incorrect because minimum altitude above the ground for acrobatic flight is 1,500 feet AGL.

3168. Answer A. (FAR 91.303)
No person may operate an aircraft in acrobatic flight within Class D airspace or on a Federal Airway. Answer (B) is incorrect because acrobatic flight is permitted in Class E airspace as long as it is not associated with a Federal Airway or an airport. Answer (C) is incorrect because acrobatic flight is permitted in Class G airspace.

3169. What is the lowest altitude permitted for acrobatic flight?

A — 1,000 feet AGL.
B — 1,500 feet AGL.
C — 2,000 feet AGL.

3169. Answer B. (FAR 91.303)
No person may operate an aircraft in acrobatic flight below an altitude of 1,500 feet above the surface.

3170. No person may operate an aircraft in acrobatic flight when the flight visibility is less than

A — 3 miles.
B — 5 miles.
C — 7 miles.

3170. Answer A. (FAR 91.303)
No person may operate an aircraft in acrobatic flight when flight visibility is less than three statute miles. Answer (B) and (C) are greater than the required minimum.

3171. A chair-type parachute must have been packed by a certificated and appropriately rated parachute rigger within the preceding

A — 60 days.
B — 90 days.
C — 120 days.

3171. Answer C. (FAR 91.307)
No pilot of a civil aircraft may allow a parachute that is available for emergency use to be carried in that aircraft unless it is an approved type, and if a chair type (canopy in back), it has been packed by a certificated and appropriately rated parachute rigger within the preceding 120 days. Answers (A) and (B) are less than the required 120 days.

3172. An approved chair-type parachute may be carried in an aircraft for emergency use if it has been packed by an appropriately rated parachute rigger within the preceding

A — 120 days.
B — 180 days.
C — 365 days.

3172. Answer A. (FAR 91.307)
No pilot of a civil aircraft may allow a parachute that is available for emergency use to be carried in that aircraft unless it is an approved type, and if a chair type (canopy in back), it has been packed by a certificated and appropriately rated parachute rigger within the preceding 120 days. Answers (B) and (C) are longer than the required maximum of 120 days.

3173. With certain exceptions, when must each occupant of an aircraft wear an approved parachute?

A — When a door is removed from the aircraft to facilitate parachute jumpers.
B — When intentionally pitching the nose of the aircraft up or down 30° or more.
C — When intentionally banking in excess of 30°.

3173. Answer B. (FAR 91.307)
Unless each occupant of the aircraft is wearing an approved parachute, no pilot of a civil aircraft, carrying any person (other than a crewmember) may execute any intentional maneuver that exceeds a nose-up or nose-down attitude of 30 degrees relative to the horizon.

3178. Which is normally prohibited when operating a restricted category civil aircraft?

A — Flight under instrument flight rules.
B — Flight over a densely populated area.
C — Flight within Class D airspace.

3178. Answer B. (FAR 91.313)
No person may operate a restricted category civil aircraft within the United States over a densely populated area. Answer (A) is incorrect because there currently are no restrictions for operating a restricted aircraft under IFR. Answer (C) is terminology found in the FAR regulating acrobatic flight and is not applicable to restricted category civil aircraft.

3179. Unless otherwise specifically authorized, no person may operate an aircraft that has an experimental certificate

A — beneath the floor of Class B airspace.
B — over a densely populated area or in a congested airway.
C — from the primary airport within Class D airspace.

3180. The responsibility for ensuring that an aircraft is maintained in an airworthy condition is primarily that of the

A — pilot in command.
B — owner or operator.
C — mechanic who performs the work.

3181. The responsibility for ensuring that maintenance personnel make the appropriate entries in the aircraft maintenance records indicating the aircraft has been approved for return to service lies with the

A — owner or operator.
B — pilot in command.
C — mechanic who performed the work.

3182. Completion of an annual inspection and the return of the aircraft to service should always be indicated by

A — the relicensing date on the Registration Certificate.
B — an appropriate notation in the aircraft maintenance records.
C — an inspection sticker placed on the instrument panel that lists the annual inspection completion date.

3183. If an alteration or repair substantially affects an aircraft's operation in flight, that aircraft must be test flown by an appropriately-rated pilot and approved for return to service prior to being operated

A — by any private pilot.
B — with passengers aboard.
C — for compensation or hire.

3179. Answer B. (FAR 91.319)
Unless otherwise authorized by the Administrator in special operating limitations, no person may operate an aircraft that has an experimental certificate over a densely populated area or in a congested airway. Answers (A) and (C) are incorrect because there are no restrictions specific to the airspace listed.

3180. Answer B. (FAR 91.403)
The owner or operator of an aircraft is primarily responsible for maintaining that aircraft in an airworthy condition. Answer (A) is incorrect because the pilot in command is only responsible for determining if the aircraft is in an airworthy condition. Answer (C) is incorrect because the certified mechanic is only responsible for the work he/she performs.

3181. Answer A. (FAR 91.405)
Each owner or operator of an aircraft shall ensure that maintenance personnel make appropriate entries in the aircraft maintenance record. Answers (B) and (C) are incorrect because it is not the responsibility of the pilot in command or mechanic to make sure the appropriate entries have been made.

3182. Answer B. (FAR 91.409)
No person may operate an aircraft unless, within the preceding 12 calendar months it has had an annual inspection by a person authorized to do that type of inspection and is entered as an annual inspection in the required maintenance records. Answer (A) is incorrect because an annual is either entered in maintenance records, or in the issuance of an airworthiness certificate. Answer (C) is wrong because it does not meet the requirement for recording an annual inspection.

3183. Answer B. (FAR 91.407)
Before any person (other than a crewmember) can fly in an aircraft that has been maintained, rebuilt, or altered in a manner that may have appreciably changed its flight characteristics or substantially affected the operation in flight, an appropriately rated pilot with at least a private pilot certificate must first conduct a test flight and log the flight in aircraft records. Answer (A) is wrong because a private pilot is a required crewmember. Answer (C) is incorrect because flying the aircraft for compensation or hire may not involve carrying passengers.

3184. Before passengers can be carried in an aircraft that has been altered in a manner that may have appreciably changed its flight characteristics, it must be flight tested by an appropriately-rated pilot who holds at least a

A — Commercial Pilot Certificate with an instrument rating.
B — Private Pilot Certificate.
C — Commercial Pilot Certificate and a mechanic's certificate.

3185. An aircraft's annual inspection was performed on July 12, this year. The next annual inspection will be due no later than

A — July 1, next year.
B — July 13, next year.
C — July 31, next year.

3186. To determine the expiration date of the last annual aircraft inspection, a person should refer to the

A — Airworthiness Certificate.
B — Registration Certificate.
C — aircraft maintenance records.

3188. What aircraft inspections are required for rental aircraft that are also used for flight instruction?

A — Annual and 100-hour inspections.
B — Biannual and 100-hour inspections.
C — Annual and 50-hour inspections.

3189. An aircraft had a 100-hour inspection when the tachometer read 1259.6. When is the next 100-hour inspection due?

A — 1349.6 hours.
B — 1359.6 hours.
C — 1369.6 hours.

3184. Answer B. (FAR 91.407)
An appropriately rated pilot with at least a private pilot certificate is authorized to flight test the aircraft. Answers (A) and (C) are incorrect because a commercial pilot with either an instrument rating or a mechanic rating is not the minimum requirement for the pilot.

3185. Answer C. (FAR 91.409)
No person may operate an aircraft unless, within the preceding 12 calendar months, it has had an annual inspection. The term "calendar month" is defined as to the end of the month. Answer (A) is incorrect because it is less than 12 months. Answer (B) is incorrect because it is less than 12 calendar months.

3186. Answer C. (FAR 91.417)
The registered owner or operator shall keep records of the maintenance, preventive maintenance, alterations, records of the 100-hour, annual, progressive, and other required or approved inspections, as appropriate, for each aircraft. This information is found in the aircraft's maintenance records. Answers (A) and (B) are incorrect because a record of maintenance is not kept on the airworthiness certificate or registration certificate.

3188. Answer A. (FAR 91.409)
No person may operate an aircraft carrying any person (other than a crewmember) for hire, or give flight instruction for hire in an aircraft, which that person provides, unless within the preceding 100-hours of time in service, the aircraft has received an annual or 100-hour inspection. Answer (B) is incorrect because a biannual inspection is not in compliance with the annual inspection requirement. Answer (C) is incorrect because 50-hour inspections are not required for all rented aircraft.

3189. Answer B. (FAR 91.409)
No person may operate an aircraft carrying any person (other than a crewmember) for hire, or give flight instruction for hire in an aircraft, which that person provides, unless within the preceding 100-hours of time in service, the aircraft has received an annual or 100-hour inspection. Answer (A) is at 90 hours and is incorrect. Answer (C) is at 110 hours and is incorrect. An aircraft can go 10 hours over the 100 hour inspection as long as it is enroute to a place where the inspection can be done. If an aircraft does go over 100 hours, that time must be subtracted from the next 100 hours.

3190. A 100-hour inspection was due at 3302.5 hours on the tachometer. The 100-hour inspection was actually done at 3309.5 hours. When is the next 100-hour inspection due?

A — 3312.5 hours.
B — 3402.5 hours.
C — 3409.5 hours.

3190. Answer B. (FAR 91.409)
The 100-hour limitation may be exceeded by not more than 10 hours while enroute to reach a place where the inspection can be done. However, the excess time used to reach a place must be included in computing the next 100 hours of time in service. Answer (A) is incorrect because although an aircraft can go 10 hours over the 100 hour inspection, it is due at the 100 hour time. Answer (C) is incorrect because any time over 10 hours that is used to get an aircraft to a place of inspection, is counted against the next 100 hour inspection.

3192. Maintenance records show the last transponder inspection was performed on September 1, 1993. The next inspection will be due no later than

A — September 30, 1994.
B — September 1, 1995.
C — September 30, 1995.

3192. Answer C. (FAR 91.413)
No person may use an ATC transponder unless, within the preceding 24 calendar months, that transponder has been tested and found to comply with the appropriate standards listed in Appendix F of Part 43. The term "calendar month" is defined as to the end of the month. Answers (A) and (B) are incorrect because they are less than 24 calendar months.

3193. Which records or documents shall the owner or operator of an aircraft keep to show compliance with an applicable Airworthiness Directive?

A — Aircraft maintenance records.
B — Airworthiness Certificate and Pilot's Operating Handbook.
C — Airworthiness and Registration Certificates.

3193. Answer A. (FAR 91.417)
The owner or operator of an aircraft shall keep a record of current status of applicable airworthiness directives (ADs) in the appropriate aircraft maintenance records. Answers (B) and (C) are not appropriate maintenance records.

3781. All operations within Class C airspace must be in

A — accordance with instrument flight rules.
B — compliance with ATC clearances and instructions.
C — an aircraft equipped with a 4096-code transponder with Mode C encoding capability.

3781. Answer C. (FAR 91.215, 91.130)
All aircraft must have an altitude encoding transponder in order to operate within Class C airspace. Answer (B) is not entirely correct because the regulations state that in order to enter Class C airspace, all you need is two-way radio contact with ATC. However, per FAR 91.123, once you receive a clearance from ATC, you cannot deviate from that clearance except in an emergency. Answer (A) is not correct because an IFR clearance is not a requirement for operations within Class C airspace.

SECTION D
NTSB 830 — AIRCRAFT ACCIDENT AND INCIDENT REPORTING

You also need to be familiar with the requirements and procedures for reporting aircraft accidents, incidents, and overdue aircraft to the National Transportation Safety Board (NTSB). The following questions covering NTSB regulations are included in this section:

3194, 3195, 3196, 3197, 3198, 3199, 3200.

3194. If an aircraft is involved in an accident which results in substantial damage to the aircraft, the nearest NTSB field office should be notified

A — immediately.
B — within 48 hours.
C — within 7 days.

3194. Answer A. (NTSB 830.5)
The operator of an aircraft shall immediately, and by the most expeditious means available, notify the nearest National Transportation Safety Board field office when an aircraft accident occurs. Answer (B) does not comply with notification requirements. Answer (C) is terminology found in NTSB 830.15 for filing reports and statements.

3195. Which incident requires an immediate notification to the nearest NTSB field office?

A — A forced landing due to engine failure.
B — Landing gear damage, due to a hard landing.
C — Flight control system malfunction or failure.

3195. Answer C. (NTSB 830.5)
The operator of an aircraft shall immediately, and by the most expeditious means available, notify the nearest National Transportation Safety Board field office when a flight control system malfunction or failure occurs. Answers (A) and (B) do not require immediate notification.

3196. Which incident would necessitate an immediate notification to the nearest NTSB field office?

A — An in-flight generator/alternator failure.
B — An in-flight fire.
C — An in-flight loss of VOR receiver capability.

3196. Answer B. (NTSB 830.5)
The operator of an aircraft shall immediately, and by the most expeditious means available, notify the nearest National Transportation Safety Board field office when a fire in flight occurs. Answers (A) and (C) do not require immediate notification.

3197. Which incident requires an immediate notification be made to the nearest NTSB field office?

A — An overdue aircraft that is believed to be involved in an accident.
B — An in-flight radio communications failure.
C — An in-flight generator or alternator failure.

3197. Answer A. (NTSB 830.5)
The operator of an aircraft shall immediately, and by the most expeditious means available, notify the nearest National Transportation Safety Board field office when an overdue aircraft is believed to be involved in an accident. Answers (B) and (C) do not require immediate notification.

3198. May aircraft wreckage be moved prior to the time the NTSB takes custody?

A — Yes, but only if moved by a federal, state, or local law enforcement officer.
B — Yes, but only to protect the wreckage from further damage.
C — No, it may not be moved under any circumstances.

3198. Answer B. (NTSB 830.10)
Prior to the time the Board or its authorized representative takes custody of aircraft wreckage, mail, or cargo, such wreckage may not be disturbed or moved except to the extent necessary to protect the wreckage from further damage.

3199. The operator of an aircraft that has been involved in an accident is required to file an accident report within how many days?

A — 5.
B — 7.
C — 10.

3200. The operator of an aircraft that has been involved in an incident is required to submit a report to the nearest field office of the NTSB

A — within 7 days.
B — within 10 days.
C — when requested.

3199. Answer C. (NTSB 830.15)
The operator of an aircraft shall file a report within 10 days after an accident, or after 7 days if an overdue aircraft is still missing. Answer (A) is less than the required 10 days. Answer (B) is wrong because it applies to aircraft that are overdue and still missing.

3200. Answer C. (NTSB 830.15)
A report on an incident for which notification is required by 830.5(a) shall be filed only when requested by an authorized representative of the Board.

SUBJECT MATTER KNOWLEDGE CODES

APPENDIX 1

To determine the knowledge area in which a particular question was incorrectly answered, compare the subject matter code(s) on AC Form 8080-2, Airmen Written Test Report, to the subject matter outline that follows. The total number of test items missed may differ from the number of subject matter codes shown on the AC Form 8080-2, since you may have missed more than one question in a certain subject matter code.

FAR 1 Definitions and Abbreviations

A01	General Definitions
A02	Abbreviations and Symbols

FAR 25 Airworthiness Standards: Transport Category Airplanes

A03	General
A04	Flight
A05	Structure
A06	Design and Construction
A07	Powerplant
A08	Equipment
A09	Operating Limitations and Information

FAR 23 Airworthiness Standards: Normal, Utility, and Acrobatic Category Aircraft

A10	General

FAR 21 Certification Procedures for Products and Parts

A11	General

FAR 39 Airworthiness Directives

A13	General
A14	Subpart B — Airworthiness Directives

FAR 43 Maintenance, Preventive Maintenance, Rebuilding, and Alteration

A15	General
A16	Appendixes

FAR 61 Certification: Pilots and Flight Instructors

A20	General
A21	Aircraft Ratings and Special Certificates
A22	Student Pilots
A23	Private Pilots
A24	Commercial Pilots
A25	Airline Transport Pilots
A26	Flight Instructors
A27	Appendix A: Practical Test Requirements for Airline Transport Pilot Certificates and Associated Class and Type Ratings
A28	Appendix B: Practical Test Requirements for Rotorcraft Airline Transport Pilot Certificates with a Helicopter Class Rating and Associated Type Ratings
A29	Recreational Pilot

FAR 63 Certification: Flight Crewmembers Other Than Pilots

A30	General
A31	Flight Engineers
A32	Flight Navigators

FAR 65 Certification: Airmen Other Than Flight Crewmembers

A40	General
A41	Aircraft Dispatchers
A44	Parachute Riggers

FAR 71 Designation of Federal Airways, Area Low Routes, Controlled Airspace, and Reporting Points

A60	General
A61	Airport Radar Service Areas
A64	Control Areas and Extensions

FAR 91 General Operating Rules

B07	General
B08	Flight Rules — General

B09	Visual Flight Rules
B10	Instrument Flight Rules
B11	Equipment, Instrument, and Certification Requirements
B12	Special Flight Operations
B13	Maintenance, Preventive Maintenance, and Alterations
B14	Large and Turbine-powered Multiengine Airplanes
B15	Additional Equipment and Operating Requirements for Large and Transport Category Aircraft
B16	Appendix A — Category II Operations: Manual, Instruments, Equipment, and Maintenance
B17	Foreign Aircraft Operations and Operations of U.S.-Registered Civil Aircraft Outside of the U.S.

FAR 97 Standard Instrument Approach Procedures

B97	General

FAR 105 Parachute Jumping

C01	General
C02	Operating Rules
C03	Parachute Equipment

FAR 108 Airplane Operator Security

C10	General

FAR 121 Certification and Operations: Domestic, Flag and Supplemental Air Carriers and Commercial Operators of Large Aircraft

D01	General
D02	Certification Rules for Domestic and Flag Air Carriers
D03	Certification Rules for Supplemental Air Carriers and Commercial Operators
D04	Rules Governing all Certificate Holders Under This Part
D05	Approval of Routes: Domestic and Flag Air Carriers
D06	Approval of Areas and Routes for Supplemental Air Carriers and Commercial Operators
D07	Manual Requirements
D08	Aircraft Requirements
D09	Airplane Performance Operating Limitations
D10	Special Airworthiness Requirements
D11	Instrument and Equipment Requirements
D12	Maintenance, Preventive Maintenance, and Alterations
D13	Airman and Crewmember Requirements
D14	Training Program
D15	Crewmember Qualifications
D16	Aircraft Dispatcher Qualifications and Duty Time Limitations: Domestic and Flag Air Carriers
D17	Flight Time Limitations and Rest Requirements: Domestic Air Carriers
D18	Flight Time Limitations: Flag Air Carriers
D19	Flight Time Limitations: Supplemental Air Carriers and Commercial Operators
D20	Flight Operations
D21	Dispatching and Flight Release Rules
D22	Records and Reports
D23	Crewmember Certificate: International
D24	Special Federal Aviation Regulation SFAR No. 14

FAR 125 Certification and Operations: Airplanes Having a Seating Capacity of 20 or More Passengers or a Maximum Payload Capacity of 6,000 Pounds or More

D30	General
D31	Certification Rules and Miscellaneous Requirements
D32	Manual Requirements
D33	Airplane Requirements
D34	Special Airworthiness Requirements
D35	Instrument and Equipment Requirements
D36	Maintenance
D37	Airman and Crewmember Requirements
D38	Flight Crewmember Requirements
D39	Flight Operations
D40	Flight Release Rules
D41	Records and Reports

FAR 135 Air Taxi Operators and Commercial Operators

E01	General
E02	Flight Operations
E03	Aircraft and Equipment
E04	VFR/IFR Operating Limitations and Weather Requirements
E05	Flight Crewmember Requirements
E06	Flight Crewmember Flight Time Limitations and Rest Requirements
E07	Crewmember Testing Requirements

Code	Description
E08	Training
E09	Airplane Performance Operating Limitations
E10	Maintenance, Preventive Maintenance, and Alterations
E11	Appendix A: Additional Airworthiness Standards for 10 or More Passenger Airplanes
E12	Special Federal Aviation Regulations SFAR No. 36
E13	Special Federal Aviation Regulations SFAR No. 38

US HMR 172 Hazardous Materials Table

Code	Description
F02	General

US HMR 175 Materials Transportation Bureau Hazardous Materials Regulations (HMR)

G01	General Information and Regulations
G02	Loading, Unloading, and Handling
G03	Specific Regulation Applicable According to Classification of Material

NTSB 830 Rules Pertaining to the Notification and Reporting of Aircraft Accidents or Incidents and Overdue Aircraft, and Preservation of Aircraft Wreckage, Mail, Cargo, and Records

Code	Description
G10	General
G11	Initial Notification of Aircraft Accidents, Incidents, and Overdue Aircraft
G12	Preservation of Aircraft Wreckage, Mail, Cargo, and Records
G13	Reporting of Aircraft Accidents, Incidents, and Overdue Aircraft

AC 61-23 Pilot's Handbook of Aeronautical Knowledge

H01	Principles of Flight
H02	Airplanes and Engines
H03	Flight Instruments
H04	Airplane Performance
H05	Weather
H06	Basic Calculations Using Navigational Computers or Electronic Calculators
H07	Navigation
H09	Appendix 1: Obtaining FAA Publications

AC 91-23 Pilot's Weight and Balance Handbook

H10	Weight and Balance Control
H11	Terms and Definitions
H12	Empty Weight Center of Gravity
H13	Index and Graphic Limits
H14	Change of Weight
H15	Control of Loading — General Aviation
H16	Control of Loading — Large Aircraft

AC 60-14 Aviation Instructor's Handbook

H20	The Learning Process
H21	Human Behavior
H22	Effective Communication
H23	The Teaching Process
H24	Teaching Methods
H25	The Instructor as a Critic
H26	Evaluation
H27	Instructional Aids
H30	Flight Instructor Characteristics and Responsibilities
H31	Techniques of Flight Instruction
H32	Planning Instructional Activity

AC 61-21 Flight Training Handbook

H50	Introduction to Flight Training
H51	Introduction to Airplanes and Engines
H52	Introduction to the Basics of Flight
H53	The Effect and Use of Controls
H54	Ground Operations
H55	Basic Flight Maneuvers
H56	Airport Traffic Patterns and Operations
H57	Takeoffs and Departure Climbs
H58	Landing Approaches and Landings
H59	Faulty Approaches and Landings
H60	Proficiency Flight Maneuvers
H61	Cross-Country Flying
H62	Emergency Flight by Reference to Instruments
H63	Night Flying
H64	Seaplane Operations
H65	Transition to Other Airplanes
H66	Principles of Flight and Performance Characteristics

AC 61-13 Basic Helicopter Handbook

H70	General Aerodynamics
H71	Aerodynamics of Flight
H72	Loads and Load Factors
H73	Function of the Controls
H74	Other Helicopter Components and Their Functions
H75	Introduction to the Helicopter Flight Manual
H76	Weight and Balance
H77	Helicopter Performance
H78	Some Hazards of Helicopter Flight

H79	Precautionary Measures and Critical Conditions
H80	Helicopter Flight Maneuvers
H81	Confined Area, Pinnacle, and Ridgeline Operations
H82	Glossary

Gyroplane Flight Training Manual — McCulloch

H90	Gyroplane Systems
H91	Gyroplane Terms
H92	Use of Flight Controls (Gyroplane)
H93	Fundamental Maneuvers of Flight (Gyroplane)
H94	Basic Flight Maneuvers (Gyroplane)

AC 61-27 Instrument Flying Handbook

I01	Training Considerations
I02	Instrument Flying: Coping with Illusions in Flight
I03	Aerodynamic Factors Related to Instrument Flying
I04	Basic Flight Instruments
I05	Attitude Instrument Flying — Airplanes
I06	Attitude Instrument Flying — Helicopters
I07	Electronic Aids to Instrument Flying
I08	Using the Navigation Instruments
I09	Radio Communications Facilities and Equipment
I10	The Federal Airways System and Controlled Airspace
I11	Air Traffic Control
I12	ATC Operations and Procedures
I13	Flight Planning
I14	Appendix: Instrument Instructor Lesson Guide — Airplanes
I15	Segment of En Route Low Altitude Chart

AC 00-6 Aviation Weather

I20	The Earth's Atmosphere
I21	Temperature
I22	Atmospheric Pressure and Altimetry
I23	Wind
I24	Moisture, Cloud Formation, and Precipitation
I25	Stable and Unstable Air
I26	Clouds
I27	Air Masses and Fronts
I28	Turbulence
I29	Icing
I30	Thunderstorms
I31	Common IFR Producers
I32	High Altitude Weather
I33	Arctic Weather
I34	Tropical Weather
I35	Soaring Weather
I36	Glossary of Weather Terms

AC 00-45 Aviation Weather Services

I40	The Aviation Weather Service Program
I41	Surface Aviation Weather Reports
I42	Pilot and Radar Reports and Satellite Pictures
I43	Aviation Weather Forecasts
I44	Surface Analysis Chart
I45	Weather Depiction Chart
I46	Radar Summary Chart
I47	Significant Weather Prognostics
I48	Winds and Temperatures Aloft
I49	Composite Moisture Stability Chart
I50	Severe Weather Outlook Chart
I51	Constant Pressure Charts
I52	Tropopause Data Chart
I53	Tables and Conversion Graphs

AIM — Airman's Information Manual

J01	Air Navigation Radio Aids
J02	Radar Services and Procedures
J03	Airport Lighting Aids
J04	Air Navigation and Obstruction Lighting
J05	Airport Marking Aids
J06	Airspace — General
J07	Uncontrolled Airspace
J08	Controlled Airspace
J09	Special Use Airspace
J10	Other Airspace Areas
J11	Service Available to Pilots
J12	Radio Communications Phraseology and Techniques
J13	Airport Operations
J14	ATC Clearance/Separations
J15	Preflight
J16	Departure Procedures
J17	En Route Procedures
J18	Arrival Procedures
J19	Pilot/Controller Roles and Responsibilities
J20	National Security and Interception Procedures
J21	Emergency Procedures — General
J22	Emergency Services Available to Pilots
J23	Distress and Urgency Procedures
J24	Two-Way Radio Communications Failure
J25	Meteorology
J26	Altimeter Setting Procedures
J27	Wake Turbulence

Code	Description
J28	Bird Hazards, and Flight Over National Refuges, Parks, and Forests
J29	Potential Flight Hazards
J30	Safety, Accident, and Hazard Reports
J31	Fitness for Flight
J32	Type of Charts Available
J33	Pilot Controller Glossary
J34	Airport/Facility Directory
J35	En Route Low Altitude Chart
J36	En Route High Altitude Chart
J37	Sectional Chart
J40	Standard Instrument Departure (SID) Chart
J41	Standard Terminal Arrival (STAR) Chart
J42	Instrument Approach Procedures
J43	Helicopter Route Chart

AC 67-2 Medical Handbook for Pilots

J52	Hypoxia
J53	Hyperventilation
J55	The Ears
J56	Alcohol
J57	Drugs and Flying
J58	Carbon Monoxide
J59	Vision
J60	Night Flight
J61	Cockpit Lighting
J62	Disorientation (Vertigo)
J63	Motion Sickness
J64	Fatigue
J65	Noise
J66	Age
J67	Some Psychological Aspects of Flying
J68	The Flying Passenger

ADDITIONAL ADVISORY CIRCULARS

K01	AC 00-24A, Thunderstorms
K02	AC 00-30B, Rules of Thumb for Avoiding or Minimizing Encounters with Clear Air Turbulence
K03	AC 00-34A, Aircraft Ground Handling and Servicing
K04	AC 00-54A, Pilot Wind Shear Guide
K11	AC 20-34D, Prevention of Retractable Landing Gear Failure
K12	AC 20-32B, Carbon Monoxide (CO) Contamination in Aircraft — Detection and Prevention
K13	AC 20-43C, Aircraft Fuel Control
K20	AC 20-103, Aircraft Engine Crankshaft Failure
K40	AC 25-4, Inertial Navigation System (INS)
L05	AC 60-22, Aeronautical Decision Making
L10	AC 61-67B, Stall and Spin Awareness Training
L15	AC 61-107, Operations of Aircraft at Altitudes Above 25,000 Feet MSL and/or MACH numbers (Mmo) Greater than .75
L34	AC 90-48C, Pilots' Role in Collision Avoidance
L42	AC 90-87, Helicopter Dynamic Rollover
L50	AC 91-6A, Water, Slush, and Snow on the Runway
L52	AC 91-13C, Cold Weather Operation of Aircraft
L53	AC 91-14D, Altimeter Setting Sources
L57	AC 91-43, Unreliable Airspeed Indications
L59	AC 91-46, Gyroscopic Instruments — Good Operating Practices
L61	AC 91-50, Importance of Transponder Operation and Altitude Reporting
L62	AC 91-51, Airplane Deice and Anti-Ice Systems
L70	AC 91-67, Minimum Equipment Requirements for General Aviation Operations Under FAR Part 91
L80	AC 103-4, Hazard Associated with Sublimation of Solid Carbon Dioxide (Dry Ice) Aboard Aircraft
L90	AC 105-2C, Sport Parachute Jumping
M01	AC 120-12A, Private Carriage Versus Common Carriage of Persons or Property
M02	AC 120-27B, Aircraft Weight and Balance Control
M08	AC 120-58, Large Aircraft Ground Deicing
M13	AC 121-195-1A, Operational Landing Distances for Wet Runways; Transport Category Airplanes
M51	AC 20-117, Hazards Following Ground Deicing and Ground Operations in Conditions Conducive to Aircraft Icing
M52	AC 00-2, Advisory Circular Checklist

American Soaring Handbook — Soaring Society of America

N01	A History of American Soaring
N02	Training
N03	Ground Launch
N04	Airplane Tow
N05	Meteorology
N06	Cross-Country and Wave Soaring
N07	Instruments and Oxygen
N08	Radio, Rope, and Wire

N09	Aerodynamics			
N10	Maintenance and Repair			

Soaring Flight Manual — Jeppesen Sanderson, Inc.

N20	Sailplane Aerodynamics
N21	Performance Considerations
N22	Flight Instruments
N23	Weather for Soaring
N24	Medical Factors
N25	Flight Publications and Airspace
N26	Aeronautical Charts and Navigation
N27	Computations for Soaring
N28	Personal Equipment
N29	Preflight and Ground Operations
N30	Aerotow Launch Procedures
N31	Ground Launch Procedures
N32	Basic Flight Maneuvers and Traffic
N33	Soaring Techniques
N34	Cross-Country Soaring

Taming The Gentle Giant — Taylor Publishing

O01	Design and Construction of Balloons
O02	Fuel Source and Supply
O03	Weight and Temperature
O04	Flight Instruments
O05	Balloon Flight Tips
O06	Glossary

Flight Instructor Manual — Balloon Federation Of America

O10	Flight Instruction Aids
O11	Human Behavior and Pilot Proficiency
O12	The Flight Check and the Designated Examiner

Propane Systems — Balloon Federation of America, 1991

O20	Propane Glossary
O21	Tanks
O22	Burners, Valves, and Hoses
O23	Refueling, Contamination, and Fuel Management
O24	Repair and Maintenance

Powerline Excerpts — Balloon Federation of America

O30	Excerpts

Balloon Ground School — Balloon Publishing Company

O46	Balloon Operations

Goodyear Airship Operations Manual

P01	Buoyancy
P02	Aerodynamics
P03	Free Ballooning
P04	Aerostatics
P05	Envelope
P06	Car
P07	Powerplant
P08	Airship Ground Handling
P11	Operating Instructions
P12	History
P13	Training

The Parachute Manual, Para Publishing

P31	Regulations
P32	The Parachute Rigger Certificate
P33	The Parachute Loft
P34	Parachute Materials
P35	Personnel Parachute Assemblies
P36	Parachute Component Parts
P37	Maintenance, Alteration, and Manufacturing Procedures
P38	Design and Construction
P39	Parachute Inspecting and packing
P40	Glossary/Index

The Parachute Manual, Vol. II, Para Publishing

P51	Parachute Regulations
P52	The Parachute Rigger's Certificate
P53	The Parachute Loft
P54	Parachute Materials
P55	Personnel parachute Assemblies
P56	Parachute Component Parts
P57	Maintenance, Alteration, and Manufacturing
P58	Parachute Design and Construction
P59	Parachute Inspection and Packing
P60	Appendix
P61	Conversion Tables
P62	Product/Manufacturer-Index
P63	Name and Manufacture Index
P64	Glossary-Index

AC 65-9A Airframe and Powerplant Mechanics General Handbook

S01	Mathematics
S02	Aircraft Drawings
S03	Aircraft Weight and Balance
S04	Fuels and Fuel Systems
S05	Fluid Lines and Fittings
S06	Aircraft Hardware, Materials, and Processes
S07	Physics
S08	Basic Electricity

Subject Matter Knowledge Codes

S09	Aircraft Generators and Motors
S10	Inspection Fundamentals
S11	Ground Handling, Safety, and Support Equipment

AC 65-12A Airframe and Powerplant Mechanics Powerplant Handbook

S12	Theory and Construction of Aircraft Engines
S13	Induction and Exhaust Systems
S14	Engine Fuel and Metering Systems
S15	Engine Ignition and Electrical Systems
S16	Engine Starting Systems
S17	Lubrication and Cooling Systems
S18	Propellers
S19	Engine Fire Protection Systems
S20	Engine Maintenance and Operation

AC 65-15A Airframe and Powerplant Mechanics Airframe Handbook

S21	Aircraft Structures
S22	Assembly and Rigging
S23	Aircraft Structural Repairs
S24	Ice and Rain Protection
S25	Hydraulic and Pneumatic Power Systems
S26	Landing Gear Systems
S27	Fire Protection Systems
S28	Aircraft Electrical Systems
S29	Aircraft Instrument Systems
S30	Communications and Navigation Systems
S31	Cabin Atmosphere Control Systems

EA-ITP-G[2] A and P Technician General Textbook — International Aviation Publishers (IAP), Inc., Second Edition

S32	Mathematics
S33	Physics
S34	Basic Electricity
S35	Electrical Generators and Motors
S36	Aircraft Drawings
S37	Weight and Balance
S38	Fluid Lines and Fittings
S39	Aircraft Hardware
S40	Corrosion and Its Control
S41	Nondestructive Inspection
S42	Ground Handling and Servicing
S43	Maintenance Forms and Records
S44	Maintenance Publications

EA-ITP-P[2] A and P Technician Powerplant Textbook — IAP, Inc., Second Edition

S45	Reciprocating Engines
S46	Turbine Engine
S47	Engine Removal and Replacement
S48	Engine Maintenance and Operation
S49	Induction and Exhaust Systems
S50	Engine fuel and fuel metering
S51	Engine Ignition and Electrical Systems
S52	Engine Lubrication and Cooling Systems
S53	Engine Fire Protection Systems
S54	Propellers

EA-ITP-A[2] A and P Technician Airframe Textbook — IAP, Inc., Second Edition

S55	Aircraft Structures
S56	Assembly and Rigging
S57	Aircraft Fabric Covering
S58	Aircraft Painting and Finishing
S59	Aircraft Metal Structural Repair
S60	Aircraft Wood and composite Structural Repair
S61	Aircraft Welding
S62	Ice and Rain Control Systems
S63	Hydraulic and Pneumatic Power Systems
S64	Aircraft Landing Gear Systems
S65	Fire Protection Systems
S66	Aircraft Electrical Systems
S67	Aircraft Instrument Systems
S68	Aircraft Fuel Systems
S69	Aircraft Cabin Atmosphere Control Systems

EA-TEP-2 Aircraft Gas Turbine Powerplants — IAP, Inc.

S70	History of Turbine Engine Development
S71	Jet Propulsion Theory
S72	Turbine Engine Design and Construction
S73	Engine Familiarization
S74	Inspection and Maintenance
S75	Lubrication Systems
S76	Fuel Systems
S77	Compressor Anti-Stall Systems
S78	Anti-Icing Systems
S79	Starter Systems
S80	Ignition Systems
S81	Engine Instrument Systems

S82	Fire/Overheat Detection and Extinguishing Systems for Turbine Engines
S83	Engine Operation

The Aircraft Gas Turbine Engine and Its Operation — United Technologies Corporation, Pratt Whitney, 1988

T01	Gas Turbine Engine Fundamentals
T02	Gas Turbine Engine Terms
T03	Gas Turbine Engine Components
T04	Gas Turbine Engine Operation
T05	Operational Characteristics of Jet Engines
T06	Gas Turbine Engine Performance

Aircraft Powerplants — McGraw-Hill, Sixth Edition

T07	Aircraft Powerplant Classification and Progress
T08	Reciprocating-Engine Construction and Nomenclature
T09	Internal-Combustion Engine Theory and Performance
T10	Lubricants and Lubricating Systems
T11	Induction Systems, Superchargers, Turbochargers, and Exhaust Systems
T12	Basic Fuel Systems and Carburetors
T13	Fuel Injection Systems
T14	Reciprocating-Engine Ignition and Starting Systems
T15	Operation, Inspection, Maintenance, and Troubleshooting of Reciprocating Engines
T16	Reciprocating-Engine Overhaul Practices
T17	Gas Turbine Engine: Theory, Construction, and Nomenclature
T18	Gas Turbine Engine: Fuels and Fuel Systems
T19	Turbine-Engine Lubricants and Lubricating Systems
T20	Ignition and Starting Systems of Gas-Turbine Engines
T21	Turbofan Engines
T22	Turboprop Engines
T23	Turboshaft Engines
T24	Gas-Turbine Operation, Inspection, Troubleshooting, Maintenance, and Overhaul
T25	Propeller Theory, Nomenclature, and Operation
T26	Turbopropellers and Control Systems
T27	Propeller Installation, Inspection, and Maintenance
T28	Engine Control System
T29	Engine Indicating and Warning Systems

EA-ATD-2 Aircraft Technical Dictionary — IAP, Inc., Sixth Edition

T30	Definitions

Aircraft Basic Science — McGraw-Hill

T31	Fundamentals of Mathematics
T32	Science Fundamentals
T33	Basic Aerodynamics
T34	Airfoils and their Applications
T35	Aircraft in Flight
T36	Aircraft Drawings
T37	Weight and Balance
T38	Aircraft Materials
T39	Fabrication Techniques and Processes
T40	Aircraft Hardware
T41	Aircraft Fluid Lines and their Fittings
T42	Federal Aviation Regulations and Publications
T43	Ground Handling and Safety
T44	Aircraft Inspection and Servicing

Aircraft Maintenance and Repair — McGraw-Hill, Fifth Edition

T45	Aircraft Systems
T46	Aircraft Hydraulic and Pneumatic Systems
T47	Aircraft Landing Gear Systems
T48	Aircraft Fuel Systems
T49	Environmental Systems
T50	Aircraft Instruments and Instrument Systems
T51	Auxiliary Systems
T52	Assembly and Rigging

EA-363 Transport Category Aircraft Systems — IAP, Inc.

T53	Types, Design Features and Configurations of Transport Aircraft
T54	Auxiliary Power Units, Pneumatic, and Environmental Control Systems
T55	Anti-Icing Systems and Rain Protection
T56	Electrical Power Systems
T57	Flight Control Systems
T58	Fuel Systems
T59	Hydraulic Systems
T60	Oxygen Systems
T61	Warning and Fire Protection Systems
T62	Communications, Instruments, and Navigational Systems
T63	Miscellaneous Aircraft Systems and Maintenance Information

Subject Matter Knowledge Codes

Aircraft Electricity and Electronics — McGraw-Hill, Fourth Edition

T64	Fundamentals of Electricity
T65	Applications of Ohm's Law
T66	Aircraft Storage Batteries
T67	Alternating Current
T68	Electrical Wire and Wiring Practices
T69	Electrical Control Devices
T70	Electric Measuring Instruments
T71	DC Generators and Related Control Circuits
T72	Alternators, Inverters, and Related Controls
T73	Electric Motors
T74	Power Distribution Systems
T75	Design and Maintenance of Aircraft Electrical Systems
T76	Radio Theory
T77	Communication and Navigation Systems
T78	Weather Warning Systems
T79	Electrical Instruments and Autopilot Systems
T80	Digital Electronics

FAA Accident Prevention Program Bulletins

V01	FAA-P-8740-2, Density Altitude
V02	FAA-P-8740-5, Weight and Balance
V03	FAA-P-8740-12, Thunderstorms
V04	FAA-P-8740-19, Flying Light Twins Safely
V05	FAA-P-8740-23, Planning your Takeoff
V06	FAA-P-8740-24, Tips on Winter Flying
V07	FAA-P-8740-25, Always Leave Yourself an Out
V08	FAA-P-8740-30, How to Obtain a Good Weather Briefing
V09	FAA-P-8740-40, Wind Shear
V10	FAA-P-8740-41, Medical Facts for Pilots
V11	FAA-P-8740-44, Impossible Turns
V12	FAA-P-8740-48, On Landings, Part I
V13	FAA-P-8740-49, On Landings, Part II
V14	FAA-P-8740-50, On Landings, Part III
V15	FAA-P-8740-51, How to Avoid a Midair Collision
V16	FAA-P-8740-52, The Silent Emergency

EA-338 Flight Theory for Pilots — IAP, Inc., Third Edition

W01	Introduction
W02	Air Flow and Airspeed Measurement
W03	Aerodynamic Forces on Airfoils
W04	Lift and Stall
W05	Drag
W06	Jet Aircraft Basic Performance
W07	Jet Aircraft Applied Performance
W08	Prop Aircraft Basic Performance
W09	Prop Aircraft Applied Performance
W10	Helicopter Aerodynamics
W11	Hazards of Low Speed Flight
W12	Takeoff Performance
W13	Landing Performance
W14	Maneuvering Performance
W15	Longitudinal Stability and Control
W16	Directional and Lateral Stability and Control
W17	High Speed Flight

Fly the Wing — Iowa State University Press/Ames, Second Edition

X01	Basic Aerodynamics
X02	High-Speed Aerodynamics
X03	High-Altitude Machs
X04	Approach Speed Control and Target Landings
X05	Preparation for Flight Training
X06	Basic Instrument Scan
X07	Takeoffs
X08	Rejected Takeoffs
X09	Climb, Cruise, and Descent
X10	Steep Turns
X11	Stalls
X12	Unusual Attitudes
X14	Maneuvers At Minimum Speed
X15	Landings: Approach Technique and Performance
X16	ILS Approaches
X17	Missed Approaches and Rejected Landings
X18	Category II and III Approaches
X19	Nonprecision and Circling Approaches
X20	Weight and Balance
X21	Flight Planning
X22	Icing
X23	Use of Anti-ice and Deice
X24	Winter Operation
X25	Thunderstorm Flight
X26	Low-Level Wind Shear

Technical Standard Orders

Y60	TSO-C23b, Parachute
Y61	TSO-C23c, Personnel Parachute Assemblies

Practical Test Standards

Z01 FAA-S-8081-6, Flight Instructor Practical Test Standards for Airplane
Z02 FAA-S-8081-7, Flight Instructor Practical Test Standards for Rotorcraft
Z03 FAA-S-8081-8, Flight Instructor Practical Test Standards for Glider

NOTE: AC 00-2, Advisory Circular Checklist, transmits the status of all FAA advisory circulars (ACs), as well as FAA internal publications and miscellaneous flight information such as AIM, Airport/Facility Directory, written test question books, practical test standards, and other material directly related to a certificate or rating. To obtain a free copy of the AC 00-2, send your request to:

U.S. Department of Transportation
Utilization and Storage Section, M-443.2
Washington, DC 20590

APPENDIX 2

LEGEND INFORMATION

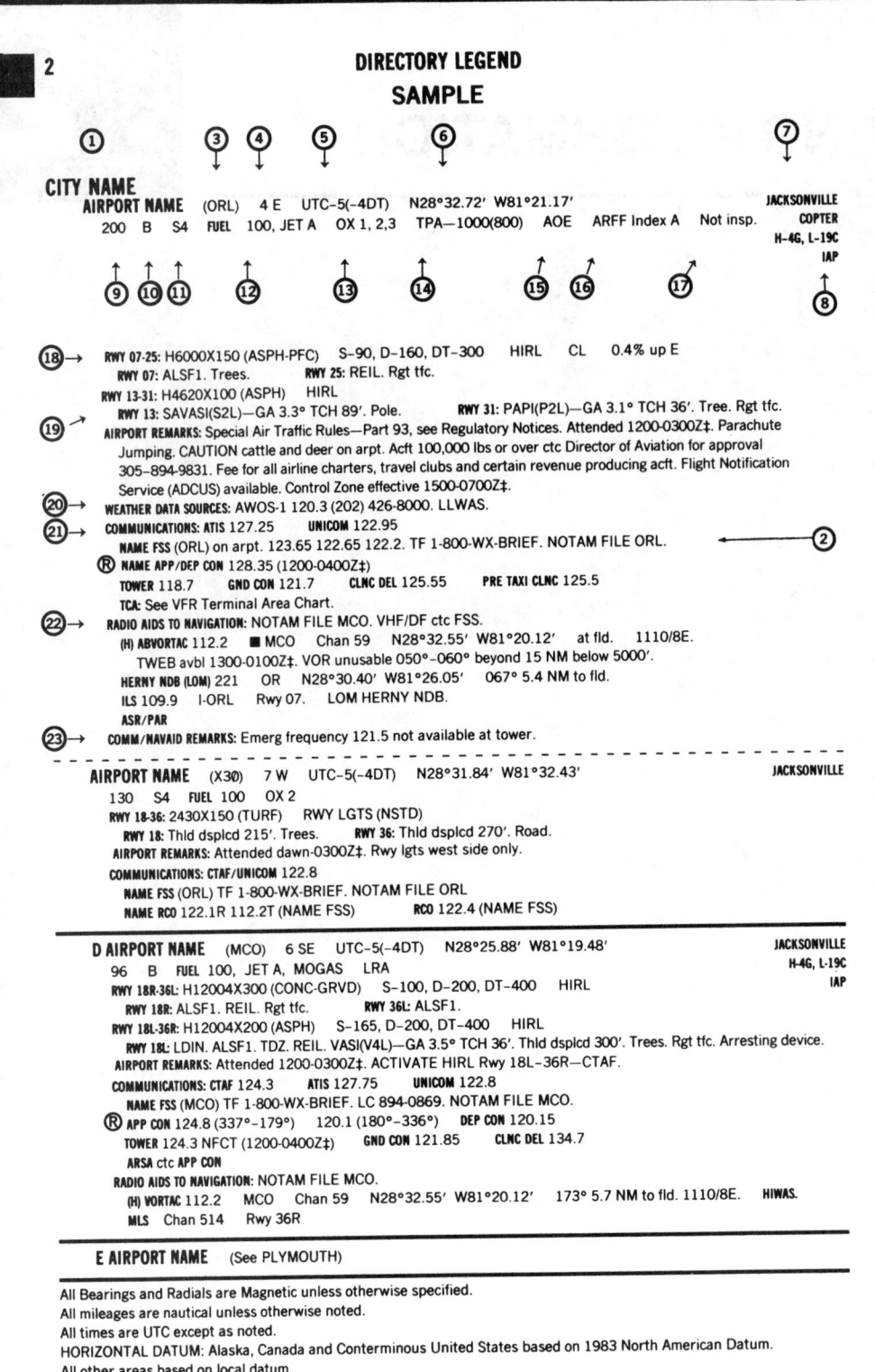

LEGEND 2.— Airport/Facility Directory.

DIRECTORY LEGEND

LEGEND

This Directory is an alphabetical listing of data on record with the FAA on all airports that are open to the public, associated terminal control facilities, air route traffic control centers and radio aids to navigation within the conterminous United States, Puerto Rico and the Virgin Islands. Airports are listed alphabetically by associated city name and cross referenced by airport name. Facilities associated with an airport, but with a different name, are listed individually under their own name, as well as under the airport with which they are associated.

The listing of an airport in this directory merely indicates the airport operator's willingness to accommodate transient aircraft, and does not represent that the facility conforms with any Federal or local standards, or that it has been approved for use on the part of the general public.

The information on obstructions is taken from reports submitted to the FAA. It has not been verified in all cases. Pilots are cautioned that objects not indicated in this tabulation (or on charts) may exist which can create a hazard to flight operation.

Detailed specifics concerning services and facilities tabulated within this directory are contained in Airman's Information Manual, Basic Flight Information and ATC Procedures.

The legend items that follow explain in detail the contents of this Directory and are keyed to the circled numbers on the sample on the preceding page.

① CITY/AIRPORT NAME

Airports and facilities in this directory are listed alphabetically by associated city and state. Where the city name is different from the airport name the city name will appear on the line above the airport name. Airports with the same associated city name will be listed alphabetically by airport name and will be separated by a dashed rule line. All others will be separated by a solid rule line.

② NOTAM SERVICE

All public use landing areas are provided NOTAM "D" (distant dissemination) and NOTAM "L" (local dissemination) service. Airport NOTAM file identifier is shown following the associated FSS data for individual airports, e.g. "NOTAM FILE IAD". See AIM, Basic Flight Information and ATC Procedures for detailed description of NOTAM's.

③ LOCATION IDENTIFIER

A three or four character code assigned to airports. These identifiers are used by ATC in lieu of the airport name in flight plans, flight strips and other written records and computer operations.

④ AIRPORT LOCATION

Airport location is expressed as distance and direction from the center of the associated city in nautical miles and cardinal points, i.e., 4 NE.

⑤ TIME CONVERSION

Hours of operation of all facilities are expressed in Coordinated Universal Time (UTC) and shown as "Z" time. The directory indicates the number of hours to be subtracted from UTC to obtain local standard time and local daylight saving time UTC–5(–4DT). The symbol ‡ indicates that during periods of Daylight Saving Time effective hours will be one hour earlier than shown. In those areas where daylight saving time is not observed that (–4DT) and ‡ will not be shown. All states observe daylight savings time except Arizona and that portion of Indiana in the Eastern Time Zone and Puerto Rico and the Virgin Islands.

⑥ GEOGRAPHIC POSITION OF AIRPORT

Positions are shown in degrees, minutes and hundredths of a minute.

⑦ CHARTS

The Sectional Chart and Low and High Altitude Enroute Chart and panel on which the airport or facility is located. Helicopter Chart locations will be indicated as, i.e., COPTER.

⑧ INSTRUMENT APPROACH PROCEDURES

IAP indicates an airport for which a prescribed (Public Use) FAA Instrument Approach Procedure has been published.

⑨ ELEVATION

Elevation is given in feet above mean sea level and is the highest point on the landing surface. When elevation is sea level it will be indicated as (00). When elevation is below sea level a minus (–) sign will precede the figure.

⑩ ROTATING LIGHT BEACON

B indicates rotating beacon is available. Rotating beacons operate dusk to dawn unless otherwise indicated in AIRPORT REMARKS.

⑪ SERVICING

S1: Minor airframe repairs.
S2: Minor airframe and minor powerplant repairs.
S3: Major airframe and minor powerplant repairs.
S4: Major airframe and major powerplant repairs.

LEGEND 3.—Airport/Facility Directory.

DIRECTORY LEGEND

⑫ FUEL

CODE	FUEL
80	Grade 80 gasoline (Red)
100	Grade 100 gasoline (Green)
100LL	100LL gasoline (low lead) (Blue)
115	Grade 115 gasoline
A	Jet A—Kerosene freeze point–40° C.
A1	Jet A-1—Kerosene freeze point–50°C.
A1+	Jet A-1—Kerosene with icing inhibitor, freeze point–50° C.

CODE	FUEL
B	Jet B—Wide-cut turbine fuel, freeze point–50° C.
B+	Jet B—Wide-cut turbine fuel with icing inhibitor, freeze point–50° C.
MOGAS	Automobile gasoline which is to be used as aircraft fuel.

NOTE: Automobile Gasoline. Certain automobile gasoline may be used in specific aircraft engines if a FAA supplemental type cetificate has been obtained. Automobile gasoline which is to be used in aircraft engines will be identified as "MOGAS", however, the grade/type and other octane rating will not be published.

Data shown on fuel availability represents the most recent information the publisher has been able to acquire. Because of a variety of factors, the fuel listed may not always be obtainable by transient civil pilots. Confirmation of availability of fuel should be made directly with fuel dispensers at locations where refueling is planned.

⑬ OXYGEN

OX 1 High Pressure
OX 2 Low Pressure
OX 3 High Pressure—Replacement Bottles
OX 4 Low Pressure—Replacement Bottles

⑭ TRAFFIC PATTERN ALTITUDE

Traffic Pattern Altitude (TPA)—The first figure shown is TPA above mean sea level. The second figure in parentheses is TPA above airport elevation.

⑮ AIRPORT OF ENTRY, LANDING RIGHTS, AND CUSTOMS USER FEE AIRPORTS

U.S. CUSTOMS USER FEE AIRPORT—Private Aircraft operators are frequently required to pay the costs associated with customs processing.

AOE—Airport of Entry—A customs Airport of Entry where permission from U.S. Customs is not required, however, at least one hour advance notice of arrival must be furnished.

LRA—Landing Rights Airport—Application for permission to land must be submitted in advance to U.S. Customs. At least one hour advance notice of arrival must be furnished.

NOTE: Advance notice of arrival at both an AOE and LRA airport may be included in the flight plan when filed in Canada or Mexico, where Flight Notification Service (ADCUS) is available the airport remark will indicate this service. This notice will also be treated as an application for permission to land in the case of an LRA. Although advance notice of arrival may be relayed to Customs through Mexico, Canadian, and U.S. Communications facilities by flight plan, the aircraft operator is solely responsible for insuring that Customs receives the notification. (See Customs, Immigration and Naturalization, Public Health and Agriculture Department requirements in the International Flight Information Manual for further details.)

⑯ CERTIFICATED AIRPORT (FAR 139)

Airports serving Department of Transportation certified carriers and certified under FAR, Part 139, are indicated by the ARFF index; i.e., ARFF Index A, which relates to the availability of crash, fire, rescue equipment.

FAR-PART 139 CERTIFICATED AIRPORTS
INDICES AND AIRCRAFT RESCUE AND FIRE FIGHTING EQUIPMENT REQUIREMENTS

Airport Index	Required No. Vehicles	Aircraft Length	Scheduled Departures	Agent + Water for Foam
A	1	<90'	$\geq$1	500#DC or HALON 1211 or 450#DC + 100 gal H_2O
B	1 or 2	$\geq$90', <126'	$\geq$5	Index A + 1500 gal H_2O
		$\geq$126', <159'	<5	
C	2 or 3	$\geq$126', <159'	$\geq$5	Index A + 3000 gal H_2O
		$\geq$159', <200'	<5	
D	3	$\geq$159', <200'	$\geq$5	Index A + 4000 gal H_2O
		>200'	<5	
E	3	$\geq$200'	$\geq$5	Index A + 6000 gal H_2O

> Greater Than; < Less Than; $\geq$ Equal or Greater Than; $\leq$ Equal or Less Than; H_2O–Water; DC–Dry Chemical.

LEGEND 4.—Airport/Facility Directory.

DIRECTORY LEGEND 5

NOTE: The listing of ARFF index does not necessarily assure coverage for non-air carrier operations or at other than prescribed times for air carrier. ARFF Index Ltd.—indicates ARFF coverage may or may not be available, for information contact airport manager prior to flight.

⑰ FAA INSPECTION

All airports not inspected by FAA will be identified by the note: Not insp. This indicates that the airport information has been provided by the owner or operator of the field.

⑱ RUNWAY DATA

Runway information is shown on two lines. That information common to the entire runway is shown on the first line while information concerning the runway ends are shown on the second or following line. Lengthy information will be placed in the Airport Remarks.

Runway direction, surface, length, width, weight bearing capacity, lighting, gradient and appropriate remarks are shown for each runway. Direction, length, width, lighting and remarks are shown for sealanes. The full dimensions of helipads are shown, i.e., 50X150.

RUNWAY SURFACE AND LENGTH

Runway lengths prefixed by the letter "H" indicate that the runways are hard surfaced (concrete, asphalt). If the runway length is not prefixed, the surface is sod, clay, etc. The runway surface composition is indicated in parentheses after runway length as follows:

(AFSC)—Aggregate friction seal coat	(GRVD)—Grooved	(TURF)—Turf
(ASPH)—Asphalt	(GRVL)—Gravel, or cinders	(TRTD)—Treated
(CONC)—Concrete	(PFC)—Porous friction courses	(WC)—Wire combed
(DIRT)—Dirt	(RFSC)—Rubberized friction seal coat	

RUNWAY WEIGHT BEARING CAPACITY

Runway strength data shown in this publication is derived from available information and is a realistic estimate of capability at an average level of activity. It is not intended as a maximum allowable weight or as an operating limitation. Many airport pavements are capable of supporting limited operations with gross weights of 25-50% in excess of the published figures. Permissible operating weights, insofar as runway strengths are concerned, are a matter of agreement between the owner and user. When desiring to operate into any airport at weights in excess of those published in the publication, users should contact the airport management for permission. Add 000 to figure following S, D, DT, DDT and MAX for gross weight capacity:

S—Runway weight bearing capacity for aircraft with single-wheel type landing gear, (DC-3), etc.
D—Runway weight bearing capacity for aircraft with dual-wheel type landing gear, (DC-6), etc.
DT—Runway weight bearing capacity for aircraft with dual-tandem type landing gear, (707), etc.
DDT—Runway weight bearing capacity for aircraft with double dual-tandem type landing gear, (747), etc.

Quadricycle and dual-tandem are considered virtually equal for runway weight bearing consideration, as are single-tandem and dual-wheel.

Omission of weight bearing capacity indicates information unknown.

RUNWAY LIGHTING

Lights are in operation sunset to sunrise. Lighting available by prior arrangement only or operating part of the night only and/or pilot controlled and with specific operating hours are indicated under airport remarks. Since obstructions are usually lighted, obstruction lighting is not included in this code. Unlighted obstructions on or surrounding an airport will be noted in airport remarks. Runway lights nonstandard (NSTD) are systems for which the light fixtures are not FAA approved L-800 series: color, intensity, or spacing does not meet FAA standards. Nonstandard runway lights, VASI, or any other system not listed below will be shown in airport remarks.

Temporary, emergency or limited runway edge lighting such as flares, smudge pots, lanterns or portable runway lights will also be shown in airport remarks.

Types of lighting are shown with the runway or runway end they serve.

NSTD—Light system fails to meet FAA standards.
LIRL—Low Intensity Runway Lights
MIRL—Medium Intensity Runway Lights
HIRL—High Intensity Runway Lights
RAIL—Runway Alignment Indicator Lights
REIL—Runway End Identifier Lights
CL—Centerline Lights
TDZ—Touchdown Zone Lights
ODALS—Omni Directional Approach Lighting System.
AF OVRN—Air Force Overrun 1000' Standard Approach Lighting System.
LDIN—Lead-In Lighting System.
MALS—Medium Intensity Approach Lighting System.
MALSF—Medium Intensity Approach Lighting System with Sequenced Flashing Lights.
MALSR—Medium Intensity Approach Lighting System with Runway Alignment Indicator Lights.
SALS—Short Approach Lighting System.
SALSF—Short Approach Lighting System with Sequenced Flashing Lights.
SSALS—Simplified Short Approach Lighting System.
SSALF—Simplified Short Approach Lighting System with Sequenced Flashing Lights.
SSALR—Simplified Short Approach Lighting System with Runway Alignment Indicator Lights.
ALSAF—High Intensity Approach Lighting System with Sequenced Flashing Lights
ALSF1—High Intensity Approach Lighting System with Sequenced Flashing Lights, Category I, Configuration.
ALSF2—High Intensity Approach Lighting System with Sequenced Flashing Lights, Category II, Configuration.
VASI—Visual Approach Slope Indicator System.

NOTE: Civil ALSF-2 may be operated as SSALR during favorable weather conditions.

LEGEND 5.—Airport/Facility Directory.

6 DIRECTORY LEGEND

VISUAL GLIDESLOPE INDICATORS

APAP—A system of panels, which may or may not be lighted, used for alignment of approach path.
- PNIL   APAP on left side of runway
- PNIR   APAP on right side of runway

PAPI—Precision Approach Path Indicator
- P2L   2-identical light units placed on left side of runway
- P2R   2-identical light units placed on right side of runway
- P4L   4-identical light units placed on left side of runway
- P4R   4-identical light units placed on right side of runway

PVASI—Pulsating/steady burning visual approach slope indicator, normally a single light unit projecting two colors.
- PSIL-   PVASI on left side of runway
- PSIR-   PVASI on right side of runway

SAVASI—Simplified Abbreviated Visual Approach Slope Indicator
- S2L   2-box SAVASI on left side of runway
- S2R   2-box SAVASI on right side of runway

TRCV—Tri-color visual approach slope indicator, normally a single light unit projecting three colors.
- TRIL   TRCV on left side of runway
- TRIR   TRCV on right side of runway

VASI—Visual Approach Slope Indicator
- V2L   2-box VASI on left side of runway
- V2R   2-box VASI on right side of runway
- V4L   4-box VASI on left side of runway
- V4R   4-box VASI on right side of runway
- V6L   6-box VASI on left side of runway
- V6R   6-box VASI on right side of runway
- V12   12-box VASI on both sides of runway
- V16   16-box VASI on both sides of runway

NOTE: Approach slope angle and threshold crossing height will be shown when available; i.e., –GA 3.5° TCH 37'.

PILOT CONTROL OF AIRPORT LIGHTING

Key Mike	Function
7 times within 5 seconds	Highest intensity available
5 times within 5 seconds	Medium or lower intensity (Lower REIL or REIL-Off)
3 times within 5 seconds	Lowest intensity available (Lower REIL or REIL-Off)

Available systems will be indicated in the Airport Remarks, as follows:

ACTIVATE MALSR Rwy 07, HIRL Rwy 07-25–122.8 (or CTAF).
or
ACTIVATE MIRL Rwy 18-36–122.8 (or CTAF).
or
ACTIVATE VASI and REIL, Rwy 07–122.8 (or CTAF).

Where the airport is not served by an instrument approach procedure and/or has an independent type system of different specification installed by the airport sponsor, descriptions of the type lights, method of control, and operating frequency will be explained in clear text. See AIM, "Basic Flight Information and ATC Procedures," for detailed description of pilot control of airport lighting.

RUNWAY GRADIENT

Runway gradient will be shown only when it is 0.3 percent or more. When available the direction of slope upward will be indicated, i.e., 0.5% up NW.

RUNWAY END DATA

Lighting systems such as VASI, MALSR, REIL; obstructions; displaced thresholds will be shown on the specific runway end. "Rgt tfc"—Right traffic indicates right turns should be made on landing and takeoff for specified runway end.

RUNWAY DECLARED DISTANCE INFORMATION

TORA—Take-off Run Available
TODA—Take-off Distance Available
ASDA—Accelerate-Stop Distance Available
LDA—Landing Distance Available

⑲ AIRPORT REMARKS

Landing Fee indicates landing charges for private or non-revenue producing aircraft, in addition, fees may be charged for planes that remain over a couple of hours and buy no services, or at major airline terminals for all aircraft.
Remarks—Data is confined to operational items affecting the status and usability of the airport.
Parachute Jumping.—See "PARACHUTE" tabulation for details.
Unless otherwise stated, remarks including runway ends refer to the runway's approach end.

LEGEND 6.—Airport/Facility Directory.

DIRECTORY LEGEND

⑳ WEATHER DATA SOURCES

ASOS—Automated Surface Observing System. Reports the same as an AWOS-3 plus precipitation identification and intensity, and freezing rain occurrence (future enhancement).

AWOS—Automated Weather Observing System

AWOS-A—reports altimeter setting.
AWOS-1—reports altimeter setting, wind data and usually temperature, dewpoint and density altitude.
AWOS-2—reports the same as AWOS-1 plus visibility.
AWOS-3—reports the same as AWOS-1 plus visibility and cloud/ceiling data.
See AIM, Basic Flight Information and ATC Procedures for detailed description of AWOS.

HIWAS—See RADIO AIDS TO NAVIGATION
LAWRS—Limited Aviation Weather Reporting Station where observers report cloud height, weather, obstructions to vision, temperature and dewpoint (in most cases), surface wind, altimeter and pertinent remarks.
LLWAS—indicates a Low Level Wind Shear Alert System consisting of a center field and several field perimeter anemometers.
SAWRS—identifies airports that have a Supplemental Aviation Weather Reporting Station available to pilots for current weather information.
SWSL—Supplemental Weather Service Location providing current local weather information via radio and telephone.

㉑ COMMUNICATIONS

Communications will be listed in sequence in the order shown below:
Common Traffic Advisory Frequency (CTAF), Automatic Terminal Information Service (ATIS) and Aeronautical Advisory Stations (UNICOM) along with their frequency is shown, where available, on the line following the heading "COMMUNICATIONS." When the CTAF and UNICOM is the same frequency, the frequency will be shown as CTAF/UNICOM freq.

Flight Service Station (FSS) information. The associated FSS will be shown followed by the identifier and information concerning availability of telephone service, e.g., Direct Line (DL), Local Call (LC-384-2341), Toll free call, dial (TF 800-852-7036 or TF 1-800-227-7160), Long Distance (LD 202-426-8800 or LD 1-202-555-1212) etc. The airport NOTAM file identifier will be shown as "NOTAM FILE IAD." Where the FSS is located on the field it will be indicated as "on arpt" following the identifier. Frequencies available will follow. The FSS telephone number will follow along with any significant operational information. FSS's whose name is not the same as the airport on which located will also be listed in the normal alphabetical name listing for the state in which located. Remote Communications Outlet (RCO) providing service to the airport followed by the frequency and name of the Controlling FSS.

FSS's provide information on airport conditions, radio aids and other facilities, and process flight plans. Local Airport Advisory Service is provided on the CTAF by FSS's located at non-tower airports or airports where the tower is not in operation.
(See AIM, Par. 157/158 Traffic Advisory Practices at airports where a tower is not in operation or AC 90 - 42C.)

Aviation weather briefing service is provided by FSS specialists. Flight and weather briefing services are also available by calling the telephone numbers listed.

Remote Communications Outlet (RCO)—An unmanned air/ground communications facility, remotely controlled and providing UHF or VHF communications capability to extend the service range of an FSS.

Civil Communications Frequencies—Civil communications frequencies used in the FSS air/ground system are now operated simplex on 122.0, 122.2, 122.3, 122.4, 122.6, 123.6; emergency 121.5; plus receive-only on 122.05, 122.1, 122.15, and 123.6.

   a. 122.0 is assigned as the Enroute Flight Advisory Service channel at selected FSS's.
   b. 122.2 is assigned to most FSS's as a common enroute simplex service.
   c. 123.6 is assigned as the airport advisory channel at non-tower FSS locations, however, it is still in commission at some FSS's collocated with towers to provide part time Local Airport Advisory Service.
   d. 122.1 is the primary receive-only frequency at VOR's. 122.05, 122.15 and 123.6 are assigned at selected VOR's meeting certain criteria.
   e. Some FSS's are assigned 50 kHz channels for simplex operation in the 122-123 MHz band (e.g. 122.35). Pilots using the FSS A/G system should refer to this directory or appropriate charts to determine frequencies available at the FSS or remoted facility through which they wish to communicate.

Part time FSS hours of operation are shown in remarks under facility name.

   Emergency frequency 121.5 is available at all Flight Service Stations, Towers, Approach Control and RADAR facilities, unless indicated as not available.

Frequencies published followed by the letter "T" or "R", indicate that the facility will only transmit or receive respectively on that frequency. All radio aids to navigation frequencies are transmit only.

TERMINAL SERVICES

CTAF—A program designed to get all vehicles and aircraft at uncontrolled airports on a common frequency.
ATIS—A continuous broadcast of recorded non-control information in selected areas of high activity.
UNICOM—A non-government air/ground radio communications facility utilized to provide general airport advisory service.
APP CON—Approach Control. The symbol ® indicates radar approach control.
TOWER—Control tower
GND CON—Ground Control
DEP CON—Departure Control. The symbol ® indicates radar departure control.
CLNC DEL—Clearance Delivery.
PRE TAXI CLNC—Pre taxi clearance
VFR ADVSY SVC—VFR Advisory Service. Service provided by Non-Radar Approach Control.
   Advisory Service for VFR aircraft (upon a workload basis) ctc APP CON.

LEGEND 7.—Airport/Facility Directory.

8 DIRECTORY LEGEND

STAGE II SVC—Radar Advisory and Sequencing Service for VFR aircraft
STAGE III SVC—Radar Sequencing and Separation Service for participating VFR Aircraft within a Terminal Radar Service Area (TRSA)
ARSA—Airport Radar Service Area
TCA—Radar Sequencing and Separation Service for all aircraft in a Terminal Control Area (TCA)
TOWER, APP CON and DEP CON RADIO CALL will be the same as the airport name unless indicated otherwise.

㉒ RADIO AIDS TO NAVIGATION

The Airport Facility Directory lists by facility name all Radio Aids to Navigation, except Military TACANS, that appear on National Ocean Service Visual or IFR Aeronautical Charts and those upon which the FAA has approved an Instrument Approach Procedure. All VOR, VORTAC ILS and MLS equipment in the National Airspace System has an automatic monitoring and shutdown feature in the event of malfunction. Unmonitored, as used in this publication for any navigational aid, means that FSS or tower personnel cannot observe the malfunction or shutdown signal. The NAVAID NOTAM file identifier will be shown as "NOTAM FILE IAD" and will be listed on the Radio Aids to Navigation line. When two or more NAVAIDS are listed and the NOTAM file identifier is different than shown on the Radio Aids to Navigation line, then it will be shown with the NAVAID listing. NOTAM file identifiers for ILS's and their components (e.g., NDB (LOM) are the same as the identifiers for the associated airports and are not repeated. Hazardous Inflight Weather Advisory Service (HIWAS) will be shown where this service is broadcast over selected VOR's.

NAVAID information is tabulated as indicated in the following sample:

```
                         TWEB       TACAN/DME Channel    Geographical Position              Site Elevation
NAME (L) ABVORTAC 117.55  ■ ABE    Chan 122(Y)    N40°43.60'  W75°27.30'   180°   4.1 NM to fld.   1110/8E. HIWAS.
    ↑         ↑     ↑                                                      ↑           ↑                ↑
  Class   Frequency Identifier                           Bearing and distance  Magnetic Variation   Hazardous Inflight
                                                         facility to center of airport              Weather Advisory Service
```

VOR unusable 020°-060° beyond 26 NM below 3500'

Restriction within the normal altitude/range of the navigational aid (See primary alphabetical listing for restrictions on VORTAC and VOR/DME).

Note: Those DME channel numbers with a (Y) suffix require TACAN to be placed in the "Y" mode to receive distance information.

HIWAS—Hazardous Inflight Weather Advisory Service is a continuous broadcast of inflight weather advisories including summarized SIGMETs, convective SIGMETs, AIRMETs and urgent PIREPs. HIWAS is presently broadcast over selected VOR's and will be implemented throughout the conterminous U.S.

ASR/PAR—Indicates that Surveillance (ASR) or Precision (PAR) radar instrument approach minimums are published in U.S. Government Instrument Approach Procedures.

RADIO CLASS DESIGNATIONS

VOR/DME/TACAN Standard Service Volume (SSV) Classifications

SSV Class	Altitudes	Distance (NM)
(T) Terminal	1000' to 12,000'	25
(L) Low Altitude	1000' to 18,000'	40
(H) High Altitude	1000' to 14,500'	40
	14,500' to 18,000'	100
	18,000' to 45,000'	130
	45,000' to 60,000'	100

NOTE: Additionally, (H) facilities provide (L) and (T) service volume and (L) facilities provide (T) service. Altitudes are with respect to the station's site elevation. Coverage is not available in a cone of airspace directly above the facility.

The term VOR is, operationally, a general term covering the VHF omnidirectional bearing type of facility without regard to the fact that the power, the frequency protected service volume, the equipment configuration, and operational requirements may vary between facilities at different locations.

AB _____	Automatic Weather Broadcast (also shown with ■ following frequency.)
DF _____	Direction Finding Service.
DME _____	UHF standard (TACAN compatible) distance measuring equipment.
DME(Y) _____	UHF standard (TACAN compatible) distance measuring equipment that require TACAN to be placed in the "Y" mode to receive DME.

LEGEND 8.—Airport/Facility Directory.

DIRECTORY LEGEND 9

H	Non-directional radio beacon (homing), power 50 watts to less than 2,000 watts (50 NM at all altitudes).
HH	Non-directional radio beacon (homing), power 2,000 watts or more (75 NM at all altitudes).
H-SAB	Non-directional radio beacons providing automatic transcribed weather service.
ILS	Instrument Landing System (voice, where available, on localizer channel).
ISMLS	Interim Standard Microwave Landing System.
LDA	Localizer Directional Aid.
LMM	Compass locator station when installed at middle marker site (15 NM at all altitudes).
LOM	Compass locator station when installed at outer marker site (15 NM at all altitudes).
MH	Non-directional radio beacon (homing) power less than 50 watts (25 NM at all altitudes).
MLS	Microwave Landing System
S	Simultaneous range homing signal and/or voice.
SABH	Non-directional radio beacon not authorized for IFR or ATC. Provides automatic weather broadcasts.
SDF	Simplified Direction Facility.
TACAN	UHF navigational facility-omnidirectional course and distance information.
VOR	VHF navigational facility-omnidirectional course only.
VOR/DME	Collocated VOR navigational facility and UHF standard distance measuring equipment.
VORTAC	Collocated VOR and TACAN navigational facilities.
W	Without voice on radio facility frequency.
Z	VHF station location marker at a LF radio facility.

ABBREVIATIONS

The following abbreviations are those commonly used within this Directory. Other abbreviations may be found in the Legend and are not duplicated below.

acft	aircraft		ldg	landing
apch	approach		med	medium
arpt	airport		NFCT	non-federal control tower
avbl	available		ngt	night
bcn	beacon		npi	non precision instrument
blo	below		NSTD	nonstandard
byd	beyond		ntc	notice
clsd	closed		opr	operate
ctc	contact		ops	operates/operation
dalgt	daylight		ovrn	overrun
dsplc	displace		p-line	power line
dsplcd	displaced		PPR	prior permission required
durn	duration		req	request
emerg	emergency		rqr	requires
extd	extend, extended		rgt tfc	right traffic
fld	field		rwy	runway
FSS	Flight Service Station		svc	service
ints	intensity		tmpry	temporary, temporarily
LAA	Local Airport Advisory		tkf	take-off
lgtd	lighted		tfc	traffic
lgts	lights		thld	threshold
			twr	tower

LEGEND 9.—Airport/Facility Directory.

CROSS-REFERENCE LISTING OF QUESTIONS

APPENDIX 3

Appendix 3 is a numerical listing of all airplane questions in the *Recreational Pilot and Private Pilot Written Test Book*, FAA-T-8080-15B. The listing includes the FAA question number and the answer. The cross-reference listing is to the right of the answer. It refers to the chapter and the page in the *Private Pilot Exam Study Guide* where the question is answered.

Example: 3309 C 1-9

This indicates that the answer to question 3309 is C and the question is answered in Chapter 1 page 1-9 of the Study Guide.

QUESTION	ANSWER	PAGE	QUESTION	ANSWER	PAGE	QUESTION	ANSWER	PAGE
3001	B	1-1	3035	A	10-6	3071	B	10-13
3002	B	1-1	3036	B	10-7	3072	B	10-13
3003	A	1-1	3037	C	10-7	3073	C	10-14
3004	A	1-1	3038	B	10-7	3074	B	10-14
3005	C	10-1	3039	B	10-7	3075	B	3-17
3006	A	1-4	3040	C	10-7	3076	B	10-14
3007	A	10-1	3041	A	10-8	3077	A	10-14
3008	A	10-1	3042	C	10-8	3078	A	10-14
3009	C	10-1	3043	A	10-8	3079	C	10-14
3010	A	10-2	3044	B	10-8	3080	B	10-15
3011	C	3-17	3045	B	10-8	3081	C	10-15
3012	A	3-17	3046	B	10-8	3082	C	10-15
3013	C	10-13	3047	C	10-9	3083	A	10-15
3014	A	10-2	3048	B	10-9	3084	C	10-16
3015	B	10-2	3049	C	10-9	3085	B	10-16
3016	C	10-2	3050	C	10-9	3086	A	10-16
3017	C	10-3	3051	B	10-9	3087	B	10-16
3018	B	10-3	3052	A	10-9	3088	C	10-16
3019	C	10-3	3053	C	10-10	3089	B	2-1
3020	B	10-3	3054	C	10-10	3090	B	2-1
3021	C	10-3	3055	A	10-10	3091	A	2-1
3022	C	10-4	3056	B	10-10	3092	A	2-1
3023	C	10-4	3057	B	10-11	3093	B	2-2
3024	B	10-4	3058	C	10-11	3094	C	2-2
3025	B	10-4	3059	C	10-11	3095	C	2-2
3026	C	10-5	3060	C	10-11	3096	B	10-17
3027	B	10-5	3061	C	10-11	3097	B	10-17
3028	C	10-5	3064	B	10-12	3098	A	10-17
3029	C	10-5	3065	B	10-12	3099	A	10-17
3030	A	10-5	3066	B	10-12	3100	B	10-17
3031	C	10-6	3067	A	2-14	3101	A	2-2
3032	C	10-6	3068	B	2-14	3102	C	2-2
3033	B	10-6	3069	B	2-14	3103	B	2-3
3034	A	10-6	3070	B	10-13	3104	A	2-3

QUESTION	ANSWER	PAGE	QUESTION	ANSWER	PAGE	QUESTION	ANSWER	PAGE
3105	B	2-3	3162	C	10-20	3220	A	1-3
3106	A	2-3	3163	C	10-20	3221	B	3-10
3107	B	2-14	3164	C	10-20	3222	C	3-11
3108	B	10-18	3165	A	2-19	3223	A	3-11
3109	A	10-18	3166	C	2-19	3224	A	3-16
3110	B	10-18	3167	B	10-20	3225	B	3-11
3111	A	2-26	3168	A	10-20	3226	B	3-11
3112	A	2-27	3169	B	10-21	3227	A	3-11
3113	B	2-27	3170	A	10-21	3228	A	3-12
3114	C	2-27	3171	C	10-21	3229	C	3-12
3115	B	2-27	3172	A	10-21	3230	A	3-12
3116	B	2-27	3173	B	10-21	3231	C	3-12
3117	C	6-1	3178	B	10-21	3232	B	3-12
3118	B	2-14	3179	B	10-22	3233	B	3-12
3119	A	2-15	3180	B	10-22	3234	A	3-13
3120	B	2-5	3181	A	10-22	3235	C	3-13
3121	B	2-6	3182	B	10-22	3236	A	3-13
3123	C	10-18	3183	B	10-22	3237	C	3-13
3124	A	2-15	3184	B	10-23	3238	C	3-13
3125	C	2-15	3185	C	10-23	3239	B	3-13
3126	B	2-15	3186	C	10-23	3240	B	3-14
3127	A	2-15	3187	C	9-1	3241	A	3-16
3128	B	2-16	3188	A	10-23	3242	A	3-16
3129	A	2-16	3189	B	10-23	3243	C	3-16
3130	A	2-16	3190	B	10-24	3244	C	3-14
3131	B	10-18	3191	C	2-27	3245	A	3-14
3132	C	10-19	3192	C	10-24	3246	B	3-17
3134	B	10-19	3193	A	10-24	3247	B	3-1
3135	B	10-19	3194	A	10-25	3248	C	3-1
3136	C	2-16	3195	C	10-25	3249	C	3-1
3137	A	2-16	3196	B	10-25	3250	C	3-1
3138	B	2-16	3197	A	10-25	3251	C	3-2
3139	B	2-17	3198	B	10-25	3252	A	3-2
3140	B	2-17	3199	C	10-26	3253	B	3-2
3141	A	2-17	3200	C	10-26	3254	C	3-2
3142	B	2-17	3201	A	1-2	3255	A	3-2
3143	A	2-17	3202	A	1-2	3256	A	3-3
3144	A	2-17	3203	B	1-2	3257	B	3-3
3145	C	2-18	3204	A	1-3	3258	B	3-3
3146	C	2-18	3205	A	1-3	3259	B	3-3
3147	B	2-18	3206	A	4-7	3260	B	3-3
3148	C	2-18	3207	A	1-4	3261	C	3-3
3149	B	2-18	3208	B	1-4	3262	C	3-3
3150	B	2-18	3209	B	1-4	3263	C	3-4
3151	A	2-19	3210	B	1-8	3264	C	3-4
3153	C	2-19	3211	A	1-8	3265	A	3-4
3154	B	2-19	3212	B	1-8	3266	C	3-4
3155	C	2-3	3213	A	1-4	3267	C	3-4
3156	C	2-4	3214	C	1-5	3268	C	3-4
3157	B	2-4	3215	C	1-5	3269	C	3-4
3158	B	2-4	3216	B	1-5	3270	B	3-4
3159	C	10-19	3217	B	1-6	3271	C	3-5
3160	B	10-19	3218	B	1-6	3272	C	3-5
3161	B	10-20	3219	C	1-3	3273	B	3-5

Cross-Reference Listing of Questions

QUESTION	ANSWER	PAGE	QUESTION	ANSWER	PAGE	QUESTION	ANSWER	PAGE
3274	C	3-5	3392	A	3-6	3450	C	4-3
3275	A	3-7	3393	C	3-6	3452	A	4-12
3276	C	3-7	3394	B	3-6	3453	A	5-18
3277	C	3-8	3395	B	4-1	3454	B	5-18
3278	C	3-9	3397	C	4-2	3455	A	5-18
3279	C	3-9	3398	B	4-2	3456	C	5-18
3280	B	3-9	3399	A	4-2	3457	C	5-18
3281	C	3-9	3400	A	4-2	3458	C	5-19
3282	C	3-9	3401	B	4-2	3459	A	5-19
3283	C	3-10	3402	C	4-4	3460	A	5-19
3284	B	3-10	3403	B	4-4	3461	A	5-19
3286	A	3-10	3404	A	4-4	3462	C	5-1
3287	B	1-8	3405	A	4-5	3463	B	5-2
3288	A	1-9	3406	A	4-5	3464	A	5-2
3289	C	3-18	3407	C	4-5	3465	B	5-2
3290	C	3-18	3408	A	4-5	3466	B	5-2
3291	B	3-18	3409	C	4-5	3467	A	5-3
3292	C	3-18	3410	B	4-5	3472	C	5-3
3293	C	3-18	3412	A	4-5	3473	C	5-3
3294	C	3-18	3413	A	4-6	3474	A	5-3
3295	A	3-19	3414	C	4-6	3475	B	5-4
3296	C	3-20	3415	B	4-6	3476	B	5-4
3297	A	3-20	3416	B	4-6	3478	C	5-4
3298	A	3-20	3417	C	4-7	3479	C	5-4
3299	B	3-20	3418	B	4-7	3480	C	5-4
3300	B	3-20	3419	B	4-8	3481	C	5-5
3301	A	1-6	3420	C	4-8	3482	A	5-5
3302	C	2-6	3421	C	4-6	3483	B	5-5
3303	A	2-6	3422	A	4-6	3484	B	5-6
3304	A	2-6	3423	A	4-6	3485	B	5-6
3305	A	2-6	3424	C	4-7	3486	A	5-6
3306	A	2-7	3425	A	4-8	3487	A	5-6
3307	C	2-7	3426	C	4-8	3488	C	5-7
3308	B	2-7	3427	B	4-8	3489	C	5-7
3309	C	1-9	3428	C	4-8	3490	A	5-7
3310	A	1-9	3429	C	4-9	3491	C	5-7
3311	C	1-3	3430	C	4-9	3492	A	5-8
3312	A	1-6	3431	C	4-9	3493	B	5-9
3313	A	1-7	3432	A	4-9	3494	A	5-19
3314	B	1-7	3433	B	4-9	3495	C	5-19
3315	B	1-7	3434	B	4-9	3496	A	5-20
3316	A	1-7	3435	B	4-10	3497	C	5-20
3317	A	1-3	3436	A	4-10	3498	B	5-20
3381	C	4-1	3437	B	4-10	3499	A	5-20
3382	A	4-1	3438	A	4-10	3500	B	5-9
3383	C	4-3	3439	A	4-10	3501	A	5-9
3384	A	4-4	3440	B	4-10	3502	B	5-10
3385	A	4-4	3441	B	4-11	3503	A	5-10
3386	A	3-6	3442	C	4-11	3504	C	5-10
3387	C	3-20	3443	A	4-11	3505	C	5-10
3388	B	3-6	3444	C	4-3	3506	B	5-10
3389	C	3-21	3445	B	4-11	3507	A	5-11
3390	C	3-6	3446	C	4-11	3508	B	5-11
3391	B	3-6	3447	C	4-11	3509	A	5-11

QUESTION	ANSWER	PAGE	QUESTION	ANSWER	PAGE	QUESTION	ANSWER	PAGE
3510	C	5-11	3572	B	2-24	3626	B	2-21
3511	B	5-13	3573	C	2-24	3627	B	2-21
3512	C	5-13	3574	B	2-25	3628	B	2-21
3513	B	5-13	3575	C	2-25	3629	C	6-13
3514	A	5-13	3576	A	2-25	3630	A	6-13
3515	B	5-13	3577	C	7-4	3631	C	6-13
3516	C	5-13	3578	B	7-4	3632	C	6-13
3517	B	5-14	3579	A	7-5	3633	A	6-13
3518	C	5-15	3580	C	7-5	3634	B	6-13
3519	B	5-15	3581	C	7-5	3635	A	6-14
3520	B	5-15	3582	C	7-6	3636	C	6-14
3521	A	5-15	3583	B	7-6	3637	B	6-14
3522	A	5-17	3584	C	7-7	3638	B	6-14
3523	A	5-17	3585	A	7-7	3639	B	6-14
3524	B	5-17	3586	C	7-7	3640	C	6-14
3526	A	5-20	3587	B	7-7	3641	B	6-15
3527	B	5-21	3588	C	7-7	3642	C	6-15
3528	C	5-21	3589	C	7-7	3643	NCA	6-15
3529	C	6-16	3590	A	7-8	3651	A	3-14
3530	A	6-1	3591	B	7-8	3652	A	3-14
3531	C	6-20	3592	B	7-8	3653	A	3-14
3532	B	7-1	3593	A	7-9	3654	B	3-15
3533	C	7-1	3594	B	7-9	3655	B	3-15
3534	B	6-16	3595	C	7-9	3656	A	3-15
3535	B	6-1	3596	B	7-9	3657	B	3-15
3536	C	6-1	3597	C	7-9	3658	B	9-1
3538	C	6-20	3598	C	7-5	3659	A	9-2
3539	A	7-1	3599	C	6-2	3660	C	9-2
3540	C	6-17	3600	B	6-2	3661	A	3-29
3541	C	6-17	3601	A	2-20	3662	C	3-29
3542	B	6-17	3602	B	2-20	3663	C	3-29
3543	B	6-2	3603	A	2-20	3664	B	3-30
3545	B	6-21	3604	A	6-2	3665	B	3-30
3546	A	6-21	3605	B	6-2	3666	A	3-31
3547	A	6-21	3606	A	6-11	3667	B	3-31
3548	B	6-18	3607	A	6-11	3668	C	3-34
3549	B	6-18	3608	C	6-11	3669	A	3-34
3550	C	6-22	3609	A	6-11	3670	B	3-35
3551	A	6-22	3610	A	6-12	3671	C	3-35
3552	A	7-3	3611	B	6-12	3672	B	3-35
3553	B	7-3	3612	B	6-12	3673	B	3-37
3554	C	6-19	3613	A	2-25	3674	A	3-37
3556	A	6-23	3614	A	2-25	3675	B	3-38
3559	B	7-3	3615	C	2-26	3676	A	3-38
3560	A	7-3	3616	C	5-21	3677	B	3-39
3561	C	7-4	3617	A	5-21	3678	C	3-21
3562	A	6-19	3618	A	6-12	3679	B	3-21
3563	A	6-19	3619	B	6-25	3680	B	3-22
3565	A	6-23	3620	A	2-20	3681	B	3-22
3566	A	7-4	3621	B	2-20	3682	C	3-22
3567	A	6-2	3622	A	6-12	3683	B	3-22
3568	C	6-23	3623	C	2-21	3684	C	3-22
3570	C	7-4	3624	A	2-21	3685	C	3-22
3571	C	2-23	3625	C	6-12	3686	C	3-23

Cross-Reference Listing of Questions

QUESTION	ANSWER	PAGE	QUESTION	ANSWER	PAGE	QUESTION	ANSWER	PAGE
3687	B	3-23	3788	C	2-23	3843	B	6-28
3688	A	3-23	3789	C	2-26	3844	A	8-4
3689	B	3-24	3791	C	2-28	3845	A	8-4
3690	A	3-25	3792	B	2-28	3846	A	8-4
3691	C	3-25	3793	A	2-28	3847	B	8-4
3692	C	3-25	3794	C	2-28	3848	A	8-5
3693	B	3-25	3795	C	2-29	3849	C	8-2
3694	B	3-26	3796	A	2-29	3850	B	8-3
3695	B	3-26	3797	C	2-29	3851	A	8-3
3696	C	3-26	3798	C	2-29	3852	B	8-3
3697	A	3-27	3799	A	2-23	3853	A	8-3
3698	B	3-27	3800	C	2-29	3854	A	6-28
3705	B	3-27	3801	A	2-30	3855	B	6-28
3706	B	3-27	3802	A	2-30	3856	C	6-28
3707	A	3-28	3803	B	2-30			
3708	A	3-28	3804	A	2-30			
3709	B	6-25	3805	B	2-12			
3710	B	2-4	3806	A	2-12			
3711	A	1-7	3807	A	2-12			
3712	B	8-1	3808	C	2-13			
3713	A	8-1	3809	A	2-13			
3714	C	8-1	3810	C	2-13			
3715	A	8-2	3811	A	2-30			
3716	A	8-2	3812	A	2-31			
3717	C	8-2	3813	B	2-23			
3718	B	2-7	3814	A	2-4			
3719	C	8-2	3815	A	6-24			
3759	A	2-28	3816	B	6-24			
3760	B	2-8	3817	C	6-25			
3761	A	2-8	3818	B	6-25			
3762	C	2-8	3819	B	2-31			
3763	B	2-8	3820	A	2-31			
3764	C	2-8	3821	C	2-31			
3765	B	2-8	3822	C	2-31			
3766	B	2-8	3823	A	5-21			
3767	B	2-9	3824	C	4-12			
3768	C	2-9	3825	C	4-12			
3769	B	2-9	3826	A	4-12			
3771	B	2-10	3827	C	4-12			
3772	B	2-10	3828	B	4-12			
3773	B	2-11	3829	A	4-13			
3774	B	2-11	3830	B	4-13			
3775	A	2-11	3831	B	6-15			
3776	C	2-11	3832	B	8-4			
3777	C	2-11	3833	C	2-4			
3778	C	2-11	3834	B	2-5			
3779	C	2-21	3835	A	2-5			
3780	C	2-22	3836	C	2-5			
3781	C	10-24	3837	C	2-26			
3782	C	2-22	3838	A	6-27			
3783	B	2-22	3839	C	6-27			
3785	C	2-22	3840	A	6-27			
3786	B	2-22	3841	B	6-27			
3787	C	2-22	3842	B	6-28			

Tech Star

No other aviation flight computer gives you as much capability.

- Over 25 Aviation Calculations
  (Compared with 18 to 20 With Other Computers)
- 55 Conversions Available
- Six Independent Memory Registers
- Enter Prompted Values In Any Order Or Change Them At Any Time
- Scratch Pad Allows You To Work Other Problems While An On-Screen Calculation Is Being Completed
- Weight And Balance Calculations Include Weight Shift Formulas
- Least Expensive Aviation Hand-held On The Market

$65.95 Suggested List Price

Contact Your Local Jeppesen Dealer or Call Us for Details

Prices Subject to Change Without Notice.

55 INVERNESS DRIVE EAST, ENGLEWOOD, COLORADO 80112-5498 (303) 799-9090